NATIONAL
GEOGRAPHIC
TRAVELER

paris

paris

by Lisa Davidson and Elizabeth Ayre
photography by Gilles Mingasson

National Geographic
Washington, D.C.

CONTENTS

Pages 2–3: Night falls on the City of Light.
Opposite: The café scene near the Église St.-Germain-des-Prés

TRAVELING WITH EYES OPEN

Alert travelers go with a purpose and leave with a benefit. If you travel responsibly, you can help support wildlife conservation, historic preservation, and cultural enrichment in the places you visit. You can enrich your own travel experience as well.

To be a geo-savvy traveler:

- Recognize that your presence has an impact on the places you visit.

- Spend your time and money in ways that sustain local character. (Besides, it's more interesting that way.)

- Value the destination's natural and cultural heritage.

- Respect the local customs and traditions.

- Express appreciation to local people about things you find interesting and unique to the place: its nature and scenery, music and food, historic villages and buildings.

- Vote with your wallet: Support the people who support the place, patronizing businesses that make an effort to celebrate and protect what's special there. Seek out shops, local restaurants, inns, and tour operators who love their home—who love taking care of it and showing it off. Avoid businesses that detract from the character of the place.

- Enrich yourself, taking home memories and stories to tell, knowing that you have contributed to the preservation and enhancement of the destination.

That is the type of travel now called geotourism, defined as "tourism that sustains or enhances the geographical character of a place—its environment, culture, aesthetics, heritage, and the well-being of its residents." To learn more, visit National Geographic's Center for Sustainable Destinations at *www.nationalgeographic.com/travel/sustainable.*

paris

ABOUT THE AUTHORS

Lisa Davidson is a writer and editor living in Paris. She has written for *Village France, France par Excellence,* and *World Media Network* and has published *Baboushka and Dedoushka,* a memoir of the Russian Revolution. She is currently working with *Beaux-Arts Magazine* and Paris-based publisher Gallimard.

Elizabeth Ayre is also a writer and editor living in Paris. She has written for the *International Herald Tribune, The Independent,* and *Village France* and *France par Excellence* guidebooks. She is the author of *They Don't Take No for an Answer* and editor of the journal *Variations*. She is currently working with Paris-based publisher Gallimard and runs a European network for children separated from an imprisoned parent.

Responsible for updating and writing new features for the 2011 edition, **Heidi Ellison** is an American journalist who has lived in Paris for more than 20 years. She is the founder and editor of ParisUpdate.com. Over the years, her articles on travel, art, design, architecture, and fashion have appeared in dozens of magazines and newspapers. She has also contributed to a number of guidebooks.

The authors would like to thank the following people for their collaboration in this book: David Applefield (Bridges), John Calder (Literature), Tina Isaac (Fashion), Lisa Nesselson (Cinema), Julian Nundy (Paris today), A. J. Paterson (Paris today and research on the History section), Nicolas Petty (Travelwise), and Karen Wells Verlander (Fashion).

Charting Your Trip

Paris has changed enormously in the past 25 years, leaving behind many of its provincial ways and becoming an increasingly modern, multicultural, and international metropolis. The new Paris is more user-friendly, staying open all day as the life of a bustling 21st-century city swirls around its historical core.

The pride Paris takes in its history is evident in the ongoing restoration of its monuments, which now sparkle and glow in the sunlight almost as brilliantly as the glittering lights that transform the Eiffel Tower into a giant sparkler every evening on the hour.

The new Paris, however, has not lost its legendary romantic atmosphere. Couples still canoodle on the quays of the Seine, and the ever-changing light still inspires painters and poets. Young people still come here dreaming of writing novels in garret rooms and making Hemingway's moveable feast their own. French students still argue vehemently about philosophy in cafés and then go out dancing all night.

Which brings us to one major change that most visitors will find to be a huge improvement. The (once highly accurate) clichéd image of smoky Parisian cafés, restaurants, and jazz clubs is dead forever, killed by the recently instituted law forbidding smoking in public places. Breathe deeply and enjoy your stay!

How to Get Around

Paris has an excellent transportation system. The 14 lines of the easy-to-use Métro subway system (*www.ratp.fr*) cover almost every corner of the city and are supplemented by the RER suburban train lines, which can also be used to travel within the city for the price of a Métro ticket. An extensive grid of municipal bus lines fills in any gaps not served by the Métro or RER. Almost any location in the city is within a few minutes' walk from one of these transportation options.

While the bus lines are slightly more complicated to use, they offer visitors with time to spare a wonderful way to see the city without tiring themselves out, provided that they travel in off hours (after 10 a.m. and before 5 p.m.). Every bus shelter has a map of the entire system on the outside and details of the line(s) served on the inside. Once the Métro has stopped running, at about 12:30 a.m. (1:30 a.m. on Friday and Saturday), there are two options: Take a taxi or a Noctilien

Rodin's "The Thinker"

all-night bus (shelters are marked with a big "N"), which cover the city well and run more frequently than in the past. Avoid driving in Paris; traffic jams are a given and parking scarce and expensive.

For trips out of town, you can either rent a car at a train station or airport, or take a train to your destination and rent a car on site if you need one (to tour the Loire châteaux, for example, or Champagne country). In most urban destinations, a car is not necessary. It is always wise to reserve a car in advance.

The other suburban railway system serving the Île de France is called the Transilien *(www.transilien .com/web/site)*. Destinations beyond the Île de France are well served by the SNCF *(www.sncf.com)*, the excellent national railway, which offers high-speed TGV service to major cities (three hours to Bordeaux or Marseille, for example) and slower Corail or Téoz trains to other destinations. The Eurostar *(www .eurostar.com)* zips passengers to London in two-and-a-quarter hours, while the high-speed Thalys *(www.thalys.com)* serves northern destinations, including Brussels, Cologne, and Amsterdam.

Back in Paris, the truly adventurous might want to try the Vélib' short-term bicycle rental system *(www.velib.paris.fr)*, recommended only for those who are confident cyclists and who dare to brave the tangle of traffic and sometimes frighteningly aggressive Parisian drivers. All others should abstain. A safer way to visit Paris by bicycle is to take a tour with a company like Paris à Vélo C'est Sympa *(www.parisvelosympa.com)*.

If You Have One Week

Few first-time visitors to Paris will have a hard time deciding what to do in Paris, since the major sites are so deservedly well known: the **Eiffel Tower**, the **Louvre**, the **Musée d'Orsay**, the **Orangerie**, the **Arc de Triomphe**, the **Sacré-Coeur**, the **Latin Quarter**, the **Champs-Élysées**, and the **quays of the Seine.**

NOT TO BE MISSED:

The gargoyles of
Notre-Dame 48

The glowing windows of Ste.-
Chapelle 56

Strolling the Luxembourg
Gardens 82

The eye-opening Centre
Georges-Pompidou 96

Masterpieces at Musée du
Louvre 124

A walk along the quays of the
Seine 138

Climbing the Tour Eiffel 172

Tourism Information

Main Office
25 rue des Pyramides, 75001
Tel 01 49 52 42 63
Gare de Lyon
20 boulevard Diderot, 75012
Tel 01 49 52 42 63
Gare du Nord
18 rue de Dunkerque, 75010
Tel 01 49 52 42 63
Official website:
en.parisinfo.com

City of Paris
Everything to do with life in Paris
www.paris.fr
**Paris-Île de France Regional
Tourism Office**
www.new-paris-ile-de-france.com
Paris Update
Weekly magazine with reviews
www.parisupdate.com
The Parisian
www.theparisian.org

When to Go

When you go to Paris depends on what you are looking for. Some people find the Christmas lights on the Champs-Élysées thrillingly romantic, or come in winter to avoid other tourists. "April in Paris" is beautiful, but may be cold and rainy. May and June usually have fine weather. During July and August, the city is fairly laid-back as many of its residents are on vacation, and the Métro is filled with tourists; many shops and restaurants are closed in August. September brings la rentrée—the return of vacationing Parisians— and with it an upswing in activity. Paris is lovely in the fall, when the chestnut trees turn rust-colored and children return to school.

It would take a lifetime to discover all of Paris's treasures, but if you have only one week and have never been here before, the sites mentioned above should be part of the master plan. Most of the major monuments are clustered fairly close together on either side of the Seine on the Right and Left Banks, and many are within walking distance. All can be reached in 30 to 40 minutes by Métro from the center of Paris. A Bateau-Mouche (www.bateaux-mouches.fr) ride along the Seine at the beginning of your trip or an OpenBus tour will help you get the lay of the land.

Rest & Relaxation

Visiting more than one museum a day is not recommended, except for those high in energy and artistic curiosity, especially since long lines often mean waits to get in. Plan to stop frequently in cafés or restaurants to rest and recuperate and prevent oversaturation blues. In fine weather, a good way to relax and rest your feet is a stop in the **Luxembourg** or **Tuileries Gardens.** When it rains, a film in one of Paris's dozens of cinemas might be in order (check that your English-language films are marked "VO"—for version originale—which means they are shown in the original language with French subtitles). A nap at the hotel before dinner is also recommended to keep your strength up and whet your appetite (most restaurants do not begin to serve dinner until 8 p.m.).

For blockbuster temporary art exhibitions, such as those usually held at the **Grand Palais,** it is a good idea to book online far ahead, even before you leave home. The 2010 Monet exhibition, for example, was sold out far in advance—despite offering entrance 24 hours a day.

Top Ten Local Phrases

Where is the bathroom?	Où sont les toilettes?
How much does it cost?	Combien ça coute? Or just Combien?
Where is the nearest Métro station?	Où est le Métro le plus proche?
I don't understand.	Je ne comprends pas.
Pleased to meet you.	Enchanté(e).
See you later.	A plus tard.
Thank you. You are very kind.	Merci. Vous êtes très gentil(le).
Do you know a good, inexpensive restaurant in this area?	Connaissez-vous un bon restaurant, pas trop cher, dans le quartier?
I would like to reserve a table for two.	Je voudrais réserver une table pour deux.

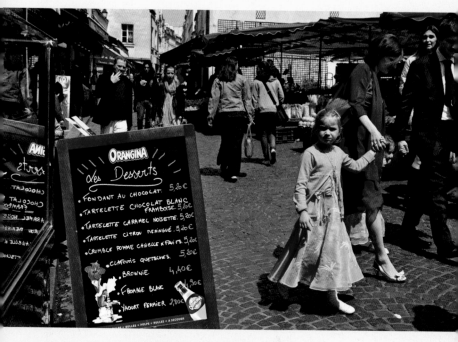

Gastronomic treats beckon at the market on Rue Mouffetard in the Latin Quarter.

If You Have More Time

Once you have taken the elevator to the top of the Eiffel Tower, seen the "Mona Lisa," admired the view of the Champs-Élysées from the Arc de Triomphe, and visited the other attractions mentioned above, that does not mean you have done Paris. If you have more than a week or are visiting for the second (or third, or fourth) time, hundreds of other things remain to do, beginning with visits to smaller museums like the **Marmottan-Monet,** near the Bois de Boulogne, or the **Musée Gustave-Moreau,** in the 9th arrondissement.

Cooking classes, many of which include market visits, are a wonderful way to immerse yourself in French culture—or join the crowds in Sunday-morning food markets like the **Marché d'Aligre** near Bastille. Flea markets are another option. The permanent ones on the outskirts of Paris are open every weekend, but temporary flea markets are often held in different neighborhoods (check the "Brocantes" section of weekly events guide *Pariscope*). During the week, the **Village Saint-Paul** in the Marais is a peaceful haven for antique hunters. Other options are to explore Paris's many beautiful parks or join a walking or biking tour.

The possibilities for out-of-town excursions are almost limitless as well. **Versailles** is the most obvious, but there are many other châteaus that can be visited on a day trip from Paris: **Fontainebleau, Chantilly,** and **Malmaison** among them. A number of fascinating sites are only an hour or so away by train and can be visited in one day, among them **Provins, Giverny,** and the stunning **Chartres Cathedral.**

History & Culture

Above: A clock approaches the eleventh hour at the Musée d'Orsay. Opposite: Stained-glass windows at Notre-Dame

Paris Today

"Paris vaut bien une messe" (Paris is well worth a mass), said King Henri IV on converting to Catholicism in 1593. Then as now it would have been hard to disagree. Paris was the political heart of France, and since then has more often than not been the political as well as the geographical heart of Europe.

Known as the City of Light, Paris is considered by many people to be the world's most beautiful city. Its monuments and treasures are better preserved than those of any rival city. But Paris is much more than that. It is an international city that controls the larger part of France's economy, the third most successful in the European Union, after Germany and the United Kingdom.

The French capital for over a thousand years, Paris was central to the establishment of the modern French state, which developed out of the initial domain of the Capetian kings (roughly Paris to Orléans) over some six centuries. The city is the governmental, economic, and cultural axis around which French society has revolved, a trend that has grown since the French Revolution. This historic trend has been diluted by a series of decentralization measures, and Marseille, Lyon, Bordeaux, and other major cities have developed their own identities and clout as a result. Yet France remains the creation of a capital of which it has often been a mere extension—in other words, as the saying goes, when Paris sneezes, France catches cold.

The Importance of "Bonjour"

Walk up to a French person in the Parisian street and say, "Excuse me, where is the Louvre?" and the response is likely to be an intense stare, followed by a pause for effect, and *"Bonjour."* Not saying *"bonjour"* as you enter a shop or before you launch into whatever you want to say is considered extremely rude. So be a good visitor and say instead, *"Bonjour, Madame/ Monsieur* [far more polite and respectful]. *Parlez-vous anglais?"* If the answer is affirmative, then ask your question. You may make a friend for life.

The Paris Region & Its Economy

Paris is blessed with great natural assets: Straddling the middle reaches of the Seine, the city lies at the center of Europe's greatest sedimentary basin (the Bassin Parisien). The basin's agricultural resources, which exploit the rich alluvial soils of its plains and low plateaus, have traditionally been the backbone of the French economy. The Paris region dominates a wide area extending from Normandy in the west, around Picardy and Champagne to the north and east, and through the Beauce country of Chartres between the Seine and the Loire to the south. Within this broad geographic area, today's Région d'Île-de-France (one of 22 French metropolitan regions) covers a little over 4,500 square miles (12,000 sq km), forming a threefold concentric ring of eight *départements* (out of a total of 95 départements in mainland France) around the capital, which, since 1976, has resumed its status of commune with its own mayor.

The elegant displays of the Galeries Lafayette make it an iconic shopping destination.

EXPERIENCE: The Personal Touch at B&Bs

How to meet the French? Those who are not naturally chatty could try staying in a bed and breakfast. Parisians who operate B&Bs are generally those who are most interested in meeting foreigners. Some sit down with arriving guests for a drink and a snack in their living room or enjoy getting to know them over breakfast. Try booking through these agencies, whose members have signed the city of Paris's "Quality Charter" specifying standards: **Alcôve & Agapes: Paris Bed &**

Breakfast (tel 01 44 85 06 05, www .bed-and-breakfast-in-paris.com), **Association Française BAB France** (tel 01 34 19 90 00, www.bedbreak.com), **Fleurs de Soleil** (tel 08 26 62 03 22, www .fleursdesoleil.fr), **Good Morning Paris** (tel 01 47 07 28 29, www.goodmorningparis.fr), **Une Chambre en Ville** (tel 01 44 06 96 71, www.chambre-ville.com), **2binparis** (tel 01 82 88 01 45, www.2binparis.com). The city's official B&B site: **Hôtes Qualité Paris** (www.hotesqualiteparis.fr).

One of the great victories of Paris has been to contain the city proper within the Périphérique ring road, keeping the city a manageable size. With a clean, extensive, efficient, and constantly modernized transport system, this means that few journeys across town take more than 40 minutes.

The Parisian Population

The city's population began to stabilize during the 1920s and now counts 2.2 million inhabitants, while the suburbs began their rapid expansion. Some 3 million people a day travel from the suburbs into Paris to work. The city is constantly evolving; only about one in three Parisians was born in the capital. Immigration also has influenced the city's demographics. From the mid-1950s to the 1970s, labor shortages led to massive recruitment campaigns in North Africa and poorer European regions like southern Italy, Spain, and Greece. Today one Parisian in seven is of foreign nationality, the predominant groups being Africans, Algerians, and Tunisians.

Paris is divided into 20 districts called *arrondissements,* which spiral out in a circle from the center (Châtelet) like a snail shell. Parisians tend to identify strongly with their own *quartier* (neighborhood), whether it be the stodgier 16th arrondissement or one of the lively multiethnic areas of Belleville, Chinatown, or Ménilmontant to the east.

Many American, Japanese, and European nationals opt for the inner-city arrondissements of the center or west. Those from Southeast Asia (primarily Cambodia, Laos, and Vietnam) have gravitated to the 13th; many Chinese and Turks live in the 10th; many people from sub-Saharan Africa or Algeria are in the 18th; and many from sub-Saharan Africa or China in the 19th. The Belleville district straddling four arrondissements (10th, 11th, 19th, 20th) is a melting pot of the various ethnic and religious groups.

The Paris population is young, with twice as many single people as families with children. Most Paris apartments are extremely small (over half have only two rooms or less); the housing shortage (construction has shifted from residential to office building in many areas) and exorbitant prices have exacerbated the problem, driving many Parisians, both well-off and less well-off, into the suburbs.

Parisian Life

One of the municipal priorities is to maintain the city's diversity. In practical terms, this means a commitment made in 2001 to create 3,500 new public housing units, seen as a source of vitality, per year. Meanwhile, certain districts of working-class arrondissements to the east are attracting fairly well-off young people, encouraged by lower real-estate prices and the villagelike feel of these neighborhoods. This demographic shift has both negative and positive impacts: Locals welcome the trendy new shops, bars, and restaurants the *bobos* (bourgeois bohemians) bring, yet often bemoan the watering down of the neighborhood's original character.

The bobos have also been active in creating residents' associations and campaigning for more green spaces and bicycle lanes, much to the chagrin of architects and shop owners who maintain that they're an obstacle to the capital's economic development and risk turning Paris into a "pedestrianized museum." But they seem to have Paris's Socialist mayor Bertrand Delanoë on their side. One of his most memorable contributions has been the creation of Paris Plages, a month-long summer operation that transforms stretches of the Right and Left Bank and the Bassin de la Villette with small strips of sand, palm trees, deck chairs, food stands, beach volleyball courts, and swimming pools. This and a host of restored museums, new restaurants and bars, and improved transportation have injected new life into this ever changing but eternal city. ■

A young couple takes a skating break on the Pont Neuf.

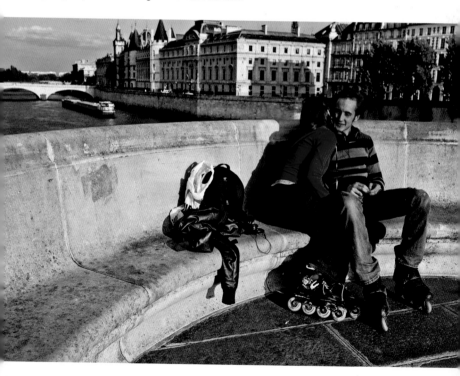

History of Paris

The history of Paris is very much present throughout the city today. Various quarters—the Napoleonic Opéra area or the 17th-century Marais, for example—bear the mark of Parisian rulers.

The Celts

The site where Paris is today was occupied from as early as the fifth or fourth millennium B.C. until the early Iron Age (circa 800–700 B.C.). Neolithic humans inhabited the island that would become Île de la Cité, as well as a rocky spur on the left bank that served as an observation point. The island subsequently was abandoned, probably due to climatic changes, until around 250–225 B.C., when a

Gallic leader Vercingétorix surrenders to Caesar, in a painting by Lionel Royer (1899).

Celtic tribe called the Parisii settled there. The Parisii lived mainly from river trade until approximately 90 B.C., when they began to mint high-quality gold coins. This continued until the Romans arrived in the middle of the first century B.C.

In 53 B.C., seizing upon its strategic geographical position, Julius Caesar used the island as his base during his campaign to quell the insurrection of the neighboring Senones. According to Caesar's *Gallic War*, by 52 B.C., the Celt Vercingétorix had convinced the Parisii to revolt against the Romans. When Caesar's lieutenant Labienus and four legions arrived to crush them, the Gauls (Gaul was the Roman name for France) set fire to the Cité and destroyed its bridges. Labienus then surrounded the Gallic positions, killing the Celtic general Camulogenus and routing the other Gauls. (Historians are divided over where the battle took place; it may have occurred on the plain of Grenelle.)

Lutetia, as it was known, flourished under the Romans. The settlement was reconstructed and a wall built around it in the early second century A.D. Rustic Gallic dwellings were

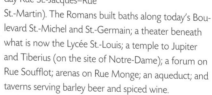

Toward the mid-third century, Lutetia became a Christian center through the efforts of Saint Denis, the city's first bishop.

replaced with homes built along actual streets. A new city sprang up across the Petit Pont on the left bank, around the cardo, the main north–south street of the Roman city (the present-day Rue St.-Jacques–Rue St.-Martin). The Romans built baths along today's Boulevard St.-Michel and St.-Germain; a theater beneath what is now the Lycée St.-Louis; a temple to Jupiter and Tiberius (on the site of Notre-Dame); a forum on Rue Soufflot; arenas on Rue Monge; an aqueduct; and taverns serving barley beer and spiced wine.

Toward the mid-third century, Lutetia became a Christian center through the efforts of Saint Denis, the city's first bishop. For years, the Romans tolerated Denis as he converted followers and founded churches. But eventually they clamped down on Christianity and ordered his arrest. According to legend, Denis was beaten, thrown to the lions, and crucified. Refusing to abjure his faith, he was dragged to the Mont des Martyrs (later Montmartre) and beheaded. He then rose, picked up his head, and carried it to a village north of Paris. The Basilica of St.-Denis was later built on the site of the martyr's tomb, and Denis became the patron saint of France.

Christianity & Barbarism

Constantine I made Christianity the official religion of the Empire in 313. His nephew Julian the

Apostate, who rose to the imperial throne in 361, would play a large role in promoting Paris as an imperial city (although a third-century decree renamed Lutetia "Paris," Julian continued to call it Lutetia). He also did a great deal to defend Gaul from barbarian invasions until he was killed in battle in 363. Over the next century, Roman power weakened, and by the early fifth century it had virtually collapsed.

Middle Ages

The Merovingians: The Frankish king Merovech (*R.447–457*) and his son Childeric I (*R.457–481*) proved loyal allies of Rome against Attila the Hun and other invaders. As the Empire disintegrated, Childeric's son Clovis (*R.481–511*) formally added the Roman provinces of western Gaul to his realm in Flanders, thus establishing the Frankish Kingdom, the forerunner of the modern French state. The educated Gallo-Romans found themselves subject to the crude culture of the bloodthirsty Merovingians—called the "long-haired kings" because cutting their hair was seen as a disgrace that barred them from the throne.

In 486, Clovis triumphed over the Romans at Soissons. A pagan, he married a Catholic, Clothilda of Burgundy, in 491 and was baptized at Reims. Clovis made Paris his capital in 508. Three years later he died, and the Merovingian kingdom was divided into four parts. One of Clovis's descendants, Dagobert (*R.628–639*), established the annual Fair of St.-Denis outside Paris in 635, and the city once again became a leading commercial and cultural center.

By Philippe the Fair's reign (1285–1314), Paris was the site of political decision making and the main seat of royalty.

The Carolingians: Dagobert's descendants, nicknamed *"les rois fainéant"* or "do-nothing kings," allowed power to slip into the hands of the palace mayors, and Pepin the Short had himself elected king in 751. His bastard son Charlemagne became king of the Franks in 768 and in 30 years, reconquered a large part of the old western Roman Empire. In December 800, he was crowned emperor by the Pope, choosing Aachen (Aix-la-Chapelle) as the capital of his Holy Roman Empire.

In the ninth century, Paris became a target for Viking raiders in quest of plunder, and the city was repeatedly attacked from 845 to 885. Charlemagne's great empire had now split into three kingdoms, and was too disrupted to organize effective resistance. Disgruntled nobles and clergy, therefore, turned to the warrior Robert the Strong, Count of Anjou and Blois. He was killed by Vikings, and his son Eudes (Odo) became Count of Paris (under the Carolingians, palace mayors were replaced by hereditary counts). Parisians placed their trust in Eudes, then restored the Roman walls around the Île de la Cité and built two *châtelets*, or castles.

The Capetians: After Charles III (the Fat) was deposed in 887, the nobles set a precedent by electing Count Eudes king instead of the legitimate Carolingian heir. When the last Carolingian king—Louis V—died, Hugues Capet (Count of Paris) was elected king in 987 and crowned at Noyon. The Capetian dynasty ruled from Paris, imbuing the city with a prestige unknown since Clovis. Trade and commerce expanded on the right bank. The powerful abbeys and fairs at St.-Denis and St.-Germain played a key role in the development, as did Abbot Suger, a shrewd administrator who commissioned the new basilica of St.-Denis—France's first Gothic building—in 1136.

The royal domains doubled during the reign of Philippe-Auguste (1180–1223), who took a great interest in Paris. He backed a University of Paris charter, paved the main streets, built a market at Les Halles, and laid the Louvre's foundations. Before embarking on the Crusades, Philippe-Auguste ordered the expansion of the city's protective wall, which was to encompass areas on both banks of the Seine. Vestiges of the wall can be seen in the Latin Quarter and the Marais.

Saint Geneviève

When word spread that Attila and his Huns were headed toward Paris in 451, the people panicked and made ready to flee. A young Gallo-Roman woman from Nanterre, named Geneviève, urged the inhabitants to remain, pray to God, and do works of penance to avert the invasion. Luckily for Geneviève, Attila's plan was not to ransack Paris, but to reach the Loire at Orléans and attack the Visigoths. Geneviève was credited with a miracle and proclaimed the savior of Paris. As Saint Geneviève, she was said to continue to protect the city through her relics.

Philippe-Auguste's grandson, Louis IX (R.1226–1270), was known as Saint Louis for his piety. He commissioned Ste.-Chapelle to house part of the True Cross and the Crown of Thorns. By Philippe the Fair's reign (1285–1314), Paris was the site of political decision making and the main seat of royalty. Philippe made the Parlement of Paris a legitimate court of law (not a governing body), and convoked the first French Estates-General. He also built the magnificent Salle des Gens d'Armes in the Conciergerie. His three sons ascended the throne in succession, following his death in 1314; the last, Charles IV, died in 1328 without leaving a male heir.

House of Valois

Edward III of England (Philippe IV's grandson) believed he had a better right to the French throne than the late king's cousin, Philippe de Valois. This claim was denied on the grounds of a new addition to the Salic Law forbidding matrilineal inheritance. (Edward was the son of Philippe IV's daughter.) Philippe de Valois (Philippe VI, R.1328–1350) claimed the throne, launching the Valois Dynasty and precipitating the onset of the Hundred Years' War between England and France.

During this war, Parisians became instrumental in politics, as the king appealed regularly for financial support in raising war revenues. The period was marked by strife, with the Black Death claiming nearly a third of the French population in 1348. Étienne Marcel, who was Merchant Provost, had become a spokesman for Parisians, who were angry over government corruption and the court's lavish lifestyle. He assembled 3,000 armed men and invaded the Île de la Cité palace in 1358, slitting the throats of two advisers of the future Charles V as the boy looked on. The event was said to have traumatized Charles V (the Wise, R.1364–1380), who later moved the royal residence to the more secure Louvre. Charles V beautified Paris, with garden layouts, palaces, and private mansions. He also extended the city walls and built the Bastille in eastern Paris.

Late Middle Ages & Renaissance: France had long been at war with England. Following the Battle of Agincourt in 1415, the English, in alliance with the dukes of

Burgundy, appeared victorious. From 1420 to 1436, Paris was under English rule, and Henry VI of England was anointed King of France in Paris in 1431. Famine and rebellions afflicted the besieged city and wolves roamed the streets. Charles VII (R.1422–1461) finally liberated Paris and retook his capital.

France made an impressive recovery during the late 15th and early 16th centuries. The restored House of Valois regained its royal authority, and the economy began to expand. Printing was introduced, and perfumes, ladies' underwear, and forks were imported. The kings, influenced by Italian urban concepts integrating beauty with functional design, took a growing interest in their city. Gothic designs, such as the Église St.-Séverin, the Hôtel de Sens, and the Hôtel de Cluny, were added to the cityscape.

François I (R.1515–1547), an ostentatious patron of the arts who expanded royal absolutism and fostered intellectual freedom, declared Paris his residence in 1528. The city became more cosmopolitan, and artists such as Leonardo da Vinci and Benvenuto Cellini worked at his court. François renovated the Louvre; built superb castles at Chambord, Blois, and Fontainebleau; commissioned the lavish Hôtel de Ville; and drew up many of the main streets. Renaissance art found new expression in the Fontaine des Innocents, the St.-Eustache church, and the Tuileries Palace.

St. Bartholomew's Day Massacre: The Protestant Reformation began in Wittenberg in 1517, with Martin Luther's protest of the Church's sale of indulgences. In Paris, many intellectuals, princes, and wealthy merchants embraced the ideas behind the Reformation, in contrast to the capital's heavily Catholic lower classes.

Catherine de Médicis, the wife of François I's successor, Henri II (R.1547–1559), wielded immense power. She played the two ideological groups off each other, permitting an armed conflict to develop that led to the first of the Religious Wars.

> Absolute monarchy—by divine right—reached its apogee under Louis XIV, "the Sun King," who inherited the throne at the age of five.

Religious strife and paranoia were exacerbated by factional fighting between the Huguenot Prince de Condé and the Catholic Duc de Guise. Accused heretics were burned at the Place Maubert. The planting of a rumor that Huguenots (French Calvinist Protestants) were planning to "cut the king's throat, kill his brothers, and pillage the city of Paris" led to the St. Bartholomew's Day Massacre of August 24, 1572, during which Catholic mobs turned on Protestants. Approximately 5,000 were killed in the capital alone.

Henri III's (R.1574–1589) proposal of compromise made him hugely unpopular. His immediate heir was the Protestant Henri de Navarre, but the population backed Henri, Duc de Guise, who became leader of the Catholic League. A revolt broke out following the latter's assassination in 1588, and Henri III and Henri de Navarre besieged Paris. When a League monk assassinated Henri III in 1589, Henri de Navarre (IV) became king, founding the Bourbon dynasty.

Henri IV: Henri IV's (R.1589–1610) Protestantism remained an obstacle to his recognition by royalist Catholics who held Paris against him. In 1593 he converted to Catholicism, a step that all but completed his great task of unifying a fractious

The tombs of French monarchs Henri II and Catherine de Médicis in the Cathédrale St.-Denis

country. A year later, he was anointed at Chartres and entered the capital on March 22, 1594. He then sought to consolidate royal power. Henri IV completed the Pont Neuf (the first Paris bridge that was not lined with houses or shops, but with sidewalks and benches); commissioned the Place Dauphine; and laid out royal squares.

But the Catholic League had not forgiven its old opponent, and—after more than 20 assassination attempts—Henri IV was stabbed to death by the fanatic François Ravaillac, in May 1610, while caught in a traffic jam on the Rue de la Ferronnerie.

Ancien Régime

Louis XIII: Henri IV's son Louis XIII (R.1610–1643) was only eight at the time of his father's death. His domineering mother, Marie de Médicis, served as regent until Louis XIII assumed power in 1617. The real head of his government was Cardinal Richelieu (who became Chief Minister in 1624), a shrewd administrator whose centralizing policies—along with those of his successor Cardinal Mazarin—paved the way for royal absolutism. He commissioned the Palais Cardinal (later the Palais-Royal), rebuilt the Sorbonne, and founded the Académie Française. The Counter-Reformation fostered the construction of convents, chapels, and churches such as Val-de-Grâce, built in 1638 to commemorate the "miraculous" birth of Louis XIII's son, the future Louis XIV (Anne of Austria's first child at the age of 37).

Rebellious Stirrings: Absolute monarchy—by divine right—reached its apogee under Louis XIV (R.1643–1715), "the Sun King," who inherited the throne at the age of five. The Parlement sought to check the young king's power by drawing up a constitution; the aristocratic opposition wanted shared power, but was fraught with dissension. Rumors that taxes were to be paid in proportion to income resulted in panic and protest. In July 1648, Chief Minister Cardinal Mazarin, co-regent for Louis with Anne of Austria, declared that the young king would not repay his debts.

The Fronde, a series of rebellions by nobles and their supporters against absolutism and tax policy, spread violence in Paris from 1648 to 1653, with troops led by the Prince de Condé besieging the city and blocking its food supply. Louis assumed full power in 1661 following Mazarin's death, and a desire for order ultimately permitted the king's absolutism to flourish.

The Sun King: The 23-year-old Louis embarked on a series of wars to establish France's supremacy in Europe. At first he delegated important affairs of state to

Anne of Austria and the infant Louis XIV in an anonymous 17th-century painting.

Mazarin's successor, Jean-Baptiste Colbert, who sought to replenish the royal treasury and make Paris more secure. He introduced an anticorruption campaign, created the Lieutenant General of Police, and organized firefighting. He also ordered the city's reconstruction according to a classical ideal, resulting in the Place Vendôme, Place des Victoires, the Invalides, and the Observatory.

But Louis's attention was focused less on Paris than on Versailles. The Sun King poured vast amounts of money into the palace and moved his court there in 1682, where political power was out of the reach of street movements. Almost 10,000 people worked in the vast palace and its expanse of formal gardens, a virtual city of servants and courtiers. By keeping the aristocracy under his supervision, Louis also severed the independence of high nobles, who were reduced to squabbling over who would—literally—wipe the royal behind.

But financing wars and the king's extravagance put a strain on the economy, as did the exodus of skilled artisans and merchants after the king revoked the Edict of Nantes (which granted Huguenots religious and civil liberties) in 1685. To meet rising expenses, Colbert had been forced to revert to short-term expedients to increase taxation revenue. The root of financial problems, however, was the tax collection system itself more than expenditures. Louis XIV's legacy was a modern system of government financed by a semi-medieval taxation system.

Cour des Miracles

During the 15th, 16th, and 17th centuries, war and the plague spawned masses of homeless people in France. Many came to Paris, gravitating toward the side streets just inside Charles V's Wall. By day, they made a living as beggars, pretending to be crippled, maimed, blind, and orphaned, or worked the crowds alongside the swindlers and thieves. At night, they disappeared into the alleyways, miraculously cured—hence the area's name, Cour des Miracles.

The Cour des Miracles was shut down by police in 1667, with the so-called cripples leading the flight from the security forces.

Louis XV: After Louis XIV's death in 1715, the court and young Louis XV (R.1715–1774) moved back to Paris under the regent Philippe d'Orléans, a dissipated rake who allowed the great noble families to regain their former independence. Parisians sought to forget the austerity of Louis XIV's final years, opting for bright colors and a dash of frivolity. This was the age of Watteau's lighthearted paintings and Charles Perrault's fairy tales.

A period of political stability followed under the king's chief adviser, André de Fleury, with overseas trade and improved transportation boosting commercial development. Paris grew on both banks, with the stylish new faubourgs (quarters outside the old walls) of St.-Germain and St.-Honoré. After de Fleury's death in 1743, Louis XV took over as head of government. He commissioned the Place Louis XV (now the Place de la Concorde), the Ste.-Geneviève Church (Panthéon), the Odéon theater, the École Militaire, and the Champ de Mars.

Where the Ghosts Are

With more than 2,000 years of history, the city of Paris cannot help but be haunted by a few ghosts. The prime real estate that is the Tuileries Garden, for example, is said to be haunted by a butcher known as Jean l'Ecorcheur (John the Skinner). His assassination was supposedly ordered by Queen Catherine des Médicis, who built the Tuileries Palace, because he knew too much about her occult activities. "I shall return," he told his assassin. He is said to have appeared to Marie-Antoinette when she was imprisoned in the palace, to Napoleon just before the Battle of Waterloo, and to the Communards who burned the palace down in 1870.

On the Left Bank, the Luxembourg Gardens are visited by a man in a frock coat who may invite visitors to a concert. Beware: The concert took place a century ago. Another park with a ghostly presence is the Parc de Montsouris, haunted by the wailing of the headless corpse of Isauré de Montsouris, who was decapitated by a band of thieves in 831. And, of course, many legends surround the Père-Lachaise Cemetery, where black masses and human sacrifices are said to have taken place. And watch out if you spy a huge red cat there with an unusual gait—it may not be what it appears.

The Enlightenment: Louis XV's lack of character resulted in nearly 50 years of weak government. He sought distraction in hunting and in women, one of whom was his famous mistress, the Marquise de Pompadour. She was a friend of Denis Diderot, who recruited the major French thinkers of the Enlightenment to write the *Encyclopédie*, a remarkable compendium of ideas championing skepticism and rationalism. The first volume was published in 1751.

The 18th century brought great interest in reform, as political and financial structures were not keeping pace with social changes. Montaigne, Descartes, Newton, and others had laid the groundwork for unorthodox ideas—stifled under Louis XIV but now flourishing. By mid-century, revolutionary ideas on science and philosophy circulated through the fashionable salons held by influential women such as Madame Geoffrin.

French Revolution

Louis XVI's Government: The Parlements became the center of opposition to Louis XIV's weaker successors. The Parlement of Paris saw itself as the defender of constitutional liberties, and although Louis XVI (*R.*1774–1792) tried to enact reforms, the Parlement continued to spread opposition and revolutionary ideas.

To gain favor with the people, the king appointed Jacques Necker as Director General of Finances in 1777. Necker was a popular figure, an ally of the commoners. The French government was on the verge of bankruptcy, due in part to expenses incurred by France during the American Revolution. In 1785, work began on the Fermiers Généraux (Tax Collectors) wall around Paris. Heavy taxes were levied on goods entering and leaving the city, fueling popular discontent. The *vingtième*, a tax on one-twentieth of all incomes, had been introduced in 1749, but the nobility refused to pay, and the clergy led the opposition to the tax.

Third Estate: After attempts to avert bankruptcy failed, Louis XVI was forced to convene the Estates-General to try to raise new taxes. The Estates-General was composed of the clergy (First Estate); the nobility (Second Estate); and the commoners (Third Estate), each voting as a block. Its meeting in May 1789—for the first time since 1614—marked the abdication of absolute monarchy and the empowerment of the Third Estate. A new kind of revolution was to emerge, one no longer led by the Parlements, nobility, and clergy. The hidden impetus was the supply and price of food—primarily bread—following the disastrous harvest of 1788.

Representing 96 percent of the population, the Third Estate proclaimed itself the National Assembly on June 17. When their meeting hall was closed, the deputies adjourned to a nearby *jeu de paume*, or indoor tennis court, and took an oath (June 20) to meet until a constitution was drafted. Troops, largely foreign, continued to pour into Paris and Versailles, and on July 11 Necker was dismissed and replaced by Queen Marie-Antoinette's favorite, the Baron de Breteuil.

Revolt Against the Monarchy: On July 14, orators at the Palais-Royal incited the people to take up arms. They attacked Les Invalides to procure munitions, then stormed the Bastille's armory. Refusing to surrender, the governor was killed and his head was paraded around Paris on a pike to mark the victory. Louis XVI proceeded to the Hôtel de Ville, where he accepted the tricolor cockade from the new municipal government, or commune.

In October, angry Parisians marched to Versailles to protest high bread prices—when Marie-Antoinette allegedly told them to try brioche instead. In Paris, political clubs guided the National Assembly in drafting a constitution. The king and queen fled the city on June 20, 1791, but were recognized at Varennes and brought to the Tuileries Palace in humiliation. The king accepted the constitution, thus creating a limited monarchy.

> By [the mid-18th century], revolutionary ideas on science and philosophy circulated through the fashionable salons.

Exasperation of Parisians with the government led to the radicalization of the *sans-culottes* ("without breeches"; the lower classes wore trousers instead of aristocratic breeches) in 1792. On August 10, 1792, when a demand that Louis XVI be deposed was refused, they attacked the Tuileries, and an insurrectionary commune replaced the legally elected one.

Reign of Terror: Mobs stormed the prisons during the September massacres, killing nearly 2,000 suspected traitors. The monarchy was abolished on September 22, 1792—the first day of Year 1 of the French Republic, according to the new revolutionary calendar. The king was tried for treason and guillotined on January 21, 1793; Marie-Antoinette followed him nine months later. The Reign of Terror, ostensibly a campaign against foreign spies directed by the Committee of Public Safety—which included the revolutionary leaders Maximilien Robespierre and Louis Saint-Just—was in reality an attempt to purge "enemies from within." Thousands were guillotined, including Robespierre himself, in July 1794.

The National Convention, which had been elected to draw up a new constitution, set up a five-man Directory, fraught with internal dissension and dependent on the army to maintain control. The Directory was overthrown by a coup d'état in November 1799, and army hero Napoleon Bonaparte (R.1804–1814) was declared First Consul.

19th-Century Paris

First Empire: Napoleon's popularity rose as peace returned, and he quickly shaped France into a powerful, centralized state. Although he distrusted Paris and considered shifting the imperial seat to Lyon, he understood the capital's key position. He set about marking it with his imperial stamp following his coronation on December 2, 1804—building new boulevards, palaces, and imposing Roman-style monuments, such as the Arc de Triomphe, the Madeleine, and the Bourse. He also expanded the Louvre's collections with booty from abroad.

While pursuing military campaigns, Napoleon boosted the economy and trade, established the Code Napoleon for civil law, set up the Grandes Écoles, and revamped the administrative system. But the success of his initial campaigns waned, particularly after the catastrophic invasion of Russia in 1812. In early 1814, Paris was occupied by the allied troops of Russia, Austria, Prussia, and Great Britain, and Napoleon was exiled to Elba. King Louis XVIII (Louis XVI's gout-afflicted brother; R.1814–1824) was restored to the throne with Talleyrand's help, but fled when Napoleon escaped from Elba a year later for his Hundred Days' Rule. Napoleon was crushed in the Waterloo Campaign (June 12–18) and was banished to the island of St. Helena by the British government.

> Although [Napoleon] distrusted Paris and considered shifting the imperial seat to Lyon, he understood the capital's key position.

The Revolution of 1830: Louis XVIII returned to Paris on July 8. His chief ministers initially were moderates, but the ultraroyalists eventually got the upper hand. Electoral laws were revised to favor the wealthy and civil liberties were curbed. Louis's successor, the reactionary Charles X (R.1824–1830), went further, dissolving the liberal Chamber of Deputies in May 1830, banning the press, and modifying electoral laws to favor property owners. On July 27, newspapers published defiantly; barricades soon went up and insurrection committees formed. A new provisional government ordered the tricolor raised, and three days of fighting ensued—the famous Trois Glorieuses (July 27–29)—forcing Charles into exile.

July Monarchy & Revolution: During the reign of Louis-Philippe (R.1830–1848), dubbed "the citizen king," class divisions became even more entrenched. Wealthy families could afford to live in spacious new districts like the 8th arrondissement, while the poor were packed into central districts like St.-Merri.

A painting by Lejeune depicts the 1800 Battle of Marengo, an early Napoleonic victory.

On February 23, 1848, troops opened fire on a crowd on the Boulevard des Capucines, killing more than 40. Parisians erected barricades and tore up paving stones on the Place Vendôme and the Rue Royale. Louis-Philippe abdicated the next day.

The provisional government, presided over by Alphonse Lamartine, included "Albert the mechanic"—the people's representative. It abolished slavery in the colonies and the death penalty for political crimes, decreed freedom of expression, granted universal suffrage to men, and set up national workshops on construction sites throughout France to ease unemployment.

In April 1848, a conservative commission was voted in, and Parisian revolutionaries and socialists took to the streets. On May 21, the national workshops were suppressed. The next day, rioting broke out to shouts of *"Du pain ou du plomb!"*—"Bread or lead!"—ending in a bloodbath that killed 3,000.

Second Empire: In late 1848, elections overwhelmingly brought Louis-Napoleon Bonaparte (the emperor's nephew) to power as France's first president. He carried out a coup d'état three years later (the constitution forbade running for a second term of office), and the following year he was installed as Napoleon III (*R.*1852–1870). Paris saw it as the triumph of order.

Louis-Napoleon's plans to modernize the city reflected this sense of order. He called upon Baron Haussmann, Prefect of Paris, to oversee the major projects (see p. 166).

New market halls at Les Halles were built, the Palais-Garnier commissioned, and the sewer system expanded. By the end of the Second Empire, Paris was a showcase for industrial exhibitions and the economy was thriving. But the euphoria was shattered when Napoleon III, recognizing that Prussia's rise posed a threat to France, declared war, precipitating the disastrous Franco-Prussian War of 1870.

Paris Commune: Following Napoleon III's military defeat at Sedan, September 2, 1870, and the fall of the imperial regime, a new Republic—proclaimed on September 4, 1870—prepared to face the advancing Prussians. By late September, the capital's troops numbered 500,000 (two-thirds of whom were grossly inexperienced). Although 30,000 cattle and 180,000 sheep were kept in the Bois de Boulogne as a backup food supply, the besieged Parisians went hungry that winter. Horses, dogs, cats, rats—even a few beasts from the zoo at the Jardin des Plantes—were eaten in the effort to survive.

Adolphe Thiers's government negotiated a temporary armistice with Bismarck on January 28, 1871. Terms included the surrender of Alsace and much of Lorraine, and many Parisians saw the armistice as a betrayal. On March 18, Thiers sent troops to confiscate 227 guns from the National Guard in Montmartre. The people refused to give up the guns, and when the troops sent to remove them started fraternizing with the crowd, two of their generals were executed. On March 28, the Commune of Paris was proclaimed, its principal demand being that Paris have a municipal government within a French

Charles de Gaulle leads a march down the Champs-Élysées, 1944.

democratic republic. The Commune laid out plans for compulsory primary education and workers' cooperatives.

Bloody Week & Its Aftermath: Thiers and the Versailles troops began a ferocious, five-week siege of Paris to suppress the Commune, culminating in Bloody Week (May 22–28). The greatly outnumbered Communards barricaded the streets, and shot many suspected of not resisting the troops. The government retook the city in a brutal assault, and on May 28, the Commune was defeated. Thousands of Communards were shot in reprisal; 147 were executed against the Federalists' Wall of Père-Lachaise Cemetery, with the death toll estimated at anywhere from 17,000 to 35,000.

Despite a mutual wariness between Parisians and the French government, one long-term impact of the siege was a surge in patriotism, which found expression in such spectacular new monuments as the Grand Palais and the Eiffel Tower—the centerpiece of the 1889 Universal Exposition marking the centenary of the French Revolution.

> In 1936, Léon Blum brought Radical Socialists, Socialists, and Communists together in a Popular Front government.

20th-Century Paris

Belle Epoque & World War I: During the belle epoque, Paris became as dynamic as it had been under Haussmann. The 1889 exposition featuring the Eiffel Tower was outdone only by the 1900 exposition, when the opening of the first Métro line launched the new century. Paris was the world's cultural capital, and artists, writers, and musicians were laying the foundations of the modern era.

The expansion was halted by the onset of war. By September 2, 1914, the Germans were 15 miles outside Paris. Five days later, 4,000 men were shuttled to the front in taxis. Following the Battle of the Marne, a German retreat was ordered and trench warfare began. In four years, Paris was hit by 746 bombs. Big Bertha, the huge cannon in the St.-Gobain forest 88 miles (140 km) away, lobbed more than 300 shells, each weighing 400 pounds, on the city. Morale in Paris had been badly damaged by the 1916 Battle of Verdun, when France suffered 163,000 dead and 320,000 wounded. Propaganda campaigns sought to boost morale, but the tide only really turned when the formidable Georges Clemenceau became prime minister in 1917 and led his country to victory.

Postwar Paris: The victory parade on Bastille Day in 1919 marked the end of a nightmare, yet the postwar years were harsh. The Depression exacerbated political crises, and on February 6, 1934, right-wing forces rallied protesters ranging from war veterans to Fascists on the Place de la Concorde, ostensibly against government corruption. Riots broke out, and police killed 15 and injured 1,500, including several "war heroes." Five days later, unions organized a massive strike in support of democracy. In 1936, Léon Blum brought Radical Socialists, Socialists, and Communists together in a Popular Front government, inaugurating collective bargaining and a 40-hour work week.

France and Britain declared war on Germany in September 1939. During the subsequent "Phoney War"—with the side having declared war awaiting attack—truckloads of art left the Louvre for Chambord, the stained-glass windows of Ste.-Chapelle were removed, and gas masks were distributed. Germany attacked France on May 10, 1940, forcing many Parisians into exodus. Paris was declared an open city and the government left for Bordeaux. On June 14, Paris fell.

Marshal Pétain, who became prime minister, demanded an armistice, triggering Charles de Gaulle's June 18 call from London to shore up "Free French" resistance. (De Gaulle, then Undersecretary of State for War, was sentenced to death in absentia by a Vichy court.) The armistice was signed, the Third Republic was dissolved, and Pétain became Head of State of the government of unoccupied France (now at Vichy), with more legal authority than any leader since Bonaparte.

The Occupation: The Germans occupied 60 percent of France, which became an ally in the Holocaust. There is no proof that Vichy acted under Nazi pressure to enact racial laws in 1940, yet it imposed a broader definition of a Jew than the Germans had. The laws also lowered the age of children subject to deportation.

During the Occupation, average Parisians were deprived of cars; bread, sugar, and other staples were rationed. Vegetable patches sprang up on rooftops. Street signs were in German, and the swastika flew over the Hôtel de Ville and the Eiffel Tower.

The Germans required the registration of all Jewish persons and launched anti-Jewish propaganda campaigns. An exhibit called "The Jew and France," designed to instruct the public on how to recognize Jews, featured a huge poster depicting a Shylock-like caricature of a Jewish man. All Jewish people over the age of six were forced to wear a yellow star in the occupied zone. They were barred from public places, many important jobs, and morning shopping hours, and had to ride in the last Métro car, dubbed "the Synagogue." Police sweeps in the Paris region began in May 1941, when Jewish men, at first mostly foreign, were rounded up. The first deportation train left for Germany in March 1942, half of the men being French Jews. During La Grande Rafle in July 1942, more than 8,000 people, including 4,115 children, were rounded up at the Vélodrome d'Hiver bicycle stadium in the 15th arrondissement. During the same period, the first French victims died in the gas chambers at Auschwitz.

The organized Resistance hid many Jewish people and helped them escape. Although one-third of French Jews were deported and killed, two-thirds were saved, largely through the efforts of French citizens and the Resistance.

> Hitler had instructed German Commander General von Choltitz to reduce the city to ashes . . . but he did not carry out the order.

The Liberation: The Allies landed in Normandy on June 6, 1944, and by August they were fast approaching Paris. An insurrection was launched on August 19, resulting in heavy casualties on both sides. Hitler had instructed German Commander General von Choltitz to reduce the city to ashes in case of defeat, but he did not carry out the order.

On the evening of August 24, an advance detachment from General Leclerc's Second Armored Division burst through the city to the Hôtel de Ville, and hundreds of church bells pealed above the roofs of Paris. On August 25, the main body of Leclerc's

President Nicolas Sarkozy delivers a speech in front of a French-made Airbus A380.

Division, in conjunction with the American 4th Infantry Division, liberated the city. The French flag was hoisted over the Eiffel Tower.

Modern France: De Gaulle emerged as the postwar leader of France, but in 1946 he brusquely withdrew during political maneuvering in forming the Fourth Republic. He was called back in 1958 during an uprising led by right-wing elements determined to keep Algeria as a French colony. De Gaulle prevailed, forming the Fifth Republic and becoming its first president. Algeria was proclaimed independent, and Paris at last began to enjoy prosperity.

This lasted until May 1968, when students demonstrated massively against France's obsolete educational system. Workers joined the movement and called a general strike that nearly paralyzed the country. Ten months after this upheaval, De Gaulle resigned, and Georges Pompidou was elected president, succeeded by Valéry Giscard d'Estaing. The latter's projects for Paris included the Musée d'Orsay. In 1981 Socialist François Mitterrand came to power, instituting a series of *grands travaux*. His Bibliothèque Nationale de France was completed after his death in 1996.

Former Paris mayor Jacques Chirac became president in 1995, and was followed by current right-of-center President Nicolas Sarkozy, who is having rather more success in opening up French markets and pushing through reforms than his predecessors. Socialist Bertrand Delanoë, elected mayor of Paris in 2001, however, has remained popular. ■

The Arts

Paris, the most visited city in the world, certainly owes its fame to its monuments and its history. But above all, this vibrant city basks in a rich cultural heritage and continues to attract leading exponents of literature, art, dance, theater, and opera.

Literature

Paris has always drawn writers looking for recognition and inspiration at the center of European intellectual society.

From the 15th to the 17th centuries, the long-established University of Paris was the home of scholastic philosophy, which tried to reconcile the thinking of Greek

Visitors climb the Louvre's floating staircase.

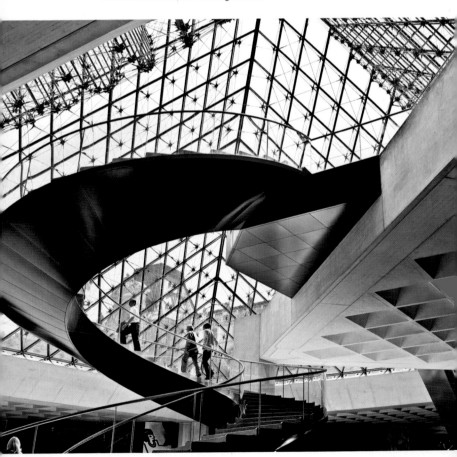

philosophers—particularly Aristotle and Plato—with Christian orthodoxy. It also played a part in the French Inquisition, forcing independent thinkers like 17th-century philosopher René Descartes to choose their words carefully to avoid prosecution. But theater flourished under Louis XIV. The plays of Jean Racine and Pierre Corneille elegantly retold the ancient Greek stories using classical French verse, while the satirist Molière amused his aristocratic audiences with plays depicting the pretensions and ambitions of the growing middle classes.

18th Century: Eighteenth-century literature was greatly influenced by a young aristocrat, François-Marie Arouet, who eventually went too far in his satires and was sent to the Bastille. There he changed his name to Voltaire. Upon his release, Voltaire became enormously popular, but was nonetheless forced to spend most of his life in exile. His contemporaries, Denis Diderot, Jean

> **In [19th-century] Paris there were strong personal links and friendships between creative artists.**

le Rond d'Alembert, and their circle, stayed on in Paris, producing the first French *Encyclopédie*. They became the center of the Enlightenment, which gradually brought intellectual tolerance to France.

Many of the next generation's circle of aristocratic and liberal French writers, whose works circulated through the famous literary salons, died while serving in Napoleon's armies. The most famous was Stendhal (Henri Marie Beyle), whose historical romances were the first important 19th-century French novels.

19th Century: After 1830, the French novel progressed from Honoré de Balzac through Gustave Flaubert, Victor Hugo, Émile Zola, and Marcel Proust to achieve a new form that described everyday life, investigated character, and propagated social and political ideas, thus enabling a massive, newly literate readership to understand more about the world around it.

Artists and poets were regarded in a new light, suddenly becoming important and influential social leaders. Some 19th-century poets, such as Charles Pierre Baudelaire and Théophile Gautier, shocked society by probing the darker sides of human nature, and were even prosecuted for their work. However, as the notoriety only increased sales, they received more benefit than harm. In Paris particularly, there were strong personal links and friendships between creative artists of all kinds, so that ideas spread rapidly, encouraging the emergence of new styles in painting, literature, and music. With the rise of the comfortable middle classes, survival was no longer the only aim in life, and artists led the way in prescribing the pursuit of pleasure as a new goal.

Throughout the middle years of the 19th century, Paris became a haven for intellectual and artistic refugees from all over Europe, such as Karl Marx, Richard Wagner, and Heinrich Heine, although some—among them Victor Hugo—who angered the monarchy were forced to flee the country. Talk of new systems in art, literature, philosophy, politics, and everyday institutions dominated the conversations at café tables from Montmartre to Montparnasse, bolstering the city's reputation as an artistic and intellectual center.

20th Century: Impressionism, which started in painting, also affected literary and musical techniques. The burgeoning modernism of the first decade of the 20th century took many forms—symbolism, imagism, cubism, and others—which André Breton employed in his surrealist school, perhaps the most successful of the modernist art movements.

Engineering Marvels

England astonished the world in 1851 with the Crystal Palace, built for the first Great Exhibition to showcase British goods and technical know-how. The French immediately began planning their own world's fair. The first of five *expositions*, most of which were based around the Champ de Mars, was held in 1867 (see p. 174).

The greatest French fair was the one held in 1889, when 28 million visitors came to marvel at the glittering cast-iron and glass structures covering the site and to look up amazed at the Tour Eiffel.

When American Sylvia Beach established her Shakespeare and Company bookshop on the Left Bank in 1919, Paris also became a haven for British and American writers, and she was the first to publish James Joyce's *Ulysses*. Dubbed "the lost generation" by Gertrude Stein, the Americans included popular novelists like journalist Ernest Hemingway and F. Scott Fitzgerald; literary magazine editors like the Crosbys and the Jolases, who published in Paris and in England; and others like James Joyce and Henry Miller, whose works were too outspoken and sexually frank to be published in their own, English-speaking countries. The poet T.S. Eliot collected material in Paris for his magazine *The Criterion,* and author and journalist Cyril Connolly came for the wine, food, and culture, and to get published by Jack Kahane's Obelisk Press (which was the first to publish Miller's controversial *Tropic of Cancer*).

Women writers such as Colette and Anaïs Nin also made their mark with their explicit descriptions of love and sex, setting the groundwork for later women who would challenge the predominantly male domain of erotic literature.

Post World War I: In the 1930s, antifascists and Jews fleeing Italy and Germany joined the expatriate Americans still in Paris. These included André Gide, André Malraux, Roger Martin du Gard, Jean Cocteau, Franz Werfel, Erich Remarque, and Odön von Horvath. During the war, a great many writers were either killed serving in the French army, in the Resistance, in concentration camps, or shot at borders. But throughout the war, a considerable underground press continued publishing works such as Vercors's novel *The Silence of the Sea,* about passive resistance to the Germans, and Paul Éluard's passionate poem *Liberté,* which was dropped on Paris by the Royal Air Force.

Literary Café Life from Postwar Paris to the Present: After the war, a new generation of writers, philosophers, and intellectuals that included Jean-Paul Sartre, Albert Camus, Boris Vian, and Simone de Beauvoir came to prominence. They, in turn, were followed by what became known as the *"nouveau roman,"* a legacy of surrealism. New theater also flourished in the plays written by such major figures as Samuel Beckett, Arthur Adamov, and Eugène Ionesco, who continued in the vein initiated by Antonin Artaud.

Today's Shakespeare and Company bookstore is a fixture of the Latin Quarter.

These writers, some not French-born, were soon joined by other expatriates from America and Britain, who produced small magazines in English for another new movement in literature, the "Beat" writers (whose starting place was thus as much in Paris as in San Francisco).

Although there has been a decline in literary café life in the last few decades, cafés like La Coupole, Flore, and Brasserie Lipp in St.-Germain, where Sartre held court, still recall the heyday of this vibrant past. One of the more recent literary discoveries—and source of scandal—is novelist and poet Michel Houellebecq, who wrote *Atomized* and *The Possibility of an Island*. Paris seems alive with a creativity that still lures artists today, and the city still has a reputation for recognizing talent.

Art

The art scene in Paris is as diverse and international as its literature, with galleries and exhibitions showing work by artists from Africa, Asia, America, and Europe.

Parisian Galleries: Art is alive and well in Paris, if the several hundred galleries in the city are any indication. Most are concentrated in three main areas:

The Panthéon Bouddhique in the Musée Guimet contains stone carvings and bodhisattvas.

St.-Germain-des-Prés, the Marais, and the 8th arrondissement, just behind the Champs-Élysées, which is now filled with galleries showing more recognized artists.

New artists are most likely to be found in the Marais area near Rue Vieille-du-Temple and in the 13th arrondissement. Generally speaking, more established artists exhibit in the dozens of galleries clustered around the Rue de Seine and the Rue Guénégaud in the St.-Germain neighborhood. A group of new galleries, primarily promoting conceptual art and *art contemporain,* has banded together on Rue Louise-Weiss in the 13th arrondissement, behind the four towers of the Bibliothèque de France.

It is possible to see artwork outside the galleries. A number of artists display their work in the square at Montmartre, though you'll have to sift through the purely commercial tourist work. There are also several artists' associations that organize *portes ouvertes,* or open houses, welcoming the public into their studios (usually in May and October). The Génie de la Bastille was the first of these, but others have sprung up in the 13th and 20th arrondissements, and in the suburbs of Ivry, Montreuil, and Montrouge, where many artists have moved to escape Paris's high rents.

Several publications (mostly in French) provide information about current shows, including the weekly *Pariscope,* the monthly *Beaux Arts Magazine, Art Press,* and a gallery guide that is available free of charge at galleries. This guide provides a map of the St.-Germain and Marais neighborhoods, with locations and dates of the *vernissages* (openings). The Drouot auction house puts out *La Gazette de l'Hôtel Drouot,* which features information about upcoming auctions and news on exhibitions and galleries.

Architecture

The architectural history of Paris is densely layered. Time and time again old buildings and monuments have been knocked down, or transformed or reused to make way for new ones. For example, vestiges of the Bastille prison were used to build the Concorde Bridge and the Théâtre du Marais (no longer standing), and stones from the Roman baths and Left Bank dwellings were used in medieval times to build a medieval defensive wall on the Île de la Cité.

Paris's earliest architectural elements are over 2,000 years old, dating from the time when the original settlement of Lutetia was only a backwater at the outer reaches of the Roman Empire. The ruins of two characteristic structures remain from this period: the heavily restored 16,000-seat Arena (rediscovered in the 19th century) and the baths of Cluny, now part of the Museé de Cluny.

Gothic & Medieval Architecture: The Île de France is the cradle of Gothic architecture, with its luminous churches heightened by their Gothic arches. In 1136, the Basilica of St.-Denis was begun, which was the first Gothic building to combine flying buttresses and ribbed vaulting; it was followed by the Cathedral of Notre-Dame in 1163, and the Flamboyant Gothic-style masterpiece, Ste.-Chapelle, built by Pierre de Montreuil in the following century. The Hôtel de Sens and the Hôtel de Cluny are among the few examples of secular Gothic architecture left in Paris.

Medieval architecture persisted in Paris long after the Renaissance had replaced it elsewhere. Although King François I brought back Renaissance ideas in architecture from his military campaigns in Italy, he only utilized them in the Loire Valley châteaus. Meanwhile, Paris continued to build Flamboyant Gothic buildings for nearly five centuries; they include the Tour St.-Jacques (1509–1523), the St.-Merri Church (1520–1552), and the St.-Gervais Church (1494–1657). Henri IV initiated the great royal squares, the first being today's Place des Vosges.

EXPERIENCE: Gallery Hopping

To really immerse yourself in Paris's impressive art scene, try a day or two of gallery hopping. Most high-end art galleries are clustered around Avenue Matignon and Rue du Faubourg-St.-Honoré in the 8th arrondissement. This is where Flemish Old Masters, 18th-century French furniture, and Picasso and other 20th-century masters can be found. One of the latest additions is the **Gagosian Gallery** (4 rue de Ponthieu, 75008, tel 01 45 63 98 06), specialist in big-name contemporary artists. On the Left Bank, the area around Rue de Seine and Rue Mazarine is home to many 20th-century art and design galleries, as well as contemporary galleries, one of the hottest at the moment being **Kamel Mennour** (47 rue Saint André des Arts, 75006, tel 01 56 24 03 63). The upper Rue Vieille du Temple between Rue des Francs Bourgeois and Rue de Bretagne is a hotbed for trendy galleries, among them **Galerie Rabouan Moussion** (121 rue Vieille du Temple, 75003, tel 01 48 87 75 91), which shows cutting-edge work by Russian artists. New galleries in the Belleville area include **Galerie Suzanne Tarasiève** (Passage de l'Atlas/5, Villa Marcel Lods, 75019, tel 01 45 86 02 02).

17th, 18th, & 19th Centuries: The fashionable quarter in the 17th century remained the Marais, where a number of lavish mansions—the Hôtel de Sully and the Hôtel Salé (now the Musée Picasso)—still stand. During the Ancien Régime (France's system of government before the Revolution), some of the greatest architects worked under royal patronage. Salomon de Brosse constructed the Palais de Luxembourg, François Mansart created his eponymous roofline and windows, and Louis Le Vau built Vaux-le-Vicomte. This era also saw the development of formal landscaping, its leading proponent being André Le Nôtre.

> **Paris was radically transformed . . . when Baron Haussmann . . . set about modernizing the city during the Second Empire.**

During the 18th century, the aristocracy migrated to the Faubourg St.-Germain, where many *hôtels particuliers,* or private mansions, were built in the rococo style; most of these are now embassies and government institutions.

There was little new building during the Revolution. Churches were either torn down or converted. Many were deconsecrated and used as warehouses or Temples of Reason. Paris was radically transformed, however, when Baron Haussmann, Prefect of Paris under Napoleon III, set about modernizing the city during the Second Empire (see p. 166). He tore down dilapidated houses, replacing them with entire blocks of apartment buildings, and sliced wide boulevards through old neighborhoods. Another legacy of 19th-century architecture were the exuberant iron structures dramatically exemplified by the Eiffel Tower.

Modern Architecture: Technical innovations and a new design aesthetic, devised by Le Corbusier, contributed to the more geometric and functional style of the modern movement after World War I. There are few of Le Corbusier's designs in Paris, although his influence was widespread.

Postwar Paris was marked by experiments in high-rise developments, where entire neighborhoods, particularly in the 19th arrondissement, were replaced by impersonal slabs of apartment buildings. President Mitterrand's *grands travaux* had a great impact on the face of the city, with some of the more admirable monuments including the Louvre Pyramid, the Grande Arche de La Défense, and the Institut du Monde Arabe; others—such as the Opéra-Bastille or the stark towers of the new Bibliothèque de France—are more controversial.

Cinema

In France, and Paris in particular, an appreciation of the cinema is regarded as a key component of the good life. France has a long tradition of serious writing about cinema. The monthly journals *Positif* and *Cahiers du Cinéma* have been in business for nearly half a century, each voicing occasionally sharp divisions in taste. Every major general-interest magazine includes extensive movie criticism and director profiles.

The French government encourages its citizens to go to the movies by offering discounts to students, the elderly, members of the military, members of families with three or more children, and the unemployed, while several movie houses offer unlimited access passes at very reasonable rates per month. Whereas box office statistics in the United States are less than scientific, in France the National Center for Cinema (CNC) accounts for every last ticket sold, a percent of which is funneled into future productions of French movies (the *avance sur recettes* system).

The sheer choice of films in Paris is spectacular—some 376 screens in around 88 theaters—from the latest Hollywood megaproduction to first-person documentaries shot in Super-8 or video formats and blown up for commercial release. Although the art house and repertory cinemas remain far more vital in Paris than in any other city on Earth—in

I. M. Pei's glass pyramid entrance to the Louvre contrasts with the facade of the older buildings.

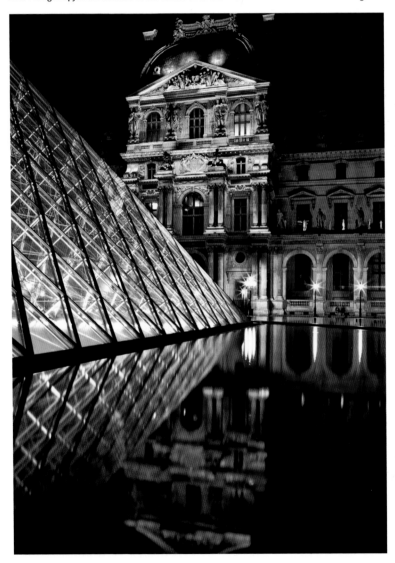

Paris, one cinema in five is classed as "art and experimental"—there are also megacinema chains, such as the giants Gaumont and MK2, which threaten independent theater owners (although both run art movies in addition to commercial releases).

In addition to the small art house cinemas and state-of-the-art multiplexes, there is Studio 28 in Montmartre, where Luis Buñuel and Salvador Dalí's notorious surrealist masterpiece *An Andalusian Dog* premiered in 1928, and the huge, lavishly decorated Grand Rex cinema with its star-spangled ceiling, which offers a backstage tour that includes an elevator ride behind the giant screen while a movie is showing. The reopened Cinémathèque Française in a Frank Gehry building on Rue de Bercy offers a series of retrospectives and cinema-related exhibitions. The city also organizes annual festivals like the Paris Cinéma and Cinéma au Clair de la Lune.

Purely French Cinema: Although the vast majority of viewers under the age of 25 think "American" when they think "Let's go to the movies," French cinema is back in vogue. In the 1990s, the share of the box office in France for French-made films dropped to 34.5 percent, with 53.8 percent of the moviegoing public opting for American releases, and dipped to below 30 percent in 2000. But in 2001, French moviegoers led a mass revolt against the bulwark of Hollywood productions when record numbers hit movie houses to see a variety of films produced by a domestic film industry that has reinvented itself. The strength of French cinema, regarded as being the champion of European film creativity today, is its diversity. The French have always excelled at more intimate movies, such as those by François Ozon *(Under the Sand, Eight Women)*, but they're now also recording commercial and artistic successes, with everything from lighthearted comedies (Jean-Pierre Jeunet's *Amélie*, Agnès Bacri's *Le Goût des Autres*) to New Wave-inspired pieces by directors like Jacques Rivette *(Va Savoir)*; thrillers (Hitchcock-influenced numbers like *With a Friend Like Harry* by Dominik Moll); hardline detective films; and action movies, spearheaded by Luc Besson, director of Hollywood-influenced movies like *La Femme Nikita* and *The Professional.*

EXPERIENCE:
The World of Dance

The diverse program of the annual multi-arts Autumn Festival *(www .festival-automne.com)* is a good opportunity to view dance from around the globe, but dance lovers can view international dance troupes in the auditorium of the **Musée du Quai Branly** (see p. 175). The **Maison de la Culture du Japon** *(www.mcjp.fr)* includes dance such as the Jiutamai song and dance of the geishas as part of its varied program of cinema, theater, and exhibitions. The Parc de La Villette (see pp. 208–209) hosts WIP, an urban dance workshop that holds frequent free or low-priced performances.

Theater, Dance, & Opera
Ever since Les Confrères de la Passion established the city's first permanent theater in 1547 at the Hôtel du Duc de Bourgogne (see the commemorative plaque at 29 rue Étienne Marcel), the dramatic arts have diversified. They now range from street theater in summer to grandly produced plays, performed everywhere from tiny cellars to sumptuous surroundings. The 1960s counterculture and Culture Minister André Malraux's decentralization plan succeeded in broadening the appeal of theater, and plays everywhere are enjoying increased popularity.

The Théâtre Rive Gauche hosts plays in Montparnasse.

This recent revolution, however, has not dented the deference accorded to the traditional Comédie Française (referred to as the House of Molière), created by Louis XIV in 1680, seven years after Molière's death. This prestigious symbol of French culture purveys classics by Molière, Pierre Corneille, and Jean Racine (see p. 35), as well as plays by such modern authors and playwrights as Jean Genet, Stefan Zweig, Marguerite Duras, and Tom Stoppard.

Contemporary Theater: Contemporary directors such as Ariane Mnouchkine and Peter Brook have opted out of commercial crowd-pleasers to pursue exciting, independent theater. Mnouchkine at the Théâtre du Soleil uses this spacious venue— a transformed armaments factory—to intrigue audiences with evocative plays.

Such unconventional use of space characterizes many Parisian theaters, drawing directors from abroad, such as self-exiled Englishman Peter Brook, whose Théâtre des Bouffes du Nord is exceptional. Together with Micheline Rozan, he founded the Centre International de Recherche Théâtral (CIRT) in 1970 and Le Centre International de Créations Théâtrales in 1974. It stages Shakespearean plays, the classic Indian work *The Mahabharata*, vaudeville, and new works in a historic theater deliberately kept in a state of disrepair. Some of his innovative techniques include incorporating technology in the form of television screens along with the usual staging of a play.

France's commitment to continuing cross-cultural exchange was exemplified by

Harold Pinter's first-time direction of *Ashes to Ashes;* Oscar-winning French actress Juliette Binoche's off–West End appearance in London; and Paris-based playwright Yasmina Reza's *Art,* which has been translated into 35 languages. Resident English-language theater companies, including Dear Conjunction and the On Stage Theater Company, present bilingual productions of well-known plays, as well as their own creations. Another important theater in the artistic exchange between France and the rest of the world is the MC 93 in Bobigny, whose eclectic international program has featured American choreographer Lucinda Childs, English producer Deborah Warner, and Irish actress Fiona Shaw.

Dance: As Europe's undisputed dance capital, Paris has a rich selection of festivals, events, spectacles, and dance forms ranging from tango and ballet to hip-hop and contemporary dance.

The Palais-Garnier, home of the Ballet de l'Opéra National de Paris, has been used almost exclusively for ballet since 1990. Generous sponsorship by the Ministry of Culture permits extravagant tributes to George Balanchine and Jerome Robbins, alongside standards like *Giselle* and *Swan Lake,* and performances by the Bolshoi Ballet. Since 1973, Carolyn Carlson, Angelin Preljocaj, Jean-Claude Gallotta, and the late Merce Cunningham have revitalized the modern dance repertoire.

> When the Opéra National de Paris-Bastille opened in 1990, it shifted the main opera program away from the Palais-Garnier.

The Théâtre de la Ville, backed by the city of Paris, is a dedicated promoter of contemporary dance. It hosts the late Pina Bausch's Wuppertaler Tanztheater almost every year, as well as other regulars, including Belgian choreographer Anne Teresa De Keersmaeker and her company Rosas. Poetry, texts, and slide projections are often interwoven with her dances.

Opera: When the Opéra National de Paris-Bastille opened in 1990, it shifted the main opera program away from its previous home at the Palais-Garnier. The Royal Academy of Music and Dance (known as l'Opéra), founded in 1669, had monopolized the theatrical and lyrical arts for decades, along with La Comédie Française.

The ingenious use of music and mime in Parisian fairground theaters laid the foundation for today's Opéra Comique, created over 200 years ago. The present building, the Salle Favart, opened on December 7, 1898. A number of operas, including Georges Bizet's *Carmen,* Claude Debussy's *Pelléas and Mélisande,* and François Boïeldieu's *La Dame Blanche,* have premiered at the Salle Favart, which was recently renovated and is a charming venue for lyrical theater. In contrast, the vast Opéra-Bastille has also staged *Carmen* as well as weightier productions.

Another leading musical theater is the Châtelet-Théâtre Musical de Paris, which has built its reputation with major conductors and directors, staging operatic productions rivaling those of other, more famous, opera houses. Today it presents mostly musicals like *Show Boat* and *My Fair Lady.*

The Théâtre des Champs-Élysées provides a distinguished backdrop—worth seeing for its sculpted facade and beautiful interiors alone—for operas, operas in concert, dance recitals, chamber music, and orchestral concerts. ■

The essence of Paris: the boat-shaped Île de la Cité—long a seat of power—and the Île St.-Louis, a preserve of 17th-century elegance

The Islands

Statues adorn Notre-Dame's facade.

The Islands

Paris, in essence, was created by the Seine, which was once twice as large. At one time, a string of islands stretched along the river; now, as a result of natural changes in the river's course and human intervention, there are only two—the Île de la Cité and the Île St.-Louis.

Île de la Cité

"The Île de la Cité is the head, heart, and very marrow of Paris," wrote Victor Hugo in *Notre-Dame de Paris*. Indeed, the Île de la Cité—the geographical center of Paris, itself the cultural center of France—was the birthplace of the city and the site of its original settlement.

Strategic positioning played a key role in the Île de la Cité's development. Not only was it situated along a major Bronze Age trade route for English tin bound for Central Europe and the Mediterranean, but it also served as a refuge in times of war. During the prosperous time of the ancient Romans, who arrived in 53 B.C. and named the settlement Lutetia Parisiorum, the town

Seine

❶

Square du
Vert Galant

PONT NEUF

Place
Dauphine

QUAI DE L'HORLOGE

La Conciergerie

QUAI DE LA CORSE

PONT AU CHANGE

PONT NOTRE-DAME

PONT D'ARCOLE

RUE DE HARLAY

❷

Ste.-Chapelle

QUAI DES ORFÈVRES

BOULEVARD DU PALAIS

Cité

❸

PLACE
LOUIS
LÉPINE

RUE DE LUTÈCE

RUE DE LA CITÉ

RUE D'ARCOLE

QUAI AUX FLEURS

ÎLE DE LA CITÉ

PONT ST-MICHEL

QUAI DU MARCHÉ NEUF

PETIT PONT

PLACE DU
PARVIS
NOTRE-DAME

PONT AU DOUBLE

PONT ST-LOUIS

SQUARE
JEAN XXIII

Notre-Dame

PONT DE L'ARCHEVÊCHÉ

Mémoria
de la
Déportation

Paris

Seine

Area of map detail

0		200 meters
0		200 yards

spread onto what is now the Left Bank. This golden age lasted about 300 years, until tribes from the outer Rhine invaded in the late third century, and the inhabitants fled back to the Cité. The Romans, Franks, and Capetian kings all expanded the original settlement.

The Île de la Cité has always been an important administrative and religious center. The original seat of the Roman governor is today's Palais de Justice, where judges still dispense justice some 2,000 years later, and both the Conciergerie (the notorious revolutionary prison; see p. 60) and the glorious Ste.-Chapelle (see pp. 56–58) are to be found within its walls.

Despite the hordes of tourists and unsightly tour buses everywhere, especially around the parvis of Notre-Dame, the Île de la Cité has many charming and secluded getaways. Examples include the Marché aux Fleurs (Flower Market) on the Place Louis-Lépine, the Square du Vert Galant on the far western edge of the island, and the narrow streets off the Quai aux

❶ Pont Neuf ❷ Palais de Justice
❸ Marché aux Fleurs

NOT TO BE MISSED:

The spires of Notre-Dame 48–53

Lunch in the Place Dauphine 54

A picnic in the Square du Vert Galant 54

The colorful Marché aux Fleurs 54

Historic Hôtel de Jassaud (Île St.-Louis) 55

The windows of Ste.-Chapelle 56–58

La Conciergerie 60

Fleurs, such as the lovely Rue des Ursins, with its Gothic building that was once the home of the Aga Khan. Although the building is not open to the public, it is a fascinating pastiche of architectural elements. Just beyond, there is a splendid view down the Rue des Chantres of the spire of Notre-Dame (see pp. 48–53).

Walk around the back of the cathedral for a spectacular view of the flying buttresses; either illuminated at night or rising over the pale blossoms of spring, this is truly one of the city's most memorable sights.

Île St.-Louis

The different histories of the two islands have contributed to their diverse characters. The Île St.-Louis was a quiet, unoccupied island until 17th-century entrepreneurs came up with one of the first planned development projects, achieving a coherent architectural whole that is strikingly well preserved today. This island remains delightfully free of traffic, major shops, Métro stations, and cinemas, and a leisurely stroll around its streets will reveal many discreet vestiges of 17th-century elegance. ■

Notre-Dame

Notre-Dame stands out as a symbol of Paris itself. Like the city, it sprang up along the banks of the Seine, its magnificent west facade rising up like "a vast symphony of stone," as Victor Hugo described it. The cathedral's site is rich in history. It stands over the ruins of a Gallo-Roman temple to Jupiter, a fourth-century church, and a sixth-century basilica, in whose foundations were found 12 stones originally used in the construction of the Roman temple.

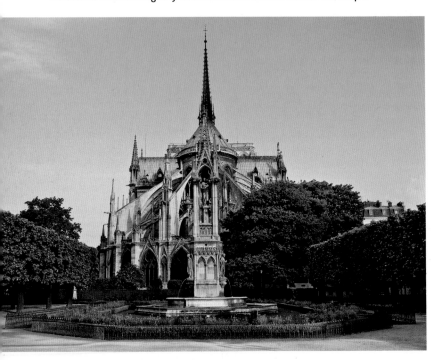

Greenery flanks the eastern facade of Notre-Dame.

Notre-Dame
- Map p. 46
- Place du Parvis Notre-Dame, Île de la Cité
- 01 42 34 56 10
- Métro: Cité

www.cathedrale deparis.com

By the 12th century, the basilica was in ruins, and Maurice de Sully (who was elected bishop of Paris in 1160) decided to replace it with a superb cathedral to rival the basilica at St.-Denis. Pope Alexander III laid the first stone in 1163, beginning what would become one of the masterpieces of French Gothic design. Work proceeded swiftly, funded by the vast sums Sully collected from the king, the clergy, the nobles, and the poor. When completed, the cathedral dominated all of religious architecture in the Île de France, as the Paris region is called, and had a sweeping impact throughout Europe.

Restoration

Notre-Dame's present appearance is largely the result of

19th-century restoration. In the 17th and 18th centuries, the Gothic style was no longer in vogue, and the cathedral suffered greatly as a result. Under Louis XIV (R.1643–1715), the chancel screen was partly destroyed, the 13th-century stained-glass windows were replaced with clear glass trimmed in blue and gold, and the rood screen and tombs disappeared. (A fragment of the rood screen, "La Descente aux Limbes," is in the Louvre.)

During the Revolutionary period, the church was pillaged and transformed into a Temple of Reason. Revolutionaries melted down the Treasury, burned the liberty flame on the altar, and smashed the 28 statues of the kings of Judea in the King's Gallery—mistakenly believed to represent the kings of France. Miraculously, 21 of the heads were subsequently found and are now preserved in the Musée de Cluny (see pp. 66–67), except for the head of King David, which is in the Metropolitan Museum of Art in New York.

By 1804, the cathedral was so dilapidated that when Napoleon I crowned himself emperor here, huge tapestries and drapings were hung to mask the damage, and plans were made to demolish it. As Victor Hugo wrote in 1831 in *Notre-Dame de Paris,* "On the face of this queen of our cathedrals, next to a wrinkle you will always find a scar. *Tempus edax, homo edacior.* Which I would freely translate: Time is blind, man is stupid." The publication of Hugo's book inspired efforts to save the cathedral and launched a movement to raise money for its restoration.

The 19th-century architect Eugène Viollet-le-Duc spent nearly 20 years restoring the statuary and glass, although his zealous efforts have been criticized. He added the 295-foot (90 m) steeple embroidered with graceful floral motifs, and replaced the sculptures on the western facade and the southern transept, reserving the most delicate work for the bays, which ultimately only succeed in approximating those of the 12th century.

Flying Buttresses

The soaring roofs of earlier churches had hidden supports, but by the high Gothic era, the dramatic flying buttress had evolved to support particularly high-flying cathedral roofs. Typically, the freestanding half arch of a flying buttress carried the thrust of a roof or vault to a distant pier, which allowed the building's walls to be much thinner than they would otherwise need to be in order to support the weight of the roof. Piers were often decorated with their own fanciful spires.

Notre-Dame's famous single-arch flying buttresses, so typical of a high Gothic cathedral, were originally built between 1220 and 1230. Each incorporates a channel to allow rainwater to run off. Those at the east end have a span of 49 feet (15 m). The chapels between the buttresses date from 1250–1325.

Portals

Three portals grace the west facade of Notre-Dame; from left to right, they represent the Virgin Mary, the Last Judgment, and Saint Anne. The statues decorating the portals once were brilliantly painted and stood out against a gilt background. The Saint Anne portal contains the oldest, carved about 1170.

Framing the portals are two elegant towers (the left is slightly higher than the right), each pierced by lancets more than 50 feet (15 m) high, and decorated with gargoyles that lurk behind the large upper gallery between them.

Rose Windows

The size and brilliance of Notre-Dame's glorious rose windows testify to the splendor of Gothic architecture. The **North Rose,** 69 feet (21 m) in diameter, with its nearly intact 13th-century glass, features Old Testament

West Rose window

Portal of the Virgin Mary

The spire

Notre-Dame's nave was completed at the end of the 12th century.

North Rose window

Notre-Dame

Treasury

⊕ Closed Sun. a.m.

💲 €

Towers

✉ Rue du Cloître
Notre-Dame

☎ 01 53 10 07 02

⊕ Closed Jan. 1,
May 1, & Dec. 25

💲 €€

figures surrounding the Virgin.

Facing the Seine is the 43-foot-high (13 m) **South Rose,** which was greatly restored in 1737; it depicts Christ surrounded by saints, apostles, and angels. The bays of the nave and the gallery rosettes were redone in 1965 by Jacques Le Chevallier, who imbued the dismal, 19th-century *grisaille* glass with the original medieval colors—rich red and blue tones—and materials.

Treasures

The cathedral's sculpted works include 13th-century architect Jean Ravy's ancient choir-screen carvings; Nicolas Coustou's "Pietà"; and Antoine Coysevox's statue of Louis XIV. Against the southeast pillar of the transept stands a 14th-century statue of the Virgin and Child, known as "Notre-Dame de Paris." Religious

paintings by Charles Le Brun are in the side chapels. The cathedral's treasures include the **Crown of Thorns,** a **Holy Nail,** and a fragment of the **True Cross** from Ste.-Chapelle (see pp. 56–58). These are only on public display once a year, when they are brought out and paraded before the congregation on Good Friday. Other treasures include Saint Louis's rib.

Notre-Dame's famous gargoyles were sculpted in the 19th century.

The early 18th-century organ on the western wall was restored in 1992, and features 6,000 pipes, 110 stops, and 5 keyboards—the largest in France. Climb up to the **south tower** platform for a stunning view of the spire, the flying buttresses, the gargoyles, and the city. The entrance to the stairs is from the base of the north tower.

in front of the church, derived from the word for paradise) is six times larger than it was in the Middle Ages. The plaques on the ground indicate the old layout of the streets and city landmarks. Where the statue of Charlemagne now stands was the site of the seventh-century Hôtel Dieu, the oldest hospital in France. Patients in the hospital

Archaeological Crypt

✉ Place du Parvis Notre-Dame

☎ 01 55 42 50 10

🕐 Closed Mon.

💲 €

Quays of the Seine: Walkers In, Cars Out

Appreciating Notre-Dame from the walkways of the Seine is one of the pleasures of Paris. The banks of the Seine are one of UNESCO's 100 World Heritage Sites, but the highways running along them have long blighted this beautiful spot for strollers. The city of Paris is now in the planning stages of a project that would "civilize" the banks of the Seine without closing the roads entirely (they are already closed to automobiles on

Sundays during the day). On the Right Bank, more traffic lights will be installed, the sidewalks will be widened here and there to slow down cars.

On the Left Bank, automobile traffic will be banned on the stretch between the Pont de l'Alma and the Musée d'Orsay and replaced by walking and biking lanes, gardens, greenhouses, and sports facilities. Artificial island parks will float on the Seine near the Port des Invalides.

Although they seem the very essence of medieval art, the cathedral's gargoyles date only to the 19th century and the restoration efforts of Viollet-le-Duc. The term "gargoyle" comes from the word for gullet, and in fact some of the creatures, those at the higher levels, do serve as waterspouts. Others are more purely sculptural. All were created by the obscure artist Victor Pyanet. Viollet-le-Duc called them "chimeras," and over the years the individual monsters have had a variety of nicknames—among them, "The Vampire" and "The Devourer."

Parvis of Notre-Dame

The present parvis (the court

weren't grouped according to sex or disease until the 18th century, and up to six people shared each bed. A new **Hôtel Dieu**—the one now on the northern side of the cathedral's parvis—was built between 1868 and 1877, after Baron Georges-Eugène Haussmann (see pp. 166–167) razed the area.

Archaeological Crypt: Before leaving, don't miss a visit to the Archaeological Crypt (accessed by stairs opposite the cathedral) to get a feel for the Gallo-Roman fortifications beneath the parvis. To the left are the ruins of rooms that used a heating system called a hypocaust. ■

A Walk Around the Islands

The islands are the heart of medieval Paris. The lively, bustling Île de la Cité is crammed with architectural gems, such as the magnificent Notre-Dame cathedral. In striking contrast, the smaller, quieter Île St.-Louis offers a peaceful village atmosphere, its shaded embankment lined with elegant private mansions as silent witnesses to a bygone era.

Place Dauphine on Île de la Cité

Begin at Point Zero on the parvis at Notre-Dame to view the cathedral in all its Gothic glory, whether wrapped in fog or washed with sun. **Notre-Dame ❶** (see pp. 48–53) is the city's largest church. Point Zero, dating from 1769 (although the bronze star is new), is the spot from which all road distances throughout the country are gauged.

When you reach the edge of the parvis, follow the Quai du Marché-Neuf, then turn right on Boulevard du Palais to see the glorious **Ste.-Chapelle ❷** (see pp. 56–58), a fine example of high Gothic architecture.

Backtrack and turn right on Quai des Orfèvres, formerly the Île de Galilée until it was attached to the Île de la Cité in 1310. Walk along the quayside for a more scenic route, past the **Palais de Justice** on your right and on past the Pont Neuf, Paris's oldest bridge, to the beautiful **Square du Vert Galant.**

Opposite the statue of Henri IV, take Rue Henri-Robert, which leads to the **Place**

NOT TO BE MISSED:

Notre-Dame • Ste.-Chapelle • Square du Vert Galant • La Conciergerie • Mémorial de la Déportation • Hôtel de Lauzun (Île St.-Louis)

Dauphine ❸. One of the few areas of the islands to have escaped Haussmann's dramatic redevelopment scheme in the 19th century, the square is very central, yet intensely private. The din of cars rushing over the Pont Neuf fades as you step into the secluded Place Dauphine, where actors Yves Montand and Simone Signoret once lived. Turn left onto Rue de Harlay at the end of the square, then right on Quai de l'Horloge. Follow this past the towers of **La Conciergerie ❹** (see p. 60), where Paris's oldest public clock (1370) still runs today.

Now follow the Quai de la Corse to the **Marché aux Fleurs** (Flower Market). Camellias, orchids, jasmine, and bamboo fill shops and stalls. (This is joined by a bird market on Sundays.) Proceed along the Quai aux Fleurs, taking a right onto Rue de la Colombe, then left on Rue des Ursins before rejoining the Quai aux Fleurs.

Go farther down the quay to the subterranean **Mémorial de la Déportation** (Deportation Memorial) ❺ *(Square de l'Île de France, Métro: Cité),* a stark edifice commemorating the Jewish people who were deported to concentration camps during World War II. It is faced with stone quarried from all the mountain ranges in France. Narrow staircases lead down to a high-walled platform, where the river beyond the iron bars and a portcullis evoke a powerful sense of the loss of freedom. Inside the crypt are two side galleries. Here, a series of small niches in the walls, inscribed with the names of the various concentration camps, contain urns with soil from the camps and ashes from the crematoriums.

A long, dark gallery studded with glass chips symbolizing the tens of thousands of deportees from France holds the remains of an unknown deportee taken from the necropolis of the Struthof concentration camp.

Île St.-Louis

Cross over the Pont St.-Louis to reach the Île St.-Louis. The island was divided in two by a canal (Rue Poulletier) during the 14th century to reinforce the protection of the Charles V Wall. Louis XIII and his mother, Marie de Médicis, undertook the unification of the two islands—called Île Notre-Dame and Île aux Vaches—and the embellishment of the area in the 17th century.

Reunited in 1614, the island underwent massive construction from 1620 to 1650, and was rechristened Île St.-Louis in 1726. The instability of the land hampered building

efforts: Some dwellings lean to the left or right, or have subsided, but in general they support one another.

The views from the island's quays are fabulous, and, if you get hungry, go to **Berthillon's** at 31 rue St.-Louis en l'Île to sample some of their marvelous ice creams and sorbets. Other landmarks to look for include the **Hôtel de Jassaud 6** at 19 quai de Bourbon, where French sculptor Camille Claudel lived in a ground-floor studio at the rear of the courtyard; and the **Hôtel de Lauzun 7** at 17 quai d'Anjou, with its gilded dolphin water spouts. It was here that the poet Charles Baudelaire wrote much of *Les Fleurs du Mal (The Flowers of Evil)*, published in 1857. Baudelaire also first spotted his lover Jeanne Duval—his "Black Venus"—from the window. The **Hôtel Lambert 8** at 2 rue St.-Louis-en-l'Île is now a private residence.

▲ See also area map pp. 46–47
► Notre-Dame parvis
🕒 Allow 4 hours
↔ 2.7 miles (4.3 km)
► Hôtel Lambert

Ste.-Chapelle

A true jewel in the heart of Paris, Ste.-Chapelle is a glorious example of the high Gothic style and is universally recognized as a masterpiece of architecture and stained glass.

Saint Louis (King Louis IX) had this luminous chapel constructed in just six years, from 1242 to 1248, and it is generally attributed to Pierre de Montreuil (who died in 1267). It is essentially an enormous reliquary, built to house the Crown of Thorns, which Louis had purchased from the Emperor of Constantinople, Baldwin II, in 1239.

Although Louis was undoubtedly a religious man—he was canonized 27 years after his death—his motives for constructing Ste.-Chapelle were decidedly political. Louis was just 12 years old when his father, Louis VIII, died. His mother, Blanche de Castille, ruled as regent until his majority. His ascension to the throne was contested, and in a period when kings ruled by divine right, the Crown of Thorns—the most prized religious relic of all—represented a potent symbol for Louis's claim to the throne. Indeed, it was such an important relic (although never officially recognized by the Vatican) that it cost three times more than the construction of Ste.-Chapelle itself. The crown was brought to France and placed in the church in a magnificent reliquary, which disappeared during the Revolution; most of the relics, however, were saved, and are now held in the Treasury of Notre-Dame (see p. 52).

Sculptures in Ste.-Chapelle depict the 12 Apostles.

Lower Chapel

The spectacular chapel is divided into two levels: the dark, richly decorated lower chapel, reserved for the palace servants, and the stunning upper chapel, used exclusively by the royal family, visiting dignitaries, and heads of state. The vibrant red and blue colors in the lower chapel date from the 19th century when attempts were made to reproduce the original medieval decoration. The windows are small because the lower chapel supports the upper chapel. Unfortunately, the 14th- and 15th-century tombstones on the chapel's floor have been worn almost bare by nearly 900,000 annual visitors.

Upper Chapel

The effect on entering the upper chapel is breathtaking. The walls are a mosaic of colored light that streams in through the 50-foot-high (15 m) windows. The 15 stained-glass windows in this chapel are the oldest in Paris, with two-thirds of them dating from the 13th century; together, they include over 1,100 scenes. With the exception of the three windows behind the altar (Saint John the Evangelist, the Passion of Christ, and Saint John the Baptist), and the window immediately to the right on entering the chapel (which recounts the story of the relics), all the others depict scenes from the Old Testament.

Ste.-Chapelle
- Map p. 46
- 4 boulevard du Palais, Île de la Cité
- 01 53 40 60 80
- Closed 1 p.m.–2 p.m., Jan. 1, May 1, Dec. 25
- €€
- Métro: Cité, St.-Michel, Châtelet
www.monum.fr

Stained Glass

In medieval times, as in the present, church leaders were responsible for religious education. During the golden age of stained glass—the 12th and 13th centuries—the church building itself, through its windows and statuary, transmitted this knowledge. The stained-glass windows functioned as immense picture books from which a mostly illiterate population could "read" the biblical stories. The scenes are designed to be read from left to right, and bottom to top.

Stained glass can be traced to ancient times; clear glass was used in Roman baths, and they were experts in making colored-glass vases and cups. The technique of using colored glass and lead together appeared later. Stained-glass windows were not an important element of Romanesque architecture; with the development of the Gothic rib-vaulted roof, walls no longer carried the vertical thrust of the building, allowing builders to create large openings between the pillars that could be filled with stained glass.

The basic techniques for making stained-glass windows have changed little: Colored and clear glass are cut to a pattern, then painted with grisaille (iron oxide) before being baked in a kiln. Then the pieces are assembled with lead strips to create mosaics. In the 12th and 13th centuries, a limited number of colors were used, and glassmakers juxtaposed the bright reds and blues to create jewel-like colors, achieving the unique style seen in many Gothic churches. By the mid-15th century, glassmakers began to imitate paintings by modeling forms, introducing a three-dimensional effect. The glass was still beautiful, but it had lost some of its essential nature; it no longer filtered a mosaic of brilliant colors, but became more like a semi-opaque reproduction of a canvas on glass.

The style of the **Rose Window** is markedly different from the other windows; made in 1485 (200 years later than the others), it represents the Apocalypse. It's a good idea to bring along binoculars for viewing the upper windows.

The windows barely escaped destruction during the Revolution, when the church was deconsecrated. For 35 years, from 1802 to 1837, the chapel was converted into a warehouse for archives; the bottom 15 feet (4.5 m) of each window was removed, and filing cabinets rose 25 feet (7.5 m) up the walls. The missing sections of the windows were eventually re-created as exact copies of the originals, but mistakes were inevitably made.

Sculptures

The sculptures in Ste.-Chapelle depict the 12 Apostles, the

spiritual pillars of the church, each placed on one of the structural pillars of the chapel. The two alcoves on either side of the chapel were reserved for King Louis (on the left) and his mother (on the right). Louis's wife, Queen Marguerite, overshadowed by her mother-in-law, presumably sat with her husband. The king entered through the main doors, which led directly to the royal apartments in the Conciergerie. ∎

Ste.-Chapelle's famous Rose Window

EXPERIENCE: On & Off the Beaten Track

Wandering the streets of Paris is always a rewarding experience: You might stumble across a medieval tower in a back street, for example, or a charming little square with an old fountain. Even more rewarding are the many walking tours offered throughout the city that allow you to follow your interests while also benefiting from the expertise and insider knowledge of your guide.

Major Sites

Paris Walks (*www.paris-walks.com*) offers regular tours of many Paris neighborhoods. Its Monday walk from March to November covers Île de la Cité and Notre-Dame. Participants learn to read the stories embedded in medieval stone and discuss how the cathedral was built. The walk also takes in ancient back streets, the flower market, gardens, hidden courtyards, and the Mémorial de la Déportation on the islands.

Other tours cover the major sites and topics, from the Marais and Montmartre to the French Revolution and Hemingway's Paris.

Paris Perspectives (*www.parisperspectives.com*) presents some similar tours with specialized themes, including "Hemingway's Lost Generation: The Latin Quarter," as well as specialized views of the city like "Synagogues and Jewish History in the Marais" and "Poison and Passion: 17th-Century Culture in the Marais." All tours are led with verve by American Pamela Grant, who has a degree in art history and has passed the French government's rigorous French National Guide examination.

African and African-American Sites

Special-interest tours that will take you off the beaten track are available from **Walking the Spirit** (*www.walkingthespirit.com*), with tours focusing on the history and lives of African-Americans and Africans in Paris. You might see the theater where Josephine Baker wowed the French, the building James Baldwin lived in, or the café where Richard Wright wrote. Other tours take in the food markets of Little Africa.

INSIDER TIP:

Take a walk on the Viaduc des Arts (1–129 avenue Daumesnil). The vaults beneath the viaduct house studios.

—ROSEMARY BAILEY
National Geographic author

Da Vinci Code Tours

Ever since *The Da Vinci Code* came out, there has been great demand from visitors to see the Rose Line in St.-Sulpice, the inverted pyramid in the Carrousel du Louvre, and other places associated with the novel. **Classic Walks** (*classicwalksparis.com*) offers a *Da Vinci Code* tour as well as a number of others, including a World War II tour, bicycle tours, and Segway tours.

For the Gourmand

Context Travel (*www.context-travel.com/city/Paris/all_walking_tours*) has a full range of high-end specialist tours with such themes as chocolate, Paris art galleries, gardens of Paris, and the Centre Pompidou, and will also arrange custom tours to suit the special interests of visitors. For foodies, their "Baguette to Bistro: Culinary Traditions of Paris by Mouth" takes small groups to some of Paris's top shops for chocolate, spices, baguettes, cheese, wine, meat, and more.

On the Run

Joggers who don't know where to run in the city or who want to kill two birds with one stone and see the sights while running will appreciate **Paris Running Tour** (*www.parisrunningtour.com*). Visitors are accompanied by a coach who is a serious runner and can choose from various scenic areas like the Canal St.-Martin or the Left Bank with runs of varying levels of difficulty.

La Conciergerie

The Conciergerie was part of the royal palace from the 10th century to 1378, before it became the center of the Paris judicial system. Philippe IV (R.1285–1314) constructed most of the medieval buildings standing today, although they were extensively renovated in the 19th century. After Charles V moved the royal residence to the Louvre Palace (see p. 124), he appointed a concierge, or keeper, to act as his steward, and the complex became a prison.

La Conciergerie
🅰 Map p. 46
✉ 2 boulevard du Palais
☎ 01 53 40 60 97
🕐 Closed Jan. 1, May 1, Dec. 25.
💲 €€
Ⓜ Métro: Cité, St.-Michel, Châtelet

www.monum.fr

Medieval Secular Architecture

You will enter the impressive **Salle des Gens d'Armes,** one of the largest—and finest—examples of medieval secular architecture, across the courtyard from the main entrance on Quai de l'Horloge. Its name means "men at arms," and the word *gendarmes* (police) is derived from it. This hall served as the refectory for the palace staff. Rue de Paris, at the far western end of this room, contained prison cells and is named for the executioner, who was traditionally known as Monsieur de Paris. The royal banquet hall upstairs burned down and was reconstructed in 1622 as the **Salles des Pas Perdus.** It is now a lobby for lawyers and clients awaiting their turn in the courts.

Medieval Fireplaces

Thousands ate each day at the Conciergerie. Each of the four fireplaces in the medieval kitchens had a function: One was for soups, another for stews, a third for meat. No one is sure about the fourth.

The 13th-century crenelated **Tour Bonbec** (meaning "chatter tower") was once used as a torture chamber. Although it is no longer a prison, people are still held in custody here—away from the tourist circuit.

Revolutionary Tribunal

During the Revolution, the Revolutionary Tribunal sentenced more than 2,700 people to die under the so-called democratic blade of the guillotine (previously, the nobility died by the sword; common criminals were whipped, sulfur placed on their open wounds, then they were hanged, drawn, and quartered).

Incarceration here did not follow the new democracy, however. Walk upstairs to see the three reconstructed cells, which illustrate what money could buy: The *pailleux*, or penniless prisoners, slept on straw on the floor; *à la pistole* meant real beds; while prisoners of rank had their own furniture and servants. Queen Marie-Antoinette's cell has been reconstructed, and a chapel of atonement now stands on part of the original cell. Ironically, her accusers, Maximilien Robespierre and Georges Danton, followed her to prison and then the guillotine within a few months. ∎

The seat of French university life for centuries, with the Sorbonne and the Collège de France, bookshops, libraries, and cafés

Quartier Latin

Postcards in the Latin Quarter

Quartier Latin

Since the founding of the Sorbonne in the 13th century, the Quartier Latin (Latin Quarter) has been synonymous with university life, and was once the greatest seat of learning in Europe. The area's very name is derived from medieval university instruction in Low Latin. The area is still in perpetual motion, with students milling about in the streets and cafés or browsing in the Gibert Jeune bookshop.

The Latin Quarter encompasses the neighborhoods around St.-Séverin, Montagne
Ste.-Geneviève, and Place St.-Michel, with
its fountain of the saint slaying a dragon.
If it is your first visit to the area, try not
to approach the Latin Quarter from the
commercial Boulevard St.-Michel, as the
fast-food restaurants and clothing outlets
detract from the area's mythical status.
Instead, enter across the quays from Notre-
Dame, through the Square Viviani.

Next to the square is the largely touristy
Shakespeare and Company bookstore, not
to be confused with the former avant-garde
publishing house on Rue de l'Odéon owned
by Sylvia Beach (see p. 36), who first published
James Joyce's *Ulysses*. Some streets—such as
Rue de la Parcheminerie (originally Rue des
Escrivains, or Street of Writers)—reflect the
literary tradition of the Latin Quarter in their
names, although not all do; the nearby Rue de
Bièvre, for example, was named for the arm
of the river that flowed through the
quarter to the Seine.

Historic Area

The Latin Quarter is one
of Paris's more historic
areas. Here, you can wend
your way past Roman ruins,
such as the Arènes de Lutèce
amphitheater (see p. 74), or
the third-century baths (now part
of the Musée National du Moyen
Âge et des Thermes de Cluny; see

❶ Odéon-Théâtre de l'Europe ❷ Site of
former Sylvia Beach bookstore (Shakespeare
and Company), 12 rue de l'Odéon ❸ Café
Procope ❹ Gallo-Roman baths ❺ Caveau
des Oubliettes ❻ St.-Julien-le-Pauvre
❼ Square Viviani ❽ Shakespeare and
Company bookstore, Rue de la Bûcherie
❾ Bibliothèque Ste.-Geneviève ❿ Lycée
Henri IV ⓫ Philippe-Auguste Wall

> ## NOT TO BE MISSED:
>
> **The unicorn tapestries at the
> Musée de Cluny 66–67**
>
> **France's great men and women at
> the Panthéon 69**
>
> **The galleries in the hall of evolution
> at the Muséum National d'Histoire
> Naturelle 70**
>
> **A stroll through the Jardin des
> Plantes 70–71**
>
> **Browsing at Shakespeare and
> Company bookstore 75**
>
> **The striking interior of St.-Étienne-
> du-Mont 76**

pp. 66–67), up to Montagne Ste.-Geneviève,
named after the city's patron saint. Saint Geneviève was instrumental in unifying Paris (see
p. 21), and her importance is reflected in the
area, particularly around the St.-Étienne-du-
Mont Church, which has the only surviving
rood screen in Paris. The church stands where
the basilica of St.-Pierre-St.-Paul, built to
commemorate the unity of France, was once
located. Next door is the Panthéon (see p.
69), originally commissioned to be a church
for Saint Geneviève, but transformed during
the Revolution into a temple for "great men"
(and a token woman, physicist Marie Curie).

Down the other side of the hill, to the
east, lies the café-lined Place de la Contres-
carpe (named after the embankments of
Philippe-Auguste's fortifications), and the Rue
Mouffetard, one of the oldest streets, which
has a great open-air market *(closed Mon.)*.

Few visitors venture farther east, where
Paris's principal mosque (see pp. 75–76)
lies opposite the Jardin des Plantes (see pp.
70–71). The intriguing Institut du Monde
Arabe (Arab Cultural Institute; see p. 75)
overlooks the Seine near the open-air Tino
Rossi sculpture garden (see p. 205). ∎

St.-Séverin & Montagne Ste.-Geneviève Areas

The St.-Séverin and Ste.-Geneviève neighborhoods are among the oldest areas in Paris, with such medieval streets as Rue du Fouarre and Rue Galande. The former was named for the *fouarre*—or hay—on which students would sit while listening to lectures.

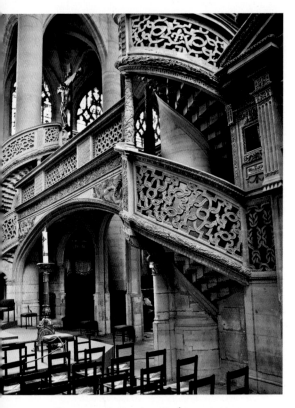

The asymmetrical interior of St.-Étienne-du-Mont

Caveau des Oubliettes

- Map p. 62
- 52 rue Galande
- 01 46 34 23 09
- Métro: St.-Michel

www.caveaudes oubliettes.fr

St.-Séverin Area

One of the most famous historic figures of this area was the 12th-century philosopher and theologian Pierre Abélard (1079–1142). Following his rift with the canons for challenging monastic discipline, Abélard was ousted from the Notre-Dame cloister. He moved to the Left Bank, taking 3,000 students with him. (See p. 114 for an account of his love affair with Héloïse.)

St.-Julien-le-Pauvre: Rue Galande was lined with infamous cabarets during the 18th century. The **Caveau des Oubliettes** was one of the rare spots where only old French songs were featured; now jazz and country have been added to the repertoire, and La Guillotine pub on the ground floor is a far cry from the old-style cabaret. But the guillotine on which Kennedy placed his head when he visited in 1960 is still on display (a remnant of the museum of torture that was once here).

Off Rue Galande is St.-Julien-le-Pauvre. One of the three oldest churches in Paris, it was built between 1165 and 1220. Originally a stopping point for travelers en route to the famous pilgrimage site of Santiago de Compostela in Spain, during the later Middle Ages rowdy student assemblies gathered here. Its simple Gothic style bears traces of the Romanesque period, and the beautiful chancel is enclosed by a wooden iconostasis (icon screen) and two beautifully carved pillars.

Square Viviani & Église St.-Séverin:

Next door, the lovely Square Viviani has a superb view of Notre-Dame, a contemporary fountain inspired by Saint Julien, and a false acacia tree (circa 1601) lying against a ruined stone buttress. Don't miss the Flamboyant Gothic **St.-Séverin Church,** one of the most beautiful sacred buildings in Paris, with its spiraling vaults, softly lit against brilliant stained glass in the apse.

Montagne Ste.-Geneviève Area

The area around Montagne Ste.-Geneviève, the Roman city mirroring the Gallo-Roman settlement on the Île de la Cité, is filled with winding streets climbing up the hill.

Well-preserved vestiges of the **Gallo-Roman baths** can be found at the corner of Rue des Écoles and Boulevard St.-Michel. Circle around them to the east, up Rue de Cluny and past Square Paul-Painlevé separating the **Musée de Cluny** (see pp. 66–67)

and the **Sorbonne** (see p. 68). On the corner of Rue des Écoles and Rue de la Sorbonne stood a convent, where the great poet and rogue François Villon grew up; he assassinated a priest in 1455 and was subsequently banished from Paris. The name Sorbonne is used interchangeably with the Université de Paris, but is actually the name of the most famous of its colleges. Farther up Rue St.-Jacques is the **Panthéon** (see p. 69), dating from 1754.

On the north side of the Place du Panthéon is the **Bibliothèque Ste.-Geneviève**—the only great monastic library in Paris spared during the Revolution. It has a fine collection of medieval manuscripts. Behind the Panthéon is one of Paris's more intriguing churches, **St.-Étienne-du-Mont** (see p. 76). Across the street is the prestigious **Lycée Henri IV,** the site of the sixth-century basilica built by Clovis following his victory over the Visigoths. Down the street on Rue Clovis is a section of the **Philippe-Auguste Wall** (see p. 21). ∎

Église St.-Séverin

- Map p. 62
- 3 rue des Prêtres St.-Séverin
- 01 42 34 93 50
- Métro: St.-Michel

www.saint-severin .com

Bibliothèque Ste.-Geneviève

- Map p. 62
- 10 place du Panthéon
- 01 44 41 97 97
- Closed Sun.
- Métro: Maubert-Mutualité RER (B): Luxembourg,

www.bsg .univ-paris1.fr

Philippe-Auguste Wall

- Map p. 62
- 3 rue Clovis
- Métro: Cardinal Lemoine

EXPERIENCE: Restaurants with Terraces

Few experiences are more Parisian than dining outside in fine weather and watching the people go by. Finding a table at a restaurant with a terrace is not easy, however. Try one of the following, but book in advance. Not far from the Jardin des Plantes is **Chez Lena et Mimile** (32 rue du Tournefort, 75005, tel 01 47 07 72 47, €€): It has traditional and fusion dishes and an elevated terrace with a view. Nearby, **Chantairelle** (17 rue Laplace,

75005, tel 01 46 33 18 59, €€) offers traditional French cuisine and a peaceful, off-street terrace. **Le Pavillon du Lac** (Parc des Buttes Chaumont, Place Armand Carrel, 75019, tel 01 42 00 07 21, €€/€€€), recently renovated, is set in a park. **Le Relais du Parc** (55–57 ave. Raymond Poincaré, 75016, tel 01 44 05 66 10, €€€), in the 16th arrondissement, has a menu by super-chef Alain Ducasse and a courtyard terrace.

Musée de Cluny

The remarkable Musée National du Moyen Âge is actually two museums in one: the 15th-century Hôtel de Cluny, which houses the medieval collections and the world-famous "Lady with the Unicorn" tapestries; and the third-century baths, the oldest and most complete vestiges of the Roman occupation in Paris.

Hôtel de Cluny & Baths

The medieval building, constructed between 1480 and 1510 as a temporary residence for visiting religious dignitaries from the wealthy Abbey of Cluny,

Five of the unicorn tapestries at Cluny may illustrate the senses: in this instance, sight.

is one of the oldest surviving examples of civil architecture in Paris. The building stands around a cobblestone courtyard, and visitors used to enter through the exterior, turreted staircase—a distinguishing feature of well-to-do medieval homes.

What is unique about Cluny is that the abbots chose to build their mansion on land abutting the ruins of a Gallo-Roman bath, one of three that existed during the second and third centuries in what was then Lutetia.

The baths contained three large rooms: the **caldarium** (hot room), now in ruins; the **tepidarium** (warm room), which had bathtubs in various alcoves; and the **frigidarium** (cold room). All were once lined with magnificent mosaics. The walls and floors of the caldarium were heated by a system of lead and terra-cotta pipes that were fed from furnaces in the cellars. The 45-foot-high (13.5 m) frigidarium has been restored and is now used as a venue for temporary exhibitions. The room was so well designed that even in the hottest days of summer, this immense hall remains cool. The **underground vaults,** which once housed the furnaces for heating the baths, can be visited on certain days (*inquire at the entrance*).

Tapestries

In medieval Europe, tapestries developed as a way to cover cold, drafty stone walls. They were easily transported and served to decorate and capture heat in châteaus and churches. They usually depicted moral, historical, floral, and biblical themes, and displayed a person's wealth through their sumptuous fabrics and elaborate designs.

The earliest surviving tapestry from a Paris workshop is the great set of hangings known as the "Apocalypse of Angers" (circa 1375), on view in the city of Angers. After the French defeat at Agincourt in 1415, Arras became the center of tapestry weaving, largely because of the extravagant patronage of the Burgundian dukes. In the 17th century, the tapestry industry flourished once again in Paris with the Gobelins Manufacture, which produced panels of unprecedented technical perfection.

Medieval Collections

The first few rooms are devoted to tapestries, some splendid stained glass, and chests. These lead to the Roman baths via Room VIII, which houses the spectacular **King's Gallery—** 21 of the 28 heads that once stood atop the figures lining the front of Notre-Dame (see pp. 48–53). Although the sculptures represent biblical figures, they were mistaken for the kings of France during the Revolution, and the heads were decapitated and left among the debris. Only in 1977 did they turn up, during excavations under a bank. This gallery is now the highlight of the room, which also displays Romanesque sculptures. The oldest sculpture in Paris, the "Pilier des Nautes" ("Boatmen's Pillar"), dating from the first century A.D., stands in the next room, near the frigidarium.

The upper floor contains a collection of precious metalwork, including the "Golden Rose of Basel," a delicate, wrought-iron piece made in 1330, and several exceptional altarpieces.

Room XIII, a specially designed rotunda, displays the museum's most famous works, the "Lady with the Unicorn" tapestries (circa 15th century, southern Netherlands). The unicorn motif, which was popular in medieval imagery, symbolized chastity and purity.

INSIDER TIP:

After visiting the tapestries, duck into a cozy bistro on nearby Boulevard St.-Germain and treat yourself to a steamy *soupe à l'oignon.*

—ANNE RANDERSON
National Geographic contributor

The museum's **medieval gardens** take you back in time through the Forest of the Unicorn, representing untamed nature, and gardens symbolic of nature tamed: the kitchen garden, the medicinal plants, the heavenly garden (flowers symbolizing the Virgin Mary), and the love garden (courtly and sensual love). ∎

Musée de Cluny

- 🅰 Map p. 62
- ✉ 6 place Paul Painlevé
- ☎ 01 53 73 78 00
- 🕐 Closed Tues., Jan. 1, May 1, Dec. 25
- 💲 €€
- 🚇 Métro: St.-Michel, Odéon, Cluny

www.musee-moyenage.fr

The Sorbonne & the Collège de France

The Sorbonne was like a quasi-state within a state for centuries, playing a major political role, while the Collège de France gave priority to educational freedom.

The Sorbonne
- Map p. 62
- 47 rue des Écoles
- 01 40 46 22 11
- By appt. only
- Métro: St.-Michel, Cluny RER: Luxembourg

www.sorbonne.fr

Collège de France
- 11 place Marcellin Berthelot
- 01 44 27 12 11
- Métro: St.-Michel, Maubert-Mutualité, Cluny

www.college-de-france.fr

The Sorbonne

The Sorbonne was founded in 1253 as a residence hall for 16 theology students, and eventually became a major center for religious education.

Strikes have been a feature of the Sorbonne since its earliest days. In 1231 the institution went on strike for two years, demanding (and winning) independence from the bishops of Paris. Some 750 years later, the violence that swept through the Latin Quarter in May 1968 was triggered by the arrest of student leaders from this same institution, protesting against a rigid, repressive, and overcrowded university system. Today, the courtyard is open to the public; the chapel, which houses the tomb of Cardinal Richelieu (see p. 23), can be visited during temporary exhibitions and on December 4, the anniversary of Richelieu's death.

INSIDER TIP:

For secondhand, discounted books and records, visit the *librairies* for students around the Sorbonne.

—ANNE RANDERSON
National Geographic contributor

Collège de France

The Collège de France is an unorthodox institution. An average 5,000 auditors follow the diverse lectures given by one of the 52 professors. Classes are free, there are no prerequisites, no academic credits are given, and the college awards no diplomas. Instead, anyone, from students to the merely curious, can attend lectures on topics ranging from molecular biology to Byzantine civilization. ■

Victor Hugo

Victor Hugo (1802–1885) was France's greatest 19th-century literary icon. He was the closest France ever came to producing a writer whose stature could be compared to that of Homer, Shakespeare, or Dante, and his works were said to have helped trigger revolutions—notably the 1830 Revolution (see p. 28). His plays revolutionized French theater, knocking it out of the fettered forms of Corneille and Racine.

Hugo turned to politics, but politics turned on him—after trying to foil Napoleon III's coup in 1851, he dodged arrest, and was subsequently exiled for 18 years, returning in 1870.

A half million people poured into the streets of Paris to mourn when he died in 1885. His body, after lying in state at the Arc de Triomphe, was taken to the Panthéon in a pauper's hearse as a sign of solidarity with the common man.

The Panthéon

The Panthéon, now a shrine "to distinguished men from a grateful nation," was constructed by Louis XV. In 1744 the king fell ill and vowed to construct a church dedicated to Saint Geneviève, if she would come to his aid. He recovered, and in 1754 commissioned Jacques Germain Soufflot to build a vast church that would "combine Greek beauty with Gothic space and light."

The Panthéon is an architectural wonder and a monument to great figures in French culture.

Soufflot's immense structure was an unprecedented feat of engineering. The subsoil was honeycombed with wells and quarries that required considerable shoring up. The first stone was laid in 1764 in the king's presence, although the church was only completed in 1790—the year all monastic orders were abolished. It was then declared to be a "temple to the Nation," and author Voltaire, philosopher Jean-Jacques Rousseau, and politician Honoré Mirabeau were buried there. It became a church again several times during the 19th century, but was finally made into a mortuary for French heroes in 1885 during the state funeral for Victor Hugo (see opposite). You can see the tombs of novelist Émile Zola (1830–1902) and physicist Marie Curie (1859–1906). The remains of author Alexandre Dumas (1802–1870) were moved here in 2002, with four men dressed as the Musketeers flanking the coffin. ■

The Panthéon
- 🅰 Map p. 62
- ✉ Place du Panthéon
- ☎ 01 44 32 18 00
- 💲 €€
- 🚇 Métro: Cardinal Lemoine RER: Luxembourg

www.monum.fr

Jardin des Plantes

The oldest garden in Paris was not designed for the pleasure of its inhabitants, but as a research garden for botanists, doctors, and pharmacists. It was created in 1635 as the royal medicinal garden for Louis XIII, but came into its own in 1739, when naturalist Georges Buffon was appointed director. The garden became the natural history museum in 1793, and over the next 30 years an assortment of animals was introduced.

Once medicinal plantings, the gardens of the Jardin des Plantes are now open to the public.

Jardin des Plantes

 Map pp. 62–63

✉ 36 rue Geoffroy St.-Hilaire. Main entrance: 57 rue Cuvier

☎ 01 40 79 56 01

 Métro: Austerlitz, Jussieu

www.jardindes plantes.net

Muséum National d'Histoire Naturelle

By 1965, the crumbling zoology gallery was closed and remained a dusty hulk until 1994, when it finally reopened after a major renovation project. The results are spectacular: Visitors enter the dramatically lit **Grande Galerie de l'Évolution,** a sort of giant Noah's Ark of mounted animals parading down the center of the building. On the lower floor, marine animals are suspended as if still swimming in the sea; the 54-foot (16.5 m) skeleton of a whale hangs in midair. Two floors of galleries upstairs explore evolution, the environment, and the effects of pollution.

The museum's facelift retained some of the existing metal-frame structure, which is brilliantly incorporated into the new design. A discovery room introduces fossils and the natural sciences to children under 12, while older kids can explore displays in the science laboratory.

The Gardens

The handsome greenhouses, the oldest dating to 1714, have been renovated and were reopened to the public in 2010. The new theme is biodiversity, and the first three greenhouses respectively present the flora of a rainforest (in an art deco building), the desert, and New Caledonia. The last one offers an overview of the history of plant life.

Three majestic avenues, lined with trees, lead elegantly away from the museum past a series of meticulously planted flower beds. Elsewhere, the geometric formality gives way to a less rigid layout. To the north lies the Ménagerie and an 18th-century labyrinth, which leads to a bronze gazebo called the **Gloriette de Buffon,** the oldest metallic structure in Paris (circa 1786). Nearby is the **Alpine** temperature can vary as much as 35°F from one spot to another. Two thousand different species of plants, classified by region, flourish in this lush environment.

The Ménagerie

One of the oldest zoos in the world, this opened in 1794 with animals from the royal collections, and became so popular by 1827 that the arrival of a giraffe—the first ever on French soil—was a major event of the year, drawing 600,000 Parisians. Today, the rustic quarters have an undeniable charm. Recently, the 12-acre (5 ha) zoo was saved from the claws of real estate developers by being classified a historical monument. The drawback, however, is that nothing can be changed from the original design; even renovations to bring

Muséum National d'Histoire Naturelle
- ✉ 36 rue Geoffroy St.-Hilaire
- ☎ 01 40 79 30 00
- 🕐 Closed Tues.
- 💲 €€

www.mnhn.fr

Ménagerie
- ✉ 57 rue Cuvier
- ☎ 01 40 79 37 94
- 💲 €€

www.mnhn.fr

A Home for Fashion and Design

If you have noticed what looks like a massive green carbuncle stuck to the side of an otherwise nondescript concrete building on the Left Bank riverside, about a block from the Jardin des Plantes, do not be alarmed: It is not a mutant giant of the species come to devour Paris, but a new architectural addition, designed by in-vogue architects Jakob+MacFarlane, to a hundred-year-old customs warehouse. This is **Docks en Seine/Cité de la Mode et du Design** (*34 quai d'Austerlitz, 75013*), a site for fairs and concept stores devoted to cutting-edge fashion, design, and the arts. It is also home to the French Fashion Institute. Public walkways offer a glimpse of the Seine from inside the building's green glass bubble.

Garden (*closed Nov.–March*). Not easy to find, this discreet haven is buried almost 10 feet (3 m) lower than the rest of the Jardin des Plantes to provide a more varied terrain. The gardeners have somehow created a mysterious microclimate of small valleys and hills in the garden, where the in more modern zookeeping methods are ruled out. This, combined with a lack of funds, means that some of the buildings are sadly dilapidated. The curators have taken this in their stride, specializing instead on the smaller primates, reptiles, birds of prey, and snow leopards. ∎

Subterranean Paris

Paris has an underground life that is just as active as the one above ground. Although the catacombs are one of the most frequently visited underground sites (see Denfert-Rochereau, p. 201), there are lesser known crypts in unexpected places—for example, beneath the July Column at Place de la Bastille (see p. 119), where victims from the 1830 and 1840 revolutions are buried, or under the St.-Sulpice Church (see p. 83).

Many Métro stops, such as Cité, reflect the style of the streets above.

The city also has sewer tours; a nuclear-fallout shelter underneath the Sorbonne; a French Resistance hideout underneath that; and many underground quarries, rivers, canals, and even a lake (beneath Place de l'Opéra). Lastly, there are the streamlined Métro and RER, whose rubber tires whoosh from station to station, sometimes surfacing molelike from underground tunnels into the light, but always returning to the dark recesses beneath the streets.

Quarries, Sewers, Pipes & Water

Paris was built with gypsum and limestone extracted from its subsoil. The Left Bank alone has 186 miles (299 km) of underground tunnels (not open to the public). However, intensive mining has caused subsidence, and although the quarries are no longer exploited and many buildings are reinforced by pilings, several houses are collapsing in areas like Montmartre. (Ironically, this has helped to spare the area from overdevelopment.) Efforts to shore up the limestone quarries are under way, and an inspection team constantly monitors the limestone for fissures and flaws.

If you take a tour of the sewers, you will enter the most malodorous of Paris's museums. In these tours you will learn about sewer- and water-treatment systems, Monsieur Poubelle (for whom the French garbage can is named), and purification equipment. Sewers (égouts) generally run under the middle of streets, although on broader avenues they run underneath the sidewalks. These tunnels feature plaques with the names of the streets above. Larger mains contain pipes for drinking and industrial-use water; pneumatic tubes once used by the post office to speed the delivery of letters and light packages—two are still in use today; telephone and telegraph cables; traffic-signal cables; and pipes for compressed air.

The city's first springwater-fed public fountain opened in 1184, but it was Baron Haussmann (see p. 166) who introduced the modern system. In 1852 his right-hand man, Eugène Belgrand, began diverting springs that currently supply half the city with its drinking water. Inhabitants also rely on water pumped from the Seine and Marne Rivers. The two-tiered, part subterranean Montsouris Reservoir has a capacity of 3.25 million cubic feet (94 million liters) and supplies some of eastern Paris

with water. To ensure that the reservoir supply is fresh enough for consumption, trout swim in the turquoise waters.

The Métro

The Métro is the fastest way to get around the city; its speed and design make Paris seem as if it could fit into the palm of your hand. Its stops function as reference points for the city. When construction on the Métro began during the 19th century, bones, teeth, and tusks of mammoths were found near the Montmartre Cemetery and under Square Montholon. From the start, the Métro was designed for *intra muras* Paris only, and the trains deliberately traveled on the right so they could never be hooked up to trains that went outside the city.

The Métro has well over 300 stations; the busiest is St.-Lazare, the deepest is Abbesses, and the one with the most intersecting lines is République. In the late 1960s, the Louvre station was transformed with copies of works from the museum, and the vogue for theme-based stations took off.

Don't miss the replicas from the nearby Musée Rodin at the Varenne station; illustrations of the storming of the prison at the Bastille station; exhibits of engineering feats at Arts et Métiers; and the art nouveau entrances at Porte Dauphine and Abbesses.

EXPERIENCE: Coolest Métro Stations

You can create your own fascinating tour of Paris simply by visiting some of the city's most fascinating Métro stops.

Not all are alike. Some have been decorated in accordance with their location: **Louvre-Rivoli** is a tasteful mini-museum furnished with reproductions of works from the Louvre, while **Varenne** has statues by Rodin. **Gare de Lyon,** on the newest line, no. 14, has a tropical garden; the **Arts et Métier** stop looks like the

inside of a submarine; and the **Concorde** station has the Declaration of the Rights of Man written out on its tiled walls.

Perhaps the coolest of all are the ghost stations. Keep your eyes peeled as the trains on line 8 or 9 pass between **Strasbourg-Saint-Denis** and **République** to see the long-closed St.-Martin station, its tiles now covered in graffiti. ADEMAS (*ademas.assoc.free*) takes you on tours of the Métro, including a ghost station.

More Places to Visit in the Quartier Latin

Arènes de Lutèce

Hidden away behind the modern buildings of the Jussieu University are the vestiges of the Lutetia Arena, a second-century Roman amphitheater designed to seat 15,000 spectators, the second largest in Gaul. The Romans used the natural slope of what is now called Montagne Ste.-Geneviève (see p. 65) for the 35 tiers of stone seats and placed the stage to the east, where performers would receive the last rays of the setting sun.

Few of the original stones remain: The theater eroded away after Parisians carted off handy building materials to build the walls of the Île de la Cité, and over the centuries the arena gradually filled in with debris. By the 19th century, most people believed that the ancient arena was more legend than reality, but Baron Haussmann uncovered the substructure of the arena when he extended Rue Monge in 1869. True to form, he dug up and destroyed about two-thirds of the arena so that a bus depot could use the grounds. In 1883, Victor Hugo led a determined campaign to save the remaining ruins, and the site was finally restored in 1917; only about one-third of today's arena, however, is original.

🗺 Map p. 62 ✉ 49 rue Monge 🚇 Métro: Cardinal Lemoine

INSIDER TIP:

For a great view of Paris, go to the Institut du Monde Arabe in the Latin Quarter and head to its rooftop café/ restaurant for a real visual *délice* (treat).

—ANNE RANDERSON
National Geographic contributor

Scams to Watch Out For

Tourists are the preferred victims of street scammers. A favorite scam often encountered near museums goes like this: A person walking toward you suddenly spies something on the ground and picks it up. The scammer approaches you and shows you a "solid gold" ring, says he or she does not want it and offers to sell it to you for, say, €20. Many scammers, especially around the Centre Pompidou, carry clipboards and pretend to be collecting for charity. Another trick involves a long, complicated explanation about being robbed or having undergone some other traumatic experience and not having the money to go home. In all of these cases, and anything similar, just say *non*, politely but very firmly, and walk away.

Carrefour de l'Odéon

Near the statue of the revolutionary leader Georges Jacques Danton (marking the site of his former home, from which he was arrested in March 1794 and later guil-lotined), the Carrefour de l'Odéon is a busy crossroads that stretches south to the **Odéon-Théâtre de l'Europe** and north to the famous **Café Procope**—the oldest café in Paris *(13 rue de l'Ancienne-Comédie, tel 01 40 46 79 00)*. Here, Jean le Rond d'Alembert and Denis Diderot began work on their famous *Encyclopédie* in 1727, and Benjamin Franklin met with Louis XVI to draw up the agreement for the budding American Republic.

Rue de l'Ancienne-Comédie continues to the bustling Rue St.-André-des-Arts. The beautiful, neoclassic Odéon-Théâtre de l'Europe is best viewed from its entrance at the Place de l'Odéon. It was here that Pierre Beaumarchais's *Mariage de Figaro* was first performed in 1784;

considered subversive, the play cost Beaumarchais a year's imprisonment.

Down the street, at 12 rue de l'Odéon, was
Sylvia Beach's bookstore and lending library,
the famous **Shakespeare and Company,**
once the home of the Left Bank expatriate
American literary community after 1920. Beach
was the first to publish the complete version
of Irish writer James Joyce's *Ulysses* in 1922,
launching the literary event of the decade and
nearly making her bankrupt in the process.
Despite Joyce's subsequent sale of the book
to Random House for a $45,000 advance in
1932, he never offered her any of the profits.
Gertrude Stein was one of the first to subscribe
to Beach's lending library, but was so appalled
by the publication of *Ulysses,* which she
considered obscene, that she informed Beach
that she would thereafter borrow solely from
the American Library on the Right Bank. (The
current bookstore of the same name is at 37
rue de la Bûcherie.)

 Map p. 62 Métro: Odéon

Institut du Monde Arabe

Inaugurated in 1987, the steel-and-glass
Institut du Monde Arabe is a joint Franco-
Arab project designed to encourage cultural
links between the West and the Arab world.
Twenty Arab states participated in this building, which includes permanent and temporary exhibition areas, a library, a bookstore,
conference rooms, an auditorium, and a
spectacular rooftop restaurant and café (the
view alone is worth the trip).

The widely acclaimed architecture is meant
to symbolize a crossroads: The northern or
"Western" side facing the Seine is a sleek,
transparent wall, while the inner, enclosed
courtyard reflects ancient Arab influence
through the innovative, high-tech reinterpre-
tation of the traditional *moucharaby* (carved
wooden screens). The 1,600 aluminum prisms
open and close electronically to regulate the
amount of sunlight streaming into the building.
The permanent collection occupies three floors

and showcases the many scientific and cultural
breakthroughs achieved by Arab scientists and
astronomers. *www.imarabe.org*

 Map p. 62 1 rue des Fossés-St.-
Bernard 01 40 51 38 38 Closed Mon.
 €€ Métro: Jussieu, Cardinal Lemoine,
Sully-Morland

Mosquée de Paris

Paris's principal mosque for the Algerian-
dominated Muslim community encompasses
a religious center, marked by a striking
green-and-white minaret jutting 85 feet
(26 m) into the air; the Institut d'Études
Musulmanes, where Arabo-Islamic language
and culture are taught; and the beautiful

The Institut du Monde Arabe

Moorish tearoom, restaurant, and Turkish baths.

Inaugurated in 1926 to commemorate the Muslim war effort, the mosque was built by Charles Heubès, Robert Fournez, and Maurice Mantout. The most gifted Tunisian, Moroccan, and Algerian craftsmen were summoned to layer the edifice with lovely marble, tiles, mosaics, damask, cedarwood, and fountains made of porphyry. The Grand Patio inside the mosque was inspired by the Alhambra in Granada, Spain, and features woodwork in cedar and eucalyptus, a mosaic frieze bearing verses of the Koran, and a beautiful fountain. The outdoor tearoom, where you can drink mint tea, is perfect on a hot, sunny day.

www.mosquee-de-paris.org

🄰 Map p. 62 ✉ Place du Puits de l'Ermite (mosque) or 39 rue Geoffroy-St.-Hilaire (tearoom, Turkish baths, restaurant, boutique) ☎ 01 45 35 97 33 (mosque); 01 43 31 18 14 (tearoom, restaurant, baths, boutique) 🕒 Closed during Muslim holidays (Ramadan varies from year to year, call for information) 🄼 Métro: Censier Daubenton

St.-Étienne-du-Mont

St.-Étienne-du-Mont is not one of the best-known churches in Paris, yet it is one of the most monumental and unusual. The church, with its highly original, three-tiered facade and asymmetrical interior, has the only remaining rood screen (a crucifix supported on a screen separating the nave from the chancel) in Paris; the tombs of Jean Racine and Blaise Pascal; an elaborate organ loft; a baroque pulpit supported by a figure of Samson; and the reliquary of Saint Geneviève in an elaborate chapel.

According to legend, one of Geneviève's miracles included restoring her mother's sight by washing her eyes with well water; this is depicted in one of the church's stained-glass windows. Until the French Revolution (when the relics were melted down and the saint's remains burned on the Place de la

INSIDER TIP:

Regular English-language readings from notable writers take place in Shakespeare and Company (see p. 75), a treasure trove of new and secondhand books.

—ROSEMARY BAILEY
National Geographic Books author

Grève), the jewel-studded reliquary was a source of great veneration. In times of floods and epidemics, it was carried in a flower-strewn procession to Notre-Dame after a day of atonement.

The Renaissance rood screen, flanked by two openwork spiral staircases, is magnificent. The cloister's main gallery, the Chapelle des Catéchismes (through the sacristy), is lined with magnificent 16th- and 17th-century stained-glass windows. www.saintetiennedumont.fr

🄰 Map p. 62 ✉ Place Ste.-Geneviève ☎ 01 43 54 11 79 🕒 Closed Mon. & noon–2:30 p.m. Sat. & Sun. 🄼 Métro: Cardinal Lemoine

Hemingway's Paris

When Ernest Hemingway and his wife moved to Paris in 1921, they lived in a primitive apartment on Rue Cardinal Lemoine. That area later became part of the fond memories of the protagonist of "The Snows of Kilimanjaro." "There never was another part of Paris that he loved like that, the sprawling trees, the old white plastered houses painted brown below, the long green of the autobus in that round square, the purple flower dye upon the paving, the sudden drop down the hill of the rue Cardinal Lemoine to the River, and the other way the narrow crowded world of the rue Mouffetard."

Two bustling neighborhoods that were once symbolic of the intelligentsia and artistic communities of Paris

St.-Germain
& Montparnasse

On the Rue de la Gaîté, Montparnasse

St.-Germain & Montparnasse

Paris's legendary St.-Germain-des-Prés Quarter sprang up in the ninth century around a famous Benedictine abbey, and is now an area of boutiques, jazz cellars, bookstores, and bistros. Montparnasse, another literary hub, was also the onetime capital of cubism.

The Église St.-Germain-des-Prés was the heart of an abbey whose agricultural domain stretched east to the Petit Pont, encompassing today's 6th and 7th arrondissements. The Romanesque church—the oldest in Paris—holds the remains of 17th-century philosopher and mathematician René Descartes, the founder of modern philosophy. Appropriately, the 20th-century existentialist philosopher Jean-Paul Sartre—the ubiquitous king of the "gauche caviar," or elite leftists—used to come to the nearby Café de Flore to write, vacillate, and chat with novelist Simone de Beauvoir and friends. Other intellectuals, such as Raymond Aron, drank at Les Deux Magots café or ate at the Brasserie Lipp (see p. 243), making St.-Germain-des-Prés synonymous with Parisian intellectual life.

Once Bohemian, Now Upscale

Montparnasse was the birthplace of what went on to become the École de Paris. Its effervescent energy lured writers, artists, and bohemians from all over the world. Ernest Hemingway, F. Scott Fitzgerald, John Rodrigo Dos Passos, and Edna St. Vincent Millay frequented the brasseries and bars; James Whistler lived nearby; Lenin played chess at the Closerie des Lilas; American poet Hart Crane was arrested for punching a waiter at Le Select; and Kiki, the exotic 1920s "Queen of Montparnasse," aroused them all with her raspy voice and seductive show.

La Ruche was a refuge for many artists, particularly those from Central Europe, including Constantin Brancusi, Ossip Zadkine, Chaim Soutine, and Marc Chagall. Some were living in dire poverty and thus spent hours each day in cafés simply to escape the cold. Unfortunately, the advent of central heating killed off much of café life.

The famous late-night bookstore and art gallery La Hune is still open, as are dozens of bookshops scattered through the streets of St.-Germain. This area is also where France's leading publishing houses are located. But today's St.-Germain is ruled more by consumerism, with Right Bank fashion moguls encroaching on the formerly sacrosanct literary hub: Armani has bought out the legendary Drugstore Publicis; Cartier replaced a great classical music shop; Louis Vuitton is at 6 place St.-Germain-des-Prés; and even the Flore has its own accessories boutique. Nevertheless, St.-Germain is still a wonderful area to visit. Don't miss the art galleries that line Rue de Seine, Rue Bonaparte, and Rue des Beaux-Arts, and the Musée Delacroix. And be sure to sit around the octagonal basin in the peaceful Jardin du Luxembourg; and to watch the sun

Paris

Area of map detail

slip into the Seine from the Pont des Arts.

Although Montparnasse's heyday is over, you can still get a glimmer of what the excitement was like along the strip—at La Coupole (see p. 86) and Closerie des Lilas (see p. 88). ■

① Tour Montparnasse **②** Closerie des Lilas **③** Marché St.-Germain **④** École Nationale Supérieure des Beaux-Arts

NOT TO BE MISSED:

A concert in the Église Saint-Germain-des-Prés **80**

Visiting the graves of the famous at Montparnasse Cemetery **85**

A drink at Hemingway's old bar, La Coupole **86**

0   500 meters

0   500 yards

Église St.-Germain-des-Prés

Heeding the advice of Saint Germain, who was soon to be Bishop of Paris, the Merovingian Childebert ordered a basilica and monastery to be built in 543 and dedicated to Saint Vincent (the patron saint of wine growers) and the Holy Cross. The basilica, with its magnificent mosaics and gilded-bronze roof, was nicknamed St.-Germain le Doré (St.-Germain the Gilded).

St.-Germain-des-Prés's 11th-century bell tower

Église St.-Germain-des-Prés

🅜 Map p. 79
✉ Place St.-Germain
☎ 01 55 42 81 33
Ⓜ Métro: St.-Germain-des-Prés

www.eglise-sgp.org

The Normans destroyed the abbey, but it was rebuilt as a Romanesque church around 1000; its 11th-century bell tower is the oldest in Paris. The church was consecrated in 1163 by Pope Alexander III. (Maurice de Sully, the Bishop of Paris, was barred from the ceremony to assert the abbey's independence from the bishop.) The church was expanded in 1245 with the Chapelle de la Vièrge and the cloister, vestiges of which can be seen in the small square outside.

Later History

In June 1789, revolutionaries attacked the abbey prison to free soldiers detained for refusing to fire on striking workers in the Faubourg St.-Antoine. The following year, the church was converted into a saltpeter warehouse. The former church prison, along with **St.-Joseph-des-Carmes** (*70 rue de Vaugirard*), was where the September massacres (see p. 27) began. It was also where Charlotte Corday, who murdered the revolutionary Jean-Paul Marat, was imprisoned during the Terror. In 1794, 15 tons of gunpowder stored in the dining hall exploded, devastating nearly everything.

The church was restored during the 19th century, largely due to efforts by Victor Hugo. Jean Auguste Ingres's student, Hippolyte Flandrin, completed frescoes on the walls of the nave. The columns of the 12th-century chancel are from the Merovingian basilica. In a side chapel to the right of the choir is the **tomb of René Descartes** (who died in 1650). The cloister's small garden has a bronze sculpture of a woman's head by Picasso. ∎

Around the Rue de Seine

Two cultural institutions grace the streets near Place Furstenberg, one of Paris's most romantic squares: the Delacroix Museum and the Institut de France, home to the Académie Française.

Musée Delacroix

The Delacroix Museum is housed in the building where the painter lived until his death in 1863. Delacroix moved here in 1857 while painting the murals in the St.-Sulpice Church. The museum provides a more intimate look at the artist. The collection is laid out in Delacroix's apartment and garden studio, with works displayed on a rotating basis. They include the artist's smaller works, religious paintings like the exceptional "Madeleine in the Desert," and portraits. There are also the artist's palettes, and lithographs, engravings, and objects that Delacroix brought back from North Africa. The renovated garden features the trees and interplay of colors Delacroix prized.

Institut de France

The Collège des Quatre Nations, the predecessor of the Institut de France, was built by money bequeathed by Cardinal Mazarin in 1661 as a school for provincial children. Its layout—two half-moon wings designed by Louis Le Vau—reflects the influence of Italian architecture. The building, given to the Institut de France in 1806, comprises five academies.

The **Académie Française,** the oldest and the most famous, was founded by Cardinal Richelieu in 1635. Membership is limited to 40 individuals known as *les immortels.*

Orson Welles, Peter Ustinov, and Vaclav Havel have all held positions at the **Académie des Beaux-Arts**. The baroque chapel encloses Mazarin's tomb, and the east wing houses the **Bibliothèque Mazarine,** France's first public library. Nearby is the **École Nationale Supérieure des Beaux-Arts** *(14 rue Bonaparte),* Paris's main fine arts school, housed in the vestiges of the Petits-Augustins convent, commissioned by Marguerite de Valois in 1608; its holds temporary exhibitions *(closed Mon.).* ∎

Musée Delacroix

- 🅰 Map p. 79
- ✉ 6 rue de Furstenberg
- ☎ 01 44 41 86 50
- 🕐 Closed Tues.
- 💲 €
- 🚇 Métro: St.-Germain-des-Prés

www.musee-delacroix.fr

Institut de France

- 🅰 Map p. 79
- ✉ 23 quai de Conti
- ☎ 01 44 41 44 41
- 🚇 Métro: St.-Michel

www.institut-de-france.fr

Edible Jewels

Designer pastries presented as edible jewels are all the rage in Paris these days. Across the Boulevard St.-Germain from the Musée Delacroix is **Pierre Hermé** *(72 rue Bonaparte, 75006, tel 01 43 54 47 77),* who invents such treasures as white-truffle macaroons (in season), while **Pain du Sucre** *(14 rue Rambuteau, 75003, tel 01 45 74 68 92)* offers heart-shaped soft-centered chocolate cakes. At Philippe Conticini's **La Pâtisserie des Rêves** *(bakery: 93 rue du Bac, 75007, tel 01 42 84 00 82; tearoom: 111 rue de Longchamp, 75016; tel 01 47 04 00 24),* a specialty is a deconstructed Saint Honoré with the whipped cream on the side.

Palais du Luxembourg

Mention Luxembourg to most Parisians, and they will probably describe the elegant 59-acre (24 ha) park, the only real green space in the entire 6th arrondissement, rather than the palace of the same name. For generations, the park has been one of the city's most popular.

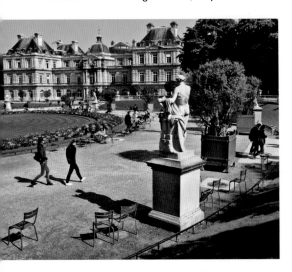

Backed by the palace, the Luxembourg Gardens are popular with walkers and families.

Palais du Luxembourg

- 🅰 Map p. 79
- ✉ 15 rue de Vaugirard
- ☎ 01 42 34 20 00
- 🕐 Interior visits guided tour only; book through Caisse Nationale de Monuments Historiques (tel 01 44 54 19 49). Gardens open daily from dawn to dusk.
- 🚇 Métro: St.-Sulpice, Odéon RER (B): Luxembourg

www.senat.fr

Italian-style Mansion

Both the palace and the gardens were created in the early 17th century by the self-aggrandizing Marie de Médicis after her husband, King Henri IV, was killed. Nostalgic for the Pitti Palace, her childhood home in Florence—and especially the Boboli Gardens—she asked architect Salomon de Brosse to re-create an Italian-style mansion on the property she bought from the Duc de Luxembourg. He retained the smaller building, the Petit Luxembourg (now the official residence of the President of the Senate), and constructed an opulent dwelling

for which she commissioned a series of 24 monumental paintings by Rubens depicting the major events of her life (now displayed in the Louvre). In 1630, after only five years in her lavish palace, she was forced into exile by her son, Louis XIII, on the so-called Day of Dupes.

Gardens

Marie de Médicis' devotion to her garden is visible in the 2,000 elm trees, orchards, and formal flower beds she planted. Although the gardens were re-landscaped by Chalgrin in the 19th century, they retain the formal layout; to this day, the park is impeccably maintained, and a gorgeous palette is created by rotating the flower species through the seasons.

The **Médicis Fountain** is one of the prettiest spots in the park, where 100-year-old plane trees shade the long pool. A number of statues dot the park including a small replica of Auguste Bartholdi's "Statue of Liberty." There's no better place to spend an afternoon with small children, as the park has a separate children's play area, with pony rides, swings, slides, and rides; a classic puppet show; and a merry-go-round constructed from plans by Charles Garnier (designer of the Opéra Garnier). ■

St.-Sulpice & Quartier

On a sunny spring day, with the pink-blossomed chestnut trees in full bloom, the Place St.-Sulpice is one of Paris's loveliest squares. The best place to appreciate the monumental Fountain of Four Bishops (Joachim Visconti, 1844) and the imposing Église St.-Sulpice is from one of the tables spilling out on the sidewalk around the Café de la Mairie.

The Church

Église St.-Sulpice is a surprisingly austere yet grandiose structure that took more than 135 years to build (which may explain the two mismatched towers flanking the colonnaded facade). The first stone was laid in 1646 to replace an earlier 13th-century building, but work stopped 20 years later due to lack of funds. Construction started again in the 18th century and proceeded haphazardly until the north tower was completed in 1778. The highlight of St.-Sulpice is Eugène Delacroix's decoration of the **Chapelle des Sts.-Anges,** which took ten years to finish. The tormented scenes of "Jacob Wrestling with the Angel" and "Heliodorus Driven from the Temple" were the artist's last great masterpieces.

Surrounding Streets

A famous *maison close* (brothel) at 36 rue St.-Sulpice once catered to high-class clientele in the very shadow of the church. The brothel is gone, but the colonnaded facade with yellow and green tiles still marks its place.

The streets around **Place St.-Sulpice** are lined with classy clothes shops, florists, lingerie shops, and bookstores. The area—a shopper's paradise—stretches as far as Sèvres-Babylone, where the renovated **Bon Marché** department store has a chic and expensive new look; the food display on the ground floor alone is worth the trip. Just behind the church is the **Marché St.-Germain,** its covered markets filled today with shops and trendy bars that make this a pale version of the famous medieval fair once held here. ■

Église St.-Sulpice
- Map p. 79
- Place St.-Sulpice
- 01 42 34 59 98
- Free guided tour every Sun. at 3 p.m.
- Métro: St.-Sulpice

www.paroisse-saint-sulpice-paris.org

Hidden Treasure: Picasso's Studio

Picasso's "Guernica" was painted while he was living not far from St.-Sulpice in the Grenier des Grands-Augustins (*7 rue des Grands-Augustins, 75006, tel 01 43 54 09 00*) in a building with a long and illustrious history. In 1610, the nine-year-old Louis XIII was crowned King of France there immediately after his father, Henri IV, was assassinated. Honoré de Balzac's short story "Le Chef-d'œuvre Inconnu," published in 1831, is set in the studio of an artist in the same building. A version of the story illustrated by Picasso was published in 1931, a few years before he moved in. The studio's previous resident had been the actor Jean-Louis Barrault, star of Marcel Carné's famous film, *Les Enfants du Paradis (Children of Paradise),* who rehearsed in the atelier with his first theater company. This handsome space has reproductions of Picasso's illustrations and can be visited by appointment.

Cemeteries

For centuries, Parisians buried their dead in the Cimetière des Innocents (Sts.-Innocents Cemetery) next to the teeming marketplace of Les Halles. It was the main cemetery for over 20 parishes in Paris, particularly for those that did not have their own cemeteries, for the destitute, and for those who died in the Hôtel-Dieu hospital. Burials were in a common grave that held up to 1,500 bodies; when this was full, another was dug nearby.

The beautiful Père-Lachaise Cemetery contains a multitude of interesting tombs.

By the late 18th century, the stench had become intolerable, and the grisly contents of the cemetery (the remains of nearly six million people) were transported in convoys to the catacombs near Denfert-Rochereau (see p. 201). The cemeteries within the walls of the city were then closed, replaced by the cemeteries of Père-Lachaise, Montparnasse, and Montmartre.

Cimetière du Père-Lachaise

Père-Lachaise (8 boulevard de Ménilmontant, tel 01 55 25 82 10, Métro: Père-Lachaise,

Philippe-Auguste) attracts more people than any other cemetery in Paris—more than two million visitors every year. It is named after the Jesuit priest de La Chaise, Louis XIV's confessor, who owned the land here between 1665 and 1709. In 1803, architect Alexandre Brongniart redesigned the layout for a cemetery. Drawing his inspiration from English-style gardens, he integrated romantically landscaped paths and exuberant funerary statuary, which nevertheless failed to excite Parisians. The cemetery opened on May 21, 1804, but there were only 2,000 tombs by 1815, partly because it was considered too remote. Ingenious Parisian government officials figured that if they transferred the remains of a few famous people, celebrity-conscious Parisians would soon follow. In 1817 the remains of playwright Molière and poet Jean de La Fontaine, along with Héloïse and Abélard (see p. 114), were brought to the cemetery; by 1828, there were over 33,000 tombs, and several lots were purchased to expand the growing site, creating today's 109-acre (44 ha) cemetery—the largest green area in Paris, with the exception of the Bois de Boulogne and the Bois de Vincennes.

The cemetery is laid out according to numbered divisions. The lower section is a romantic, tangled forest of tombs and sepulchers, arranged along dirt paths and cobblestone lanes. The upper section has a severe, geometric-grid layout. Maps are available at the cemetery's entrance; these indicate the most famous (though not easy to find) tombs—you may have to poke around off the main path. There are a multitude of interesting tombs, and the most intriguing are not always the graves of the famous. Many celebrities are buried here, including Frédéric Chopin and Oscar Wilde. The grave of the late Doors' singer Jim Morrison has become something of a shrine to his fans. A series of monuments near the Mur des Fédérés, or Federalists' Wall, form a moving homage to the French victims who died in Nazi concentration camps, especially the severe bronze monument representing three skeletal figures, a tribute to the dead of Buchenwald-Dora.

Cimetière de Montparnasse

An abbey necropolis has existed on the site of the Montparnasse Cemetery (3 boulevard Edgar-Quinet, tel 01 44 10 86 50, Métro: Edgar-Quinet, Raspail) since 1654, but it became a municipal cemetery only in 1824. Divided into the Petit Cimetière and the Grand Cimetière, it is the smallest of the three Paris cemeteries, and at first sight is less romantic than Père-Lachaise. Yet along the gridded

avenues lie the remains of many of France's intellectual and artistic elite, along with a profusion of fascinating funerary art. Charles Baudelaire's tomb, for example, features the bust of the 19th-century poet perched above a gigantic bat, contemplating a stone sculpture of his own body below. Constantin Brancusi is also buried here: Several of his sculptures, including "The Kiss," stand atop tombs. Serge Gainsbourg, Jean-Paul Sartre, and Simone de Beauvoir are all interred here.

Cimetière de Montmartre

Montmartre Cemetery (20 avenue Rachel, tel 01 53 42 36 30, Métro: Place Clichy) was initially a sinister place, where the destitute were thrown into common graves. Redesigned in 1879, it now contains the remains of many in the arts, including Edgar Degas, Émile Zola, and Vaslav Nijinsky.

The famed Cimetière de Montmartre

La Coupole

In the 1930s, La Coupole was *the* brasserie in which to see and be seen, drawing some of the 20th century's most famous intellectuals. Hemingway and Jean Cocteau were frequent guests. Today, this *bar Américain* par excellence preserves its classic elegance.

La Coupole has been a fashionable hot spot for decades in Montparnasse.

La Coupole

⬛ Map p. 79

✉ 102
boulevard du
Montparnasse

☎ 01 43 20 14 20

🚇 Métro:
Montparnasse-
Bienvenüe

www.flobrasseries
.com

La Coupole has its hours and seasons, though you can eat at any time, day or night. But it is best during oyster season (all months containing the letter "r"). Try to lunch or dine as late as possible; people tend to linger. Its fabled bar menu serves up odd blends like the eponymous house concoction (rum, Noilly Prat, grenadine, and Grand Marnier).

The Coupole may have lost some of its soul and its culinary status since it was taken over by the Flo Brasseries chain, but it has retained its marvelous art nouveau and art deco decor, with the stunning cubist-style mosaic floor and the famous 33 columns painted by neighborhood artists (most of whose names would not be recognized today) in exchange for free drinks. And it still features giant sprays of gladiolas, courtly waiters who seem devoted to treating each customer like a VIP, and a bustling ambience that conjures the ghosts of customers past, among them Samuel Beckett, Ernest Hemingway, and Salvador Dalí.

In the era of the cellphone, you can no longer enjoy the thrill of seeing your name paraded by on a small chalkboard when a phone call comes in for you, but you can still doodle on your placemat, as Swiss sculptor Alberto Giacometti used to do. ∎

Southeast Montparnasse

A short walk from the expanses of the Luxembourg Gardens are two diverse pieces of Parisian culture. The Zadkine Museum honors the sculptor who lived in Paris for decades. Nearby, the Paris Observatory offers a glimpse into the distinguished history of French astronomy.

Musée Zadkine

This small house and flower-filled garden, just a few blocks from the Luxembourg Gardens, is where the Russian-born sculptor Ossip Zadkine lived from 1928 until his death in 1967. It has remained almost unchanged, with sculptures spread over five rooms and scattered around the secluded garden. Several important pieces are on display, including his most famous sculpture, "Ville Détruite" ("The Destroyed City").

Observatoire de Paris

The Observatoire de Paris, founded in 1667 and completed in 1672, is the oldest observatory in the world still operating. Constructed by Claude Perrault (older brother of the fairy-tale author, Charles Perrault, who published the original *Cinderella*), the building's conception and architectural layout mirrors the cosmos: The main body of the edifice is oriented toward the four cardinal points, and the walls of the two octagonal towers on the southern facade indicate the sun's position during the summer and winter solstices.

Here the moon's surface was charted (1679), the metric weights and measures system devised (1791), Neptune discovered by Leverrier (1846), and the speed of light determined (18th century). The observatory remains a research center for astronomy and related services, but the building's interior can no longer be visited by outsiders. ∎

INSIDER TIP:

On a summer afternoon, join the locals by ordering a kir (chilled white wine with crème de cassis) at a traditional bistro.

—ANNE RANDERSON
National Geographic contributor

Musée Zadkine
- Map p. 79
- 100 bis rue d'Assas
- 01 55 42 77 20
- Closed Mon.
- Métro: Vavin, Notre-Dame des Champs RER (B): Port-Royal

www.paris.fr/musees/zadkine

Observatoire de Paris
- Map p. 79
- 61 avenue de l'Observatoire
- RER (B): Port-Royal

www.obspm.fr

Tour Montparnasse
- Map p. 79
- Place Raoul-Dautry
- 01 45 38 52 56
- €€€
- Métro: Montparnasse-Bienvenüe

www.tourmontparnasse56.com

Tour Montparnasse

Don't miss the 58-floor, 688-foot-high (210 m) Montparnasse Tower, the highest steel-and-glass monstrosity in Europe. It grew out of the old Montparnasse railway station, where the German army signed its surrender of Paris on August 25, 1944. The top of the tower has a panoramic restaurant and terrace, with a terrific view over Paris.

A Walk Through Montparnasse

You can still find traces of historic Montparnasse in some of its most famous establishments, such as the Closerie des Lilas and La Coupole, although it is no longer the vivacious center of art and literature it was in the early part of the 20th century.

Rue de la Gaîté, in Montparnasse, is known for its theaters.

Begin your walk at the Raspail Métro, turning down **Rue Campagne-Première ❶**. At No. 31 is Atelier 17, decorated with tall windows and ceramic tiles. American photographer Man Ray rented a studio here, then moved with his mistress "Queen" Kiki to the Istria Hotel next door. The Istria was home to numerous artists and writers, including Francis Picabia, Austrian poet Rainer Maria Rilke, Marcel Duchamp, and composer Erik Satie. Poet Paul Verlaine lived across the street at No. 14 (the house is no longer standing); when he moved out, he passed his room on to his companion, poet Arthur Rimbaud.

At No. 9, go through the door leading to another group of artists' studios at the back of a cobbled courtyard. Before World War I, many artists left Montmartre for Montparnasse, seeking lower rents and inspiration in the Boulevard du Montparnasse cafés. Italian artists Giorgio de Chirico and Amedeo Modigliani and painter

NOT TO BE MISSED:

**Closerie des Lilas • Rodin's "Balzac"
• La Coupole • Le Select**

James Whistler were among those who lived in this building.

Turn right on the Boulevard du Montparnasse and head for the lavender sign of the **Closerie des Lilas ❷** (see p. 243), a favorite haunt of artists and writers such as Ernest Hemingway. Arriving in Paris in 1921, Hemingway soon settled in at the Closerie, where he wrote *Big Two-Hearted River*, part of *The Sun Also Rises*, and many of his short stories. Its Cuban mahogany bar (where a plaque marks Hemingway's spot), red lamps, mirrored decor, and leather seats are just as inviting today as they were back then.

Outside the Closerie stands a statue of Marshal Ney, a hero of the French Revolutionary and Napoleonic Wars. Hemingway lived nearby at 113 rue Notre-Dame des Champs (turn left from the Closerie to continue the walk) above a sawmill, which no longer exists (even the street number has disappeared; the numbers jump from 111 to 115).

Turn left off Rue Notre-Dame des Champs on Rue de Chevreuse. At the intersection with Boulevard du Montparnasse (where the Batifol restaurant is found), stood Le Jockey—the 1920s haunt presided over by the legendary singer and artist's model, "Queen" Kiki.

Turn right on Boulevard du Montparnasse. At the Carrefour Vavin stands Rodin's famous statue **"Balzac"** (see p. 178). Cross Boulevard du Montparnasse and turn down Rue Delambre. At No. 10 is the **Auberge de Venise,** called Le Dingo in the 1920s; another expatriate hangout, it was where Hemingway first met fellow American F. Scott Fitzgerald.

Turn right on Rue du Montparnasse. The **Falstaff** (now a tacky beer bar) is on the left toward the end; it was once a favorite drinking spot for Samuel Beckett, Kiki, Man Ray, Fitzgerald, and Hemingway.

Turn right on Boulevard du Montparnasse. Ahead lies the Vavin Métro and four of the most famous cafés in the world—Le Select, La Rotonde, Le Dôme (now an upscale fish restaurant; see p. 243), and **La Coupole ❸** (see pp. 86 & 243). American critic and editor Malcolm Cowley described the first three as the "heart and nervous system of the . . . literary colony." Russian revolutionary Leon Trotsky often met up with Mexican painter Diego Rivera at La Rotonde. **Le Select,** the first café in Paris to stay open all night long, was where American poet Hart Crane picked a fight that landed him in jail for a week.

◣	See also map pp. 78–79
►	Raspail Métro
⊕	Allow 2 hours
↔	1.3 miles (2.1 km)
►	Vavin Métro

More Places to Visit in St.-Germain & Montparnasse

Carré Rive Gauche

The cream of the Paris antique trade is clustered within a few prestigious blocks of the 6th arrondissement. Bordered by the Quai Voltaire, Rue des St.-Pères, Rue de l'Université, and Rue du Bac, the Carré Rive Gauche offers shops with high-quality furniture, objets d'art, and paintings. Each of the 30 or so associated shops showcases an exceptional object relating to a theme that is selected annually for a special one-week show in mid-May. www.carrerivegauche.com

🅰 Map p. 79 🚇 Métro: Rue du Bac, Musée d'Orsay

Musée des Lettres et Manuscrits

A museum of manuscripts may sound boring, but the Musée des Lettres et Manuscrits, housed in a beautiful mansion on the Boulevard Saint-Germain, is anything but. No matter what your field of interest—history, art, science, music, or literature—something here is sure to fascinate you. Scientists will be thrilled to see Einstein's handwritten formulas, for example, or notes and calculations scribbled by Marie Curie, while history buffs can read the letter in which Charlotte Corday stated her intention to kill Marat. Literary types will love Marcel Proust's letter with a drawing to his friend and lover, the composer Reynaldo Hahn. The museum holds three temporary exhibitions per year. www.museedeslettres.fr

🅰 Map p. 79 ✉ 222 boulevard Saint-Germain ☎ 01 42 22 48 48; 🕐 Closed Mon. 💲 €€ 🚇 Métro: Rue du Bac, Sèvres-Babylone, St.-Germain-des-Prés.

La Ruche

Just outside Montparnasse, but of interest to students of art, is La Ruche ("beehive"), which celebrated its centenary in 2002–2003. It is one of the oldest artists' colonies still operating today. Sculptor Alfred Boucher salvaged the wine pavilion built by Gustave Eiffel for the Paris Universal Exposition of 1900 and converted it into La Ruche, thus baptized because the beehive-shaped rotunda's main stairway leads to ateliers (studios) where artists paint, sculpt, and write.

The polygonal building was divided into 24 triangular ateliers, each nicknamed quart de brie (slice of brie). It provided a refuge for artists like Amedeo Modigliani, Marc Chagall, and Constantin Brancusi, and writers such as Apollinaire, Max Jacob, and Blaise Cendrars, many of whom lived and worked here in dire poverty. It was also near the cafés of Montparnasse. The building, once nearly demolished, was saved by a committee headed by Chagall; it is now a classified monument and a thriving artistic hub. www.la-ruche.fr

✉ 2 passage de Dantzig 🕐 Some studios may be visited at the discretion of their occupants. 🚇 Métro: Convention

---

EXPERIENCE:
Language Exchanges

A good way not only to meet French people, but also to improve your French, is through language exchanges. Usually, the deal is that you meet up with a French speaker who wants to practice his or her English and the two of you spend half the time speaking each language. (There's no reason you could not speak English the whole time, however.) You can get started online before you even leave home by finding partners at www.mylanguageexchange .com or the French/English Language Exchange on Facebook, or go to informal language exchanges like the **Polyglot Club,** which holds gatherings every Saturday from 8 p.m. to midnight at the **Café Le Basile** (34 rue Grenelle, Métro: St-Germain-des-Prés).

The former market at Les Halles, now an underground shopping complex, but still, as Zola described it, the "belly of Paris"

Châtelet & Les Halles

Henri de Miller's modern head-and-hand sculpture, named "L'Écoute" ("Listen"), outside the Église St.-Eustache

Châtelet & Les Halles

The area around Châtelet and Les Halles, particularly the narrow back alleys and roads, is reminiscent of the cobbled streets of old Paris—bustling, crime-ridden, and foul-smelling, but vibrant.

Life and death coexisted in many medieval Parisian squares, where markets and fairs often sprang up in cemeteries because of the available free space, bringing together mime artists, jugglers, musicians, the homeless, and thieves amid the mixed smells of newly slaughtered meat and the freshest farm produce.

❶ Théâtre Musical de Paris ❷ Tour St.-Jacques ❸ Théâtre de la Ville

Paris

Area of map detail

Les Halles

Les Halles (see pp. 98–99), a market for French produce for 800 years, continues to draw in the crowds—especially around the Fontaine des Innocents (see p. 102); the surrounding gardens, terraces, and sculptures; the seedy Rue St.-Denis; and the Église St.-Eustache (see p. 102)—although the actual market was transferred south of Paris to Rungis in 1969 to ease traffic problems.

The sterile, largely subterranean modern commercial and cultural complex at Forum Les Halles that replaced the marketplace is somewhat alienating, and plans are under way for a complete transformation of the area, unlikely to be finished until 2015. The area's core has shifted east, toward the modern Centre Georges-Pompidou (also called Beaubourg; see pp. 96–97) and the neo-Renaissance Hôtel de Ville (City Hall; see p. 94). Beaubourg, originally a 12th-century village, retains a touch of medieval atmosphere, particularly in its narrow side streets. The former 17th-century Cour des Miracles (see p. 25), once a byword for vice in the red-light area of the 2nd arrondissement, is now a fun place to browse shops, enjoy street performers, and watch the world go by from terrace cafés. ■

République

PLACE
DE LA
RÉPUBLIQUE

Temple

Châtelet

The area around the Place du Châtelet (see p. 95) was associated with the powerful butchers' guilds, the tanneries, and the sinister Grand Châtelet Prison. With its twin theaters and Châtelet Fountain decorated with sphinxes around the base, it is difficult to imagine the square as it once was.

The nearby Tour St.-Jacques—the Flamboyant Gothic bell tower of the church of St.-Jacques la Boucherie—was built for the powerful 16th-century butchers' guild and served as a landmark for pilgrims en route to Santiago de Compostela in Spain. The scallop shells (coquilles) with which the pilgrims decorated their hats and capes became a symbol of the pilgrims—hence the famous dish, Coquilles St.-Jacques. In 1648, Blaise Pascal used the tower to repeat the barometric experiments he had carried out in Puy-de-Dôme, and the tower, standing in a small park, is now a weather station (closed to the public).

In contrast to Châtelet's murky past, Rue St.-Denis was once the path of the kings of France. Today it is lined instead with fast-food joints, clothing outlets, and sex shops, while its northern end is now a seedy red-light district.

NOT TO BE MISSED:

A dance performance at the Théâtre de la Ville **95**

Colorful, controversial Centre Georges-Pompidou **96–97**

Brancusi's reconstructed studio **97**

Eating prime rib at 3 a.m. **99**

Taking in a concert in the musically historic Église St.-Eustache **102**

Shopping for handmade hats on Rue Tiquetonne **102**

Hôtel de Ville

Although the current building is fairly recent, the site of the Hôtel de Ville (City Hall) has always played an essential role in the history of the capital.

Statues adorn the exterior of the Hôtel de Ville.

Hôtel de Ville

- Map p. 92
- Place de l'Hôtel de Ville (public entrance: 29 rue de Rivoli)
- For individual tours, call 01 42 76 43 43 one week in advance; for group tours, call 01 42 76 50 49 one month in advance.
- Métro: Hôtel de Ville, Châtelet

Water was vital in the development of the city's municipal administration, which originated with the powerful water merchants' guild that controlled and administered trade on the Seine, Oise, Yonne, and Marne Rivers. In the mid-13th century, Saint Louis introduced a municipal government composed of leading *échevins* (guildsmen), headed by the *prévôt des marchands* (equivalent to aldermen and a mayor) who were elected by the Parisian bourgeoisie to form the Parloir aux Bourgeois. The seal of the water merchants (an emblem depicting a boat on the river) became the symbol of Paris.

The site of municipal administration shifted from the Place du Châtelet in 1357, when the provost Étienne Marcel bought the Maison des Piliers on the Place de la Grève (*grève* means shore), the name given to the Place de l'Hôtel de Ville until 1830. This first Hôtel de Ville was the site of revolutions, celebrations, and executions from 1310 to 1830. Louis XVI was forced to kiss the tricolor cockade here in 1789, and revolutionaries Danton, Marat, and Robespierre used the hôtel as their headquarters during the Terror (see p. 27).

Water is still present in François-Xavier Lalanne's 1980s fountains flanking the busy, bright white edifice, which is frequently the home of temporary exhibitions. A lavish nativity scene is set up outside the building each Christmas. The interior has a series of beautiful reception halls, glittering chandeliers, gilding, ornate woodwork (note the seven different types of wood in the Salon Bertrand), a sumptuous grand staircase with murals of "Summer" and "Winter" by Puvis de Chavannes, and triumphant Third Republic ceiling murals.

Burned down to a stone shell in May 1871, the Hôtel de Ville was rebuilt between 1874 and 1882, its exterior replicating the French Renaissance style. ■

Place du Châtelet

With its elegant twin theaters, monumental fountain, and great view of the river, the Place du Châtelet bears little trace of its notorious former prison and the crime-ridden streets around it. It does, however, retain the names of the streets where the activities of the butchers and tanneries were carried out—Rue de la Tuerie (killing) and Rue de l'Ecorcherie (skinning).

The square is named for the Grand Châtelet fortress, constructed by Louis VI le Gros (circa 1130) to defend the Île de la Cité. The fortress stood at the entrance to the Pont au Change (Money Changing Bridge), then the city's main access.

Later the area became the seat of the courts, provostship, and prison. In 1808, Napoleon razed the fortress, replacing it with a fountain. A column was also built to commemorate the emperor's victories.

Until the Revolution, the Quai de la Mégisserie was the site of the public slaughterhouse; today, the attractive riverfront is lined with florists and shops selling caged animals, although these traditional businesses are gradually being replaced by home-decoration stores.

Between 1860 and 1862, at the request of Baron Haussmann, architect Jean-Antoine-Gabriel Davioud built two identical theaters on the square's opposite sides: the Théâtre du Châtelet (now the **Théâtre Musical de Paris**) and the **Théâtre de la Ville,** once owned by the actress Sarah Bernhardt. Today, with the bustling Châtelet Métro/RER stop far beneath its streets, the square has become one of the busiest crossroads in Paris. ■

INSIDER TIP:

At an outdoor *terrasse* around Châtelet–Les Halles, order a *café* and join Parisians in watching the people go by.

—ANNE RANDERSON
National Geographic contributor

Place du Châtelet
- Map p. 92
- Métro: Châtelet

Café Nuts and Bolts

After a day on your feet, nothing is more welcome than a stop at a café. Some are low-profile local places where working people eat a quick snack at lunchtime and residents meet in the evening. In general, cafés open early in the morning, in time to serve the traditional grand crème (large cup of coffee with milk) with croissants to people on their way to work.

Throughout the day they also serve wine, beer, pastis—a strong aniseed spirit diluted with water—and, of course, espresso (Parisians traditionally add milk to their coffee only in the morning). Drinks are cheaper *au bar* (standing at the bar) than *en salle* (sitting at a table inside). They are even more expensive if you sit at a table outside, but this increase in price never seems to worry anyone who is intent on soaking up the atmosphere.

Centre Georges-Pompidou

The Pompidou Center, renovated extensively between 1997 and 2000, is one of the city's most popular sites. Standing in the midst of Paris like a slumbering giant, its blue, green, yellow, and red pipes and ducts coiled against the gray rooftops and cityscape, Richard Rogers and Renzo Piano's arts complex spearheaded contemporary architecture in Paris in 1977, injecting an avant-garde tone into one of the city's oldest neighborhoods and causing great controversy.

The architecture of the Centre Georges-Pompidou is distinctive if not universally admired.

Since the 90-million-dollar renovation of the center (called Beaubourg by Parisians), the main foyer has been redesigned; exhibition space nearly doubled; disabled access improved; and the library (now with its own entrance) expanded and equipped with 370 computers. Drama, dance, and cinema theaters have opened on the lower level; a museum gallery, graphic arts gallery, and media collection has been added. A trendy (if overblown) restaurant (Georges)—where you'll at least get a great view—is found at the top of the six-level center.

The center still houses the **Center of Industrial Creation** (CCI), specializing in architecture, urbanization, and visual communications; the **Institute for Research and Acoustical/ Musical Coordination** (IRCAM) for contemporary music; and the **Cinema,** featuring film festivals and rare movies. It also hosts a **Children's Workshop** to foster touch, color, and artistic expression in 6- to 12-year-olds, and conferences, seminars, lectures, and debates.

On the other hand, the renovation has made for a less-democratic building: In a plan that was highly criticized by both architects, visitors now have to pay to take the escalators up for the splendid panoramic view. (If you are lucky enough to be there on the first Sunday of the month, escalator admission is free.) But the ticket gives access to the Musée National d'Art Moderne and its extraordinary collection of 20th-century works. The focus of the center now is to direct attention to the museum.

Musée National d'Art Moderne

The MNAM's extensive collection is second only to that of New York's Metropolitan Museum of Modern Art, housing some 60,000 works from the early 20th century to the present. The renovation expanded the exhibition space by 50 percent, and the contemporary display is rehung every six months (the modern galleries every year).

Visitors enter through the contemporary art section on the fourth level, which has rooms devoted to pop art, *arte povera,* and other major movements, as well as to individual artists such as Yves Klein and Jean Dubuffet. Visitors then proceed upstairs to the modern section (1905–1960),

featuring movements such as fauvism and cubism and works by Picasso, Kandinsky, Rouault, Chagall, and Matisse, among others. New acquisitions include Francis Picabia's "Dresseur d'Animaux." In general, there is more sculpture (Giacometti, in particular) and contemporary French art, and the

Brancusi's Sculpture Studio

When the Romanian-born sculptor Constantin Brancusi died in 1957, he left his studio to the French government, on condition that it be fully reconstituted. Originally on the Impasse Ronsin in the 15th arrondissement, the atelier was rebuilt at the Palais de Tokyo before being moved to the Pompidou Center in 1977, where it is now located on the plaza. On view are the artist's sketches, original plasters, bronze sculptures, stone and marble sculptures, bed, wardrobe, tools, and maquettes. Temporary exhibitions are held in the studio as well.

collections now include furniture and design. It is easier for visitors to circulate on both levels of the museum, and the ceilings have been opened up to reveal the pipes and ducts painted white, creating the impression of higher ceilings and brighter space. There are also video lounges, installation areas, and performance art spaces. ∎

Centre Georges-Pompidou

- Map p. 92
- Place Georges-Pompidou
- RCAM: entrance on Place Igor Stravinsky
- 01 44 78 12 33
- Closed Tues. Museum & exhibitions open at 11 a.m.; Atelier Brancusi opens 2 p.m.
- €€€
- Métro: Hôtel de Ville, Rambuteau

www.cnac-gp.fr

Les Halles

The forum at Les Halles is but a pale shadow of the legendary "belly of Paris" described by Émile Zola, where fishwives and market porters worked through the night to load the pavilions with the gleaming heady produce of rural France by dawn.

The mirrored facades of the Forum des Halles reflect the neighborhood.

Les Halles

 Map p. 92

Métro: Les Halles, Châtelet

Philippe-Auguste built Les Halles between 1181 and 1183, financing it partially by property confiscated from the Jewish residents he expelled in 1182. When the two large, 13th-century warehouses for drapers and weavers that formed the primitive market at Champeaux closed on Saturdays, the merchants and craftsmen set up their shops at Les Halles. (To qualify as a market porter [Fort des Halles], you had to be able to carry a load of 440 pounds [200 kg] over a distance of 164 feet [50 m].) By the mid-14th century, merchants were present three times a week. In 1851, Napoleon III instructed the architect Victor Baltard to construct cast-iron "umbrellas," and ten pavilions with cast-iron frames were built in Les Halles between 1854 and 1912. In 1936 two more were added, and by 1969, the market's popularity and resultant traffic problems forced authorities to move it south of the city to Rungis. All but two of the pavilions were destroyed, and for nearly a

Late-Night Restaurants

Paris may be an international metropolis, but surprisingly few restaurants stay open late at night. If you do not know where to find a meal after 10:30 or 11 p.m., you may find yourself going to bed hungry after the theater or a film. Your best chances will be found around Les Halles, where a number of traditional restaurants stay open until the wee hours: **La Tour Montlhéry** (a.k.a. Chez Denise, 5 rue des Prouvaires, 75001, tel 01 42 36 21 82), **La Poule au Pot** (9 rue Vauvilliers, 75001, tel 01 42 36 32 96), **Au Pied de Cochon** (6 rue Coquillière, 75001, tel 01 40 13 77 00). In the Marais, **Les Philosophes** (28 rue-Vieille-du-Temple 75004, tel 01 48 87 49 64) serves until 1 a.m. Around the Champs-Élysées: **L'Alsace** (39 avenue Champs-Élysées, 75008, tel. 01 53 93 97 00), specializing in choucroute, and the **Maison de l'Aubrac** (37 rue Marbeuf, 75008), with Auvergnate specialties, are open 24/7. Near Opéra: **Le Grand Café Capucines** (4 boulevard des Capucines, 75009, tel 01 43 12 19 00) serves shellfish and French dishes all day and night.

decade a gaping hole remained where the market once stood.

In 1979, the Les Halles reconstruction project took form, resulting in a widespread commercial and cultural boom. Today, the sprawling Métro-RER station at Châtelet–Les Halles acts as a high-speed crossroads for city commuters and shoppers. Crowds from all walks of life mill around in this vast, four-level, subterranean shopping complex, which also includes a photography exhibition space, gymnasium, pool, tropical greenhouse, movie complex and lounge, video library, record-lending library, center for music and dance, and billiards room.

The Renovation

Now, just 30 years after the building of the controversial Forum des Halles, with its mirrored "upside-down-umbrella" aboveground structures, all this is set to change. A massive renovation project, beginning with the gardens, finally got started in 2010. After several years of architectural competitions, heated consultations with the public, and refinements of the winning project, the new Les Halles will now finally begin to take shape. Architect David Mangin will oversee the master plan, which includes a reorganization of the Métro-RER transport hub, a new garden, and a transparent roof, known as "La Canopée," which will cover the shopping center. Judging from artists' renderings of the project, designed by Patrick Berger and Jacques Anziutti, the gently undulating yellow roof, which will incorporate solar panels and rainwater tanks, will look something like a giant spaceship that has landed in the center of Paris, glowing green at night.

The garden will include two new playgrounds, described as "the Wizard of Oz meets the Mario brothers," the first part of which is set to open in mid-2011. The project includes a public library, a conservatory, and two cafés fronting the park. ∎

Neighborhood Markets

For local color, nothing beats a morning at one of the many food markets scattered throughout Paris. You will be tempted by the brilliant displays of red and yellow peppers, slithering stacks of mysterious sea creatures, and countless different cheeses; extra encouragement comes from the boisterous sellers hawking their produce.

The market on Rue Mouffetard attracts locals and visitors to the Latin Quarter.

Every neighborhood has its own market. A few are still housed in old, covered buildings and, while some are permanent, others are set up for only two or three mornings a week. Although the markets are less crowded and the food is fresher early in the morning, there are good bargains at the end of the day, when vendors sell off their last few pounds of fruit cheap. Don't pick up the food yourself, however; point out what you want and tell the vendors, and let them handle their merchandise themselves.

Permanent & Temporary Markets

The permanent (regular) markets are closed on Sunday afternoons, Mondays, and also during several hours at lunchtime. The Marché d'Aligre, on Place d'Aligre, is one of the cheapest in Paris. It has lots of exotic goods, like North African spices, as well as many secondhand clothes stalls. The covered Marché des Enfants Rouges, the city's oldest (1615), is also a popular lunch spot, offering shoppers a choice of French, Italian, and Moroccan specialties.

Another colorful market extends along the lower end of Rue Mouffetard; it would look like a film set if it weren't for all the tourists.

For true Left Bank chic, try the Buci Market on Rue de Seine and Rue de Buci, where a quintessentially Parisian clientele crowds the busy (and expensive) stands on Sunday morning. And for organic Left Bank chic, the Marché Biologique on Boulevard Raspail offers high-priced free-range poultry and chemical-free produce. Other permanent market streets include Rue Montorgueil, a holdover from Les Halles; Rue du Poteau, a great, little known food market; and Rue Poncelet.

The largest temporary market stretches endlessly along Boulevard Richard Lenoir on Thursday and Sunday mornings. As with most neighborhood markets, locals usually return to the same vendors, but as prices and quality vary, take time to shop around. Afternoon markets include Saint Eustache–Les Halles market (Thursday afternoon) and Place Baudoyer (Wednesday afternoon).

Specialty Markets

Paris also has its share of specialty markets. In the shadow of the Paris law courts on the Île de la Cité is the flower market (see p. 54). (see p. 54)

On Sunday a bird market also takes place here, and the air is filled with their trilling and squawking.

If you want antique or secondhand books, try the book market on Rue Brancion, near the Parc Georges Brassens, on Saturday and Sunday. The serious book collectors arrive early to browse through the weekly selection.

INSIDER TIP:

The market on Boulevard Auguste Blanqui, near Butte-aux-Cailles, stretches out of sight and is a sensory feast.

—PATRICIA DANIELS
National Geographic contributing editor

The area at the base of Montmartre is the place to find fabrics. There are two main stores. Marché St.-Pierre *(2 rue Charles Nodier)*, a four-floor free-for-all, has the best prices for silks, wools, and furnishing fabrics. Across the street is the more sedate and expensive Reine *(5 place St.-Pierre)*. All around are smaller fabric outlets, selling everything from buttons to bolts of exotic African and Middle Eastern fabrics.

EXPERIENCE: Finding the Markets

Join the Parisians in shopping for produce, cheese, or charcuterie at one of Paris's many neighborhood markets. For hours and closing days, check www.paris.fr.

Markets

Marché d'Aligre *(Métro: Ledru-Rollin)*
Rue Mouffetard market *(Métro: Censier Daubenton)*
Marché Biologique *(Sun. a.m., Métro: Sêvres-Babylone)*
Rue Montorgueil market *(Métro: Les Halles, Étienne-Marcel)*
Rue du Poteau market *(Métro: Jules Joffrin)*

Rue Poncelet market *(Métro: Ternes)*
Boulevard Richard Lenoir market *(Thurs. & Sun. a.m., Métro: Bastille, Richard Lenoir)*
Place Baudoyer *(Wed. p.m., Sat. a.m., Métro: Hôtel-de-Ville)*
Marché des Enfants Rouges *(Métro: Temple)*
Rue Brancion *(Sat. & Sun., Métro: Porte de Vanves)*
Marché St.-Pierre and Reine *(Métro: Barbès-Rochechouart, Anvers)*
Saint Eustaches–Les Halles *(Thurs. p.m. & Sun. a.m., Métro: Les Halles)*

More Places to Visit in Châtelet & Les Halles

Fontaine des Innocents

Completed by Jean Goujon in 1549, this is Paris's only Renaissance fountain. (where the Cimetière des Innocents was once located; see p. 84) With its delicate bas-reliefs of nymphs and angels, the fountain is a great meeting place for lovers, skateboarders, punks, and bums alike. Although the surrounding square has suffered encroachment by McDonald's, Pizza Hut, Naf Naf, and other eyesores, it still offers proof of human creativity through performing musicians and entrancing mime artists.

🅰 Map p. 92 ✉ Square des Innocents
🚇 Châtelet–Les Halles

Where to Buy a Handmade Hat

Here's an original idea for a souvenir of a trip to Paris: a handmade hat. Drop by the Les Halles shop of Anthony Peto (56 rue Tiquetonne, 75002, tel 01 40 26 60 68, www.anthonypeto.com), a British haberdasher with a sense of humor (from his website's FAQ section: "Are your hats for men or women?" "Yes"; "Will hats ever come back into fashion?" "No") for a fitting and to choose your preferred style and fabric. The chapeau can be as eccentric or traditional as you wish. Your new headgear will be ready in one week for between €110 and €150.

Église St.-Eustache

Gothic and classical in plan and layout and Renaissance in decoration, this 16th-century church is second in size in Paris only to Notre-Dame. It was named for a Roman general who was said to have converted to Christianity after seeing a cross between a stag's antlers. (Note the stag's head beneath the gable point on the beautiful Renaissance transept facade.) During the Revolution, the church was converted into a secular Temple of Agriculture—a fitting transformation given its proximity to the former food market.

Many famous historical persons have made their mark on St.-Eustache. For example, it is where Molière was baptized (1622); Louis XIV made his first Communion (1649); and where Jean Colbert, Minister of Finance to Louis XIV, is buried (see statues of "Colbert and Abundance" by Antoine Coysevox). The funeral service for poet Jean de La Fontaine was held here (1695).

Many notable musicians are associated with the church. Here, Hector Berlioz attended the performance by 950 musicians of his massive choral/symphonic work Te Deum (1855); Franz Liszt's Grand Mass premiered here (1866); and Charles Gounod directed the choir. Indeed, the church's fine acoustics have ensured a long history of organ and choral music; concerts are still held regularly on the premises (check Pariscope for information).

Antoine Soulignac's 17th-century stained-glass windows are remarkable. There are also paintings by the school of Rubens ("Disciples at Emmaüs") and Simon Vouet ("Saint Eustache the Martyr"), and a somewhat jarringly naive sculpture by Raymond Mason.

Around the church, on Rue Montorgueil, garden stalls, butchers' shops, and boutiques give a hint of the former, bustling Les Halles market quarter. Rue du Jour has been usurped by Agnès B. and other fashionable boutiques, although the magnificent portal of the **Hôtel des Abbés de Royaumont** on this street is worth a detour.

Nighthawks gather at nearby **Le Pied de Cochon** at 6 rue Coquillère for hearty food, served until dawn (see sidebar p. 99). www.saint-eustache.org

🅰 Map p. 92 ✉ rue du Jour
🚇 Les Halles, Châtelet

A vast outdoor museum, with well-groomed squares, quiet gardens, and elaborate architectural designs

Le Marais & Bastille

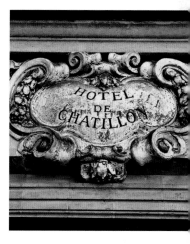

The historic Marais neighborhood preserves many old decorative details.

Le Marais & Bastille

Until the 13th century, the area around Rue St.-Antoine was a marsh, giving the Marais (meaning "swamp") its name. Fed by the flooding of the Seine, it was used for market gardening. The quarter was gradually converted into a residential area; several convents were established, followed by lords' country homes, or *courtilles,* and royal residences.

The religious orders, who subsisted on the market gardens in the 14th century, sold their properties to members of the nobility who were seeking land outside the city walls. By the late 15th century, the old nobility, or *noblesse d'épée,* was firmly implanted in the quarter.

In the 16th century, there was an influx of newly ennobled financial and intellectual bour-geoisie—the *noblesse de robe*—which supplied the crown with much required funds by purchasing expensive titles. The royalty left after Henri II's death in 1559, but the aristocracy remained, erecting a number of superb mansions. In the late 17th century, after the court moved to Versailles, Le Marais began to fall into decline because of its remote eastern location, and by 1815, the area had become more synonymous with the *petite bourgeoisie.*

The square of the Place des Vosges (see pp. 106–107) replaced the Maison Royale des Tournelles, long the residence of the kings of France, encompassing a huge house and gardens surrounded by a wall and many small tournelles, or towers. Formerly called the Place Royale, the Place des Vosges was built by Henri IV in 1605. It spearheaded the development of the elegant Marais area, filled with sumptuous *hôtels particuliers* reminiscent of tiny, individual castles, including the Hôtel de Sully (see p. 116), the Hôtel de Rohan (a new museum of French history; see p. 117), the Hôtel de Sens (see p. 120), the Hôtel Salé (home of the Musée Picasso; see pp. 110–111), and the Hôtel Carnavalet (see p. 113).

Architectural Tradition

Le Marais escaped the major urbanization overhaul during the 1960s, as Culture Minister André Malraux decreed that it be restored, given its historic value. The architectural traditions were successfully preserved, and the area is dense with elabo-rate doorways, windows, inner courtyards, bas-reliefs (such as the "Horses of Apollo" at the Hôtel de Rohan), and original street names carved in stone. Historic landmarks include vestiges of the Philippe-Auguste Wall, the Porte Clisson, and the nearby Place de la Bastille. However, fashion designers and yuppies have moved into the neighborhood, and the resulting gentrification has glazed over much of the area's charm.

The conversion of the former *hammam* (Turkish baths) on Rue des Rosiers in the old Jewish quarter into a clothing store is a potent illustration of the area's changing character. ■

1 Porte Clisson **2** Crédit Munici-
pal **3** Hôtel des Ambassadeurs de
Hollande **4** Hôtel de Rohan **5** Hôtel
Libéral Bruand **6** Hôtel de Sully
7 Musée d'Art et d'Histoire du
Judaïsme **8** Memorial de la Shoah

PLACE
DE LA
RÉPUBLIQUE

République

Temple

RUE DU TEMPLE

SQUARE DU
TEMPLE

BLVD DU TEMPLE

Filles du
Calvaire

BOULEVARD DES FILLES DU CALVAIRE

St.-Sébastien
Froissart

RUE DES ARCHIVES

RUE DU TEMPLE

RUE RAMBUTEAU

7

1

4

Musée
Picasso

RUE DU TEMPLE

RUE DES
FRANCS

2

Musée
Cognacq-Jay

5

SQUARE
G. CAIN

BOURGEOIS

RUE DES ARCHIVES

3

JEWISH
QUARTER

Musée
Carnavalet

Chemin
Vert

BLVD. BEAUMARCHAIS

RUE DE L'OBAU

Hôtel
de Ville

RUE DE RIVOLI

QUAI DE L'HÔTEL DE VILLE

8

St.-Paul

Pont
Marie

Hôtel
de Sens

6

Place des
Vosges

RUE ST.-ANTOINE

Bastille

Place de la
Bastille

QUAI DES CÉLESTINS

PONT MARIE

PORT DES CÉLESTINS

BOULEVARD HENRI IV

Opéra de
Paris-Bastille

BOURDON

BOULEVARD DE LA BASTILLE

Sully
Morland

PONT DE SULLY

BOULEVARD MORLAND

QUAI HENRI IV

Bassin
de l'Arsenal

BLVD

PORT HENRI IV

PONT MORLAND

Quai de
la Rapée

Seine

PONT
D'AUSTERLITZ

VOIE MAZAS

| 0 | 400 meters |
| 0 | 400 yards |

Paris

Seine

Area of map detail

Place des Vosges

The Place des Vosges (originally the Place Royale, but rebaptized in 1800) was Paris's first open-air square, with a striking, redbrick symmetry of 36 pavilions, 9 on a side, each with 4 arcades and steeply pitched slate roofs. Following Louis d'Orléans's death in 1407, it became Crown property. When Charles VI moved there the Place was expanded to include dwellings, chapels, parks, and meadows (hence the nearby Rue du Foin, meaning "hay").

Striking redbrick buildings surround the open-air Place des Vosges.

Charles VII, Louis XI, Charles VIII, Louis XII, François I, and Henri II all resided here. Four years after Henri II's death in a jousting accident on the Cours St.-Antoine (near the current Place des Vosges) in 1559, his wife, Catherine de Médicis, moved the royal residence to the Louvre and ordered the Hôtel des Tournelles to be torn down. The square subsequently became a horse market.

Although Henri IV originally intended to convert the square into silk workshops to ease France's dependence on Italian imports, he decided instead in 1605 to build the Place Royale

there, providing a square for public festivities that was otherwise lacking in Paris. The large southern pavilion, the **Pavillon du Roi,** served as a model for the others, with the **Pavillon de la Reine** opposite on the north side.

Henri IV was assassinated in 1610 before the square's inauguration in 1612. The inauguration celebrated a fantastic double wedding between Louis XIII (Henri IV's successor, whose statue stands in the square) and Anne of Austria, and between Princess Elisabeth of France and the future Philippe IV. Thirteen hundred horsemen paraded to the sounds of 150 trumpets and 80 musettes, oboes, and violins; torchbearers streamed through the streets of Paris at night, while fireworks were fired over the Bastille.

Thereafter, the square became a stopping-off spot for foreign envoys en route to the Louvre and a hub for luminaries such as financier Maximilien Sully and the Princesses de Rohan and de Guéménée.

Each of the numbered residences has its own story. No. 1: Built with Crown money, the Pavillon du Roi was never a royal residence, but was rented out. No. 1B: The famous literary hostess Madame de Sévigné was born here in 1626. No. 4: The Marquis de Favras, who was accused of having plotted the kidnapping of Louis XVI and the murder of Lafayette, Commander of the National Guard, lived here in 1789. No. 6: Victor Hugo lived here from 1832 to 1848, writing *Les Chants du Crépuscule* and *Ruy Blas*. In the early 20th century, the building was converted

into a museum, the **Maison de Victor Hugo** *(tel 01 42 72 10 16, www.musee-hugo.paris.fr, closed Mon.)*, containing the four-poster bed in which he died. No. 7: The entrance to the Petit Hôtel Sully, used by its owner, the Duc de Sully in the 17th century to reach the Place Royale. No. 8: The writers Théophile Gautier and Alphonse Daudet lived on the second floor in the mid-19th century. No. 9: The 19th-century tragedian Rachel (Élisa Félix) lived here in 1857; it is now the l'Ambroisie restaurant. No. 21: Cardinal Richelieu lived here from 1615 to 1623.

In 1818 the statue of Louis XIII in the square replaced a bronze one erected in 1639 by Cardinal Richelieu. Today, the square is trimmed with linden trees, and you can stretch out on grass—a rarity in Paris as this is often forbidden elsewhere. Sunday afternoons are great for strolling around the arcades, listening to a variety of music, and browsing in the small stores. ■

Place des Vosges

 Map p. 105

Métro: Bastille, Chemin Vert, St.-Paul

EXPERIENCE: Brunch à la Française

The French idea of brunch bears little resemblance to the American original. In most Paris restaurants offering brunch, customers are served a bewildering overload of dishes all at once: salad, eggs, pastries, French toast and/or pancakes, smoked salmon or ham, sometimes followed by a main course and usually by dessert. Arrive with an appetite, because you'll need it.

Some popular Sunday brunch spots—which are sure to be packed, usually with a lively crowd of youngish bobo (bourgeois-bohemian) types—are the **Des**

Gars dans la Cuisine *(72 rue Vieille du Temple, 75003, tel 01 42 74 88 26)*, a few blocks west of the Place des Vosges, and **Café Charlot** *(38 rue de Bretagne, 75003, tel 01 44 54 03 30)* also in the Marais. For a wonderful English-style brunch, try the **Rose Bakery** *(30 rue Debelleyme, 75003, tel 01 49 96 54 01 or 46 rue des Martyrs, 75009, tel 01 42 82 12 80)*, near the Musée Picasso, but be prepared to wait for a table.

For an excellent Moroccan brunch, try **404** *(69 rue des Gravilliers, 75003, tel 01 42 74 57 81)*, also in the Marais.

Streets of Paris

For centuries, travel was arduous through Paris's dark, muddy streets, then unmarked and unnumbered. Store signs came into use by the 15th century, and these served as addresses. At first they were unwieldy sheet-metal plaques suspended on a long iron arm. By the mid-18th century, signs were smaller and fixed above the stores. Some wonderful store signs can be seen at the Musée Carnavalet (see p. 113).

The streets of Paris, such as Rue Mouffetard, are filled with eye-catching details.

Street Names

In 1728, street names were ordered to appear on corners; plaques went up all over the city, with names also carved into stone on street corner buildings. In 1844, the blue, enameled iron plaques currently in use began to appear. Many streets have been named and renamed—after noted merchants or residents, such as Galande; surrounding villages, like Belleville or Charonne; churches; professions (Coutellerie for the knifemaking area); landmarks like fountains or horse markets (Cul-de-sac du Ha! Ha!, now Cul-de-sac-Royale St.-Antoine); store signs (Chat Qui Pêche, Pot-de-Fer); historic milestones and events (Avenue Quatre-Septembre); heroes; victories; leaders; and even Métro stations. The new streets around the Bibliothèque

Nationale de France in 1994 were named after writers such as François Mauriac and Raymond Aron.

In certain areas, such as Le Marais, you can still see the stone street name underneath the blue plaque. Political upheavals would sometimes upend street names: Rue de Berlin became Rue de Liège after World War I, for example. Sometimes, the names shocked residents—for example, Rue Pélican was originally a den of iniquity called Rue Poil-au-Con (a coarse reference to hairy buttocks); others merely evolved through wordplay (Rue de la Croix became Rue Eugène-Delacroix in 1868).

Lighting the City of Light

In 1318, only three public lanterns lit Paris at night, one at the Grand Châtelet fortress-prison; another at the Nesle Tower to guide sailors; and the last at the Cimetière des Innocents—the "lantern of the dead." In the first half of the 16th century, Louis XII, François I, and Henri II ordered candles to be placed in one window of each home—yet 15 people on average were murdered in the streets each night. In 1662 a mobile lighting system was adopted for those wishing to move about town at night. Porters bearing wax torches (and charging per layer of wax consumed) or oil lamps accompanied people to their doors, even if they lived several flights up.

Under Louis XIV (R.1643–1715), 3,000 lanterns were placed in the streets; these in turn were gradually replaced by oil-fueled, reflecting street lamps. There were 13,000 by 1837, and 240 lamplighters lit them as night approached, taking only three-quarters of an hour. Gas lighting spread quickly during the Restoration, with 8,000 gas lamps by 1845. Electricity first lit the Place de l'Opéra in 1878.

More recently, high-tech lighting systems using halogen lamps to bring out sculpture and details have upgraded bridges. The Eiffel Tower, in contrast to more traditional floodlighting, now glows from the inside and sparkles every hour after dark.

What to Look For

Paris is best seen at a slow stroll—as you go along, look up at the rooftop gardens,

The blue, enameled plaque of the Place des Victoires is typical of Paris's old street signs.

spilasters, caryatids, and mosaics. You'll also find a series of cityscape frescoes scattered throughout Paris. The idea for frescoes stemmed from 1930s ads painted onto walls billing the aperitif "Dubo Dubon Dubonnet"—still visible on some streets in the city— or the chocolate drink Banania. In the 1970s, artists were commissioned to decorate walls with trompe l'oeil frescoes or figures. The murals come and go over the years, with new ones being added throughout the city— like the man climbing stairs accompanied by a pianist and violinist at Métro Etienne Marcel, and the blue-and-purple greenhouse at 60 rue de Reuilly in the 12th.

Wolves & Bad Boys

One of the pleasures of sign-spotting in Paris is finding some of the more eccentric street names, such as:
Rue de l'Arbre Sec (Dry Tree St., 1st arrondissement) from tales of Marco Polo
Rue des Deux Boules (Two Balls St., 1st arrondissement) probably named after a shop sign
Rue des Mauvais Garçons (Bad Boys St., 4th arrondissement)

Rue Dieu (God St., 10th arrondissement) named after General Dieu
Rue Brèche aux Loups (Wolf Gap St., 12th arrondissement)
Rue Vineuse (Winey St., 16th arrondissement) King Louis XIII liked to stop by and drink the wine made by the convent there.
Rue Poulet (Chicken Street, 18th arrondissement)

Musée Picasso

With its sphinx-guarded entrance, the Musée Picasso has the largest collection of works by Picasso in the world and gives a strong sense of the freshness and inventiveness that permeated every medium he touched. It reopens in early 2012 after extensive renovations.

Musée Picasso
- 🅰 Map p. 105
- ✉ Hôtel Salé, 5 rue de Thorigny
- ☎ 01 42 71 25 21
- 🕐 Closed until 2012
- Ⓜ Métro: St.-Sébastian Froissart, Chemin Vert
- **www.musee-picasso .fr**

Hôtel Salé

The Musée Picasso is located in the Hôtel Salé, built by Jean Boullier in 1656 for a salt-tax collector named Pierre Aubert de Fontenay. ("*Salé*" means "salty," but it also means "very expensive"—probably because salted meat was considered more valuable than poorly salted meat—and indeed, this hôtel particulier was extremely expensive to build.) Aubert, a nouveau riche who made his fortune

The Hôtel Salé is an elegant setting for Picasso's work.

as a tax collector, displayed his rather ostentatious taste in the grandiose ironwork staircase, encompassed by winged figures bearing garlands of fruit framing medallions, and the Salon de Jupiter, with its cherubs, garlands, and two medallions with reclining gods. The decoration is the work of the sculptor Martin Desjardins.

Following Aubert's death, the hôtel was rented out to various parties, including the Venetian Embassy and Leclerc de Juigné. The last archbishop of Paris before the Revolution, de Juigné covered up the nude sculptures on the walls. The hôtel was pillaged during the Revolution, then sold and rented to two art schools, the École Centrale des Arts et Manufactures and the École des Métiers d'Art. The City of Paris acquired the mansion in 1964 and leased it to the State, which considered making it a costume museum. Picasso's death in 1973, however, prompted a search for a proper museum to display his works, and the Hôtel Salé was selected in 1976.

Picasso's Legacy

Picasso liked to joke that he was the world's greatest collector of Picassos, and indeed he kept much of his own output during his nearly 80 years of artistic production. Born in Málaga in 1881, Picasso left Spain at the age of 23 for France. Because of his close affinity with France, he lived most of his life here. After a 1934 visit to Spain, he vowed never to return because of his opposition to Franco.

After Picasso's death in Mougins, his heirs donated his artworks in lieu of paying estate duties, and this allowed the State to have first choice in selecting the works that now form the bulk of the museum's collection. Their choices were not always the finest of Picasso's works but are representative of his prolific output.

The Art

In all, the collection totals 203 paintings, 158 sculptures, 28 tableaux reliefs, 16 paper collages, 88 ceramic pieces, and over 3,000 prints and drawings, ranging from "The Girl with Bare Feet" (painted in 1895, when Picasso was 14) to his later works. Picasso kept many of his masterpieces, and although many had traveled for temporary exhibitions, some had never been seen.

The number of works and their diversity mark the originality of this museum. Paintings trace Picasso's career: his movement into his blue period, which followed the suicide of a friend, Casagemas; the rose period, when he accentuated volume and the simplification and disproportion of features typical of Iberian art; and the impact of his discovery of African and Oceanic art. Works show the influence of Cézanne's cubism, with its simplified volumes, before Picasso moved on to his own more complex

use of volume; his revolutionary incorporation of everyday items; his thematic works, which revolved around minotauromachy (minotaur fighting), crucifixion, and the *corrida* (bullfight); and his movement from painting and sculpture to paper collage and tableau relief.

The museum also holds Picasso's personal collection, including works by Paul Cézanne, Henri Matisse, Georges Braque, André Dérain, Pierre Renoir, and Douanier Rousseau, along with his collection of primitive art. The splendid furniture and chandeliers are by Diego Giacometti, the Swiss artist Alberto's brother.

After renovations, the area devoted to collections and exhibitions will be tripled; 500 of Picasso's works will be hung on three floors, and the museum will be accessible to the disabled. ∎

EXPERIENCE:
Vintage Craze

You don't have to pay top dollar for high fashion. Do as the Parisians do—pick up last year's Saint Laurent and Dior fashions at the city's many *dépôts-ventes*, consignment shops. Or join a younger crowd at trendy vintage shops, many of them located in the Marais. About a block from the Picasso Museum, **Violette et Léonie** *(27 rue de Poitou and 1 rue de Saintonge, 75003, tel 01 44 59 87 35, www.violetteetleonie.com)* offers a good selection of recent clothing, while the more far-out (both stylistically and geographically) **GoldyMama** *(14 rue du Surmelin, 75020, tel 01 40 30 08 00, www.goldymama.com)* offers vintage designer clothing and embellished used garments.

Jewish Quarter

Jewish people have lived in Paris since the sixth century, as recorded by Gregory of Tours. They were believed to have come with the Romans as merchants or craftsmen. The first Jewish quarter in Paris was not created, however, until 1119 along Rue de la Juiverie (now Rue de la Cité).

The bustling Rue des Rosiers offers stores with traditional Jewish food.

Jewish Quarter
🅰 Map p. 105
🚇 Métro: St.-Paul

Musée d'Art et d'Histoire du Judaïsme
✉ Hôtel de Saint-Aignan, 71 rue du Temple
☎ 01 53 01 86 60
🕐 Closed Sat., some Jewish holidays
💲 €€
🚇 Métro: Rambuteau, Hôtel de Ville

www.mahj.org

Following Philippe-Auguste's expulsion of the Jews in 1182, there was a new influx in 1198, with some returning to the Left Bank, and others gravitating toward the Right Bank and Rue St.-Bon. Over the centuries, Jews were repeatedly expelled and then allowed to return. They were granted citizenship in 1791 during the Revolution. In 1871 the Jewish community numbered 25,000.

In the late 19th century, an influx of Jews from Central and Eastern Europe settled in and around **Rue des Rosiers.** Sephardic Jews from Egypt, Algeria, Tunisia, and Morocco, arriving between 1950 and 1962, spread the community far beyond this initial area. Today, the more traditional section of the quarter has been squeezed down to the western end of Rue des Rosiers.

The old **Jewish boys' school** (*École des Hospitalières, 10 rue des Hospitalières-St.-Gervais*), where 165 students were rounded up and deported, is adjacent; N'OUBLIEZ PAS ("Do not forget") is engraved on the wall.

The **Musée d'Art et d'Histoire du Judaïsme** explores Jewish heritage. In 2005 a new Holocaust Memorial opened, the **Memorial de la Shoah** (*17 rue Geoffroy l'Asnier, www.memorialdela shoah.org*), with a "Wall of Names" and documentation center. ■

Musée Carnavalet

This Renaissance-style museum devoted to Parisian history is housed in the Hôtel Carnavalet, where celebrated letter-writer Madame de Sévigné once lived. Originally built for the president of the parliament in 1548, it was acquired by the widow of Henri III's tutor, Kernevenoy, who was nicknamed Carnavalet (a corruption of his name).

The Museum

As he was razing Paris and pushing the poor out toward the suburbs, Baron Haussmann (see pp. 166–167) asked the City of Paris in 1866 to acquire the Musée Carnavalet for storing the interiors of buildings he dismantled. The mansion was expanded, Renaissance-style galleries were built, and architectural elements, such as the Nazareth archway (from the old Palais de la Cité), were added. The museum's collection is displayed in two buildings—the remodeled Hôtel Carnavalet has collections dating from the origins of Paris to the Revolution; and the adjacent Hôtel Le Peletier de St.-Fargeau has the world's largest collection of portraits, objects, and memorabilia from the Revolutionary period and after.

The Collections

The rooms are arranged chronologically to illustrate the changing face of Paris. Exhibitions range from the city's origins to the 16th-century Renaissance influence; 17th-century decorative ensembles; the French Revolution; the Second Empire; and the belle epoque. You'll also find such curiosities as Marcel Proust's bedroom, a scale model of a guillotine, and objects belonging to Voltaire and Rousseau. Don't miss Charles Le Brun's painted ceiling in the Hôtel de la Rivière, the Louis XV Bouvier collection, and Demarteau's salon by Boucher and Fragonard. The Orangerie houses Neolithic canoes and other Gallo-Roman finds and hosts temporary exhibits as well as concerts. ■

Musée Carnavalet

🗺 Map p. 105
✉ 23 rue de Sévigné
☎ 01 44 59 58 58
🕐 Closed Mon.
💲 €€ for special exhibitions
Ⓜ Métro: St.-Paul, Chemin Vert

www.carnavalet.paris.fr

The secluded gardens of the Musée Carnavalet

Great Parisian Love Affairs

Time seems to stand still for lovers in Paris. Passion—as intangible and ephemeral as the charms of the city itself—has created such timeless pairs as sculptors Auguste Rodin and Camille Claudel (see p. 179) and writers Anaïs Nin and Henry Miller. The fame of these historic liaisons is such that for many, the capital is synonymous with love itself.

Jacques-Louis David's painting highlights the moment in 1804 when Napoleon made an empress of his beloved wife, Josephine.

Love United in Death: Héloïse & Abélard

One of the earliest recorded pairs of lovers reposes in the Père-Lachaise Cemetery. Sometime around 1118, a man named Fulbert offered scholar Peter Abélard (1079–1142) hospitality in his home on the Île de la Cité in exchange for ensuring Héloïse's (his 17-year-old niece) education. Despite their age difference (Abélard was 39), the two fell in love and married secretly. Outraged, Fulbert laid a trap for Abélard and had him castrated. Héloïse, who died 24 years after her lover, had arranged for the two to be united

in death by being buried in the same coffin; a disapproving nun thwarted her plans and placed them in separate coffins. Héloïse's wish was finally granted in 1817, when their remains were united in the neo-Gothic tomb at Père-Lachaise (see p. 84).

Royal Mistress: Henri II & Diane de Poitiers

Although the initials of Henri II (1519–1559) and Catherine de Médicis carved throughout the south wing of the Cour Carrée in the Louvre seem to imply a great devotion between the monarchs, the intertwined letters "H" and "C" were actually an expression of Henri's deep attachment to his mistress, Diane de Poitiers, who was 20 years his senior. The insignia was therefore meant to be read as a double "D" for Diane, not "C" for Catherine. When Henri granted Diane the revenue from a tax on church bells, Rabelais famously quipped: "The king hung the bells of the realm around the neck of his mare." The queen was relegated to near obscurity until the king died, at which time she took her revenge by ousting Diane from her beloved château of Chenonceau in the Loire Valley.

Unrequited Love: Napoleon & Josephine

Napoleon Bonaparte, the man who conquered most of Europe, had trouble conquering the woman he loved. On March 9, 1796, he married Josephine de Beauharnais in a simple civil ceremony. What began as a marriage of convenience for Josephine—a widowed aristocrat seeking security in the troubled years after the Revolution—was a true affair of the heart for the future emperor of France, who was passionately in love with his wife. He ended one of his many ardent letters to her with these words: "I shall see you in three hours. Until then, *mio dolce amor,* a thousand kisses; but give me none in return, for they set my blood on fire." They spent their happiest moments together at the Château de Malmaison (see p. 232), but he divorced her in 1809 when she could not produce an heir. Napoleon continued to bankroll her extravagant lifestyle, however, while pleading with her to limit her spending. Despite his support, she owed three million francs at her death in 1814.

The Romantics: George Sand & Frédéric Chopin

The 19th century was the era of the Romantics. A leading figure of the times,

writer George Sand (born Amandine-Aurore-Lucie Dupin in 1804), led a wild, bohemian life in Paris after leaving her oafish husband in the countryside. She embarked on a tempestuous, short-lived love affair with French poet Alfred de Musset, followed by her most famous liaison with Polish composer Frédéric Chopin.

The two were part of the community of Romantic artists and writers who lived in the area known as La Nouvelle Athènes, just south of Montmartre. They broke off their affair in 1847 when he fell ill with tuberculosis and grew impatient with her hovering maternal solicitude. Traces of this famous couple are visible at the Musée de la Vie Romantique *(16 rue Chaptal, tel 01 55 31 95 67, www.vie-romantique.paris .fr, closed Mon., Métro: St.-Georges or Pigalle),* with Chopin memorabilia and a re-creation of Sand's drawing room.

INSIDER TIP:

Being a real Parisian means having no second thoughts whatsoever about indulging in a world of guilty pleasures.

—TARAS GRESCOE
National Geographic Traveler *magazine writer*

The Eroticists: Henry Miller & Anaïs Nin

The film *Henry and June* (1990) shows something of the stormy ménage à trois between American writer Henry Miller, his wife June, and the French erotic writer, Anaïs Nin, during the 1930s. The three of them embarked on an exploration of sexual libertinism that gave birth to a new form of literature, resulting in Miller's *Tropic of Cancer,* published in the 1930s in France but not until 1961 in the United States, and Nin's *Diaries* (in which she chronicled her sexual experiences) and *Delta of Venus.* Miller rented a house at 18 Villa Seurat, which he shared with Nin from time to time.

A Walk Around the Old Marais

The sheer density of the historical and architectural wealth in Paris's best preserved quarter is overwhelming, requiring several days to visit all of its museums, hôtels particuliers, squares, and various sites.

Begin at Place de la Bastille and walk down Rue St.-Antoine, past Beaumarchais's statue on your right. Turn right on Rue de Birague to enter **Place des Vosges** ❶ (see p. 106) via the king's pavilion, and right again under the arcades to visit the stores and galleries,

NOT TO BE MISSED:

Place des Vosges • Place du Marché Ste.-Catherine • Musée Carnavalet • Square Georges Cain • Musée Picasso • Rue des Rosiers

noting the illustrious residences. Exit at No. 7 through the passageway into the beautiful French-style gardens and Renaissance building of **Hôtel de Sully,** which organizes regular photography exhibitions. The passageway may be closed at night; if so, return to Rue de Birague to reach Rue St.-Antoine.

Turn right on Rue St.-Antoine and right again on Rue Caron. Continue to **Place du Marché Ste.-Catherine,** once a 13th-century Augustinian priory. Cross the square and turn left on the tranquil Rue de Jarente. No. 6 leads to a charming, villagelike wing off the street. From there, turn right onto Rue de Sévigné, and then left onto Rue des Francs-Bourgeois. (Rue des Poulies, "pulleys," between Rue Vieille-du-Temple and Rue Payenne, was named for the looms of medieval weavers' workshops.) No. 23, now a chic clothing store, was a former belle epoque *boulangerie.*

Visit the **Musée Carnavalet** ❷ (see p. 113) before continuing down Rue des Francs-Bourgeois. Note the lovely quadrangular watchtower bearing the letters S.C. on its base, marking the limits of the estates of the Convent of Ste.-Catherine-du-Val-des-Écoliers from which the land was bought. It is part of one of the Marais' oldest mansions, the **Hôtel de Lamoignon** (now the Bibliothèque Historique

The elegant older buildings and squares of the Marais make it ideal for walking.

JARDIN ST.-AIGNAN

Rambuteau Musée d'Art et d'Histoire du Judaïsme

Hôtel Guénégaud **6**

Cathédrale Ste.-Croix

St.-Sébastien Froissart

RUE DES ARCHIVES

RUE VIEILLE DU TEMPLE

RUE DES QUATRE FILS

RUE DU TEMPLE

RUE RAMBUTEAU

Archives Nationales

Hôtel de Soubise (Porte Clisson) **7**

Hôtel de Rohan

Crédit Municipal

Demeure de Jacques Coeure

N. D. des Blancs-Manteaux

Musée Bricard

Maison de Jean Hérouët

Musée Cognacq-Jay **3**

Hôtel des Ambassadeurs de Hollande **8**

Musée Kwok On **9**

Hôtel de Lamoignon

Hôtel de Ville

Synagogue

St.-Gervais-St.-Protais

Lycée St.-Germain

Hôtel de Beauvais

St.-Paul

Memorial de la Shoah

Cité Int des Arts

Pont Marie

Hôtel de Sens

Lycée Charlemagne

St.-Paul-St.-Louis

PONT LOUIS PHILIPPE

PONT MARIE

VOIE GEORGES POMPIDOU

QUAI DES CELESTINS

Seine

Île St.-Louis

RUE DE RIVOLI

RUE PAVÉE

RUE ST.-PAUL

RUE DES ROSIERS

RUE DES FRANCS BOURGEOIS

RUE DE SÉVIGNÉ

RUE PAYENNE

SQ. G. CAIN

Musée Picasso **4**

RUE DE THORIGNY

RUE DE TURENNE

St.-Denys du St.-Sacrement

RUE DU PARC ROYAL

Musée Carnavalet **2**

RUE DE TURENNE

PL. DU MARCHÉ STE.-CATHERINE

RUE DE SÉVIGNÉ

RUE DE BIRAGUE

PLACE DES VOSGES **1**

SQUARE LOUIS XIII

Maison de Victor Hugo

Hôtel de Sully

RUE ST.-ANTOINE

Ste.-Marie

Colonne de Juillet

RUE DE LA MULE

RUE DU PAS DE LA MULE

Chemin Vert

BOULEVARD BEAUMARCHAIS

Bréguet Sabin

RUE DU CHEMIN VERT

BOULEVARD RICHARD LENOIR

Bastille

PLACE DE LA BASTILLE

START

RUE DU FAUBOURG ST.-ANTOINE

BOULEVARD HENRI IV

BLVD. BOURDON

BLVD. DE LA BASTILLE

Opéra de Paris-Bastille

Village-St.-Paul

0 — 200 meters
0 — 200 yards

de la Ville de Paris—the History Library of Paris). Hector Guimard built the synagogue at 10 rue Pavée; he fled to the United States with his American-Jewish wife during the rise of Nazism in Europe.

Turn right on Rue Payenne. The **Square Georges Cain,** a splendid small park with ruins and monuments, holds the **Musée Lapidaire de Paris** (Stone Museum of Paris), a cemetery for old stones. Look through the fence of **Musée Cognacq-Jay ❸** (see p. 120) at No. 11 on the left side of the street; note the keel-shaped roof of the Swedish Cultural Center next door, where the governess of Marie-Antoinette's children once lived. The courtyard of No. 13 is particularly exquisite in summer.

Take a left on Rue du Parc-Royal, opposite Square Léopold Achille, and continue to Place de Thorigny. The **Hôtel Libéral Bruand** at 1 rue de la Perle has a lock museum with

> ☒ See also area map p. 105
> ▶ Place de la Bastille
> 🕓 Allow 3 hours
> ↔ 1.5 miles (2.4 km)
> ▶ Rue des Rosiers

locks, door handles, and metal fastenings from Roman times to the belle epoque, including refined pieces from various royal châteaus. Take a right onto Rue de Thorigny for the **Musée Picasso ❹** (see pp. 110–111). Backtrack and continue down Rue de la Perle, taking a detour at the corner of Rue Vieille-du-Temple (left) for the **Hôtel de Rohan ❺,** the site of the new Maison de l'Histoire de France, set to open at the end of 2011 (see sidebar p. 118). Walk along Rue des Quatre-Fils (the continuation of Rue de la Perle after the Vieille-du-Temple intersection) toward the **Hôtel Guénégaud ❻** on the right. This 17th-century mansion, now the Musée de la Chasse et de la Nature—Museum of Hunting and Nature *(62 rue des Archives, tel 01 53 01 92 40, closed Mon., Métro: Rambuteau),* with its small, beautiful formal garden, is the only Mansart-designed hôtel particulier still fully intact.

Gateway to Rue des Rosiers

Turn left on Rue des Archives—No. 58 is the great **Porte Clisson** ❼ (built between 1372 and 1375), flanked by two Gothic turrets. Built on Templar grounds, it was the gateway to the manor house of Olivier de Clisson, Constable of France and companion-in-arms to the warrior Du Guesclin, and it is one of the city's oldest remaining structures. The Guise family, the most powerful in the Marais, obtained the mansion in the 16th century, using it as their headquarters during the Wars of Religion; the St. Bartholomew's Day Massacre (see p. 22) was probably plotted here. The mansion was reconstructed by François de Rohan, Prince of Soubise, and the Clisson gateway was incorporated. In the early 19th century, the mansion became state property, and Napoleon annexed Rue des

---

Housing the History of France

The Hôtel de Rohan, a beautiful 18th-century mansion in the Marais that is currently home to the Archives Nationale, is being transformed into the new **Maison de l'Histoire de France** *(60 rue des Francs Bourgeois, 75003).* The gardens are set to open in spring of 2011, and the first exhibition should be held by the end of 2011—that is, if French historians have stopped arguing by then about the contents and viewpoint of what some have termed a "dangerous project" because of the possibility of a one-sided view of history being presented.

L'As du Falafel on Rue des Rosiers has the best falafel sandwiches in town, including chickpea fritters, hummus, pickled cabbage, and harissa.

—BARBARA A. NOE
National Geographic Books senior editor

Quatre-Fils and Rue des Archives to store the national archives in 1808.

Take a left on Rue des Francs-Bourgeois. On the right at No. 55 is the Mont de Piété or **Crédit Municipal,** a government-run pawnshop, auction house, and bank created in 1777. Enter the courtyard on the right to see the remains of one of Philippe-Auguste's 20 towers from the 800-year-old wall, preserved thanks to Victor Hugo's intervention. Continue to the graceful Renaissance-style tower on the corner of Rue Vieille-du-Temple and Rue des Francs-Bourgeois, home of Jehan Hérouet, Louis XII's treasurer.

Turn right onto Rue Vieille-du-Temple, which has a stupendous door facade (No. 47) with Renaudin's Medusa head and the Hôtel Amelot de Bisseuil, also known as the **Hôtel des Ambassadeurs de Hollande** ❽, where Beaumarchais lived and wrote *The Marriage of Figaro.* Although never an embassy, it was from 1720 to 1727 home to a Protestant chaplain from the Dutch embassy, who held services after the Edict of Nantes was revoked. One of Benjamin Franklin's relatives was wed here, and Madame Necker, the future Madame de Stael, a Protestant, was baptized here in 1766. Knock and you may be permitted inside to see a 1660 bas-relief of "Romulus and Remus" and four large sundials on the walls.

As you exit, turn right and then left onto **Rue des Rosiers** ❾ (see p. 112), the heart of the medieval Jewish Quarter. Traces of the Philippe-Auguste Wall can be found at Nos. 8, 10, and 14.

Place de la Bastille

The golden spirit of liberty gleams in the sun by day, and the illuminated July Column shines beaconlike at night. Place de la Bastille is not significant for what stands here today—cafés, movie theaters, and an opera house (Opéra de Paris-Bastille) that looks like a beached silver whale—but for its history. Intended as a square for the people, it is still the scene of many political and social demonstrations.

Every year, on July 14, the entire city celebrates Bastille Day, with major fireworks held on the 13th and street dances and a military parade along the Champs-Élysées on the 14th.

The original eight-towered fortress, now destroyed, with its moat, drawbridge, and crenelated walls, was built during the 14th century to ward off English attacks from the east and protect the Hôtel St.-Pol (Charles V's residence). The Café Français (*3 place de la Bastille*) now stands where the medieval gate was. Pinkish cobblestones indicate the precise location of the Bastille, which never played a military role except during the Fronde (see p. 24); instead, it was a State prison from the days of Cardinal Richelieu.

A series of illustrious figures were imprisoned here in the 17th and 18th centuries, in surprisingly comfortable conditions—the Cardinal de Rohan hosted a dinner party for 20 here; the Marquis de Sade had his own wine brought in from Provence; and Voltaire praised the food upon his release. Because the prison was expensive to run, Necker, Minister of Finance to Louis XVI, planned to tear down the Bastille (and replace it with Place Louis XVI), but Revolutionary fervor did it for him.

The July Column stands in front of the opera house.

The July Column

The July Column was inspired by Trajan's column in Rome, and commemorates those who died during the July 1830 Revolution. Beneath the column is a gallery where victims' remains from the 1830 and 1848 Revolutions lie. ∎

Place de la Bastille

⬛ Map p. 105
🚇 Métro: Bastille

More Places to Visit in Le Marais & Bastille

Bassin de l'Arsenal

Leisure boats are docked in a basin that occupies what used to be part of the ancient moats of the Bastille. The southern extremity of Canal St.-Martin (see sidebar p. 210) rises from underneath Place de la Bastille, flanked by a lovely garden on the eastern bank.

🅰 Map p. 105 ✉ Between Boulevards Bourdon and de la Bastille 🚇 Métro: Bastille

INSIDER TIP:

Take a canal ride with Canauxrama *(www.canauxrama .com)* beneath the Place de la Bastille to Parc de la Villete.

—BARBARA A. NOE
National Geographic senior editor

Hôtel de Sens

One of the few great medieval private residences in Paris, this beautiful, half-civilian, half-military mansion (circa 1475) overlook-ing the Seine provides a fine example of the transitional period between Gothic and Renaissance styles. The architect remains unknown, although it was possibly a joint project of Tristan de Salazar, Archbishop of Sens at the time, and Martin Cham-biges, who designed the transept for Sens cathedral. In 1605 Henri IV housed his former wife, Queen Margot, here, and it was later used for various businesses. The gable next to the tower on the left still holds the orange-size shell that was lobbed at the mansion during the 1830 Revolution.

The City of Paris purchased the Hôtel de Sens in 1911 and began to restore it in 1929. In 1961 it was turned into the Forney Library of Decorative and Fine Arts; its stunning reading room is open to the public.

🅰 Map p. 105 ✉ 1 rue du Figuier ☎ 01 42 78 14 60 🕐 Closed Sun.–Mon. 💲 Free; special exhibits € 🚇 Métro: St.-Paul, Pont Marie

Musée Cognacq-Jay

The museum, with its collection of 18th-century European paintings and furniture, was assembled by Ernest Cognacq and his wife, Louise Jay (founders of the Samaritaine department store). All of the objects were part of Cognacq's personal collection, which was bequeathed to the City of Paris in 1928 and includes works by Fragonard, Boucher, Chardin, Reynolds, Guardi, Canaletto, and Watteau. There is also an extremely rare col-lection of jeweled and enameled snuffboxes.

🅰 Map p. 105 ✉ Hôtel Donon, 8 rue Elzévir ☎ 01 40 27 07 21 🕐 Closed Mon. 💲 Free; special exhibits € 🚇 Métro: St.-Paul

EXPERIENCE: Dancing at the Firehouse

The traditional thing to do in Paris on Bastille Day is to go to a *bal des pompiers* (firemen's ball), which are held in firehouse courtyards on the evenings of July 13 and 14. The most popular are held in the *casernes* (firehouses) at 21 rue du Jour (near Les Halles), 9 rue de Sévigné (in the Marais), and 28 rue Blanche (near Pigalle).

Most of these balls are like big open-air clubs with music provided by DJs, rather than the corny accordion bands of the firemen's balls of the past. Go early (around 8 p.m.) to avoid waiting in long lines. The firemen ask for a small entry donation and sell drinks at reason-able prices.

If you stay until closing time at 4 a.m., you may well see a few spontaneous strip-teases, both male and female.

One of the world's largest museums, and the premier attraction in a stately neighborhood built up through centuries of royal rule

The Louvre & Palais-Royal

Detail of the Alexandre III bridge

The Louvre & Palais-Royal

The monarchy may be long gone, but almost everything in this neighborhood is a reminder of centuries of royal rule. Although the Louvre is now a museum, it was originally constructed as a fortress to protect Paris from foreign invaders. For nearly 600 years it was the royal residence; each king (and emperor, for that matter) altered, expanded, and renovated the work of his predecessors.

As the palace expanded, so did its surrounding streets. The gardens were extended westward; the Tuileries Palace was constructed outside the old city walls, then linked to the Louvre; the Palais-Royal, a former royal residence (see p. 141) was constructed; and Rue de Rivoli (see p. 142) was laid out.

As the Louvre museum was formed from royal collections, so the Bibliothèque Nationale (see p. 165) began as a royal library, when Charles V brought his personal library of 973 works to the palace in 1373. After being stored in a lavish palace on Rue de Richelieu, the library outgrew its original premises; the books have been transferred to the new Bibliothèque de France (on Quai de la Gare), which opened in 1997, while prints, photographs, maps, and musical scores remain in the older building.

During the 19th century, France wavered between royal rule and revolution, and much of the action was staged in and around the Louvre. Louis XVI was held captive in the Tuileries Palace before being beheaded, and revolutionaries gathered in the Palais-Royal gardens, where the first call to arms was sounded. During the Commune of 1870–71, the Tuileries Palace, the symbol of royal oppression, was burned down. Afterward, a relative peace settled over Paris, and this neighborhood once again attracted the rich and fashionable.

Although the streets are now lined with tourist shops, a few exclusive establishments remain. It is easy to escape the noise of the nearby streets in the recently renovated Jardin des Tuileries (see p. 137), or the even more discreet gardens of the Palais-Royal, which are completely shut off from traffic.

The Louvre has been revived both above and below ground. I. M. Pei's controversial 1989 pyramid was the first of many manifestations of this major facelift. An entire subterranean city stretches out beyond the museum, with the Carrousel du Louvre—a vast, elegant, underground complex, complete with shops, parking, and a food court. An inverted glass pyramid echoes Pei's main entrance, providing light to the entire underground area.

Paris

Area of map detail

NOT TO BE MISSED:

The Tuileries gardens lie west of the Louvre toward the Place de la Concorde and the 8th arrondissement. Two museums flank the gardens, overlooking the Concorde: the Jeu de Paume, now an exhibition center for photography; and the Orangerie (see p. 140), which houses Monet's famous water lilies paintings and other Impressionist art. ■

❶ Carrousel du Louvre

Musée du Louvre

The huge "Grand Louvre" modernization project, initiated by President François Mitterrand in 1981, has transformed this magnificent museum both inside and out. The first step was I. M. Pei's glass pyramid, which created space, light, and a much needed main entrance; the next steps reorganized the collections and exhibition spaces.

I. M. Pei's once controversial glass pyramid marks the main entrance to the Louvre museum.

The Louvre began in 1190, when King Philippe-Auguste constructed a massive fortress surrounded by a wall and towers on the western edge of Paris before setting out on a crusade. In the 14th century, Charles V commissioned Raymond du Temple to turn the medieval keep into a royal residence. It expanded under two visionary Renaissance builders: Kings François I, who tore down the medieval keep; and Henri IV, who constructed the immense gallery bordering the Seine, thus linking the Louvre to the Tuileries Palace, begun in 1564 by Catherine de Médicis (for whom the Louvre was far too drafty and inelegant). The Louvre at this time consisted of a string of buildings that stretched over a quarter of a mile along the Seine—a long passageway linking the city palace to the country home. (At that time the Tuileries lay beyond the walls of Paris.)

In 1608, Henri IV opened up the palace to artists, granting them studio space, living quarters, and the status of official recognition. When Louis XIV moved his court to Versailles in 1682, the Louvre was overrun by sculptors, painters, and architects who left the palace in a pathetic state by the mid-18th century. Among them were Jean Honoré Fragonard, Jean Chardin, François Boucher, Jean-Louis David, and Guillaume Coustou, who, along with Antoine Coysevox, sculpted the famous "Horses of Marly," now wonderfully displayed in the glass-covered Cour Marly.

In 1793 the Musée Central des Arts was inaugurated at the Louvre, which then opened as a museum, marking a turning point in its history. Napoleon III realized Henri IV's dream of constructing the Richelieu Wing to mirror the Galerie du Bord de l'Eau.

The Louvre had finally achieved a state of architectural symmetry, but it didn't last long: The Tuileries Palace enclosing its western edge was burned to the ground in 1871 by the Commune.

The Louvre and its collection of royal artwork survived, the latter growing through donations and acquisitions. The museum's antiquities departments flourished in the 19th century, as excavations sponsored by the government unearthed treasures in Egypt and the Middle East. Under the terms of a now questionable agreement, the archaeological finds were divided between the various countries involved. This form of looting was justified by the argument

that without outside intervention, these prized works faced almost certain destruction.

I. M. Pei's controversial pyramid shocked many when it was unveiled in 1989 as the new main entrance to the museum, yet it is in keeping with a long tradition—architects have always been faced with the problem of integrating the palace's disparate elements.

INSIDER TIP:

Keep kids from melting down by following one of the "thematic trails" outlined on the activities section of the Louvre's website.

—PATRICIA DANIELS
*National Geographic Books
contributing editor*

The Collections

The Louvre's collections are divided into seven departments, displayed in three main sections: Sully (the Cour Carrée); Richelieu (enclosing the wing parallel to Rue de Rivoli); and Denon (the wing along the Seine), each accessible from the main entrance beneath the pyramid.

Despite the organization, the Louvre can be a daunting and tiring experience. On a first visit, pick up one of the free maps or the guidebook "Louvre First Visit" in the main hall and choose a few works of art or periods before setting out (for example, the "Winged Victory of Samothrace" and the "Mona Lisa").

Musée du Louvre
- Map p. 123
- Main entrance: Pyramide du Louvre, Cour Napoléon. Other entrances: Galerie du Carrousel, Porte des Lions (except Fri.)
- 01 40 20 50 50
- Open 9 a.m.– 6 p.m. Closed Tues. Open late Wed. & Fri. Rooms closed on a rotating basis (check before visiting).
- €€–€€€. Free 1st Sun. of each month & for under 18. Guided tour: €€. Audio guide: €€. To avoid long lines, purchase tickets in advance (tel 08 92 68 46 94 or see website) or at 500 sales outlets in France (Fnac, Virgin Megastore, etc.).
- Métro: Palais-Royal–Musée du Louvre

www.louvre.fr

The Louvre

Arc de Triomphe
du Carrousel

SECOND FLO

FIRST FLOOR

GROUND
FLOOR

Cour Marly

Cour Puget

Richelieu
Wing

Cour Napoléon

Cour
Khorsabad

Pyramid
entrance

Denon
Wing

Sully Wing

To Métro

ENTRESOL

Entrance hall (Hall
Napoléon)

Paintings/drawings

Sculpture

Objets d'art

Antiquities

Medieval
Louvre

Medieval Louvre history

Sphinx-like statues are part of the Louvre's enormous Egyptian collection.

A good place to start is in the Sully Wing, at the foundations of Philippe-Auguste's medieval keep—it's in the heart of the Louvre, kids love it, and it leads straight to the Egyptian rooms.

Antiquities

The Louvre's Egyptian treasures are displayed in the Denon Wing and in Rooms 1–30 of the Sully Wing. Greek, Etruscan, and Roman antiquities can be found in the entresol level of the Denon Wing, and on the ground and first floors of the Denon and Sully Wings (Rooms A, B, and 4–44). Parts of the entresol level of the Denon Wing are currently closed for renovation.

Egyptian Department:

For years, this collection of nearly 55,000 objects (of which about one-tenth is exhibited), the largest collection of Egyptian antiquities after the Cairo Museum, was seriously cramped for space. The recently renovated and expanded section is now worthy of these masterpieces, which are so rich that curators have created a twofold display. The ground floor (Rooms 1–19) is arranged thematically and the upper floor

French Father of Egyptology

Jean François Champollion (1790–1832) is considered the French father of Egyptology. He played a major role in deciphering the hieroglyphic text of the Rosetta Stone, thereby unlocking the mysteries of the Egyptian language. He was appointed the first curator of the Louvre's Egyptian Department in 1826.

(Rooms 20–30) is organized chronologically, from prehistory to the Roman conquest.

The first few rooms are devoted to specific aspects of Egyptian life—writing, fishing, farming, music, games, jewelry, and funeral rituals. A spectacular room follows, with a row of 20-foot-high (7 m) palm- and papyrus-shaped columns of pink granite and huge statues

INSIDER TIP:

In the basement of the Louvre you'll find the remains of the original royal castle—including the dungeon—dating from 1190 to the 16th century.

—BARBARA A. NOE
*National Geographic Books
senior editor*

of Ramses II (Room 12). While friezes are everywhere throughout the Egyptian collection, this room contains one of the loveliest, a limestone relief of Ramses II among the gods (1275 B.C., 19th dynasty). The world of the dead is displayed in the dramatic Crypt of Osiris, providing a good overview of Egyptian religious practices. Animal mummies—from an 8-foot (3 m) crocodile to a tiny, mummified scarab—are featured in one of the last rooms in the display.

The collection continues in chronological order on the upper floor. The first object is one of the oldest: a pre-dynastic ivory

dagger from Gebel El-Arak. This sophisticated ceremonial knife was sculpted more than 5,000 years ago. The following rooms trace the rise of the First Kingdom, the era in which the pyramids were built, the cult of the pharaoh grew, and a centralized government developed. "The Seated Scribe" is in this section (Room 22), as well as a radiant, surprisingly tender, wooden sculpture, "Anonymous Couple." The famous Amarna period is illustrated by a colossal statue of Akhenaten (Room 25). Although his reign lasted only 16 years, and his capital Amarna was destroyed, the pharaoh's influence can be seen in the more lifelike, expressive art of later dynasties. The New Kingdom (1554–1075 B.C.) was a golden age for the arts in ancient Egypt, especially during the reigns of the Tuthmoses, Amenophis, and Ramsesid kings, as illustrated by the painted limestone relief of Seti I and the goddess Hathor.

The Greco-Roman period began in 332 B.C. with the conquest by Alexander the Great, ending a period of Egyptian rule that lasted over 3,000 years. Room 29 contains one of the last masterpieces of Egyptian art, a magnificent gold jewel representing the triad of Osiris (god of the dead), Isis (goddess of the throne), and Horus (god in the form of a falcon), their son.

To continue this chronological tour, visit the sections devoted to Egypt under Roman control and to Coptic art on the entresol level at the Denon Wing (temporarily closed). There are a number of

Etymology of "Louvre"

No one knows the origin of the word "Louvre," or *Lupara* in Latin. Theories suggest it came from the words for leper house, watchtower, or Saxon fortress, or that it was named for a pack of wolves *(loups)* that lurked in the area.

The Louvre's collection stretches from preclassical Greece to the final years of the Roman Empire (both temporarily closed). The section devoted to the preclassical era has several remarkable examples from the Geometric (650–480 B.C.) and Archaic (circa 900 B.C.) periods. The Cycladic sculptures are especially striking: The pared-down, almost abstract idols look like sculptures from our own century.

Antiquities from the classical and Hellenistic periods are on the ground floor of the Sully Wing (Rooms 7–17). During the classical period, the reputation of Greek artists spread, and they were in demand from Persia to Rome. Figures came to life—for example,

funerary statues and mummies, as well as the striking funerary portraits from Faiyum—so realistic that they were initially considered fakes. On the opposite side of the Cour Visconti is the collection of Coptic art, dating from the early centuries of the Christian era.

Among the Louvre's most obscure treasures are the Coptic fabrics that date from the second century A.D. and include the brilliantly colored, complex "Sabine Shawl." The Bawit Room contains a reconstruction of the Coptic Church of Bawit (sixth–seventh centuries A.D.), discovered in 1900, and now believed to represent only a small part of the original monastery's structure.

Greek Antiquities: Two lovely women reign over this department: the "Venus de Milo" and the "Winged Victory of Samothrace." The former may be more famous, but the latter is quite simply breathtaking. She stands ready to take flight from the top of the monumental staircase, looking as though she had been sculpted by the wind itself.

The Louvre's "Venus de Milo" is almost as famous for what she lacks (arms) as for what she has (grace and beauty).

in the Frieze of the Panathenaic Procession, 447–406 B.C., as artists explored the ideals of beauty, form, and emotional expression.

The Hellenistic period began with the death of Alexander the Great and the breakup of his immense empire. This period ushered in a more experimental style, and sculptors worked to capture a broader range of human experience and movement. The

Treasures in Wartime

Evacuated during World Wars I and II, the Louvre's treasures were packed up in unmarked crates and moved to safety (many works went to the Château of Chambord in the Loire Valley). During World War II, almost all the works had left Paris by September 1, 1939.

"Winged Victory of Samothrace," which commemorated a naval victory, is an incomparable example of this command of motion. It is dated at 190 B.C., but was only discovered in 1863. The sensuality, dignity, and simplicity of the "Venus de Milo" (Room 16) circa 100 B.C., on the other hand, echoes the ideals of the earlier classical era.

The Greek collection continues on the first floor, with displays of bronzes and stoneware (Rooms 32–44). Among the fine works is a cache of 109 pieces of silver and gold found at Boscoreale, near Pompeii, as well as the collection

of Greek ceramics in the recently opened Campana Gallery. No examples of Greek painting have survived, but these vases, from the geometric-style funerary urns and amphorae of the eighth century B.C. to the classical masterpieces, give some indication of what it may have looked like. The golden age of Greek pottery was from the mid-sixth to the mid-fifth century B.C., with the development of the so-called red-figure technique (replacing the earlier black-figure technique). A krater (bowl for mixing wine and water) illustrated by Euphronios (510 B.C.) shows the refinement in painting at this time, with attention to anatomical detail and emotional expression.

Etruscan Antiquities:

There's something intriguing about the distant, cheerful smiles on the faces of many Etruscan sculptures, and their civilization remains a compelling mystery. It thrived for ten centuries, from about 1000 B.C. to the early years of the Christian era, and was the most sophisticated culture in pre-Roman Italy. Although the Etruscans thrived at the same time as the Greeks, they developed a unique artistic style. This was revealed in their skill with bronze- and metalworking, and is best seen in their delicate jewelry and elegant bronze mirrors detailed with engraved scenes.

The painted terra-cotta "Sarcophagus of a Married Couple" (Denon Wing, Room 18) is another of the Louvre's masterpieces; equality between husband and wife, as reflected in this sculpture, was one of the more extraordinary aspects of their society; women had more independence there than anywhere else in classical antiquity.

Roman Antiquities:

Although Roman artists constantly copied Greek sculptures, their art was more than just a watered-down version of Hellenistic Greek art. The Roman Empire encompassed many different countries and cultures, and Rome itself was filled with foreign artists. They integrated elements from both the Etruscan and Greek cultures, adapting the styles to their own less mythical, more factual concerns, namely the glorification of the State and the great patrician families.

Portraiture took on a new dimension in Roman art, as the classical ideal of abstract beauty was replaced by more realistic and representative images. Portraits were so popular that the heads were often sculpted separately and placed on a kind of standard-issue body (for example, the statue of "Augustus," Room 23).

Wealthy Romans decorated their homes with lavish frescoes and mosaics. The mosaic on the floor of Room 31 once decorated the Constantine Villa near Antioch; it dates from the fourth century A.D.

Painting

The Louvre's paintings are divided into four sections: French works from the 14th

The "Mona Lisa" holds court on the first floor, Salle des États.

through the 19th centuries, Italian, Northern European, and other European paintings.

French Painting: The French paintings on the first floor of the Denon Wing and the second floor of the Sully and Richelieu Wings cover every major period, from the early medieval and Renaissance periods through the mid-19th century. (Works after this date are found in the Musée d'Orsay; see pp. 180–184.) The collection starts with the oldest surviving easel painting, "Portrait of Jean le Bon" (circa 1350). The Renaissance came to France via King Charles VIII and King

EXPERIENCE: To Your Brushes!

Visitors to Paris often have the urge to do what the Impressionists did: set up an easel *en plein air* and paint the passersby, the bridges over the Seine, and the city's famous pearly gray light. For those who would like some guidance, a number of specialist schools offer both indoor and outdoor courses in the arts.

Painting in the Place du Tertre, Montmartre

Artist and French teacher **Brigitte Isaeff** *(tel 06 73 54 07 52, brigitte-isaeff-language-learning.blogspot.com, €€€€€)* has had the bright idea of killing two birds with one stone by teaching French through art study. After a presentation and discussion of the work of a few French artists, students do their own artworks and discuss them in six half-day classes.

The **Atelier Alupi** *(18 rue Pernety, 75014, tel 06 78 26 82 94, www.atelieralupi.com, €€€€€)* has ongoing courses in drawing and painting, but visitors can attend as few or as many sessions as they like. Its one-day or one-week Paris Cityscape Art Workshop takes students into the streets to paint in the city's food markets, for example, or on bridges over the Seine.

The **Paris American Academy** *(www.paris americanacademy.fr, €€€€€)* offers an intensive four-week summer workshop in fine arts (painting and drawing), with both studio courses and sketching sessions in museums, parks, markets, and the streets to allow students to copy famous artworks and draw from life. A crash course in French is included.

For experienced artists who just want an atmospheric place to draw from a life model and meet other artists, the **Académie de la Grande Chaumière** *(14 rue de la Grande Chaumière, 75006, tel 01 43 26 13 72, www.grande-chaumiere.fr)* is an open studio in Montparnasse where the likes of Modigliani and Gauguin once sat on the same wooden stools still used today. Just show up with your own materials *(Mon., Tues., Thurs. & Fri. 2 p.m.–5 p.m., Wed. 7 p.m.–10 p.m., Sat. 1 p.m.–5 p.m., closed Aug., €€€)*.

Visitors who prefer to see the sights through a lens might want to improve their photography skills at the **Spéos Paris Photographic Institute** *(8 rue Jules-Vallès, 75011, tel 01 40 09 18 58, www.speos.fr, €€€€€)*, which offers a variety of summer workshops suitable for visitors, with courses on portrait, studio, and commercial photography and more.

Those who want to learn more about art but aren't interested in practicing themselves can choose from the lectures and museum visits offered by **Paris Art Studies** *(1 rue Jacques-Cœur, 75004, tel 06 86 58 98 09, www.parisartstudies.com, €€€€€)* and given by art gallery owner Chris Boïcos, who has garnered a loyal following of Anglophones who admire his inspired lectures.

François I (portrait of François I by Jean Clouet, Room 7). Although Italy and France battled incessantly, the French kings easily admitted the superiority of Italian culture, bringing both its art and artists (such as Leonardo da Vinci) back to France. French painting in the 17th century moved toward realism, illustrated especially in Room 28 with George de la Tour's "The Cheat."

Rooms 50–73 concentrate on the first half of the 19th century. The last few rooms (63–73) contain landscapes by painters like Jean-Baptiste Corot, who prefigured the Impressionists.

The French collection does not end with this chronological sequence, however; large-format paintings hanging in two adjoining rooms (75 and 77) in the Denon Wing (first floor) illustrate the two conflicting schools of painting in the 19th century—neoclassicism and Romanticism. Painters clashed over the merits of the two: the idealized, cold, and rational beauty of the first (represented by Jacques-Louis David, the court chronicler for the Napoleonic era; in "The Oath of the Horatii," 1784, and "The Coronation of Napoleon I," 1804), and the emotion and individualism of the latter (as spearheaded by Eugène Delacroix in "The Death of Sardanapalus," 1827). The Romantics sought their subjects from contemporary events: Théodore Géricault created an international scandal by illustrating an actual shipwreck in "Raft of the Medusa" (Room 77), with its accompanying themes of treachery and cannibalism.

European Painting: Northern European painting is exhibited in the Richelieu Wing, and includes 15th-century Dutch works by Jan van Eyck. The Galerie Médicis contains a rather overwhelming series of canvases (nearly 330 square yards, or 275 sq m) by Peter Paul Rubens, created for the Luxembourg Palace, ordered by Marie de Médicis. There are also a number of works by Rembrandt van Rijn, including the lovely "Bathsheba," and two masterpieces by Jan Vermeer, "The Lacemaker" and "The Astronomer."

INSIDER TIP:

Hungry after your visit? The upscale brasserie Le Fumoir (6 rue de l'Amiral de Coligny), just steps away, has a fun, buzzy atmosphere.

—JANE SUNDERLAND
National Geographic contributing editor

The Italian collection (Denon Wing, first floor, Rooms 1–13) begins with the painters Giovanni Cimabue and Giotto (Room 3), whose work profoundly influenced the development of the Renaissance. Thirty years after Cimabue's "Virgin and Child," Giotto's "Saint Francis of Assisi Receiving the Stigmata" created a new style, placing more realistic figures within space and using rudimentary notions of perspective (defined by

Filippo Brunelleschi in the 1420s). The collection continues with the Quattrocento artists: Paolo Uccello, Andrea Mantegna, and Domenico Ghirlandaio.

There are several paintings by Leonardo da Vinci in the Grande Galerie: "The Virgin of the Rocks" and "Saint John the Baptist," for example—as intriguing as the "Mona Lisa," (the first has been the subject of much attention since it was featured in *The Da Vinci Code*). One room is dedicated entirely to the "Mona Lisa" (typically barricaded by crowds) and Veronese's colossal "Marriage Feast at Cana," surrounded by other Italian Renaissance masterpieces.

Near Eastern Antiquities: Covering northern Africa to the borders of India, the Oriental antiquities encompass the world's earliest known

civilizations, from which sprang many technological and philosophical inventions—wheeled vehicles, astronomical models, musical systems, and the birth of writing, not to mention a set of laws (recorded on the *Code of Hammurabi* in the Cour Khorsabad, Room 3) that formed the basis of the Greek and Roman legal systems.

The Louvre's extensive collection covers four distinct regions and periods: Mesopotamia; ancient Iran; the Levant (all located on the ground floor in the Richelieu and Sully Wings; Rooms A–D and 1–21); and the Islamic arts (being renovated and set to reopen in 2012 in the Denon Wing). Most of the displays came from 19th-century French excavation projects that unearthed long-lost palaces and cities, including the winged bulls from the palace of King Sargon II of Assyria (720 B.C.) and the winged

French sculpture adorns the luminous Marly courtyard.

archers and monumental, bull-headed capitals from the palace of Darius in Susa (late sixth century B.C.).

Sculpture

Even on a gloomy winter's day, the Marly and Puget courtyards, covered by skylights, create an ideal setting for outdoor sculpture. Those in the Cour Marly were created for Louis XIV's private château at Marly. During the Revolution, the "Horses of Marly" were placed on the Place de la Concorde, but they were moved to the Louvre in 1984; cast models now stand in their original setting.

French sculpture begins in rooms around the Cour Marly with works from the 12th century and continues through the Romanesque and Gothic eras; many pieces came from French churches. One of the oddest is the actual-size funeral cortege of the 15th-century "Tomb of Philippe Pot" (Room 10), with eight hooded mourners bearing the deceased.

The Denon Wing houses a smaller collection of sculpture from Italy, Germany, the Netherlands, and Spain, including Michelangelo's two "Slaves" and other celebrated Italian work from the 16th and 17th centuries, such as Antonio Canova's "Psyche Revived by Cupid's Kiss."

Objets d'Art

The objets d'art collection contains works ranging from the Middle Ages through the 19th century. The term "objets

> ### Louvre Staff
>
> A staff of 2,000—curators, guards, and technical specialists, among others—keep the Louvre running. Close to 65 curators watch over the 440,000 works of art, of which only about 35,000 are on display at any one time.

d'art" designates everything from religious relics and enamels to tapestries, jewels, and furniture—the everyday items of the aristocracy. All are located on the first floor of the Richelieu and Sully Wings. The glittering Galerie d'Apollon has now reopened after extensive renovation, and it displays magnificent painted ceilings.

Part of the objets d'art department and one of the Louvre's more obscure treasures are the Napoleon III apartments, which were opened to the public when the Finance Ministry moved to the Quai de Bercy.

Prints & Drawings

Temporary displays draw on this collection located on the first floor of the Denon Wing (Rooms 9–11), which has some 120,000 works—treasures such as illuminated manuscripts, drawings by Leonardo da Vinci, Delacroix's Moroccan sketchbook, and studies by Rembrandt.

The Chalcographie shop, which sells engravings made from original copper plates, is located under the pyramid. ■

Three Museums of the Arts

Three museums occupy the Rohan and Marsan Wings of the Louvre: the Decorative Arts Museum, the Fashion and Textile Museum, and the Advertising Museum, all administered by the Union Centrale des Arts Décoratifs (UCAD, or Central Union for the Decorative Arts). Along with the rest of the Louvre, these museums have been redesigned to add more space.

Rohan & Marsan Wings of the Louvre

 Map p. 123

 Palais du Louvre, 107 rue de Rivoli

☎ 01 44 55 57 50

🕐 Closed Mon.

💲 €€

 Métro: Palais-Royal–Musée du Louvre, Tuileries, Pyramides

www.ucad.fr

Musée des Arts Décoratifs

The Decorative Arts Museum, part of the Louvre since 1905, presents an extraordinarily rich collection of some 220,000 works from the Middle Ages to the 20th century—including ceramics, glassware, jewelry, furniture, wallpaper, drawings, and toys.

The exhibition is not arranged chronologically; it is organized into a fine arts section and a decorative arts section. Best of all is the Galerie des Bijoux, a dramatic glass bridge between two rooms.

Musée de la Mode et du Textile

The Fashion and Textile Museum's permanent collection explores major trends in fashion through the ages. Clothing from the 17th to the 19th centuries, fashion accessories, and rare fabrics are on display, as are major contributions from 20th-century haute couture artists and contemporary fashion designers. The curators rotate the collection with thematic displays that are changed each year.

Musée de la Publicité

The Advertising Museum was created in 1978. It contains nearly 50,000 posters from around the world, ranging from the mid-18th century to 1949; in addition, it has 50,000 contemporary posters donated by agencies and designers, and 20,000 contemporary publicity films. ∎

EXPERIENCE: Paris's Feathered Inhabitants

Bird-watchers do not have to leave Paris to give their binoculars a workout. The some 60 species that nest in the City of Light, including kingfishers and sparrowhawks, can be spotted everywhere from stadiums to urban parks of all sizes (such as the Tuileries gardens and the Bois de Vincennes), cemeteries, and vacant lots.

Over 150 species, including migrators, can be seen in the city. Many of them enjoy the same sites as tourists: The common kestrel *(Falco tinnunculus)*, for example, prefers high-end real estate and builds nests in niches in Notre-Dame (you may see them soaring around the spires), the Eiffel Tower, and the Sacré-Coeur. One couple has even nested on the balcony of an apartment.

The most active local birders' association, **CORIF** (Centre Ornithologique Ile-de-France; *tel 01 48 60 13 00, www .corif.net)*, organizes numerous tours in and around Paris. Reservations required. Tours are in French, but bird names are international!

Jardin des Tuileries

The view west from the Louvre encompasses one of the most impressive alignments of monuments in any city. This symmetry starts with the Arc de Triomphe du Carrousel, framed by the two wings of the Louvre, and continues past the Luxor Obelisk at the Place de la Concorde to the Arc de Triomphe and the Grande Arche de La Défense, 5 miles (8 km) beyond.

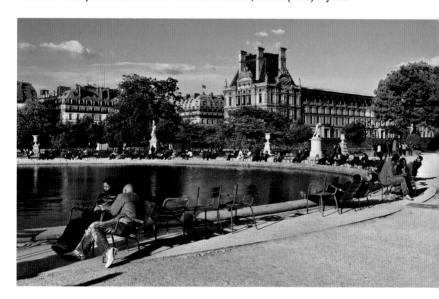

The Tuileries gardens link the Louvre to the Place de la Concorde.

When the Tuileries was created by André Le Nôtre in 1666, it was outside the city walls—a place where aristocrats came to see and be seen and enjoy royal festivities and fireworks. As part of the Grand Louvre project, completed in late 1997, the adjoining gardens were given a face-lift to emphasize the east–west axis and link the new Louvre parvis (square) to the gardens on the west.

The original design, which called for a more formal garden near the Louvre, gradually becoming more wooded toward Place de la Concorde, was reinstated. The beginning of the gardens' eastern edge, marked by the Arc de Triomphe du Carrousel added by Napoleon, is enclosed within the long wings of the Louvre. Seen through this arch, the Luxor Obelisk (see p. 147) and the Arc de Triomphe are perfectly aligned. Replanting has restored Le Nôtre's original design, and cafés, pony rides, and a summer funfair give a pleasure garden atmosphere.

Hidden away among hedges of yew near the Louvre is a sculpture garden with 20 bronzes by Aristide Maillol. ∎

Jardin des Tuileries

🅰 Map pp. 122–123

🅼 Métro: Palais-Royal–Musée du Louvre, Tuileries, Pyramides, Concorde

Bridges & Quays of Paris

Stand on the Pont de la Concorde at night, with the Assemblée Nationale illuminated at one end and the imposing Madeleine Church in the distance at the other, and you can see why Paris is called the City of Light. Or wander along the quays to explore the 36 other bridges spanning the Seine, where lovers, traffic, history, politics, and art all converge. The city's splendor and its traditions are reflected, quite literally, in the waters of the Seine.

The exuberant, ornate Alexandre III bridge was built in the late 19th century.

Paris's two islands, the Île de la Cité and the Île St.-Louis, are connected to the rest of the city by eight and five bridges respectively, with one footbridge—the Pont St.-Louis—joining the two islands behind Notre-Dame. The Pont de Sully, at the quaint eastern tip of the Île St.-Louis, took its name from the celebrated duke, minister, and friend of Henri IV, who masterfully directed the royal finances in the late 16th century.

Majestic Pont Neuf

Just west of the Latin Quarter, between the Quai des Grands Augustins and the Quai de la Mégisserie and straddling the western end of the Île de la Cité, sits the majestic Pont Neuf and its 12 perfect arches. One of Paris's loveliest bridges, it is also the oldest remaining one—despite its name, which means "new bridge." It was inaugurated in 1607 under the direction of Henri IV, who is immortalized in bronze on horseback on the bridge. The Pont Neuf was the first bridge to be lined with sidewalks rather than dwellings; it immediately became the center of Paris, a fashionable strolling place. In the mid-1990s, the artist Christo chose this bridge to wrap in miles of cloth.

Unusual & Artistic Bridges

The Pont des Arts, a few hundred yards farther west, is a wooden footbridge that attracts the city's romantic souls, especially at sunset.

The 348-foot-long (106 m) Passerelle de Solferino links the Louvre complex with the Musée d'Orsay via the Jardin des Tuileries. The new, metal arched-suspension bridge includes a two-tiered walkway built from exotic wood; it is the only Parisian bridge accessible from both the river and street levels.

Winged horses, cherubs, nymphs, gold-leaf swords (regilded for the 1989 bicentennial and repainted in gold in 1997), and other art nouveau details grace the Pont Alexandre III, Paris's most celebrated and photographed bridge. It was named after Tsar Alexander III, whose son laid the first stone in 1896 (see p. 149).

Cult Bridges: the Pont de l'Alma & the Pont de Bir-Hakeim

The area around the Pont de l'Alma and the tunnel that passes underneath it is now heavily visited by tourists drawn to the site where Diana, Princess of Wales, was killed in 1997. The Pont de l'Alma has a sculpture of a Second Empire soldier, known as the Zouave, which is used to measure the level of the Seine. During the major flood of 1910, the water reached as high as his beard.

At the foot of the bridge on the Right Bank sits the gold-encrusted Statue of Liberty flame, cast from the original mold. A scale replica of the entire statue now greets river visitors to

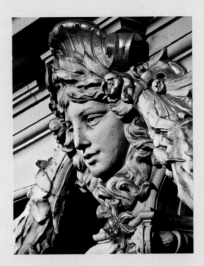

Gilded details brighten the Alexandre III bridge, a highlight of boat trips on the Seine.

Paris as they sail under the Pont de Grenelle.

Farther west, the Seine is straddled by the gray-metal stanchions of the Pont de Bir-Hakeim. In the 1970s, it gained cultlike status with the movie *Last Tango in Paris*.

The sleek Charles-de-Gaulle bridge, inaugurated in 1998, spans the Seine between the Pont d'Austerlitz and the Pont de Bercy, and a new footbridge links the Bibliothèque François Mitterrand with the Parc de Bercy.

EXPERIENCE: Getting Married in Paris

What could be more romantic than exchanging vows in the City of Light? French red tape and residency requirements make a civil ceremony difficult, so it is wise to have legal requirements taken care of at home and then arrange a church wedding (at the American Church, for example, or the American Cathedral) or a symbolic ceremony in Paris. A number of wedding planners can help organize weddings in spectacular settings, among them **Weddings in France** (*www*

.weddingsinfrance.com), **Pièce Montée** (the name of the traditional French wedding cake, *www.piecemontee.com*), or **Bulle et Tulle** (*www.bulle-et-tulle.com*). Or be creative and organize your own ceremony: For those on a tight budget, on the Pont des Arts at sunset or on a bateau-mouche as it cruises the Seine, for example, or for those on a big budget, by renting out the **Musée Jacquemart-André** (*tel 01 45 62 16 40*), housed in an elegant 19th-century mansion.

Around the Tuileries

Flanking the Tuileries gardens are two small but important museums: the Musée de l'Orangerie, containing Impressionist masterpieces, and the Jeu de Paume, once tennis courts, and now a center for photography exhibitions.

Musée de l'Orangerie

- ▲ Map p. 122
- ✉ Jardin des Tuileries, Place de la Concorde
- ☎ 01 44 77 80 07
- ⊕ Closed Tues.
- 💲 €€
- Ⓜ Métro: Concorde

www.musee-orangerie.fr

Galerie Nationale du Jeu de Paume

- ▲ Map p. 122
- ✉ Jardin des Tuileries, Place de la Concorde
- ☎ 01 47 03 12 50
- ⊕ Closed Mon.
- 💲 €€
- Ⓜ Métro: Concorde

www.jeudepaume.org

Musée de l'Orangerie

Claude Monet's "Water Lilies" have made the Musée de l'Orangerie famous. However, this small gem of a museum also boasts 144 masterpieces by other School of Paris artists—from the Impressionists to artists of the 1930s.

The Orangerie building was constructed in 1852 as a winter shelter for the orange trees lining the Tuileries walkways. It now houses the remarkable Walter-Guillaume Collection. Paul Guillaume amassed this collection of works by the School of Paris

INSIDER TIP:

À la mode **may mean a scoop of ice cream to you, but in Paris you can take it as a compliment: It means you're fashionable.**

—ANNE RANDERSON
National Geographic contributor

painters and opened a gallery in 1914 in Paris, enthusiastically supporting such avant-garde painters as Chaim Soutine and Maurice Utrillo. The exhibit reflects his pioneering stance as a collector and supporter of modern art, with 22 works by Soutine, and others by Cézanne, Matisse, Modigliani,

and Picasso. Guillaume's wife, Domenica, donated the works to the government in 1977 on condition that the paintings remain together.

Monet's "Water Lilies," in beautifully restored oval rooms, are the highlight. The French politician Georges Clemenceau helped Monet get the commission to paint these enormous murals in 1914 as a gift to France. Throughout World War I, Monet remained absorbed by the elusive patterns and luminous colors of this theme. The specially designed oval rooms containing the murals, often referred to as the Sistine Chapel of Impressionism, were inaugurated in 1927, less than a year after the painter's death.

Galerie Nationale du Jeu de Paume

Napoleon III constructed the Jeu de Paume between 1861 and 1862 as an indoor tennis court. Used as an exhibition space in 1909, it was co-opted by the Nazis as a temporary storehouse for plundered art. Immediately after the war, it became one of the world's finest Impressionist museums. In 1986 the collection was moved to the Musée d'Orsay (see p. 180), and its light, spacious rooms now house the Centre Nationale de la Photographie, with a range of exhibitions. ∎

Palais-Royal

The Palais-Royal was indeed a royal palace at one time. The original structure (not the gardens behind) was built by Cardinal Richelieu in 1636, thus its name, the Palais Cardinal. Today it holds government offices and surrounds a quiet park.

Daniel Buren's black-and-white columns were added to the Palais-Royal in the 1980s.

Louis XIV lived here as a child for some time, before fleeing to escape the Fronde (see p. 24). He was never fond of Paris and was happy to hand over the city property to his brother, Philippe d'Orléans. Much to the disdain of Philippe's aristocratic kin, his deeply debt-ridden son (also named Philippe) went on to construct 180 arcades and shops on the site.

This new Palais-Royal opened with great fanfare in 1784 and soon drew merchants, intellectuals, and houses of ill repute. When the puritanically minded Louis-Philippe was crowned in 1830, he closed down this hotbed of vice, causing fashionable Parisians to move to other neighborhoods.

By the time Colette and Jean Cocteau had become residents (at 9 rue de Beaujolais and 36 rue de Montpensier, respectively), the gardens had become an island of serenity in the heart of Paris. The former palace, burned during the Commune and restored, is now home to government institutions.

The Palais-Royal's most recent controversy was the installation of Daniel Buren's short, black-and-white striped columns at the south end of the gardens. At the other end is one of Paris's loveliest restaurants, the elegant 18th-century Grand Véfour (see p. 247). Between these, today's gardens form one of the city's most peaceful public parks, overlooked by quaint arcaded shops. ∎

Palais-Royal

- Map p. 123
- Place du Palais-Royal
- Métro: Palais-Royal–Musée du Louvre

More Places to Visit in the Louvre & Palais-Royal

Comédie Française

The theater troupe inspired by the playwright Molière found a home in the 1790s next to the Palais-Royal and has remained there ever since, making it one of the world's oldest established theaters. Created in 1680 by Louis XIV, this state-subsidized company performs primarily classic and modern French plays, such as those by Molière, Racine, and Feydeau. However, in recent years newer playwrights, including Tennesee Williams, have taken their place among the classics. (See p. 259). *www.comedie-francaise.fr*

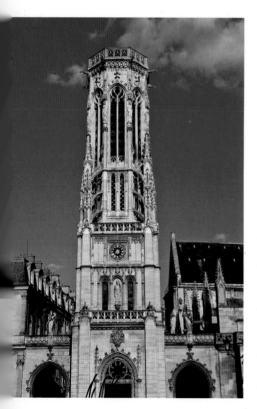

The St.-Germain l'Auxerrois church contains original Gothic structures.

🅰 Map p. 123 ✉ Place Colette
☎ 01 44 58 15 15 🚇 Métro: Palais-Royal–Musée du Louvre

Place des Victoires

Maréchal de la Feuillade, a fawning court follower, created this square solely as a backdrop for a gilded statue of Louis XIV. Melted down during the Revolution, the statue was replaced in 1822. Now mainly a quiet shopping area, the square's shops have been colonized by Japanese designers, including Kenzo.
🅰 Map p. 123 🚇 Métro: Louvre-Rivoli, Bourse

Rue de Rivoli

Always packed with tourists because of its proximity to the Louvre, Rue de Rivoli was built by Napoleon to provide the city with another east–west axis to ease the traffic along the existing Rue St.-Honoré. The covered arcades, completed in 1835, were an innovation at the time, providing pedestrians with protection from both the weather and carriages. Today, souvenir shops share the elegant facades with old-time luxury hotels like the Meurice. Two English bookshops, W. H. Smith and Galignani, are also here, as well as the Angélina tearoom at No. 226, famous in particular for its hot chocolate.
🅰 Map pp. 122–123 🚇 Métro: Concorde, Tuileries, Palais-Royal–Musée du Louvre

St.-Germain l'Auxerrois

This church, opposite the eastern end of the Louvre, was the royal parish for the Valois kings while they resided in the palace across the street. Most of the original decoration has disappeared, with the exception of the superb Flamboyant Gothic porch (circa 1435), the only original one left in Paris.
🅰 Map p. 123 ✉ Place du Louvre
☎ 01 42 60 13 96 🚇 Métro: Louvre-Rivoli

The fabled avenue long called the Triumphal Way and its well-heeled neighbors

Champs-Élysées & 16th Arrondissement

Carvings from the Musée National des Arts Asiatiques-Guimet

Champs-Élysées & 16th Arrondissement

No first-time visitor to Paris wants to miss the mythical Champs-Élysées, the famous Arc de Triomphe, or the glitter of lights around the Place de la Concorde, which symbolize the French sense of grandeur in the most ostentatious way. A stroll through the nearby 16th Arrondissement (see pp. 154–157) takes you to some handsome buildings and museums.

NOT TO BE MISSED:

An exhibition at the Grand Palais 148

The permanent collection at the Petit Palais 149

Haute-couture shopping on the Avenue Montaigne 149

The Arc de Triomphe 149, 152

Taking in art deco and art nouveau architecture 154–155

A wine-tasting class at the Musée du Vin 156–157

Impressionist art at the Musée Marmottan-Monet 157

The Champs-Élysées area is a relatively recent neighborhood, developed mostly during the Second Empire (1852–1870). Under Napoleon III, Adolphe Alphand's gardens and parks (such as the Parc de Monceau; see p. 158) transformed the western edge of Paris into a respectable, residential neighborhood.

The international heart of haute couture was created in Paris's 8th arrondissement by Englishman Charles Worth during the Second Empire, and is still firmly clustered around the Champs-Élysées.

The Faubourg St.-Honoré, running parallel to the Champs-Élysées to the north, is lined with art galleries and elegant shops, including Hermès at No. 24 (leather goods, silk scarves,

and clothes). At No. 55 is the Palais de l'Élysée, the official presidential residence since 1873. It is open to the public during the Journées des Patrimoine (National Heritage Weekend), usually around the second weekend of September.

16th Arrondissement

Much of the 16th arrondissement, especially near the Champs-Élysées, is occupied by banks, multinationals, over-priced hotels, and fashion designers. The southern part of this arrondissement, including the former villages of Passy and Auteuil, is just as snooty but still has a neighborly feel, however exclusive. Connoisseurs of art will enjoy the area's wealth of art nouveau and art deco buildings as well as the fabulous Impressionist collection at the Musée Marmottan-Monet. ∎

Paris

Area of map detail

16th Arrondissement, see map on page 154–155

Seine

❶ Théâtre des Champs-Élysées
❷ Théâtre du Rond-Point ❸ Théâtre
Marigny ❹ Palais de l'Élysée
❺ Musée Cernuschi

Champs-Élysées

Napoleon III returned from London determined to bring the space and greenery of British gardens to the French capital; employing Adolphe Alphand, he overhauled the Champs-Élysées. Once the promenade of elegant aristocrats and the bourgeoisie, its buildings today range from the Palais de l'Élysée, the official presidential residence since 1873, to movie theaters, fast-food emporiums, airline agencies, and megastores.

A fountain at the Place de la Concorde frames a distant view of the Eiffel Tower.

Place de la Concorde

Once the site of Revolutionary bloodbaths, today's Place de la Concorde is framed by the American Embassy and the luxurious Hôtel Crillon, and offers a breathtaking view up the Champs-Élysées toward the Arc de Triomphe.

The Place de la Concorde was laid out in 1757 by the royal architect Jacques-Ange Gabriel as a backdrop for an equestrian statue of Louis XV. As opposed to Paris's other royal squares (Place des Victoires and Place Dauphine, for example), which were enclosed, Gabriel constructed buildings on one side only, leaving intact the view from the Tuileries Palace up the Champs-Élysées to the Rond-Point. His two colonnaded buildings—now the Crillon hotel and the Ministère de la Marine (where Marie-Antoinette once kept a secret apartment)—mirror the facade of the National Assembly across the river. Louis's statue was pulled down during the Revolution, and the Place Louis-XV was rebaptized the Place de la Révolution. During the Terror, more than 1,200 people were guillotined here, including Louis XVI, Maximilien Robespierre, and Marie-Antoinette.

The Obelisk: After a series of name changes, the square was renamed the Place de la Concorde in 1795. Louis-Philippe erected statues and fountains representing the great cities of France and placed a central monument in the square—a 3,300-year-old obelisk, a twin of the one that stands in front of the Temple of Luxor, given to France in 1829 by Egyptian Viceroy Mohammed Ali.

Some 200,000 Parisians cheered as the engineer Le Bas and his 120-strong team raised the obelisk in 1836. Their exploit is recorded on the obelisk's base, which is the best place to appreciate the square's sweeping view of the Louvre's pyramid (to the east), and the Champs-Élysées extending west toward La Défense, framed by copies of the "Horses of Marly." The originals are now in the Louvre (see p. 124).

Champs-Élysées

When it was created by André Le Nôtre in 1667 for Louis XIV, the Champs-Élysées was meant to be a visual extension of the Tuileries gardens. It was not yet the classy neighborhood it was to become, and the fields and undergrowth served as a meeting place for the city's riffraff. The Champs-Élysées is divided into two sections: the pretty, garden-lined avenue that leads from Place de la Concorde to the Rond-Point, and the commercial area from the Rond-Point to the Arc de Triomphe.

In the 1830s, architect Jacques Hittorff began to transform this unpopulated area of Paris. Over 1,200 gas lamps were installed, and the area became a giant

Place de la Concorde
🅰 Map p. 145
Ⓜ Métro: Concorde

Champs-Élysées
🅰 Map pp. 144–145
Ⓜ Métro: Concorde, Champs-Élysées–Clemenceau, Franklin D. Roosevelt, George V, Charles de Gaulle–Étoile

Where to Slunch

Traditionally, the French are rigid in their eating habits: breakfast in the morning, lunch at 1 p.m., and supper (dinner) between 8 p.m. and 10:30 p.m. Trying to eat in a restaurant outside of those times has always been difficult. Those rules are breaking down in Paris, however, as outside influences change eating habits (American-style hamburgers are popping up on more and more menus). The latest trend is slunch (between supper and lunch, at around 5 p.m.), which comes in the form of a trayful of small dishes, all served at the same time for diners to choose from.

Just off the Champs-Élysées in the Grand Palais, the **Mini Palais** (*Avenue Winston Churchill, tel 01 42 56 42 42*), with a menu by superstar chef Eric Frechon, offers a gourmet slunch. For those who crave a real, high-quality American hamburger and/or who want to eat at anytime they feel like it between noon and 12:30 a.m. (1 a.m. on weekends), that old faithful **Joe Allen** (*30 rue Pierre Lescot, 75001, tel 01 42 36 70 13*) is the best bet.

Grand Palais

- ⚠ Map p. 145
- ✉ Entrance on Avenue Général Eisenhower
- ☎ 01 44 13 17 17
- 🕐 Closed Tues.
- 💲 €€€
- 🚇 Métro: Champs-Élysées–Clemenceau

www.rmn.fr/
galeries-nationales-
grand-palais

Palais de la Découverte

- ✉ Grand Palais, entrance on Avenue Franklin D. Roosevelt
- ☎ 01 56 43 20 20
- 🕐 Closed Mon.
- 💲 €€
- 🚇 Métro: Champs-Élysées–Clemenceau

www.palais-
decouverte.fr

Petit Palais

- ⚠ Map p. 145
- ✉ Avenue Winston Churchill
- ☎ 01 53 43 40 00
- 🕐 Closed Mon.
- 🚇 Métro: Champs-Élysées–Clemenceau

www.petitpalais.
paris.fr

playground, filled with formal gardens, fountains, and restaurants. All that remains of these former pleasure pavilions are two expensive restaurants, Ledoyen (see p. 250) and Laurent. The gardens of the **Élysées Palace** (the presidential residence) border the northern edge of Avenue Gabriel.

During the 1914 Occupation of Paris, Russian troops set up their tents along the Champs-Élysées, devastating the area; it took the city two years to repair the damage.

West of the Rond-Point stretches what the French like to call the most beautiful avenue in the world, still considered the

INSIDER TIP:

Be careful at sidewalk cafés on the Champs-Élysées, where purse snatchers prey on unwary tourists.

—ANNE RANDERSON
National Geographic contributor

obligatory route for all important gatherings, departures, and returns. For example, the July 14 military parades, with their low-flying jets, pass here; it marks the finish line of the annual Tour de France bicycle race and the starting point of the Paris Marathon.

However, the Champs-Élysées' reputation tends to outshine its reality. Despite a face-lift in the 1990s that removed parking and expanded the already huge

sidewalks, it has been invaded by flashy car dealerships, fast-food restaurants, and giant movie complexes.

Universal Exposition Monuments

These three legacies of the 1900 Universal Exposition were conceived as monuments to French art. The 1889 Universal Exposition was so successful that immediately after it closed, plans were laid for another in 1900. This time, the city decided to build permanent structures.

Grand Palais: The Grand Palais, which replaced the Palais de l'Industrie of 1885, is a huge iron-and-glass structure with a classical stone facade. Exuberant ironwork, the colossal bronze statues of Apollo's chariot drawn by flying horses, and a seemingly endless glass roof are characteristic of the art nouveau style of its time.

The Grand Palais has hosted many major exhibitions, including the 1905 Salon d'Automne that launched the fauves group of artists. The Grand Palais's exhibition space, which has hosted innumerable art fairs over the years, reopened in 2005 after a 12-year closure, with its magnificent glass roof completely restored.

The **Galeries Nationales du Grand Palais** host international art shows. At the **Palais de la Découverte,** the Grand Palais science museum, interactive exhibits explore such diverse topics as animal communication, Earth's origins, and meteorology.

Petit Palais: The Petit Palais was also built for the 1900 exposition; it now belongs to the City of Paris and houses a mixed collection ranging from Chinese porcelain to 19th-century paintings. The beautifully renovated building has an interior garden and pools.

Pont Alexandre III: Another vestige of the 1900 exposition is the Pont Alexandre III, an extravagant structure with gilded statues dedicated to friendship between Russia and France. Tsar Nicholas II laid the first stone on October 7, 1896, and it was completed two years later.

Avenue Montaigne

Branching off from the Champs-Élysées and home to one of the most famous *bals populaires* (dance halls) in the mid-1800s, the ultra-chic Avenue Montaigne is lined with luxury shops, palatial hotels, and the haute couture houses of some of France's leading fashion names, including Chanel and Christian Dior. Givenchy's shop is on the nearby Avenue George V.

Arc de Triomphe

Parisians still call the square surrounding the Arc de Triomphe l'Étoile ("the star"), despite its name changing in 1970 to the Place Charles de Gaulle. It gets its name from the 12 avenues radiating from it. At its center stands the Arc de Triomphe, a striking landmark in the middle of Paris's longest vista.

In 1806, Napoleon commissioned a monument from the

The Arc de Triomphe looms over a circle at the center of 12 intersecting avenues.

architect Jean-François Chalgrin to honor his Grande Armée and the victory of Austerlitz. In keeping with the Napoleonic sense of grandeur, the Arc de Triomphe is 164 feet high (50 m) and 147 feet wide (45 m)—the largest arch of its kind ever built. It was finally completed in 1836.

Its bas-relief sculptures include the famous "Départ des Volontaires," or "La Marseillaise," a winged figure leading soldiers into battle, by François Rude; and its friezes depict the departure of the French armies (eastern side) and their return (western side).

The 12 avenues radiating out from the arc and the 12 matching
(continued on p. 152)

Arc de Triomphe

- Map p. 144
- Place Charles de Gaulle
- 01 55 37 73 77
- €€ (includes museum)
- Métro: Charles-de-Gaulle–Étoile

**www.arc-de-triomphe.
monuments-
nationaux.fr**

Paris, Capital of Chic

France's reputation as the world's luxury capital remains untarnished. New York, London, and Milan may have their own unique styles, but Paris is the only true center of classic haute couture.

Models stalk the runway during a Christian Dior spring show in Paris.

Fashion for the New Millennium

The new buzzwords: luxury and functionality. Women are no longer afraid to wear clothes at work that would previously have been considered more suitable for the opera than the office. Meanwhile, the invasion of foreign designers continues unabated: for instance, London-schooled Italian designer Ricardo Tisci reigns at Givenchy. Why do top designers flock to Paris? They are given creative freedom and can rely on a network of incomparable craftsmen to give form to their visions.

Parisian Haute Couture

Designers' dazzling collections may seem remote and dauntingly priced—few can afford extravagances such as handmade designs that sell for $10,000 and higher—but their inspiration will inevitably trickle down into ready-to-wear and accessories in boutiques around the world.

The haute couture collections unveiled in January and July demonstrate the pivotal role Paris plays as the center of creative fashion. Expression is at its peak, with designers choosing eccentric locations to play up the clothes

INSIDER TIP:

Department stores dress windows for the winter holidays in a unique French fashion, mixing whimsy and style.

—SHEILA BUCKMASTER
National Geographic Books contributing editor

on view. What counts? Virtuosity in technique, detail, and color, and—most of all—the "theater of the moment"—the *spectacle*.

The great couture tradition was founded in the mid-20th century by the likes of Coco Chanel, Christian Dior, Hubert de Givenchy, and Pierre Cardin, names that convey the difference between what is French and what is the Rest of the World. (The master of them all, the late Yves Saint Laurent, retired in 2002 with a retrospective of his 40-year contribution to the field.)

New York fashion is about practicality and

Brocade shoes in a shop window

versatility, featuring clothing that travels from office to evening; London fashion is more eccentric; and in Milan, the focus is on the beauty, quality, and salability of fabrics. That leaves the out-and-out sheer romantic glamour to Paris.

Less Is More

French style—the much-admired way French women have of carrying themselves, wearing a scarf, and pulling a look together in a seemingly effortless, innate manner—is the subject of much study and imitation; it can sometimes be learned, but it can never be bought.

As with many other nationalities, the French have embraced the American fashion influence, but their approach to style as an art form can be seen as much on Parisian streets as on the catwalks at fashion houses. For the past few seasons, Chanel has mixed curious forms of sportswear with its classically chic suits. Unlike her Anglo-Saxon counterpart—whose buying habits tend toward quantity and all-purpose wear—the Frenchwoman (particularly the Parisian) usually buys fewer, higher-ticket items, such as an excellent pair of shoes, a top-quality handbag, or

a colorful silk scarf, and has no qualms about wearing the same thing twice or more in one week, as a designer piece will look just as chic on the hundredth wearing. Accessories do not have to match, and the sharpest dressers adhere to the no-more-than-two-colors rule. Handbags by such Paris-based designers as Vuitton, Hermès, Longchamp, and Lancel have been particularly hot items recently.

France is not a country where dressing for success has become politicized. Most Frenchwomen dress to accent their femininity, even playing it to their advantage in a business context: They don't worry that high hemlines or figure-revealing clothes might interfere with being taken seriously, any more than the average Frenchman worries whether offering a compliment will result in being slapped with a lawsuit.

Cathedrale St.-Alexandre-Nevsky

- Map p. 144–145
- 12 rue Daru
- 01 42 27 37 34
- Open 3–5 p.m. Tues., Fri., & Sun.
- Métro: Courcelles

hôtels (residences) surrounding the Place were not part of the original design, but were introduced by Baron Eugène Haussmann (see p. 166). The result is perhaps monumental in a way he never intended: The 12 streets converging at the Étoile now create a huge traffic jam.

Over the years, the Arc de Triomphe has symbolized all that is great and glorious in France: Napoleon's ashes passed under the arch on their way to Les Invalides, as did Victor Hugo's funeral cortege. The conquering armies—the Prussians in 1871 and the Germans in 1940—that marched here were succeeded by France's heroic liberators, such as Gen. Charles de Gaulle, who led the Allied victory march along the avenue before thousands of jubilant Parisians on August 26, 1944 (see p. 30).

An unknown soldier's tomb was placed here in 1920, and every evening at 6:30 veterans relight the flame. An underground walkway at the end of the Champs-Élysées leading underneath the Place Charles-de-Gaulle provides a safe passage to the Arc de Triomphe, where the view from the top overlooks Haussmann's design.

Beneath the viewing platform is a small museum with an exhibition on the history of the building of the monument and mementoes of Napoleon and World War I.

Cathédrale St.-Alexandre-Nevsky

The heart of Little Russia, this onion-domed, Russian Orthodox cathedral was constructed in 1861 and is based on a Greek-cross floor plan. The inside is lined with impressive frescoes and icons, and the tympanum is covered with mosaics on a gilded background. ■

Parisians relax in the sun in the Parc Monceau, near the Cathédrale St.-Alexandre-Nevsky.

EXPERIENCE: Learning La Cuisine Française

Where better to learn to cook than in Paris? Other national cuisines may have their advocates, and rightly so, but French cooking techniques remain the gold standard for chefs around the world. And, in the past 20 years or so, French chefs have become far less rigid and are experimenting with international influences of all sorts, reviving and enriching their national cuisine.

In Paris, there are dozens of options for learning to cook, from one-off demonstrations or hands-on classes for the amateur to serious professional programs, almost all of them available in English. Best of all, participants get to eat the results. Choose one that suits your interests and time constraints.

Few dishes are more quintessentially French than garlicky escargots (snails).

Cordon Bleu & Escoffier

The granddaddy of them all is the Cordon Bleu (8 rue Léon Delhomme, 75015, tel 01 53 68 22 50, www.cordonbleu .edu/paris), which offers a variety of diplomas and certificates for those who wish to become career chefs or sommeliers, with the possibility of internships in Parisian restaurants. The school also offers short-term cooking and wine-tasting demonstrations and courses for amateurs.

The **Ritz Escoffier School** (15 place Vendôme, 75001, tel 01 43 16 30 50, www.ritzparis.com) was named after Auguste Escoffier, who laid down many of the rules for French cooking in his Le Guide Culinaire and was the first head chef of the Ritz Paris. Located in a nicely decorated room in the basement of the Ritz, near the kitchen, this school offers diploma courses for professionals and individual workshops for foodies.

Ducasse & Others

Internationally renowned chef Alain Ducasse may be the Escoffier of today, but only time will tell. He is passing on his expertise through the **École de Cuisine Alain Ducasse** (64 rue du Ranelagh, 75016, 01 44 90 91 00, www .ecolecuisine-alainducasse.com), which offers classes with chefs trained by Ducasse in different cooking styles and by guest chefs who share their skills in such varied cuisines as Indian or Basque. Courses are in French, but translation can be arranged on request.

For a quick, fun cooking class, ranging from 30 minutes to 4 hours, on a wide range of topics, try the **Atelier des Chefs** (several locations, tel 01 49 70 97 50, www.atelierdeschefs.fr). It offers a wide variety of classes to choose from and is easy to book online.

French Home Cooking

If you are looking for a homier experience with a professional approach, **Marguerite's Elegant Home Cooking** (tel 01 42 04 74 00, www.elegant cooking.com) offers just that. Students meet their teacher at an outdoor market to learn about French products and buy the ingredients for the meal they will cook. They then go to a family home to cook the meal in a professional kitchen with four two-person cooking stations. The whole group then sits down in the family dining room to enjoy the fruits of their lesson together.

16th Arrondissement

Despite its reputation as a refuge for the rich and as an opulent but boring neighborhood, the 16th arrondissement has a wealth of museums, a few remaining traces of its former village life, and the most concentrated number of art nouveau and art deco buildings in Paris. Comfortably wedged between the Seine on one side and the Bois de Boulogne on the other, the 16th arrondissement is the neighborhood favored by both old and new money.

The view from the Palais de Chaillot

This part of Paris has lured the upper classes for centuries. Catherine de Médicis often stopped on Chaillot Hill (the present-day Trocadéro, a semicircular square in front of the Palais de Chaillot) on her way from St.-Germain-en-Laye to Paris, gradually expanding the lodge that stood on the site. The wine produced by the Abbey of Passy and the Minimes de Chaillot was famous throughout the region, and vineyards lined the hills sloping toward the Seine. In the 17th century, the curative powers of Passy's spring brought upper-crust clientele to its thermal spa; today, its source still provides crystal-clear water.

Architectural Gems

More than half of Hector Guimard's art nouveau buildings are in the 16th arrondissement, particularly in Auteuil. Best known for his superb glass-and-iron Métro entrances (especially the one at the Porte Dauphine), Guimard also designed the flamboyant Castel Béranger, an art nouveau masterpiece, and several other buildings along Rue de la Fontaine. The streamlined art deco style followed in the 1920s and '30s; its chief Parisian proponent, Robert Mallet-Stevens, designed a series of town houses on an Auteuil street that now bears his name. Several small alleyways off Rue Boileau (*Métro: Exelmans*), including the Villa Cheysson and the Villa Mulhouse—originally built to house millworkers—are lined with charming houses and gardens.

The villages of Passy, Auteuil, and Chaillot were annexed to the City of Paris in 1860. For the 1937 Universal

❶ Porte Dauphine Métro ❷ Castel
Béranger ❸ Rue Boileau

Exposition the enormous
Palais de Chaillot (see
p. 156) was built in neoclassical style and decorated with
sculptures and bas-reliefs. It now
contains three museums (one,
the Musée de l'Homme, is closed
until 2012) and a theater.

East down Chaillot Hill are
two major museums: the Musée
Guimet (see p. 158), devoted to
Asian arts, and, just down the
street, the lively Musée d'Art
Moderne de la Ville de Paris (see
p. 156), both in the neoclassical
Palais de Tokyo, a structure built
for the 1937 Exposition.

Palais de Chaillot

🅰 Map p. 155

✉ 17 place du Trocadéro

☎ Musée de l'Homme: 01 44 05 72 72
Musée de la Marine: 01 53 65 69 69

🕐 Closed Tues.

💲 €€

🚇 Métro: Trocadéro

www.mnhn.fr

www.musee-marine.fr

Cité de l'Architecture et du Patrimoine

☎ 01 58 51 52 00

www.citechaillot.fr

Musée d'Art Moderne de la Ville de Paris

✉ 11 avenue du Président Wilson

☎ 01 53 67 40 00

🕐 Closed Mon.

💲 €€–€€€

🚇 Métro: Iéna

www.mamparis.fr

Site de Création Contemporaine

✉ 13 avenue du Président Wilson

☎ 01 47 23 54 01

🕐 Closed Mon.

💲 €€

🚇 Métro: Iéna

www.palaisdetokyo.com

Palais de Chaillot & Trocadéro Museums

The view from the terrace of the Palais de Chaillot across the river is one of the best in Paris. The museums inside this monument, however, are less well known—the Musée de l'Homme, Musée de la Marine,

INSIDER TIP:

Don't miss Patrick Roget's chocolate boutique (45 avenue Victor Hugo), which features fantastical chocolate sculptures.

—PATRICIA DANIELS
National Geographic Books contributing editor

and the Cité de l'Architecture et du Patrimoine, which includes newly reopened Musée des Monuments Français, a huge architecture museum. Down the hill, the Palais de Tokyo houses the Musée d'Art Moderne de la Ville de Paris and the Site de Création Contemporaine.

Cité de l'Architecture et du Patrimoine:
This revamped institution brings together the Institut Français de l'Architecture, focusing on modern architecture, and the Musée des Monuments Français, with its models of French monuments.

Musée de l'Homme:
The Musée de l'Homme, an ethnology and anthropology museum,

is closed for renovation until 2012.

Musée de la Marine: Created in 1748, this establishment is one of the oldest marine museums in the world. It contains intricate scale models of warships dating from the 17th century to the present and splendid examples of the famous tall sailing ships.

Palais de Tokyo: The **Museum of Modern Art of the City of Paris,** in the Palais de Tokyo's east wing, represents many artists of the school of Paris as well as a rich collection of fauvist and cubist works—including pieces by Matisse and Dufy and the École de Paris artists Soutine, Modigliani, and van Dongen. The Contemporary Art Department continues its ambitious temporary shows of young international artists and current art trends.

In the west wing, the **Site de Création Contemporaine**—billed as a "laboratory of contemporary art"—presents exhibitions, installations, and performances.

Musée du Vin

On the other side of Palais de Chaillot, is a 15th-century hideaway enclosing the wine cellars of the former Minimes de Chaillot monastery, which distilled one of Louis XIII's favorite vintages. Most of the buildings were destroyed during the Revolution and the cellars were forgotten until the 1950s. In 1984 they were made into a wine museum *(Rue des Eaux, tel 0145 25 63 26, www .museeduvinparis.com, closed Mon., €€€ includes a glass of wine)*. Visitors can now explore the former limestone quarries that house objects used in the making and drinking of wine and sign up for classes. Entrance to the museum is free if you lunch in the restaurant. (Reserve for theme dinners).

Musée Marmottan-Monet

Although the Musée Marmottan-Monet is now famous throughout the world for its Impressionist paintings, the museum was initially devoted to an entirely different theme: the Napoleonic era.

Jules and Paul Marmottan, father and son, were responsible for this collection, housed in a former hunting lodge, which was entirely remodeled by Marmottan senior. At the turn of the 19th century both men were interested in Napoleonic memorabilia, and they amassed a superb collection of Empire furnishings. After his father's death made him a wealthy man, Paul Marmottan became a recognized expert on Empire art. When he died in 1932, he left his mansion and entire art collection to the Institut de France.

Several later bequests transformed the Marmottan into a world-renowned Impressionist museum. The first bequest included "Impression: Sunrise," while a second in 1966, from Monet's son Michel, brought 65 works by the painter, including some of his best paintings.

A number of the "Water Lilies" paintings are exhibited downstairs, along with the images of smoke-filled train stations and brilliant fields of flowers and other works such as Alfred Sisley's "Spring in the Environs of Paris" and Paul Gauguin's "Bouquet of Flowers."

The ground-floor room contains a collection of medieval illuminated manuscripts from the Georges Wildenstein collection. ∎

Musée Marmottan-Monet

- Map p. 155
- 2 rue Louis Boilly
- 01 44 96 50 33
- Closed Mon.
- €€
- Métro: La Muette

www.marmottan .com

The Jardins du Trocadéro front the Palais de Chaillot.

More Places to Visit on the Champs-Élysées & in the 16th Arrondissement

Musée Jacquemart-André

This museum in the home of Edouard André and his wife, Nélie Jacquemart, reflects the couple's lifetime devotion to building their art collection. Famous for its Italian Renaissance works, the collection includes a rare fresco ceiling by Tiepolo, "Henri III Received in Venice by the Doge Cantarini," and Uccello's "Saint George Slaying the Dragon." There are also French and Flemish paintings (with Rembrandt's "Pilgrims of Emmaus," "Amalia von Sohms," and "Doctor Tholinx"). *www.musee-jacquemart-andre.com*
🅰 Map p. 145 ✉ 158 boulevard Haussmann ☎ 01 45 62 11 59 💲 €€ 🚇 Métro: Miromesnil, St.-Philippe du Roule

INSIDER TIP:

Try classic Guerlain fragrances (including Shalimar) at the company's 68 Champs-Élysées flagship shop.

—SHEILA BUCKMASTER
*National Geographic Traveler magazine
editor at large*

Maison de Balzac

In 1840, Honoré de Balzac, writer of *La Comédie Humaine (The Human Comedy),* was on the brink of financial ruin. He moved to this house in Passy, where he lived under the pseudonym of Monsieur de Breugnol. A museum since 1960, it displays many of his personal objects, including his writing desk, where he sometimes worked for 24 hours at a stretch. As he wrote to Madame Hanska, whom he married just before his death at the age of 51, this desk "witnessed my anguish, my miseries, my distress, my joys, my everything." Raised in Paris, Balzac set

many of his works in the French capital. *www.balzac.paris.fr*
🅰 Map p. 155 ✉ 47 rue Raynouard ☎ 01 55 74 41 80 🕐 Closed Mon. 🚇 Métro: Passy

Musée National des Arts Asiatique-Guimet

The museum's original collection came from Lyon industrialist Émile Guimet, who gathered a fantastic number of objects during his trips around the world in the late 19th century. His Egyptian collection eventually went to the Louvre, but works from the Far East remained here. A national museum since 1928, it exhibits Guimet's collection, which ranges from Afghan to Japanese works and spans eras from 2000 B.C. to the 19th century, including examples of Khmer artwork, bronze statues from India, and antique jade and porcelain from China. The galleries of the Buddhist pantheon at 19 avenue d'Iéna are devoted to the history of Far Eastern religions. *www.museeguimet.fr*
🅰 Map p. 155 ✉ 6 place d'Iéna ☎ 01 56 52 53 00 🕐 Closed Tues. 💲 €€ 🚇 Métro: Iéna

Parc de Monceau

This park is farther afield but is linked in spirit to the Second Empire, when it and much of the area surrounding the Champs-Élysées became a fashionable neighborhood. It retains something of its former 19th-century bourgeois aura, with its picturesque park, grottoes, and rockery, along with several extravagant follies (decorative constructions). The **Musée Cernuschi** *(7 avenue Velasquez, tel 01 53 96 21 50, closed Mon.),* with its wonderful collection of Asian art, is located next to the park. 🅰 Map p. 145 ✉ Boulevard Courcelles 🚇 Métro: Monceau, Courcelles

Created in the 19th century for the up-and-coming bourgeoisie, encompassing the Opéra, department stores, and theaters

Les Grands Boulevards

Covered passages link parts of the Boulevards.

Les Grands Boulevards

Les Grands Boulevards begin near the Madeleine Quarter and run eastward as far as Bastille. These wide thoroughfares form a shopping and cultural hub, including the ostentatious Opéra Garnier, luxury food stores and designer boutiques, fashion houses, cafés, theaters, and galleries.

"Là est la vie!" ("That's where life is!") proclaimed novelist Honoré de Balzac, referring to Les Grands Boulevards. Originally created by Louis XIV in the 1670s, they became the center of entertainment in the 19th century after the prudish Louis-Philippe closed down the bordellos and gambling dens at the Palais-Royal. Crowds flocked to the boulevards, the wealthy to the west of Rue Montmartre, the poor to the east.

The Boulevard des Capucines, Boulevard des Italiens, and Avenue de l'Opéra converge at the Opéra Garnier (see p. 163) in the Place de l'Opéra designed by Baron Haussmann (see pp. 166–167). It is one of Paris's most brilliant illustrations of the Napoleon III style. Napoleon III crowned the Colonne d'Austerlitz on Place Vendôme (see p. 162) with an imperial effigy of his uncle (Napoleon I) dressed as Julius Caesar. Ancient Greece inspired the series of temples previously commissioned by Napoleon I as well: La Madeleine church, a temple of glory to the Grande Armée, and La Bourse, or Paris stock exchange, a temple to finance.

The Madeleine Quarter, where Les Grands Boulevards begin, is also a modern-day temple to luxury. Rue de la Paix and Place

Vendôme were tranquil bourgeois corners until the late 19th century, when the lavish boutiques of jewelers and fashionable tailors, including the *maison de couture* of Englishman Charles Frederick Worth, moved in.

Artists were drawn to the area: The first Impressionist exhibition was held at 35 boulevard des Capucines, and the first showing of the Lumière brothers' film shorts was at No. 14

(now the Hôtel Scribe) in 1895. Musicians such as Lully (the 17th-century court composer) gravitated to the area around the now-vanished Opera House of Paris.

The elegant Square de Louvois, near the Bibliothèque Nationale (see p. 165), with its magnificent Labrouste Reading Room, now stands in place of the old Opera House. Behind it are the Vivienne and Colbert Galleries, in one of the area's remaining 19th-century covered arcades. Today, these galleries have stores, a restaurant, and a tearoom.

Place Vendôme is studded with the world's leading jewelers, the Ritz Hotel, and the Justice Ministry. Luxury shops, such as Fauchon and Hédiard, are scattered around the Madeleine, along with the famous flower market. ■

NOT TO BE MISSED:

A concert at La Madeleine 162

Window shopping for luxuries on the Place Vendôme 162

A tour of the Opéra Garnier 163

A Mona Lisa chocolate éclair at Fauchon 164

An exhibition at the Bibliothèque Nationale 165

Tea and shopping in the Galerie Vivienne 165

Exploring the arcades off the Passage des Panoramas 168

❶ Église Notre-Dame de l'Assomption ❷ La Bourse ❸ Passage des Panoramas ❹ Passage Jouffroy ❺ Passage Brady

La Madeleine & Place Vendôme

The contrasting influences of the royal family and Napoleon I both shaped two iconic locations among the Grand Boulevards: the imposing church of La Madeleine (formally the church of Saint Mary Magdalene), and the Place Vendôme.

La Madeleine
- Map p. 160
- Place de la Madeleine
- 01 44 51 69 00
- Métro: Madeleine

www.eglise-lamadeleine.com

Place Vendôme
- Map p. 160
- Métro: Opéra, Madeleine

The Madeleine

The Madeleine is one of the most famous monuments in Paris, particularly interesting for its colossal exterior and 64-foot-high (20 m) Corinthian columns. The interior is dark and lugubrious, with light coming from three domed skylights in the nave and a semicircular apse. Here celebrity weddings, funerals, and memorial services (as well as regular religious services) are held. In the vestibule is the "Baptism of Christ" (far left), a masterpiece by François Rude.

INSIDER TIP:

The roof of the Galeries Lafayette (40 boulevard Haussmann) offers stunning views of the city.

—GILLES MINGASSON
National Geographic photographer

The church was planned as part of J. A. Gabriel's layout for the Place Louis XV (today's Place de la Concorde). The original construction, begun in 1764, was razed in favor of a building modeled on the Panthéon until work was halted by the French Revolution. In 1806, Napoleon commissioned a temple to his Grande Armée and the existing structure was once more razed. However, in 1814 Louis XVIII confirmed that it should be a church and devoted the building to his guillotined brother, Louis XVI.

Place Vendôme

The Place Vendôme is superlatively spacious and luminous at night, with an imposing, imperial air. The square (called Place Louis-le-Grand until the Revolution) was originally created by Louis XIV to rival Place des Vosges. In 1792, the square's statue of Louis XIV was destroyed and replaced in 1810 by the Colonne d'Austerlitz to glorify Napoleon's military campaigns. The bronze spiral wrapped around the stone column—inspired by Trajan's column in Rome—was made from the 1,200 cannon captured at the Battle of Austerlitz (1805).

Opened in 1898 overlooking the square, the Ritz was the first hotel to have private bathtubs. Scott and Zelda Fitzgerald lived here in the 1920s. Ernest Hemingway claimed to have "liberated" the hotel with Allied soldiers in August 1944, while Coco Chanel died here. ∎

Opéra Garnier

The Opéra Garnier, built under Napoleon III, now features ballet primarily, with opera mostly staged at the Opéra de Paris-Bastille. Following an attempt on Napoleon III's life near the old opera house on Rue Le Peletier, the emperor moved the Opéra to a more secure site. Architect Charles Garnier resolved the dilemma of building the Opéra over a lake—it still lies underneath, and the fountains and pools in the basement are said to have inspired *The Phantom of the Opera*.

The over-the-top style of the Opéra Garnier is typical of Napoleon III's era.

Despite Haussmann's approval of Garnier's project in 1861, Empress Eugénie complained: "What is this style? It is no style at all, neither Greek nor Louis XVI." To which Garnier reportedly replied: "Those styles have had their day. It is Napoleon III, and for this you complain?"

The Opéra indeed epitomizes Napoleon III style: baroque, eclectic, and ridiculously extravagant, with its Apollo-crowned dome and statues of music and dance, including a copy of Carpeaux's "La Danse." The bacchanalian sculpture to the right of the entrance was branded an "ignoble saturnalia" and an "offense to public morals" (the original work

is now in the Musée d'Orsay). The Emperor's Pavilion on Rue Scribe, which once featured a ramp to allow the king to enter the royal box directly from his carriage, now provides access to a museum of props and scores.

The Opéra's interior is filled with gold leaf, precious stones, frescoes, marble, and a grandiose foyer and staircase. The five-tier auditorium has only 2,131 seats, some with no visibility, but the huge stage can accommodate up to 450 performers. The false ceiling painted by Chagall in 1964 can be seen when performances or rehearsals are not in progress.

Honey made in beehives on the roof is sold in the boutique. ∎

Opéra Garnier

- ⬛ Map p. 160
- ✉ Place de l'Opéra
- ☎ Tour info./ museum: 08 25 05 44 05
- 🕐 Closed for visits on days when there is a matinée performance or special event. Guided tours by prior arrangement.
- 💲 €€€ (for tour)
- Ⓜ Métro: Opéra

www.opera-de-paris.fr

A Walk Along Les Grands Boulevards

As you stroll along Les Grands Boulevards, originally laid out as tree-lined promenades in the 17th century, you can still get an impression of what the area looked like in its heyday.

Local passages are a shopper's paradise.

Begin your walk at the 19th-century **Café de la Paix** on the Place de l'Opéra, once frequented by Émile Zola and Guy de Maupassant. Next, visit the landmark **Opéra Garnier ①** (see p. 163).

Exiting the Opéra, turn right down Boulevard des Capucines. The Hôtel Scribe at No. 14 is where, in 1895, the Lumière brothers first showed film shorts. The refurbished **Olympia** concert hall, at No. 28, is where Edith Piaf, Jacques Brel, and the Beatles once performed.

Continue straight on Boulevard des Capucines to **La Madeleine ②** (see p. 162). On the eastern side are the wonderful, wood-paneled art nouveau public rest rooms (women's side only), with mirrored columns, stained glass, and yellow and green floral tiles (closed 11:30 a.m.–12:30 p.m.). Go around the church past the flower market (circa 1834) to **Fauchon** at 26 place de la Madeleine—Paris's most extravagant food store—then on to the more discreet **Hédiard** at No. 21 place de la Madeleine, on the opposite side of the church. Hédiard is renowned for miniature and exotic fruits and vegetables. Also on Place de la Madeleine are the Maison de la Truffe (No. 19) and Caviar Kaspia (No. 17) for caviar and pepper vodka.

Circle back in front of the church; Marcel Proust lived at 9 place de la Madeleine, where the restaurant Lucas Carton is located. Head down **Rue Royale ③** and within a few paces pass the Cité Berryer, which has a good wine shop. You're in the lap of luxury here, with the Ladurée tea salon and pastry shop, Maxim's restaurant, Lachaume florists, Lalique crystal, and Christofle flatware all nearby.

Turn left on Rue St.-Honoré. On the right is the 17th-century **Église Notre-Dame de l'Assomption ④**, the former chapel of the Convent of the Sisters of the Assumption (now the Polish Church in Paris). Continue until you reach a passage just before Rue de Castiglione, and cut left through the passage to Place Vendôme, leading to **Rue de la Paix,** the

19th-century's most glamorous shopping street.

Past the north side of the square, turn right on Rue Danielle Casanova (which becomes Rue des Petits Champs). Look to the right toward **Rue du Marché St.-Honoré** to see the glass-and-steel Marché St.-Honoré—part of BNP Paribas (a bank), it houses offices, galleries, and upscale shops, and is surrounded by lively cafés and restaurants. At 40 rue des Petits Champs, turn left into the **Passage Choiseul ❺**. Built in 1825 by Bertrand Tavernier, the glass-roofed gallery itself is attractive, although it is now a tacky arcade.

Turn right down perpendicular Passage Ste.-Anne at the Lavrut art supplies store, which leads to Rue Cherubini and Square Louvois. Cross Rue de Richelieu and enter the courtyard of the **Bibliothèque Nationale ❻** (*58 rue de Richelieu, tel 01 53 79 59 59, closed Sun.–Mon., Métro: Bourse*). Temporary exhibitions display some of the treasures of this library, initially founded with royal collections in 1666. The books have been transferred to the Bibliothèque Nationale de France–Site Tolbiac,

located in the 13th arrondissement, but the maps, musical scores, medals, prints, and photographs remain here. Turn right and enter the main building to see the spectacular **Labrouste Reading Room** created by Henri Labrouste in 1868; it's not open to the public, but you can peek through the glass doors. Continue down the corridor of the main building and exit right through the gardens. Directly opposite is the entrance to the 19th-century arcade of **Galerie Vivienne ❼**; the Galerie Colbert is perpendicular to the right. The belle epoque Grand Colbert restaurant is located here, and the tea salon in the Galerie Vivienne, A Priory Thé, is good for brunch on Sundays.

🅜 See also area map pp. 160–161
► Café de la Paix, Place de l'Opéra
🕒 3 hours
↔ 1.6 miles (2.6 km)
► Galerie Vivienne, Rue Vivienne
Take this walk during the day, as it explores several passageways that close around 7 p.m.

From Medieval to Modern: Haussmann's Paris

At the turn of the 19th century, France was coming to terms with the Revolution and the end of the monarchy, and was about to embark on an industrial revolution that would transform its society and alter the city almost beyond recognition.

Impact of the Industrial Revolution

The development of steam-powered trains, iron wheels, and tracks in the early 19th century created a railway network that linked cities. Suddenly, architects had to find a way to integrate train stations—vast, industrial buildings—into the heart of the city. New materials, including cast iron and sheet glass, solved the problem. Metal was lightweight, strong, and flexible, and glass created uniform, overhead lighting. Glass-and-iron structures were therefore perfect for museums, stations, and marketplaces. The first passageways in Paris used this type of design, as did the marketplace at Les Halles.

As industry thrived in the mid-19th century, workers from the provinces poured into the capital looking for work. Land seized from the Church and the aristocracy during the Revolution was divided up by speculators and developers, and a building boom was soon under way. By the time Louis-Napoleon Bonaparte came to power in 1848, Paris's population had doubled, and the congested city had serious housing, water supply, sanitation, and transportation problems. Inspired by the large parks and wide avenues of London, where he had lived in exile, Napoleon envisaged a new Paris. This was to be created by his prefect of the Seine, the Alsatian Baron Georges-Eugène

Georges-Eugène Haussmann studied law before entering the civil service.

Haussmann—the grandson of a Napleonic general and a longtime civil servant. Political concerns also motivated Louis-Napoleon's decision. Just a few years earlier, barricades set up in the city center by rebellious Parisians had led to the downfall of his predecessors Charles X and Louis-Philippe. Haussmann's intention was to rid the capital of the ancient, intricate warren of tiny streets and replace them with broad, clean avenues, which were much easier to control and patrol.

Haussmann's Transformations

Haussmann's plan to link the great train stations with wide avenues coincided with a changing view of the city. The newly created bourgeois classes wanted to live, work, and play in the center of the city, to enjoy the wealthy classes' privileges of theaters, museums, libraries, and department stores. Haussmann gave them what they wanted, and more. The entire urban structure was ripped apart and remodeled. The social ramifications of this upheaval were even more brutal. Those not wealthy enough to afford apartments in the lavish new neighborhoods—political troublemakers in Napoleon's eyes—were banished to outlying areas in Paris or to the suburbs.

A major aim was to facilitate traffic flow,

which Haussmann did by opening up the area and slicing wide boulevards straight through the city (including Avenue de l'Opéra, Boulevard St.-Germain, and Boulevard Haussmann) and creating large squares, such as Place de la République. These new avenues were often designed to showcase a monument, for example, the exuberant Opéra Garnier at the end of Avenue de l'Opéra. Haussmann's sweeping vision of urban renewal was contested as Paris became a gigantic, muddy construction site.

Destruction & Renewal

With the exception of the major monuments, most of the Île de la Cité was destroyed. Entire blocks of centuries-old buildings collapsed under Haussmann's demolition crews. His methods were brutal—even unscrupulous—yet his ability to see the entire city as interlinking elements was a revolutionary new approach to city planning. Nearly 25,000 houses were destroyed, replaced by 50 boulevards and streets, 75,000 new buildings, and 3 new parks: Parc Monceau, Parc Montsouris, and Parc des Buttes-Chaumont. Sewers, sidewalks, schools, hospitals, markets, and new parks went in. The new streets were lined with Haussmannian buildings, distinguished by their coherence and architectural unity (a result of strict building codes that defined every architectural element from overhangs to door widths). Haussmann also reorganized the political structure of the city, creating a town hall for each arrondissement. In just 17 years, he remodeled the entire city—a phenomenally expensive project that, for better or for worse, transformed Paris from a filthy warren of medieval streets to a modern, functioning metropolis.

Haussmann's encompassing vision of a city of broad avenues is particularly clear from above.

More Places to Visit on Les Grands Boulevards

Other Passages & Galleries

Described as "human aquariums," the glass-roofed passages and galleries of Paris run from north to south off Les Grands Boulevards, linking one area to the next. The arcades allowed shoppers to browse without fear of being splashed by mud from passing vehicles. Although there are now only about 20 left, more than 100 existed in the early 19th century.

Passage Brady: Passage Brady is a passage to India and South Asia, featuring exotic spices, fruits, vegetables, and inexpensive restaurants.

🄼 Map p. 161 ✉ Between 46 rue du Faubourg-St.-Denis and 43 rue du Faubourg St.-Martin 🚇 Métro: Château d'Eau

Passage des Panoramas: This is the first gaslit passage and second oldest arcade in Paris. (The Passage du Caire, with its three heads of Hathor reflecting the Egyptomania following Napoleon's Egyptian campaigns, is the oldest.) Opened in 1800, the Passage des Panoramas is named after the giant, circular trompe l'oeil "panorama" paintings (such as those by the American Robert Fulton) of Rome, London, and other world capitals, which once decorated the entrance. It branches off into a labyrinth of arcades—Galerie St.-Marc, Galerie des Variétés, and Galerie Feydeau. Note the Stern Engraving Company's (founded 1840) impressive store sign (No. 47) and the Napoleon III decor of the L'Arbre à Cannelle tea salon.

🄼 Map p. 161 ✉ Entrances at 11 boulevard Montmartre and 10 rue St.-Marc 🚇 Métro: Grands Boulevards

Passage Jouffroy: Adjacent to the Musée Grevin, this busy passage has storefronts containing miniatures, handcrafted toys, collector walking canes with ivory heads of dogs and lions, tea salons, and bistros; the continuing Passage Verdeau has books and lithographs.

🄼 Map p. 161 ✉ 12 boulevard Montmartre 🚇 Métro: Grands Boulevards

Musée Grévin

The Musée Grévin (wax museum) had a great impact in 1882—an age devoid of television or media images—as it enabled people to discover what celebrities looked like.

Figures now include Serge Gainsbourg, Johnny Hallyday, President Barack Obama, and historic figures like Charlemagne, Napoleon III, and Marat, whose stabbed effigy lies in the actual bathtub in which he was killed.

Don't miss the Palais des Mirages sound-and-light show (held at regular intervals throughout the day), first featured at the Paris Universal Exposition of 1900. It's a kaleidoscope of images, music, and sound effects. www.musee-grevin.com

🄼 Map p. 161 ✉ 10 boulevard Montmartre ☎ 01 47 70 85 05; 💲 €€€€ 🚇 Métro: Grands Boulevards

---

EXPERIENCE:
A Night at the Ballet

Fine wine, fine food, and fine clothing may all be hallmarks of Parisian culture, but for the full cultural experience, visitors should not pass up a trip to the **Paris Opera Ballet** (www.operadeparis .fr) at the glittering Opéra Garnier (see p. 162). This is the company, after all, that invented the five basic ballet positions. With more than 150 dancers and a sizeable budget, the ballet puts on a lavish show, presenting not only traditional ballets but works by such newer choreographers as Trisha Brown and Pina Bausch.

Where monuments, museums, and ministries occupy former aristocratic mansions with a quiet elegance

Tour Eiffel & Les Invalides

The Musée du Quai Branly

Tour Eiffel & Les Invalides

Extending west of St.-Germain-des-Prés, the elegant 7th arrondissement—a former haven of aristocratic mansions, many of which are now government buildings and embassies— prides itself on its wealth of museums and on the greatest tourist site of them all, the Eiffel Tower.

In the early 17th century, this area was a large expanse of mostly empty land; it was far from the city center and very hard to reach. The Pont Royal, constructed in 1689 to replace the 1632 Pont Rouge footbridge, linked Rue du Bac on the Left Bank to the Jardin des Tuileries (see p. 137), thus providing easier access to the Right Bank.

The 18th century ushered in a new era of development for this neighborhood as nobles returned to Paris. Many of their former mansions are now embassies and government ministries, including the magnificent Palais-Bourbon, built for the Duchesse du Bourbon and now the home of the Assemblée Nationale (see p. 176); and the beautiful Hôtel Matignon at 57 rue de Varenne, the official residence of the prime minister. The former Hôtel Biron at 77 rue de Varenne is today the Musée Rodin (see pp. 178–179), where you can visit the artist's former studio or enjoy a stroll through the gardens.

The other major museum is the Musée d'Orsay (see pp. 180–184), which is devoted to 19th-century art and holds some of the world's best known Impressionist paintings. Next door to the Orsay is the little known Musée de la Légion d'Honneur, displaying a collection of the red-rosette decorations instituted by Napoleon. France's famous emperor is forever linked to the neighborhood, as his ashes are enthroned under the gilded dome of Les Invalides, originally built by Louis XIV (see p. 177). The world's most famous monument, the Eiffel Tower (see pp. 172–173), soars 1,051 feet (320 m) above the grassy expanse of the Champ de Mars (see p. 174), on the western edge of the neighborhood.

The Y-shaped UNESCO Building behind the École Militaire (see p. 174) was considered revolutionary when inaugurated in 1958. A giant Calder mobile and a Henry Moore sculpture, "Silhouette," adorn the esplanade outside, while works by Karel Appel, Jean Arp, Matta, and Picasso are inside. Isamu Noguchi designed the lovely Japanese Zen garden, restored in 1998.

There are a few places with a more human scale—for example, the street market on Rue Cler is lined with exquisite upscale shops, and the entrance to

Tour Eiffel

PASSERELLE DEBILLY

QUAI BRANLY

5

PONT D'IÉNA

Seine

AVENUE DE

CHAMP DE MARS

PARC DU CHAMP DE MARS

QUAI BRANLY

PONT DE BIR HAKEIM

1

AVE. J. DE CHAMP DE MARS

AVENUE DE SUFFREN

Bir Hakeim

BLVD. DE GRENELLE

Dupleix

Paris

la Motte Picquet Grenelle

Seine

la Motte Picquet Grenelle

Area of map detail

29 avenue Rapp nearby is one of Paris's best examples of art nouveau architecture. For a subterranean view of the city, visit the famous Égouts (sewers; see p. 72), the entrance to which is on Place de la Résistance, opposite the Pont de l'Alma.

The Musée du Quai Branly, specializing in tribal arts, opened in 2006 and displays a huge collection of works moved from the Musée de l'Homme and the Musée des Arts d'Afrique et d'Océanie. ■

NOT TO BE MISSED:

The sparkling Tour Eiffel (on the hour, after dark until 2 a.m.) 172–173

A picnic on the Champ de Mars 174

Unusual art at the Musée du Quai Branly 175

The Musée Rodin and its exquisite garden 178–179

Impressionists at the Musée d'Orsay 180–184

❶ 29 avenue Rapp ❷ Les Égouts
❸ Rue Cler ❹ Hôtel Matignon
❺ Musée du Quai Branly

Tour Eiffel

Parisians typically greet any new monument in their urban landscape with a mixture of horror, criticism, and public dismay for a few years, after which it becomes a cherished national symbol. The Eiffel Tower is a perfect example.

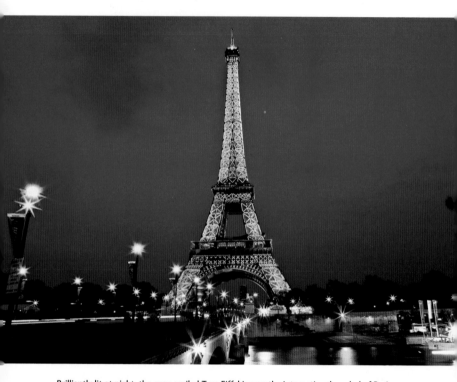

Brilliantly lit at night, the once-reviled Tour Eiffel is now the international symbol of Paris.

In 1887, Gustave Eiffel's cast-iron monument design was selected to showcase the 1889 Universal Exposition celebrating the centennial of the French Revolution. He used the same techniques for construction as in his bridges in France and abroad: All 15,000 metal parts were prefabricated and numbered for assembly, and most of the 2.5 million rivets were already in place before the tower went up. His well-laid plans and technological wizardry ensured that, with 300 steelworkers toiling 7 days a week for 26 consecutive months (and without a single fatal accident), the world's tallest building was completed just 7 days before the exhibition opened.

The Eiffel Tower was the largest and most innovative structure of its time, sending a clear message that France and French engineers intended to lead the world into the

20th century. Some critics, however, were less than enthusiastic, calling it "the hollow candlestick" and "a disgusting column of bolts and sheet metal." Guy de Maupassant was so distressed at the sight of it that he ate in its second-floor Le Jules Verne restaurant, claiming it was the only place in town he couldn't see it. Although it was slated for demolition 20 years after the exposition closed, it was unexpectedly saved by the invention of radio (or wireless) transmission, as its height made it an unrivaled setting for an antenna.

The tower offers a superb view that extends up to 45 miles (73 km) on a clear day. Ticket price varies, depending on how high you want to go and whether you take the elevator: You can walk up to the second platform. You can save time by buying tickets online, up to a day in advance, but be prepared for lines even for ticketholders. If you're willing to take the stairs to the first or second platforms, you won't have as long to wait

INSIDER TIP:

The best time to take in the view from the Eiffel Tower is late afternoon or sunset. Bring a windbreaker in spring and fall—it gets chilly on top.

—GILLES MINGASSON
National Geographic photographer

(but you'll need to be in decent physical shape to make it up the 704 steps to the second level). To go to the top (which costs more), pick up a second elevator at the second level.

The tower's nearly seven million annual visitors rarely include Parisians, who often snub it as the ultimate in kitsch, but the one-star Le Jules Verne restaurant (see p. 253) is gradually luring them back. It's expensive, but has a wonderful view and excellent cuisine. ■

Tour Eiffel

- Map p. 170
- Champ de Mars
- 01 44 11 23 23
- €€–€€€
- Métro: Bir Hakeim
  RER: Champs de Mars–Tour Eiffel

www.tour-eiffel.fr

Restaurants Open on Sunday

Parisian chefs like to relax on the weekend, so getting a good meal on a Sunday night can be a problem. Here are a few exceptions to the rule: In the Eiffel Tower itself, the pricey but stunning **Le Jules Verne** (€€€€€, *tel 01 45 55 61 44, www.lejulesverne-paris.com*); close to the Champ de Mars, **La Fontaine de Mars** (€€€, *129 rue St.- Dominique, 75007, tel 01 47 05 46 44*), a high-quality traditional bistro where President Barack Obama and his wife, Michelle, ate on a visit to Paris in 2009; in St.-Germain-des-Prés,

top chef Yves Camdeborde's excellent **Comptoir du Relais** (€€€, *9 carrefour de l'Odéon, 75006, tel 01 44 27 07 97*); in the Marais, the **Café des Musées** (€€, *49 rue de Turenne, 75003, tel 01 42 72 96 17*), with fine food for very reasonable prices, or **Glou** (€€, *101 rue Vieille du Temple, 75003, tel 01 42 74 44 32*), a trendy restaurant popular with young people; and in the 11th arrondissement, **Astier** (€€, *44 rue Jean Pierre Timbaud, 75011, tel 01 43 57 16 35*), a well-loved bistro with a wood-paneled interior and tasty food.

Champp de Mars & École Militaire

The Champ de Mars spreads out like an immense green carpet to the base of the Eiffel Tower; it actually predates the tower by 140 years. Today, it is a pleasant expanse of open grass, where children play soccer and throw frisbees, and families relax.

The Champ de Mars stretches down to the École Militaire.

École Militaire

🅰 Map p. 171

✉ École Militaire, avenue de la Motte Picquet

🚇 Métro: École Militaire
RER: Champ de Mars–Tour Eiffel

The Champ de Mars was initially laid out as a parade ground for the École Militaire, a military school founded to educate members of the impoverished nobility. Young Napoleon Bonaparte spent a year at the school (1784–1785).

The first Bastille Day was celebrated here on July 14, 1790, when crowds gathered to watch Louis XVI pay allegiance to the new constitution (see pp. 26–28). In the late 18th century, the half-mile-long Champ de Mars was transformed from parade ground to playground when the sport of horse racing was introduced from England, and it remained a racecourse until 1855.

French city planners have always had a penchant for majestic vistas, and one of the best is from the École Militaire (not open to the public), across the Champ de Mars toward the Eiffel Tower, with the outstretched wings of the Palais de Chaillot in the background. The well-manicured lawns also make a good spot for a picnic after climbing the Eiffel Tower. ∎

Festival of the Supreme Being

In June 1794, the Champ de Mars was the site for one of the Revolutionary era's spectacles, the Festival of the Supreme Being. The festival was the brainchild of Maximilien de Robespierre, who opposed the more extreme "cult of reason" movement of the Revolution. In a speech at the Festival, Robespierre declared, "The Author of Nature has bound all mortals by a boundless chain of love and happiness." The following month, he and his comrades were guillotined by a populace that blamed him for the bloody Reign of Terror.

Musée du Quai Branly

The Musée du Quai Branly, located on the Seine, opened in June 2006. Its vast collection, comprising 3,500 pieces from the Musée de l'Homme and the Musée National des Arts d'Afrique et d'Océanie, showcases ethnic art from all over the world. Jean Nouvel designed the glass-fronted structure, which echoes the shadow of the neighboring Eiffel Tower and is surrounded by a park of paths, a pool, and 200 trees.

The collection, much of it gathered by 19th-century travelers, includes stone sculptures from Sumatra, artifacts connected with initiation rites and ancestor worship from New Guinea, and aboriginal art from

INSIDER TIP:

Visit in spring to admire the Musée du Quai Branly's unique and beautiful garden.

—CHRISTEL CHERQAOUI
*National Geographic books
promotion director*

Australia. In the large collection of **African arts,** you'll find furniture, embroidery, wooden vessels, pottery, and jewelry. The **French-Indochina collection** explores farming, Buddhism, and popular religious cults.

In the **textiles collection** are pre-Columbian weavings from Paracas, painted skins from the North American plains, Bengal embroidery, and other sumptuous examples of ethnographic materials. Elsewhere, a huge number of **musical instruments,** including drums and idiophones—rigid bodies made to vibrate by concussion, shaking, scraping—are housed

in a transparent Glass Tower. A multimedia system plays the songs of the nomads of Niger, the vocal polyphonies of the Pygmies of Cameroon, the processional music of Nepal, and more.

Adding to the richness of the displays, the stories behind the artifacts are evoked by paintings, sculptures, travelers' notebooks, and watercolors painted by sailors at the turn of the 19th century (including Paul Gauguin). ■

Musée du Quai Branly

🅰 Map p. 170
✉ Rue de l'Université or Quai Branly
☎ 01 56 61 70 00
🕐 Closed Mon.
💲 €€–€€€
Ⓜ Métro: Iéna, Alma-Marceau

www.quaibranly.fr

Carvings at the Musée du Quai Branly

Assemblée Nationale

After Louis XIV's death in 1715, the many nobles who had followed the king to Versailles were delighted to return to Paris at the end of his 72-year-long rule, and several moved to this area, building ornate mansions and palaces, including one that became the Assemblée Nationale.

Assemblée Nationale

- 🅰 Map p. 171
- ✉ 126 rue de l'Université
- ☎ 01 40 63 60 00
- 🕐 Individuals can visit during the Journées du Patrimoine.
- Ⓜ Métro: Assemblée Nationale

www.assemblee-nationale.fr

The lower house of the French Parlement (Assemblée Nationale) is housed in the Palais-Bourbon; the Upper House (Sénat) is in the Palais du Luxembourg (see p. 82). Visitors can view the Hémisphère (where political debates take place) and the library, decorated by Delacroix's "History of Civilization."

The Palais-Bourbon, which houses the 577 elected deputies of the Assemblée Nationale (the government's legislative body), was built between 1722 and 1728 for the Duchesse de Bourbon; she ceded part of her property to her lover, the Marquis de Lassay, who constructed the magnificent Hôtel de Lassay next door.

The government confiscated the buildings in 1795, making them the seat of the elected assembly. Such extensive remodeling was done, including adding a neoclassical facade and a semicircular Council Chamber to replace the formal reception rooms, that only the courtyard of the original gracious mansion remains. Usually closed to the public, the Assemblée can be visited during the Journées du Patrimoine (Heritage Days, in September). ∎

INSIDER TIP:

In Paris, what you're holding in your hands isn't a menu, it's called *la carte*. A *menu* is a set lunch or dinner.

—ANNE RANDERSON
National Geographic contributor

The Assemblée's Inner Workings

The political leanings of a deputy in the French National Assembly can be read in a glance at the "hémicycle," as their chamber is called: Ever since the French Revolution, the left-wing deputies have sat to the left (from the vantage point of the president, who sits facing them) and the right-wing to the right.

The Assembly, located in the Palais Bourbon facing the Seine, is the lower house of the French Parliament. The upper house, the Senate, is located in the Luxembourg Gardens. The Assembly's 577 deputies are elected for five-year terms from metropolitan France and the French overseas departments and territories through a two-round system (if no candidate has a majority, the two top vote-winners face off in a second round of elections).

Each constituency is represented by one deputy. The French president has the power to dissolve the Assembly and call new elections (if he has not done this in the past year), but rarely does so. The Assembly, in turn, has the right to censure the government, but it has done so only once since 1958.

Les Invalides

The shining dome of the Église St.-Louis-des-Invalides is visible from all over Paris, marking the expansive collection of military museums and monuments that stands just off the Champ de Mars. Most famously, it denotes the final resting place of Napoleon I.

Originally built by Louis XIV as a hospital for his veterans, Les Invalides comprises the largest single complex of monuments in Paris, including the Musée de l'Armée, the Musée des Plans-Reliefs, the Musée de l'Ordre de la Libération, and the Église St.-Louis-des-Invalides.

After Versailles, Les Invalides ranks as the most important architectural project of Louis XIV's reign. In 1670 the king commissioned Libéral Bruant to build a military hospice on the far western edge of the Faubourg St.-Germain, where poor, infirm soldiers and aging veterans could be kept. Originally intended for 1,500 invalids, by 1690 some 6,000 men were clamoring to enter, and monarchs throughout Europe began modeling their own military hospitals on it.

The dome of Les Invalides looms over military museums.

Napoleon's Tomb

The dome of the church at Les Invalides, designed by Jules Hardouin-Mansart and completed in 1706, is a gleaming landmark in the Parisian landscape. What was designed as a royal chapel became an imperial mausoleum in 1840 when the body of Napoleon I was returned to France from Saint Helena. In 1861, his ashes were laid to rest in a porphyry tomb, inside a glass-topped crypt in the center of the dome.

Others interred in Les Invalides include Claude Rouget de Lisle, composer of *La Marseillaise*.

Military Museums

Three museums are housed within the grounds of Les Invalides. The **Musée de l'Armée** is one of the most complete military museums in the world. Its collection ranges from antiquity to World War II, including Napoleonic souvenirs. The **Musée des Plans-Reliefs** is an intriguing museum of three-dimensional scale models of fortified towns, a collection that began in 1668. The **Musée de l'Ordre de la Libération** honors those who fought for France during World War II. ■

Les Invalides

- Map p. 171
- Esplanade des Invalides
- 01 44 42 37 72
- Closed Jan. 1, May 1, Nov. 1, Dec. 25
- €€
- Métro: Varenne, La Tour Maubourg

www.invalides.org

Musée Rodin

Auguste Rodin's sculptures fill the luxurious gardens and interiors of the 18th-century Hôtel Biron, the most charming and intimate spot in this otherwise grandiose neighborhood on the Rue de Varenne.

Rodin's "The Thinker" holds a place of honor in the gardens.

Rodin is generally credited as the founding father of modern sculpture. A self-taught artist, he vehemently rejected academic conventions throughout his life.

Born into poverty, Rodin worked in obscurity on public monuments for years. He was almost 38 when his first important work, "The Age of Bronze," was exhibited in 1878 amid great controversy. It was so perfectly modeled that critics accused him of taking plaster casts directly from his model. He was finally vindicated, and the ensuing publicity catapulted him into the public eye.

Two years later he received a commission for "The Gates of Hell" (a work never completed in his lifetime), and by the time he had reached his mid-40s, he had achieved international fame. Yet nearly all of his major works created controversy, from "The Burghers of Calais" (1895) to his statue of Victor Hugo (1909), shocking his patrons with their realism, power, and emotional content. His statue of Balzac, wearing his legendary dressing gown, was considered so inappropriate that it was initially refused by the Société des Gens de Lettres (an institution of literary figures), and it remained hidden from public view for 41 years. In 1939, "Balzac" was finally placed at the Carrefour Vavin in Paris, where it now stands.

Camille Claudel

Rodin said of Camille Claudel: "I showed her where to find gold, but the gold she found was truly hers." She came to Rodin's studio as a student in 1883 and soon became his model and lover. Her face appears in some of Rodin's best work, including "The Kiss," "The Gates of Hell," and "Fugit Amor." Their liaison lasted through 1898, when it became clear that Rodin would never break his long-term relationship with Rose Beuret.

Claudel retreated into madness, living alone in her studio on the Île St.-Louis. She was interned in a mental institution in 1913, where she remained until her death in 1943. In his will, Rodin stipulated that her work be exhibited in his museum, which has such intensely emotional pieces as "Sakountala" (perhaps her most important work), "Waltz," and "L'Age Mûr," created during her separation from Rodin.

Hôtel Biron

The rococo-style Hôtel Biron was completed in 1730, and, after the Revolution, it housed the Russian Embassy and then a religious school. By 1905, it was in a dilapidated state, and its future uncertain.

INSIDER TIP:

The gardens are a destination in themselves and a lovely place of respite for visitors with tired feet.

—PATRICIA DANIELS
National Geographic contributing editor

During negotiations, a few artists were allowed to use the building as a temporary studio—Austrian poet Rainer Maria Rilke (Rodin's secretary at the time), Henri Matisse, Jean Cocteau, and lastly, Rodin, who moved there in 1908. This situation became permanent when the State purchased the property in 1911. In the early

20th century, at the height of his career, Rodin's dream of creating a museum of his work in the Hôtel Biron was approved by the State, but he died before his museum was officially inaugurated.

Rodin donated all of his own work to the State, as well as his collection of paintings and Greek and Roman sculptures. All of his major pieces are represented here—"The Thinker," "The Walking Man," "The Burghers of Calais," and others, plus a number of studies. (Rodin's home and studio, in Meudon, also contains thousands of his terra-cotta and plaster models.)

Gardens

No fewer than 27 bronzes and 40 marbles by Rodin are scattered around the Hotel Biron's lovely grounds. The 7-acre (3 ha) gardens are divided into a rose garden to the north (including the Rodin rose) and other plantings to the south. You can visit the gardens separately (*9:30–5:00 Oct.–Mar., 9:30–6:45 April–Sept., closed Mon., €*). ■

Musée Rodin

- Map p. 171
- 79 rue de Varenne
- 01 44 18 61 10
- Closed Mon.
- €€–€€€
- Métro: Varenne, Invalides

www.musee-rodin.fr

Rodin's Home & Studio

- Villa des Brillants, 19 avenue Auguste Rodin, Meudon (on the southern edge of Paris)
- 01 41 14 35 00
- Open Fri.–Sun. April–Sept.
- €

Musée d'Orsay

Although the Impressionist paintings are probably the greatest draw for visitors to the Musée d'Orsay, the museum also features decorative arts, photography, and the performing arts.

The grand Musée d'Orsay began its existence as a train station.

Musée d'Orsay
- 🅰 Map p. 171
- ✉ 1 rue de la Légion d'Honneur
- ☎ 01 40 49 48 14
- 🕐 Closed Mon.
- 💲 €€
- 🚇 Métro: Solférino RER: Musée d'Orsay

www.musee-orsay.fr

The Musée d'Orsay's building rose from a pile of ashes. The former Palais d'Orsay, home of the Conseil d'État and the Cour des Comptes, was burned during the Commune in 1871 (see pp. 30–31). Émile Zola described the scene: "The four buildings, which surrounded the great inner courtyard, had caught fire at once; and then the oil poured down the stairs to the four corners, streaming along the steps like torrents from hell." The blackened ruins were left standing for nearly 30 years. On the eve of the Paris Universal Exposition of 1900, the government agreed to allow the Orléans Railway Company to construct a train station on the site of the ruins, providing a station that was more central than the remote Austerlitz.

The problem of integrating the train terminus with its aristocratic environment was solved in 1898 by Victor Laloux, who suggested hiding the cast-iron structure under finely cut stone. He incorporated the most up-to-date technology inside the building— elevators, ramps, luggage elevators, electric traction, and even a 370-room hotel surrounding the station along the length of Rue de Bellechasse, Rue de Lille, and part of the quay.

The station and hotel were inaugurated on July 14, 1900, and their lobby was so luxurious that the painter Edouard Detaille called it—prophetically—a "Palace of Fine Arts." Train stations around the world were modeled after Orsay, including Grand Central Terminal in New York and Union Station in Washington, D.C. For nearly 40 years, the Orsay station was the hub for traffic bound for southwest France. By 1939, however, long-distance trains no longer stopped here, as the platforms were too short for the longer modern trains.

The building was then put to a number of different uses, becoming a mailing center during World War II, a holding center for returning prisoners of war, a film set (featured in Orson Welles's adaptation of Kafka's *Trial* in 1962), and a temporary auction house. In the 1960s, plans to destroy the building and replace it with a modern hotel complex had already been approved when critics lobbied to have it classified as a historical monument. It was saved in 1977 when President Valéry Giscard d'Estaing proposed transforming it into a museum devoted to all forms of 19th-century art (from 1848 to 1915), thus filling a historical gap between the collections of the Louvre Museum and the Centre Pompidou.

The ACT architecture group transformed the building itself, and a team of architects under Italian Gae Aulenti worked on its interiors. The masterful result incorporates Laloux's original cast-iron pillars and stucco decoration in a space suitable for the museum's requirements. The huge, luminous central entrance hall is divided by stone partitions and lined with galleries.

The Musée d'Orsay was officially inaugurated on December 1, 1986, by President François Mitterrand and it became the new home for Impressionist works that had been displayed at the Jeu de Paume. The Louvre transferred Salon paintings and works by artists born after 1820, and Post-Impressionist works came from the Musée National d'Art Moderne.

The Collections

The period covered by the Musée d'Orsay is important in the history of contemporary art. Academic conventions were overturned, new themes were introduced, and a radical approach to painting and

EXPERIENCE:
Kid Stuff at Museums

Many Paris museums have special activities for children, and even spaces where the kids can be parked while the parents visit an exhibition. The **Musée d'Orsay** hosts guided tours for children *(www .musee-orsay.fr/en/visit/individuals/tours)* and special activities in the summer. The **Centre Georges Pompidou** (see p. 96) has a children's gallery and special workshops. Its Studio 13/16 offers teenagers a space where they can participate in workshops or just hang out with friends. The **Louvre** (see p. 124) offers guided tours, workshops, and tours with a storyteller for children.

photography regarding color and composition appeared. The museum is organized in broad chronological sequences.

Ground Floor: The period represented here, from 1848 to 1870, is less known than that of the Impressionists, yet it was these artists who broke new ground for the generations to come. At that time, the yearly Salon (an official exhibition of art sponsored by the French government), with its staid and predictable historical and mythological paintings, was the standard by which artists were measured.

Ingres and Delacroix, who belonged to the earlier years of the century, continued as leading figures, and several of their later works (in the first rooms to the right of the entrance) illustrate the transition in academic painting. Thomas Couture and Alexandre

Cabanel exemplified the languid, classical, and uncontroversial subjects of the *pompiers* (as in "pomp" and "pompous"), although they were highly regarded in their day. To the left of the entrance are landscapes from the Barbizon school (Jean-Baptiste Camille Corot, Charles Daubigny, and Théodore Rousseau), whose work was based on an idealization of nature and a rejection of academic convention. Jean-François Millet's painting "Gleaners" perhaps best represents this humanistic spirit.

Honoré Daumier was a major figure in realism, the movement that opposed the *pompier* style. Although better known as a cartoonist, his real masterpieces (on display) are the 26 painted clay busts that ruthlessly caricatured contemporary politicians. The Realist leader was Gustave Courbet, who portrayed scenes from contemporary life with an unsentimental yet sympathetic eye (as in his "Burial at Ornans"). His most sensational painting, the sexually explicit "Origins of the World," only recently acquired, was so realistic that it had never before been shown in public.

This floor also exhibits works painted before 1870 by Impressionist artists, including Édouard Manet, whose "Olympia" caused a scandal at the 1865 Salon des Refusés (created for those turned down by the official Salon). However, it was his subject matter—criticized as an obscene portrayal of a prostitute—that shocked the critics, not his technique, and although sympathetic to other Impressionists, Manet remained

"Bathers" is one of many Cézanne paintings in the museum.

aloof from them. Works by Monet, Degas, and Fréderic Bazille illustrate their early experiments in solving the problems of light and shadow, and their work pioneered a new vision of painting.

The central aisle emphasizes 19th-century sculpture in the neo-classical tradition; the most interesting are those by Jean-Baptiste Carpeaux, whose "Dance" for the facade of the Opéra Garnier was called "an offense to public morals."

Upper Floor: Escalators go straight to the upper galleries, where room after room contains treasures from the years 1874 to 1886—a period that revolutionized painting as artists began seeing in a new way. After the Prussian Wars (1870–1871), Renoir, Monet, and Pissarro, along with Berthe Morisot and Alfred Sisley, banded together in opposition to the official Salons. The first exhibition by the Impressionist painters, held in 1874, was where the term "Impressionism" was coined, when critic Louis Leroy used it to mock Monet's painting, "Impression: Sunrise" (now in the Marmottan-Monet Museum, see p. 157). The artists proudly adopted the name themselves, continuing to exhibit until 1886.

The first gallery on this floor exhibits the Moreau-Nélaton Collection, dominated by Manet's "Déjeuner sur l'Herbe," the masterpiece of the 1863 Salon des Refusés. The next rooms are devoted to Manet and James Whistler and to the spread of Impressionism, with works by Degas ("Blue Dancers"), Monet ("Gare St.-Lazare"), Renoir ("Le Bal du Moulin de la Galette"), and others.

Paul Cézanne's works are displayed in a room in the upper gallery. Note especially "The Card Players" and "Apples and Oranges." He was less interested

in the Impressionist experiments with light, working instead on structure, color, and composition. Ridiculed by critics, Cézanne was ultimately vindicated as the forerunner of 20th-century painting; both Picasso and Matisse were heavily influenced by his work.

Cézanne appears again in the room devoted to Dr. Gachet's collection (Gachet was doctor and friend to Cézanne) in the Bellechasse Gallery, which includes such masterpieces as van Gogh's "Église d'Auvers-sur-Oise," "Portrait of the Artist," and "l'Arlésienne."

The innovative tendencies of the next generation—Gauguin and the Pont-Aven painters Odilon Redon and Paul Signac—are exhibited in the following rooms of the Bellechasse Gallery; these include

Gauguin's "La Belle Angèle," "On the Beach," and "The White Horse"; Signac's "The Red Buoy"; and Redon's "Decorative Panels."

Middle Floor: It may seem that the galleries on this floor hold solely genre works and the monumental decorations of the Third Empire, but they actually encompass a wide range of painting, decorative arts, and sculpture, with nearly a quarter of the sculpture terrace devoted to Rodin. Several works are on loan from the nearby Musée Rodin (see pp. 178–179), including the plaster versions of "The Gates of Hell" and "Balzac." Commissioned for a museum that was never built, "The Gates of Hell" was based on Dante's "Divine Comedy."

The nabi painters—Pierre Bonnard, Édouard Vuillard, and Maurice Denis—occupy several rooms on the south side of this level. They aimed to establish painting as a decorative art for embellishing day-to-day existence.

Several rooms are also dedicated to the art nouveau movement that spread throughout Europe under various names—Modern Style, Jugendstil, and Arte Joven—in the late 19th century. Objects of all kinds, from chairs to furniture, glassware, and stained glass, illustrate what was a radically new approach to design at the time. One of the most beautiful examples is the Charpentier Dining Room (circa 1900), a luscious interior of mahogany, oak, and poplar, with the characteristic floral decoration.

Photography

The museum also has several thousand images from the earliest days of photography. These are presented in rotation in exhibition rooms: Dossier 3 (ground floor) and Dossier 5 (upper floor). Interesting temporary exhibitions treat various themes or retrospectives of little-known 19th-century artists.

The museum hosts films, lectures, and lunchtime concerts in its auditorium. Special joint tickets give discounted access to the Musée de l'Orangerie or the Musée Rodin; the Orsay ticket will also give you reduced rates at the Opéra Garnier or the Gustave Moreau Museum. ∎

Salon des Refusés

Today, crowds flock to the Musée d'Orsay to see the works of Édouard Manet, Claude Monet, Vincent van Gogh, and dozens of other artists whose works are worth multiple millions. It is well known that van Gogh only sold one painting in his lifetime, but he was not the only one who struggled. At the beginning of their creators' careers, works by Manet, Whistler, Monet, and many other now-famous artists were rejected by the jurors of the official Salon, the gateway to success for artists at the time. In reaction, some of them staged the Salons des Refusés, which was even sponsored by the French government in 1863. Monet and other Impressionists also held alternative salons to show their work.

A neighborhood of narrow, sinuous streets snaking downward toward Pigalle and, in the heart of it all, the dome of Sacré-Coeur

Montmartre

Sculpture at the Musée de Montmartre

Montmartre

There is no other place in Paris quite like Montmartre. High on a hill (known to Parisians as the "Butte"), it has a unique village atmosphere, encompassing both Pigalle's neon lights and the lyrical, winding streets and charming houses just steps away. Music, art, and wine—along with a touch of the licentious and an irreverence for authority and tradition— have all contributed to the myth of Montmartre.

The Butte Montmartre has been a place of worship since earliest history: The Druids celebrated their priestly rites here, and it was also the site of a Roman temple, probably dedicated to Mercury. This area has escaped real estate development largely because the ground is riddled with tunnels from old quarries, where gypsum and limestone have been mined since Roman times.

Montmartre's hill was also punctuated with Christian edifices, such as the Royal Abbey of St.-Denis, constructed in 1136 by Louis VI and his wife, Adelaide de Savoy, in honor of the martyred saint (see p. 21). Its lands extended south into the present-day 9th arrondisse- ment and north toward the abbey. After the Revolution, the abbey's lands were sold and its buildings dismantled, except the Romanesque St.-Pierre de Montmartre Church (see p. 190), which continued to be the villagers' favored place of worship even after work on the Basilica of Sacré-Coeur (see p. 190) began in 1876. The villagers' long history of independence was demonstrated when, infuriated by Thiers's capitulation to the Prussians in 1871, they refused to hand over the cannon guarding the city, setting off a series of events that produced the Commune (see p. 30). The generals dispatched by Thiers to recover the cannon were killed, an act that would be commemo- rated on a plaque behind the basilica (on Rue Chevalier-de-la-Barre).

Montmartre's social structure was trans- formed when trainloads of people from the provinces came to the capital during the indus- trial revolution to look for work and ended up living in this inexpensive neighborhood. The

wall of the Fermiers Généraux, or toll road, where the present-day Place Pigalle is, effec- tively cut Montmartre off from the city. Incom- ing goods were levied on Pigalle's tollgate; therefore, outside the walls, wine—produced in abundance on the hills of Montmartre—was cheaper and the demand was heavy. The village was incorporated into the City of Paris in 1860 as the 18th arrondissement.

By the late 19th century, the area's numerous cabarets, brothels, and nefarious underworld activities had earned Montmartre an enduring reputation for depravity that inevi- tably attracted artists, writers, and bourgeois Parisians in search of new thrills. Artists of all types, from Eugène Delacroix, Hector Berlioz, and Vincent van Gogh to contemporary paint- ers, have come to the Butte for its charm, light, and, in the past, low rents.

0 |————| 600 meters
0 |————| 600 yards

① Lapin Agile ② Allée des Brouillards ③ Place des Abbesses ④ Folies-Bergère ⑤ Place du Tertre

Montmartre today is much as it has always been: a mix of romance, poetry, sex, and commercialism. The Moulin Rouge (see pp. 192–193) is still packed every night, and the Place du Tertre is inundated with portrait painters and the smell of crêpes from the food stands. But glimpses of a more lyrical era still survive in the labyrinth of steep, tree-lined streets encircling the Butte. From its vantage point, the busy capital below seems miles away. ■

Paris

Area of map detail

A Walk Through Montmartre

This bohemian area of Paris may have lost some of its romantic appeal, but there are times when a stroll around the quaint old streets can take you back a hundred years or more to an age when it was a renowned artists' quarter.

Sacré-Coeur rises over a Montmartre street.

NOT TO BE MISSED:

Place Pigalle • Sacré-Coeur • Place du Tertre • St.-Pierre de Montmartre Church • Allée des Brouillards

---

As the steps and steep streets may make this rather a strenuous walk, another option is to take the small train that leaves Place Blanche (opposite the Moulin Rouge at 82 boulevard de Clichy) for a 40-minute guided tour of the Butte, although some of the sites below can only be reached on foot.

Begin at the **Place Pigalle** (Métro: Pigalle), whose late-19th-century dance halls and cabarets lured Parisians in search of flash and flesh. A less classy ambience still reigns among the garish, neon-lit sex shops and seedy boulevards.

Walk east on Boulevard de Clichy and turn left up Rue des Martyrs, the street once climbed by many illustrious Christian pilgrims on their way to the Basilica of Sacré-Coeur. Turn right to reach 9 rue Yvonne le Tac. Here Saint Denis was supposedly beheaded in the third century

(see p. 21) and Ignatius of Loyola founded the order of the Jesuits in 1534. At the end of Rue Yvonne Le Tac, turn right on Rue des Trois Frères, then left at the Place Charles Dullin, past the **Théâtre de l'Atelier** (1822).

Continue to Rue de Steinkerque, over which Sacré-Coeur looms, and turn left up the street. The streets and the nearby Place St.-Pierre are lined with shops offering the best prices and widest selection of fabrics in Paris. From here, the only way to go is up—climb the steps that zigzag up the middle or the set of steps just past the funicular, or if you prefer to ride, take the funicular off to the left side (fare: one Métro ticket).

After enjoying the view and visiting **Sacré-Coeur** basilica ❶ (see p. 190), follow the tourists heading up Rue Azais to **Place du Tertre** (see p. 191), an unavoidable tourist stop on any tour of Montmartre. Take the time to explore the church of **St.-Pierre de Montmartre** ❷ (see p. 190), one of Paris's few remaining Romanesque churches.

Walk past the church down Rue du Mont Cenis (past Rue St.-Rustique) to explore the real charms of old Montmartre. Turn left on Rue Cortot to reach the **Musée de Montmartre** ❸ at No. 12 (see p. 191). Turn right on Rue des Saules to see Montmartre's last remaining vineyard, whose harvest festival takes place on the first Saturday in October. Straight ahead is the legendary **Lapin Agile** ❹ (22 rue des Saules, tel 01 46 06 85 87), the cabaret whose regulars once included Picasso and Modigliani.

Backtrack up the hill and turn right onto Rue de l'Abreuvoir. The postcard-perfect, pink house at No. 2 was immortalized by the painter Maurice Utrillo. Continue down the mysterious **Allée des Brouillards,** across the street from Renoir's onetime residence. The fountain in the nearby Square Suzanne-Buisson is reputedly where Saint Denis stopped to wash off his severed head. Go to **Avenue Junot ❺** and turn left. At No. 25 is the **Villa Léandre,** a row of impeccable houses built in 1926.

Go through the gate at No. 23 and walk down the steps to Rue Lepic. Turn left here to see one of the two remaining windmills on the Butte Montmartre—the **Moulin de la Galette ❻** of Renoir's famous painting is now a restaurant. Turn right down Rue d'Orchampt to reach **Place Émile Goudeau ❼**. Here Picasso, Max Jacob, and others lived in the Bateau-Lavoir, an old wooden warehouse, during the early 1900s.

The original building was replaced by a block of studios at 6 rue Durantin (to the right).

Continue along Rue Durantin to Rue Tholozé and turn left down the hill to No. 10. The Studio 28 Cinema made headlines in 1930 when shocked spectators pelted the screen with eggs and ink during the premiere of Luis Buñuel's classic surrealist film, *L'Age d'Or;* Buñuel's and Jean Cocteau's footprints are embedded in the hall of the cinema.

Turn left on Rue des Abbesses, where you can end the walk and rest your legs at any one of the local cafés. Or go on to the Métro at **Place des Abbesses ❽**.

> ◪ See also area map pp. 186–187
> ► Place Pigalle (Métro: Pigalle)
> ⊕ Allow 2 1/2–3 hours
> ⬌ 3 miles (4.8 km)
> ► Place des Abbesses (Métro: Abbesses)

Sacré-Coeur

Rising like a giant wedding cake in northern Paris, the Basilica of Sacré-Coeur stands on the highest point of the city and is thus the most visible of Montmartre's monuments, though one of its most recent. One of Sacré-Coeur's most striking aspects is its perpetually sparkling white stone, despite the dirt and grime of city pollution. The stone, from the Seine and Marne regions, produces a white-lime deposit when it rains.

Sacré-Coeur
- 🗺 Map p. 187
- ✉ Place du Parvis du Sacré-Coeur
- ☎ 01 53 41 89 00
- 💲 Basilica: free. Crypt and dome: €.
- Ⓜ Métro: Anvers, Abbesses, Lamarck Caulaincourt

www.sacre-coeur-montmartre.com

St.-Pierre de Montmartre
- ✉ 2 rue du Mont-Cenis
- ☎ 01 46 06 57 63
- Ⓜ Métro: Anvers, Abbesses, Lamarck Caulaincourt

The Basilica

The impetus for the construction of this Romano-Byzantine church came from the French Catholics' vow to build a basilica devoted to the Sacred Heart of Jesus after the country's humiliating defeat in the Franco-Prussian War of 1870.

Work began in 1876. The architect, Paul Abadie (a student of Eugène Viollet-le-Duc), died in 1884, and the project was completed by Lucien Magne, who added the 275-foot (84 m) campanile. Preparation of the foundations alone was an enormous engineering feat: 83 wells were dug 147 feet (45 m) deep and filled with masonry, then connected by a series of underground arches to stabilize the subsoil and compensate for quarried tunnels riddling the hillside. Twenty-eight horses were needed to draw the wagon carrying the Savoyarde bell up Montmartre's hill; one of the world's largest bells, it resonates at a high C note. Today, visitors can climb to the stained-glass gallery in the dome for a view of the church's interior.

INSIDER TIP:

Ideal for a picnic lunch, the Square de la Turlure has a magnificent view of the basilica.

—CHRISTEL CHERQAOUI
National Geographic Books promotion director

St.-Pierre de Montmartre

Residents of Montmartre continued to worship in the Church of St.-Pierre. Situated between the basilica and the Place du Tertre, this is one of the oldest churches in Paris. Open the doors of the 18th-century facade to discover the beauty of its 12th-century, Romanesque-style nave within. ∎

The white domes of Sacré-Coeur mark Paris's highest point.

Place du Tertre

The Place du Tertre and its surrounding streets are lined with souvenir shops, overpriced cafés, and portrait painters, all vying for your euros.

In the morning, before the crowds arrive, you can see traces of old Montmartre in this village square, which once housed the post-Revolution town hall. At La Mère Catherine restaurant, the word "bistro" was coined when Russian soldiers during the 1814 occupation banged on the table, shouting *"Bistro!"*—Russian for "quick."

Musée de Montmartre

The Musée de Montmartre *(12 rue Cortot, tel 01 49 25 89 37, closed Mon., €€, Métro: Lamarck Caulaincourt, www.museedemontmartre.fr)* is just behind the Place du Tertre. In the late 19th century, a number of French artists lived in this 17th-century building, including Dufy and Renoir. The museum re-creates the unique atmosphere of Montmartre's past.

Don't miss the reproduction of one of the great artistic jokes

Stalls and tourists can't erase the charm of Place du Tertre.

played on the Montmartre art scene when the author Roland Dorgelès—who despised modern art—attached a paintbrush to the tail of the donkey that belonged to the owner of the Lapin Agile cabaret. The resulting canvas, "Sunset over the Adriatic," received critical acclaim. ∎

Place du Tertre
Map pp. 187

EXPERIENCE: Connecting on the Web

For younger people (20s to 30s), who might be shy about striking up a conversation at a bistro, a great way to meet the French is to go to one of the many Thursday-night after-work parties, usually held in clubs. For an entry fee of €15–€20, you get a buffet and champagne if you arrive early, followed by dancing. Visit their websites to sign up and to get a password for reduced fees: www.urban-nights.com, www.jeudionly.fr, www.after-work-paris.com, www.before-party.com. To find like-minded French people to go out with to a film, concert, or dance class, for example, you can suggest an outing or sign up for one on *paris.onvasortir.com* (click on the British flag for English). Or try *www.meetup.com/cities/fr/paris* to join events like language exchanges and *apéros* (drinks parties).

Cabaret

Paris has continually invented and reinvented new forms of entertainment. The *cafés chantants* or *goguettes* popular during the Revolution gave way during the Second Empire and belle epoque to concert-cafés, the forerunners to the 20th-century music halls and irreverent *cabarets artistiques* launched in Montmartre at the turn of the century.

A Fine French Tradition

Talents such as balladeers Léo Ferré and Georges Brassens debuted in cabarets during the 1950s. In the 1960s, a new form of expression surfaced in the café-théâtres, which combined comedy and satire performed in close-quartered cafés (initiated by Le Royal in Montparnasse and La Vieille Grille in the Latin Quarter). The café-théâtre was responsible for launching such diverse talents as the late comedian Coluche, Gérard Depardieu, and the Théâtre du Splendide troupe (featuring Anémone and Gérard Jugnot). The tradition is alive and well today.

INSIDER TIP:

Be careful when ordering your meals in Paris: An entrée is the first course, not the main dish, called *plat principal*.

—ANNE RANDERSON
National Geographic contributor

However, the most typically French tradition in this hub of hedonism is the legendary music hall revue—a throwback to the champagne nights of the belle epoque era. The Crazy Horse Saloon *(tel 01 47 23 32 32, www.lecrazyhorseparis.com)* on Avenue George V, for instance, evolved from a Wild West-style barroom, with swinging doors and signs like "Check Your Guns Here," into a theater flaunting the wildest of risqué apparel, with features such as Betty Buttocks and Nouka Bazooka. (During the 1950s, one Crazy Horse Saloon routine featured the whip-cracking, blond dominatrix Dodo d'Hambourg, and Bertha Von Paraboum—clad merely in boots, helmet, and a swastika G-string. This made an unfortunate impression on Parisians, whose memory of German occupation was a bit too recent.)

Exoticism & Extravagance

On the Champs-Élysées, the Lido *(tel 01 40 76 56 10, www.lido.fr)* and its glittering Bluebell Girls are the closest you'll get to Las Vegas this side of the Atlantic, with extravagant megaproductions featuring lasers, video, fountains, and fire-breathing dragons. The Paradis Latin, staged in a theater designed by Gustave Eiffel, supposedly offers a traditional Parisian cabaret, driven by a feathered Latin beat.

The Folies Bergère *(tel 08 92 68 16 50, www.foliesbergere.com)*, inaugurated in 1869, is the oldest music hall; it features jugglers, wrestlers, dancers, and magicians in exotic decors. The Folies are closely associated with the legendary cabaret *artiste* Josephine Baker, but she debuted in *La Revue Nègre* at the Théâtre des Champs-Élysées in 1925. Born in St. Louis, Missouri, she was the star attraction of the Folies. Baker became a French citizen and remained in France until her death in 1975.

Moulin Rouge

We couldn't fail to mention the kitschy Moulin Rouge *(tel 01 53 09 82 82, www.moulinrouge.com)*, where today only the red windmill is original, but the feathered Doriss Girls still offer up a cancan or two. The Moulin is usually associated with the cancan (which originated in Montparnasse) due to Toulouse-Lautrec's paintings, but it is believed that it was the striptease that

The unsubtle Moulin Rouge is a staple of the Montmartre neighborhood.

actually originated here in 1893. Supposedly, during a contest between artists' models at the yearly Bal des Quat'z Arts held by the Fine Arts School students at the cabaret, one of them leaped up on a table and threw off her clothes. Outraged upon learning of this new phenomenon, the president of the Ligue Contre la Licence des Rues—the league in charge of cleaning up the streets—took the case to court. The model was arrested, sparking protests by students demanding the right to "artistic nudity." The publicity surrounding the case led to risqué sketches in neighboring cabarets as well.

Check *Pariscope* for information on cabarets, addresses, and current shows.

More Places to Visit in Montmartre

Montmartre Vineyard

The Butte was once covered with vineyards, but by the 1920s grapes were no longer harvested here. In 1929, when a vacant lot opposite the Lapin Agile was earmarked for real estate development, a group of drinking buddies came up with a plan to save the property by creating a park.

Again threatened with a building project five years later, the plotters proposed replanting the hill with vines. However, they didn't realize that the vines needed to mature for four years before producing fruit, so they gaily made plans for a harvest festival the first year. With the vines bare and the festival approaching, the good-natured but visibly incompetent group was saved when French wine growers shipped in more than 30 tons (27 tonnes) of grapes.

Today, the vineyard produces about 75 gallons (284 l) of wine each year (reputedly of dubious quality), which are auctioned off along with a painting by a local artist, with the proceeds going to charity.

Map p. 187 14 rue des Saules Métro: Lamarck Caulaincourt

Musée Gustave Moreau

Situated south of Montmartre, the Musée Gustave Moreau offers a rare glimpse into the intimate world of an artist and his workplace. It was created by and for the artist, who planned the layout and collections before his death. Considered a precursor of the surrealist movement, Moreau was a shy, financially independent painter who shunned exhibitions of his own work, instead teaching at the Fine Arts School. Among his most celebrated pupils were Georges Rouault and Henri Matisse. A marvelous clutter hangs on the museum's walls and fills the rooms of the meticulously organized family mansion. The ornate, double-spiral staircase is one of its more interesting features; the nearly 6,000 drawings and paintings include watercolors and large, mythological themes, such as "Apollo and Pegasus," "The Unicorns," and "The Descent from the Cross."
www.musee-moreau.fr

Map p. 187 14 rue de la Rochefoucauld 01 48 74 38 50 Closed Tues. € Métro: Trinité

The Montmartre vineyard slopes downhill from the Lapin Agile.

Containing two vast landscaped parks, former outlying villages, and the ambitious urban project La Défense

Around the Périphérique

The Château de Vincennes

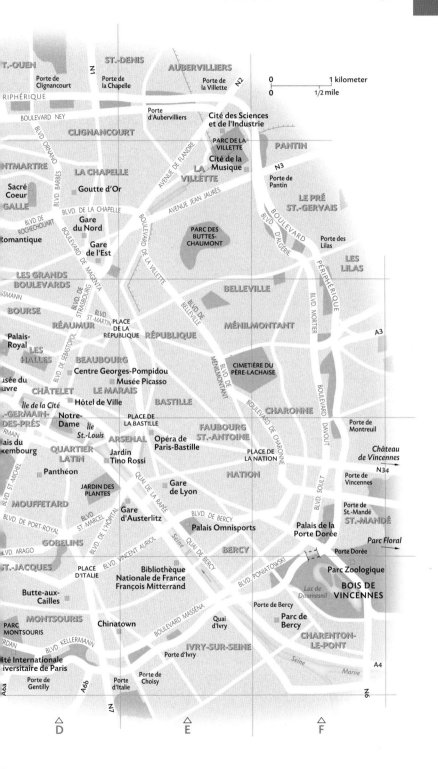

T.-OUEN
ST.-DENIS
AUBERVILLIERS

Porte de
Clignancourt
N1
Porte de
la Chapelle
Porte de
la Villette
N2

0   1 kilometer
0   1/2 mile

RIPHÉRIQUE

BOULEVARD NEY

Porte
d'Aubervilliers

Cité des Sciences
et de l'Industrie

CLIGNANCOURT

BLVD ORNANO

PARC DE LA
VILLETTE

PANTIN

NTMARTRE
LA CHAPELLE

AVENUE DE FLANDRE

Cité de la
Musique
N3

Porte de
Pantin

Sacré
Coeur
GALLE

BLVD BARBÈS

Goutte d'Or
LA
VILLETTE

LE PRÉ
ST.-GERVAIS

BLVD DE
ROCHECHOUART

BLVD. DE LA CHAPELLE

AVENUE JEAN JAURÈS

BOULEVARD

BLVD DALGERIE

Romantique

RMAIN

Gare
du Nord

BOULEVARD DE LA VILLETTE

PARC DES
BUTTES-
CHAUMONT

Porte des
Lilas

Gare
de l'Est

BOULEVARD DE MAGENTA

PÉRIPHÉRIQUE

LES
LILAS

LES GRANDS
BOULEVARDS

SMANN

BLVD. DE STRASBOURG

BELLEVILLE

BOURSE

BLVD.
ST.-MARTIN

BLVD. DE BELLEVILLE

BLVD MORTIER

A3

RÉAUMUR

PLACE
DE LA
RÉPUBLIQUE

MÉNILMONTANT

Palais-
Royal
LES
HALLES

BLVD DE SÉBASTOPOL

RÉPUBLIQUE

BEAUBOURG

Centre Georges-Pompidou

BOULEVARD

usée du
uvre

Musée Picasso

CIMETIÈRE DU
PÈRE-LACHAISE

CHÂTELET
LE MARAIS

BOULEVARD DE MÉNILMONTANT

Île de la Cité

Hôtel de Ville

BASTILLE

-GERMAIN-
DES-PRÉS

Notre-
Dame
Île
St.-Louis

PLACE DE
LA BASTILLE

CHARONNE

BOULEVARD DAVOUT

Porte de
Montreuil

lais du
xembourg

ARSENAL

FAUBOURG
ST.-ANTOINE

BOULEVARD DE CHARONNE

QUARTIER
LATIN

Opéra de
Paris-Bastille

Jardin
Tino Rossi

PLACE DE
LA NATION

Château
de Vincennes
N34

BLVD ST.-MICHEL

Panthéon

NATION

BLVD SOULT

Porte de
Vincennes

JARDIN DES
PLANTES

QUAI DE LA RAPÉE

Gare
de Lyon

Porte de
St.-Mandé
ST.-MANDÉ

MOUFFETARD

Gare
d'Austerlitz

BLVD. DE BERCY

Palais de la
Porte Dorée

BLVD. DE PORT-ROYAL

BLVD ST.-MARCEL

BLVD. DE L'HÔPITAL

Palais Omnisports

Parc Floral

BLVD. ARAGO

Seine

QUAI DE BERCY

BERCY

Porte Dorée

ST.-JACQUES

PLACE
D'ITALIE

BLVD. VINCENT AURIOL

Bibliothèque
Nationale de France
François Mitterrand

BLVD. PONIATOWSKI

Lac de
Daumesnil

Parc Zoologique

BOIS DE
VINCENNES

Butte-aux-
Cailles

Porte de Bercy

Parc de
Bercy

MONTSOURIS

Chinatown

BOULEVARD MASSÉNA

Quai
d'Ivry

CHARENTON-
LE-PONT

PARC
MONTSOURIS

RDAN

BLVD. KELLERMANN

IVRY-SUR-SEINE

Seine

A4

ité Internationale
iversitaire de Paris

Porte d'Ivry

Marne

A6a

Porte de
Gentilly

A6b

Porte
d'Italie

Porte de
Choisy

N7

N6

△
D

△
E

△
F

Around the Périphérique

The Périphérique ring road that encloses Paris sharply defines the city's limits. Many areas of the arrondissements bordering the Périphérique are somewhat off the beaten track, but form entities in and of themselves, with a degree of independence that survives to this day. If you have enough time, they are well worth a visit.

Walkers enjoy the paths of the Parc de Belleville.

Butte-aux-Cailles (see p. 202), for instance, is typical of old Paris with its narrow cobbled streets, obscure passageways, and small vine-covered town houses. Belleville, with its hamlet Ménilmontant (see pp. 206–207), served as the vineyard for the great abbeys of Paris and as a place for Parisians to go on Sundays to drink a glass of *guinguet* (a sour-tasting wine). Both were active during the Commune (see p. 30), and have been bastions of working-class agitation. Belleville has traditionally drawn waves of immigrants from the world over, and its population is the most diverse and cosmopolitan in the city, with Chinese, Arabic, African, and Turkish quarters, and colorful, ethnic markets.

The former slaughterhouses at La Villette are now part of a huge park (see pp. 208–209), a recent addition to the vast city-park system that includes the great Bois de Vincennes (see p. 203) and Bois de Boulogne (see opposite) flanking eastern and western Paris respectively. ■

Bois de Boulogne

An immense park of 2,132 acres (863 ha), the Bois de Boulogne draws people from all over the city. The two lakes (Lac Supérieur and Lac Inférieur) within the park are at different levels, connected by means of a superb waterfall.

The Bois de Boulogne was commissioned by Napoleon III. The elegant world met there during the day, while a more dubious underworld congregated at night—and still does, so certain areas are best avoided after sunset.

INSIDER TIP:

Visit the Bois de Boulogne in the early mornings, when the park is quiet and feels like the countryside.

—GILLES MINGASSON
National Geographic photographer

Graceful avenues and paths lead to the lakes through a pine forest and several oak groves. The **Jardin d'Acclimatation** has rides, miniature golf, and other activities, and in 2012 will be home to the new Louis Vuitton Foundation for Creation, housed in a cloudlike building designed by Frank Gehry.

The **Jardin Shakespeare** (*Route de Suresnes*) in the heart of the Bois encompasses a small, 300-seat open-air theater (performances in English and French). Nearby is the romantic (and expensive) **Le Pré Catalan** restaurant (see p. 254).

The **Bagatelle Garden** (*Route de Sèvres, €*) is a spectacular showcase in the spring and summer with nearly 9,000 rosebushes. The gardens also contain an impressive water lily and iris garden.

At the southern edge of the Bois, near the **Roland-Garros Stadium** (venue of tennis's French Open; *2 avenue Gordon Bennett*), is an unexpected haven: the greenhouses of **Auteuil,** which contain exotic plants, a tropical greenhouse, and a palmarium under the light of the central dome. ■

Bois de Boulogne
196 A2–4

Jardin d'Acclimatation
✉ Carrefour des Sablons or Avenue Mahatma Gandhi
☎ 01 40 67 90 82
$ €
🚇 Métro: Sablons
www.jardin dacclimatation.fr

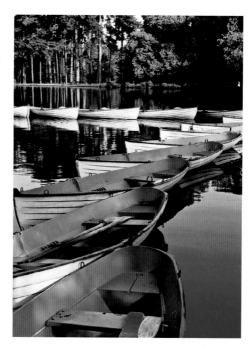

Boats await occupants at the Bois de Boulogne.

La Défense

La Défense, with its Grande Arche completing the monumental east–west axis cutting through Paris, is the French response to the Manhattan skyline.

La Défense
🅜 196 A4

La Grande Arche
✉ Parvis de la
   Défense
☎ 01 49 07 27 27
💲 €€ (€ Tues.)
www.grandearche
.com

Conceived in 1950 and begun in the early 1960s, this commercial district was designed on an American model as a functional and modern international business center for Paris.

In the early 1970s, it became a symbol of the inhumanity of modern architecture; companies snubbed the project, yet the 1980s brought a recovery with the construction of the gigantic Quatre-Temps shopping center

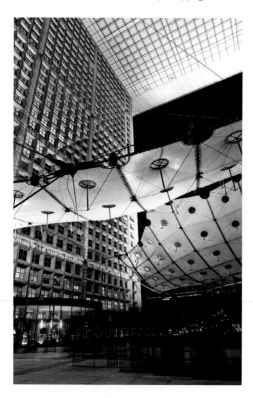

The view from beneath the Grande Arche de la Défense.

as well as a new IMAX theater.

Some berate La Défense as inhuman and sprawling; others praise it as innovative and futuristic. But it remains one of the most ambitious urban developments in Europe. Designers initially modeled their plan on similar structures in U.S. cities such as Manhattan and Chicago, but went further by eliminating traffic. The result is a two-tiered development, with the aboveground commercial and residential buildings linked by an immense esplanade, and a network of roads, trains, parking lots, and Métros below.

One of the first structures was the CNIT building, with a record-breaking 759-foot (230 m) roof span. Major trade fairs used to be held here, before moving to the Porte de Versailles. It now houses smaller shows, a hotel, and various stores and restaurants.

Concrete, glass, and steel are the rule here, but the esplanade has been brightened up with works of art that include a gigantic sculpture by Alexander Calder, a piece by Nikki de Saint-Phalle, and several playful fountains.

The crowning work, however, is **La Grande Arche.** The rooftop, at 300 feet (91.5 m), is open to the public and houses an exhibition tracing the construction of the Arche. Faced with Carrara marble, this vast, empty cube is large enough to frame Notre-Dame. ∎

Denfert-Rochereau

The 14th arrondissement is a good place to get a feel for everyday Parisian life by exploring the streets, markets, parks (particularly Montsouris), and the nearby Montparnasse Cemetery.

Paris's catacombs are literally lined with bones.

In the center of Place Denfert-Rochereau stands the "Lion of Belfort," a copy of a lion sculpted by Frédéric Auguste Bartholdi as a tribute to Alsatians during the Franco-Prussian War. North of the place, at 261 boulevard Raspail, stands the **Cartier Foundation** *(tel 01 42 18 56 50, closed Mon.)*. Constructed in 1994, the sleek, glass-and-steel structure stands in a beautiful garden and hosts art shows.

The strangest necropolis in all of Paris is the **Catacombs** (entrance on Place Denfert-Rochereau), the resting place for more than six million skeletons (and parts thereof) moved from inner-city cemeteries in the 18th and 19th centuries because of crowding and stench. Stacks of bones line miles of corridors under the city streets. ∎

Catacombs

✉ Place Denfert-Rochereau

☎ 01 43 22 47 63

🕐 Closed Mon.

💲 €€

🚇 Métro or RER: Denfert-Rochereau

www.catacombes .paris.fr

Wallace Fountains

The elegant, green cast-iron drinking fountain that graces place Denfert-Rochereau is one of 66 Wallace fountains scattered around Paris. Designed by Sir Richard Wallace as public hygiene became a prime concern under the Second Empire and Third Republic, they were placed around the city, with the first inaugurated in 1871 on Boulevard de la Villette.

The fountains are easily recognizable by their four caryatids of Simplicity, Charity, Sobriety, and Abundance, which support a dolphin-topped dome. The fountains are typical of the 19th-century style of street furniture, including benches, street lamps, and columns.

Butte-aux-Cailles

Past and present coexist in this workers' quarter, which was one of the city's many outlying villages. Locals were called *pieds mouillés* or "wet feet" as they waded barefoot across the Bièvre River (now channeled under the Rue Corvisart) into Paris to avoid paying tolls.

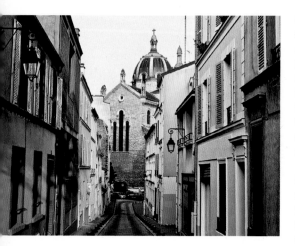

The streets of Butte-aux-Cailles have an old-fashioned feel.

Butte-aux-Cailles
- 🅰 197 D1
- ✉ Between Rue de la Butte-aux-Cailles and Rue des Cinq Diamants
- 🚇 Métro: Corvisart

The Butte-aux-Cailles became famous on November 21, 1783, when physicist Pilâtre de Rozier landed his hot-air balloon between the Moulin des Merveilles and Moulin Vieux windmills, having left the Château de La Muette 25 minutes earlier. It was the first manned free flight in a hot-air balloon, reaching an altitude of roughly 3,100 feet (945 m). The butte was a marvelous natural belvedere, overlooking the swamps, prairies, and watermills of the Bièvre Valley and the steeples of Paris.

This working-class neighborhood was one of the first to rebel during the Commune, and it still has a strong independent streak, represented by Le Temps des

Cerises restaurant (one of the rare anarchist establishments in Paris until the 1980s) and Le Merle Moqueur (dating from the Commune). The area served as a refuge for communards, and even today the Association des Amis de la Commune holds regular meetings, selling books and documents that revive the spirit of the period.

In addition to being one of the bastions of the Paris Commune, the Butte-aux-Cailles also became famous for having the last cows in Paris; there was a farm and cows near the Passage Barrault well into the first half of the 20th century. Small houses, cobbled streets, and winding lanes stand next to apartment buildings against the ultramodern backdrop of high-rises in Paris's premier **Chinatown** and the Place d'Italie, which used to be an ancient Roman crossroads.

Explore the charming, picturesque Rues Buot, Michal, de la Butte-aux-Cailles, and des Cinq Diamants, as well as the Villa Daviel, with its scenic miniature villas and cottages, and farther away, the town-house-lined Square des Peupliers.

Near Place Verlaine is an indoor-outdoor public swimming pool. Built in 1924, it has been renovated and repainted a brilliant yellow and red. It is fed by an artesian well of sulfurous water at 82°F (28°C) each day. ■

Bois de Vincennes & Château

This park is still the most popular in the eastern section of Paris. Like the Bois de Boulogne, it has a racetrack. In addition, a highly colorful Buddhist temple is located on park grounds, as well as a lake, zoo, museum, children's play area, and, of course, a château.

Once the Bois de Boulogne had been painstakingly landscaped and given to the city in 1852, Napoleon III decided to make a grand gesture in 1860 for "the workers of the 11th and 12th arrondissements," by commissioning a matching park to the east, the Bois de Vincennes. Four lakes were created, complete with romantic islands dotted with restaurants and secret grottoes.

The park's main attractions include the large **Daumesnil Lake**

Where to Run in Paris

Serious runners should find a hotel near the Bois de Vincennes, the Bois de Boulogne, the Jardin de Luxembourg, the Parc des Buttes Chaumont (warning: very hilly), the Parc Montsouris, or the Parc de Villette. While a jog along the Seine is beautiful, it is not ideal, since it is not always possible to avoid running alongside heavy traffic, except on Sundays, when the highways at water level are closed to traffic during the day. Ditto for running along the Canal St.-Martin, pleasant only on Sunday.

INSIDER TIP:

Find the bargains—or the interesting junk— of Paris early in the morning at the Porte-de-Montreuil flea market, west of the Bois de Vincennes.

—PATRICIA DANIELS
National Geographic contributor

and the nearby **Vincennes zoo** *(53 avenue de St.-Maurice, tel 01 44 75 20 10),* closed for renovation until 2014. The imposing walled **Château de Vincennes,** ringed by a moat, was a royal abode for centuries. Its 14th-century keep, once a State prison, is now a museum and recently underwent a 12-year restoration. The 16th-century chapel still has its beautiful 17th-century stained glass. Less well-known is the **Parc Floral,** a magnificently landscaped park within the park. A separate children's play area includes rides, climbing frames, and a go-cart track, while pavilions house special exhibitions and concerts.

To their great delight, kids can still experience animal life at the **Ferme Georges Ville,** a model working farm founded in 1860 by the pharmacist it is named after *(€, free on weekends).* ■

Bois de Vincennes

- 🅰 197 F1
- ✉ Avenue Daumesnil or Avenue de Gravelle

www.boisde
vincennes.com

Tibetan Temple (Kagyu Dzong)

- ✉ Route de la Ceinture du Lac Daumesnil
- ☎ 01 40 04 98 06
- 🕒 Closed Mon.
- Ⓜ Métro: Porte Dorée

www.kagyu-
dzong.org

Château de Vincennes

- 🅰 197 G2
- ✉ Avenue de Paris
- ☎ 01 48 08 31 20
- 💲 €€
- Ⓜ Métro: Château de Vincennes

www.chateau-vin-
cennes.fr

Parc Floral

- 🅰 197 G2
- ✉ Route de la Pyramide
- ☎ 01 49 57 24 84
- 💲 €
- Ⓜ Métro: Château de Vincennes

www.parcfloralde
paris.com

Parks & Gardens of Paris

Parisians often complain about the lack of open space in this dense city, yet more than 400 parks, gardens, and squares dot the urban landscape, ranging from André Le Nôtre's formal French design for the Tuileries in the 17th century, to the color-coded, postmodern André Citroën Garden at the edge of the 15th arrondissement.

The Parc des Buttes-Chaumont offers great views of the city.

Great Parisian Parks

Until the 19th century, the great gardens— Luxembourg, Palais-Royal, Tuileries—were part of royal domains. But under the Second Empire, enormous parks and small neighborhood squares began to appear all over Paris, under the impetus of Jean-Charles Alphand, Baron Georges Haussmann's chief park director. He transformed what remained of the Rouvre Forest into the Bois de Boulogne and created the Bois de Vincennes, along with the Buttes-Chaumont and Parc Montsouris.

By the early 20th century, planners were using available land for housing, and few new parks were opened up. It wasn't until the 1980s that the authorities shifted their attention back toward open spaces. In the last 20 years alone, nearly 250 acres (101 ha) of new parks have been opened, affording plenty of places to escape the noise and congestion of the city.

Lesser-Known Parks

Created by Jean-Charles Alphand during the Second Empire from a dismal gypsum quarry, the Buttes-Chaumont *(Rues Botzaris, Manin, and de Crimée, Métro: Simon Bolivar, Buttes-Chaumont)* in northeast Paris is a romantic park with steep slopes and intertwining paths, grottoes, and a famous belvedere perched at the top of a hill. There is a small lake, a bandstand for summer concerts, children's activities, and a spectacular view of the city.

A Pick of Paris's Best Gardens

Formal French gardens: Tuileries (see p. 137), Luxembourg (see p. 82)

Botanical gardens: Parc Floral de Vincennes (see p. 203), Auteuil greenhouses (see p. 199), Jardin des Plantes (see pp. 70–71)

Romantic gardens: Parc de Monceau (see p. 158), Buttes-Chaumont, Parc Montsouris, Parc de Bagatelle (see p. 199), Musée Rodin (see pp. 178–179)

Contemporary gardens: Square Tino Rossi, Parc de Bercy, Parc de Belleville (see p. 207), Parc de la Villette (see pp. 208–209)

The giants: Bois de Vincennes (see p. 203), Bois de Boulogne (see p. 199)

Parc Montsouris *(Avenue Reille/Boulevard Jourdan, RER: Cité Universitaire),* in the southern part of the city, is another of Alphand's creations, meant to mirror Buttes-Chaumont. Although it doesn't occupy as dramatic a site, it is equally romantic, with weeping willows and a lake dotted with swans. Alphand solved the problem of disguising the train lines running through the park by transforming their trenches into ravines lined with pine trees. It is a popular site with the students who live across the street at the Cité Universitaire.

A recent addition to the Paris park system is the unusual Promenade Plantée, created from a former railway viaduct. It leads from Place de la Bastille as far as the Bois de Vincennes to the east; the first part used to be a raised rail track on the viaduct and is now a landscaped footpath that crosses through several parks and an overhead bridge. Bikes are allowed in the second section, from the Jardin de Reuilly in the 12th arrondissement to the Bois de Vincennes. A classy shopping arcade called the Viaduc des Arts occupies the former arches below the viaduct.

Not far away is the Parc de Bercy, on the site of the former wine warehouses near the Bercy Stadium and the fortresslike Ministry of Finance. Fortunately, some of the hundred-year-old trees were saved along with some 18th-century ruins. The gardens include a canal, an orchard, vegetable garden, and gardens created around the four seasons.

A fine place to enjoy the Seine is at the Square Tino Rossi in the 5th arrondissement,

an open-air sculpture garden where tango and salsa dancers gather on warm evenings.

One of the most interesting parks in the Paris region is the Albert-Kahn Gardens *(14 rue du Port, Boulogne-Billancourt, tel 01 55 19 28 00, closed Mon.),* located on the western outskirts of the city. The grounds include a beautiful Japanese garden.

The green refuge of the Parc des Buttes-Chaumont

Belleville/Ménilmontant

While Belleville isn't as picturesque a butte as Montmartre, it is certainly more multicultural and dynamic—and definitely more radical. The area's population is one of the most diverse and cosmopolitan in Paris, given the successive layers of immigration. Neighboring Ménilmontant is a curious mixture of modern housing and older residences that are becoming increasingly gentrified, making the area a thriving center of alternative Paris.

The friendly Bar Aux Folies in the Belleville-Ménilmontant neighborhood

Then & Now

Incorporated into the rapidly expanding city of Paris in 1860, the former village of Belleville was a hotbed of opposition to the Empire and the last quarter to surrender its arms during the Commune. Various attempts were made to quell working-class protests, such as splitting the Belleville area up into the 11th, 19th, and 20th arrondissements.

For a long time, the butte—419 feet high (128 m)—maintained its 1930s look, a typically Parisian quarter with traditionally proletarian leanings. Yet it is continually changing, with the influx of immigrants and with countless rebuilding and renovation projects, which sometimes seem to be killing off the soul of old Belleville—some high-rise complexes have no ground floor markets or stores, for example. Sinuous side streets slope down past shops, ateliers, period bistros, and villas, and hushed gardens hide behind ornate doorways.

Belleville and its neighbor, Ménilmontant, bear traces of their rural and working-class past, when craftsmen and workers exploiting the local gypsum quarries lived at the foot of the butte. Founded in the 15th century around the vineyards run by the great abbeys of Paris, Belleville was known for its *guinguettes* (open-air cafés), and Parisians would come on Sundays to drink a sourish wine called *guinguet*. Working-class people ousted from the city by Haussmann's 19th-century upheavals sought new residences here.

Until 1914, Belleville and Ménilmontant rivaled Montmartre for its cafés, cabarets, and *bals-musettes* (dance halls with traditional French music). The Élysée Ménilmontant (no longer standing) was one of the most famous of these; Maurice Chevalier debuted here. Edith Piaf was born at 72 rue de Belleville; the Java nightclub features the original *bal-musette* setting. Rue des Envierges, lined with restaurants, bistros, and *cafés chantants*, comes alive each night.

What to See

One of the great panoramic views of the city can be found where Rue Piat, Rue du Transvaal, and Rue des Envierges converge, at the highest point of Belleville, with the Belleville Gardens below. Rue Piat led to two windmills in the last century; it now opens onto the **Parc de Belleville,** which has a spectacular view over Paris and a great children's play area.

Villa Castel off Rue du Transvaal is a beautiful alley with fabulous houses, where François Truffaut shot scenes for his film *Jules et Jim* in 1962. An open house organized by local painters is held once a year (usually in the spring), revealing magnificent courtyards, studios, and hidden gardens.

The intertwining side streets and passages between Rue de Belleville and Rue de Ménilmontant are mostly paths that once linked vineyards. Today, Rue de Ménilmontant is becoming fashionable again, particularly along the lower end near Oberkampf, where trendy bars and cafés—like Café Charbon, with the Nouveau Casino concert and club venue next door, and the intimate La Mercerie—are burgeoning. ■

Belleville/ Ménilmontant

 197 F3

✉ Belleville: centered on Rue de Belleville. Ménilmontant: centered on Rue de Ménilmontant

 Métro: Belleville: Belleville, Pyrénées; Ménilmontant: Ménilmontant

---

Back to the 18th Century

Near the Rue de Belleville lingers a remnant of a more elegant corner of the area. The chic **Manoir de Beauregard** (*43 rue des Lilas, 75019, tel 01 42 03 10 20, www .manoir-de-beauregard-paris.com, €€–€€€.*), set in a converted 18th-century hunting lodge decorated with period furniture, is something of an anomaly in this working-class neighborhood. Hostess Mary-Rose Girard welcomes her guests with tea and cake served in fine porcelain in a wood-paneled dining room. The B&B is not far from the **Parc des Buttes-Chaumont** (*map E4*)—itself worth a visit for its trees, lake, and clifftop temple.

Parc de la Villette

One of the newest redevelopment projects in Paris has also been among its most successful. Just 15 years ago, the former slaughterhouses of La Villette stood in a gigantic no-man's land in the northeast corner of Paris. Today, the 89-acre (35 ha) park contains the Cité des Sciences et de l'Industrie (Science Museum), the Cité de la Musique (Music City), the Zénith, a popular venue for pop and rock concerts, and the Grande Halle, a temporary exhibition space.

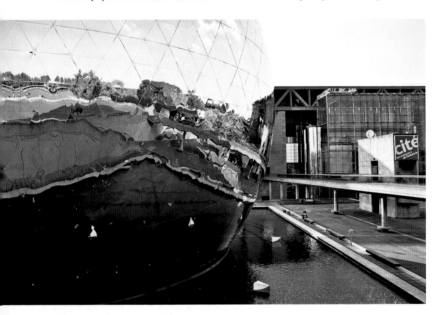

The gleaming Géode at the Cité des Sciences et de l'Industrie houses an IMAX theater.

Parc de la Villette

🅰 197 E4

✉ Quai de la Gironde

☎ 01 40 03 75 75

🚇 Métro: Porte de Pantin, Porte de la Villette

www.villette.com

Zénith

✉ 211 avenue Jean-Jaurès

🚇 Métro: Porte de Pantin

www.zenith.com

Cité des Sciences et de l'Industrie

With over three million visitors per year, the Science Museum is the park's most popular attraction. As opposed to the traditional style of French museum, which tends to be heavy on text and description, the Science Museum has plenty of interactive, hands-on exhibitions in its giant, five-level glass-and-steel building. Explora, the core, permanent exhibit, lets visitors discover the galaxies, volcanoes, man and health, the environment, energy, sound, and the ocean through a multitude of innovative displays—computerized games about space, a flight simulator, and the Greenhouse, a garden of the future.

Opened in 1986, the museum also has a planetarium for trips to outer space, a Géode sphere (a 100-seat IMAX theater, which has become the symbol of the futuristic park), the *Argonaute* full-scale submarine, and the Cinaxe, a simulated film adventure. Two sections are reserved for kids in the Cité des Enfants, a science village where children can play with interactive exhibits. One area is for 3- to 5-year-olds and another for 5- to 12-year-olds. It is best to reserve one of the 90-minute sessions when you purchase your entrance ticket.

INSIDER TIP:

A pleasant way to get to the Parc de la Villette is by renting a bicycle and following the canal de l'Ourcq. Enjoy the view!

—CHRISTEL CHERQAOUI
*National Geographic Books
promotion director*

Cité de la Musique

The **Music Museum** is one part of the Cité de la Musique, which, designed by Christian de Portzamparc, also houses a concert hall, a research center, and the Paris Conservatory. Visitors explore the displays with headsets that are activated as you walk around. Tours and hands-on workshops are available.

Other Features

Even without the museums, the vast park, designed by Swiss Bernard Tschumi, is a great place to get away from the city. It features a magical bamboo forest; wacky 20th-century, red-metal structures known as "follies" (one of which houses an information center); a children's playground with a gigantic dragon slide; and ten different thematic gardens. Don't miss the gargantuan half-buried bicycle sculpture by Claes Oldenburg. During the summer, a giant screen is set up in the park for open-air movies, and concerts are scheduled regularly.

The one remaining feature from its days as a slaughterhouse and cattle market is the **Grande Halle** (*221 avenue Jean-Jaurès, Métro: Porte de Pantin),* one of the most beautiful examples of glass-and-cast-iron architecture in Paris. Built in 1867, it originally was little more than a metal shelter for the cattle sold here. It has since been renovated with movable platforms that can be adapted to accommodate temporary exhibitions and concerts. ∎

Cité des Sciences et de l'Industrie

- ⊠ 197 E5
- ✉ 30 avenue Corentin Cariou
- ☎ 01 40 05 70 00
- ⏱ Closed Mon.
- 💲 €€€
- Ⓜ Métro: Porte de la Villette

www.cite-science.fr

La Géode

- ✉ 26 avenue Corentin Cariou
- ☎ 08 92 68 45 40
- ⏱ Closed Mon.
- 💲 €€€
- Ⓜ Métro: Porte de la Villette

www.lageode.fr

Cité de la Musique

- ⊠ 197 E4
- ✉ 221 avenue Jean-Jaurès
- ☎ 01 44 84 44 84
- ⏱ Closed Mon.
- 💲 €€€
- Ⓜ Métro: Porte de Pantin

www.cite-musique.fr

EXPERIENCE: Picnicking with the Locals

Take a break from churches and museums and relax Parisian style, with an open-air picnic. Although many people picnic along the quays of the Seine in fine weather, this venue has two main drawbacks: a lack of comfortable seating and a dearth of toilets. The Parc de Villette and Parc de Vincennes (see p. 203), with their expansive lawns, are better bets. If you picnic near the Canal St.-Martin (same drawbacks as the quays of the Seine), you might want to first stop in at **Pink Flamingo** (*67 rue Bichat, 75010, tel 01 42 02 31 70)* and order a gourmet pizza. They will give you a pink balloon so that the delivery person can find you.

More Places to Visit Around the Périphérique

Chinatown

At first sight, the stark high-rise buildings in the 13th arrondissement—known as the Choisy Triangle—form a depressing complex. Yet this is the heart of the city's thriving and colorful Chinatown, with an estimated 30,000 Asian residents and entire, transplanted cultures, complete with pagoda-fronted shops and martial arts centers. Don't miss the Tang Brothers on Avenue d'Ivry (the largest Asian supermarket in France), and the plenteous restaurants offering every type of Asian cuisine.

🅰 197 D1 🚇 Métro: Tolbiac, Porte d'Ivry

Goutte d'Or

Just east of Pigalle and Montmartre is the Goutte d'Or (Drop of Gold) district, named for the previously highly prized wine produced on its hillsides. Since the 19th century, however, it has offered some of the cheapest (and most miserable) housing in Paris. In the last few decades it has become mostly an Arab and African neighborhood, its streets teeming with a multitude of languages, dress, spicy foods, and Kabyl (ethnic Algerian) cafés.

Browse through the crowded and ultra-cheap Tati Department Store and on to the Dejean Market *(near the Château Rouge Métro)* or the open-air market on Boulevard de la Chapelle *(Wed. & Sat.)*. Every summer, the Goutte d'Or en Fête music festival features local musicians along with big names in *rai* (North African rock 'n' roll), rap, and hip hop.

🅰 197 D4 🚇 Métro: Barbès-Rochechouart

Nouvelle Athènes

Tucked into the area between Pigalle and Les Grands Boulevards is Nouvelle Athènes, where a number of 19th-century artists, including Theodore Géricault, Eugène Delacroix, and Frédéric Chopin, congregated. The fascinating **Musée Gustave Moreau** is here (see p. 194), as is the **Musée de la Vie Romantique** (see p. 115). Installed in the studio and home of painter Ary Scheffer, this museum is a tribute to the Romantic period, with memorabilia of George Sand and others. The prettiest spot, however, is the **Place St.-Georges,** featuring the gorgeous facades of the neo-Renaissance Hôtel de la Païva and the Hôtel Thiers, which organizes temporary exhibitions and houses the **Masson Fund**'s Napoleonic memorabilia *(Bibliothèque Thiers, 27 place St.-Georges, tel 01 48 78 14 33, open Thurs. & Fri. 12 p.m.–6 p.m., by appt. only).*

🅰 196 C4 🚇 Métro: St.-Georges, Pigalle

Romantic Parisian Canals

With the opening of La Villette park (see pp. 208–209) to the north, visitors who want to see the less traveled reaches of Paris near the Périphérique can do so via the city's canals. For example, a trip down the **Canal St.-Martin** leading to the Bassin de la Villette and the Canal de l'Ourcq passes through a series of eight locks, two swing bridges, and some graceful wrought-iron footbridges.

Although pleasure boats ply this 3-mile (5 km) route, the most romantic way to explore the area is on foot. The building that inspired Marcel Carné's great film *Hôtel du Nord* (1938) is at 102 quai de Jemmapes. The building was saved from destruction in the 1980s and is now a popular restaurant.

Boat cruises along the Canal St.-Martin to the Bassin de la Villette and the Canal de l'Ourcq provide a relaxing way to view the city and are operated by several companies (see p. 236); reservations are recommended.

Abbeys, castles, forests, and towns that have fed the inspiration of artists—all within easy reach of the capital

Excursions

A fountain at Versailles

Excursions

A trip away from hectic, urban Paris is a welcome break in any season (but try to avoid traveling on weekends from mid-July to the end of August, as the French tend to leave en masse for vacations then). For many first-time visitors to Paris, Versailles is a must-see. Outside of Paris the rest of the Île de France region is also studded with châteaus, such as the Italian-style Fontainebleau and Rambouillet, now a residence of the French president.

The beautiful Vaux-le-Vicomte (see p. 222) was not a royal palace, but it was so luxurious that Louis XIV's crooked finance minister, Nicolas Fouquet, was imprisoned for embezzling state funds to build it. The Château de

Chantilly's fine collection of artistic treasures includes paintings by Raphael and the stunning, medieval miniatures from the "Très Riches Heures du Duc de Berry" (see p. 232), not to mention the imposing stables

Donald, Mickey, and Minnie welcome visitors to Disneyland Paris.

built in the 18th century to house the prince of Condé's 240 horses (now a museum).

There are a few excursions within a reasonable distance of Paris that offer a unique glimpse into medieval French life: for example, the last remaining fortress at Blandy (see p. 222), near Vaux-le Vicomte; and the hilltop town of Provins (see p. 223), which hosts annual fairs with costumed actors reenacting some of the more colorful aspects of medieval life. And in the suburb of St.-Denis is the 13th-century cathedral of the same name (see p. 220), the first large Gothic building in Europe.

Monet's home and gardens at Giverny (see pp. 230–231) and the town of Auvers-sur-Oise are both landmarks for art lovers. The Abbaye de Vaux-de-Cernay (see p. 226), a 12th-century abbey that has been converted into a luxury hotel, is an obscure haven in the middle of the vast Rambouillet Forest. The original refectory is still standing, as is the roofless cathedral.

Lastly, Chartres Cathedral (see pp. 228–229), the jewel of medieval France, has the most brilliant collection of 13th-century stained glass anywhere in the world. ∎

Ourcq

Marne

la Ferté-sous-Jouarre

A4

Grand Morin

oulommiers

la Ferté-Gaucher

Béton-Bazoches

Esternay

N4

N19

Provins

Nangis

Nogent-sur-Seine

Seine

.5

Montereau-Faut-Yonne

Bray-sur-Seine

△
F

△
E

Château de Versailles

For sheer glitter, nothing beats Versailles. An extravagant palace built during Louis XIV's reign, it is not the oldest or largest of the French châteaus, but it illustrates the essence of a royal palace. Although Louis XIV (known as the Sun King) constructed the château and the famous gardens, the property had originally belonged to his father, Louis XIII. An enthusiastic hunter, Louis XIII built a lodge in 1623 in the forest; he built more spacious quarters in 1634.

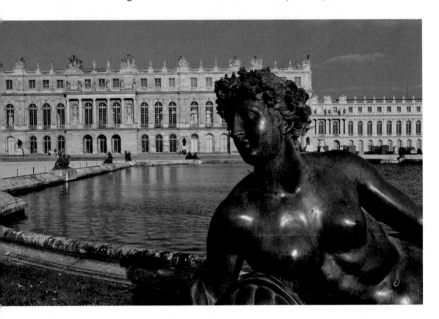

The grounds of Versailles have 32 pools and fountains.

When he died nine years later, his son Louis XIV was only five years old. The boy loved the small château, but his reasons for later spending so much time and money—and ultimately moving the court to Versailles—had more to do with the turbulent politics of the day than the château's bucolic attractions. As a child, Louis XIV had witnessed the uprising of the Fronde (see p. 24), and he remained distrustful of Parisians throughout his life. By forcing the nobles to follow him to the more isolated Château de Versailles, he could keep a close watch on them, curtailing their capacity for independent political action.

Throughout his 72-year reign, Louis XIV spent lavishly to build the château, hiring the best designers France had to offer: the architect Louis Le Vau (succeeded by Jules Hardouin-Mansart), the landscape designer André Le Nôtre, and the painter Charles Le Brun, all of whom had worked previously on the sumptuous, but ill-fated Château de Vaux-le-Vicomte (see p. 222).

The château of Versailles is inseparable from the personality of the king. (His great-grandson Louis XV and great-great-great-grandson Louis XVI made only minor alterations to his grand plan.) The finished château perfectly mirrored the ambitions of the Sun King, whose reign typified the absolutism of the monarchy, guided by the principle of *la gloire* (glory). When Versailles became the seat of government in 1682, it had to be expanded even further to house the entire court, along with all the civil servants.

Interior

The **State Apartments** give some idea of Louis XIV's practical interpretation of *la gloire*: The rooms were decorated throughout with gold and marble (quarried from every corner of his kingdom) and organized around the theme of the planets gravitating around the sun (the king's emblem). No sooner had these apartments been built than Louis XIV decided he needed more intimate quarters, so from 1684 on these rooms were designated for official functions and royal audiences, while the king resided in the old part of the château facing the Marble Court.

Everything at Versailles was ruled by protocol and etiquette—even in the king's private quarters. Courtiers fought jealously for the privilege of being received there, especially for the "Rising" and "Setting" ceremonies of the Royal Heavenly Body. The gilt-and-crimson **King's Bedchamber** is

Château de Versailles

- 🅰 212 C3
- ✉ 12 miles (19 km) southwest of Paris
- ☎ 01 30 83 78 00
- 🕐 Closed Mon.
- 💲 €€€
- 🚗 By car: A13 to exit "Versailles-Château," then follow signs. By train: from Paris-Montparnasse to Versailles-Chantiers; from Paris-St.-Lazare to Versailles-Rive Droite. RER line C to Versailles–Rive Gauche.

www.chateau versailles.fr

EXPERIENCE: King for a Night

The Château de Versailles now offers the public many of the divertissements that were once the exclusive province of its royal residents and their courtiers: operas and concerts by baroque composers like Jean-Baptiste de Lully and Henry Purcell in the Royal Opera House, strolls in the park, lavish fireworks displays, and more.

There is one event that Louis XIV missed out on, however: **Les Grandes Eaux Nocturnes.** While Louis was behind the major engineering feat required to create the multiple fountains in the château's park, he certainly never saw them in this way, lit by spectacular light installations and complete with aquatic effects, laser shows, and musical accompaniment.

Gently guided by park staff and a map, visitors are free to wander the grounds in the dark from one magical fountain spectacle to another, all of them different and surprising, and many of them hidden behind walls of greenery. The evening ends with a brilliant fireworks display over the Grand Bassin at 11 p.m., leaving just enough time to catch a train back to Paris.

Early arrivals can enjoy a **"Royal Serenade,"** a re-creation of a French ball with musicians and dancers, in the gorgeous Hall of Mirrors at 6:45 p.m. or 7:45 p.m., or picnic on the grounds before the gates to the Grandes Eaux Nocturnes open at 9 p.m. (*Sat. nights mid-June–early Sept., www.chateauversaillesspectacles.fr, €€€€€*).

now restored exactly as it was on September 1, 1715, the day the king died.

The gilded splendor of the **Queen's Room** is even more lavish, though she and the other women who lived there (two queens, two dauphines, and the wife of the king's eldest son) had even less privacy. These women gave birth to a total of 19 children, always a public affair to ensure that there were no substitutes for the royal offspring.

Nowhere is Louis XIV's quest for grandeur more evident than in the gilded, slightly gaudy **Hall of Mirrors,** a 240-foot-long room constructed by Hardouin-Mansart that runs the entire length of the central part of the château and faces the huge gardens outside. The 17 tall, arched windows are matched on the opposite wall by 17 tall French mirrors, while the coffered ceiling (decorated by Charles Le Brun) immortalizes the diplomatic and military conquests of the king over such foreign powers as Spain and Holland. More recently, during World War I, Versailles was used by the Allied War Council, and the Treaty of Versailles was signed in the Hall of Mirrors on June 28, 1919.

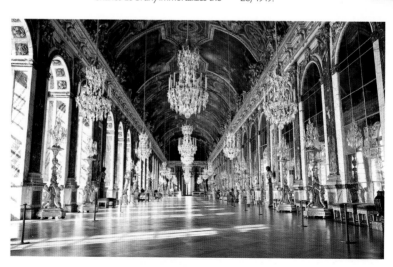

Versailles's Hall of Mirrors exemplifies the palace's glittering grandeur.

Château de Versailles

The Royal Chapel ceiling

South Parterre

Salon de Mars

Gardens

Making the most of the steep, marshy ground, André Le Nôtre designed what has been called the most perfect example of a formal French garden. In an era that believed that nature was to be mastered by man, Le Nôtre undertook immense drainage work, shifting masses of earth to form the terraces that begin with the **Parterre d'Eau** (two symmetrical pools)

just below the windows of the Hall of Mirrors and lead down to the **Bassin d'Apollon** and the **Grand Canal.**

The king was so proud of his gardens that he wrote a detailed description of the best way to visit them. Although formal in design and organized around two main axes—one running east to west, the other north to south—the gardens contain charming groves, fountains, and labyrinths

The King's Composer

Although he was Italian, Jean-Baptiste Lully (né Giovanni Battista Lulli in 1632) is considered the leading composer of French Baroque music. He started his career as a scullery boy for the Duchess of Montpensier, a fabulously rich cousin of Louis XIV, but eventually worked his way to the court as a dancer and later became the king's favorite composer. Today you can hear his music and that of other Baroque composers in the lavish Royal Opera in the Château de Versailles, designed by architect Ange-Jacques Gabriel and decorated with multiple crystal chandeliers by Augustin Pajou. Performers include top international artists such as Jordi Savall, Cecilia Bartoli, and Nathalie Dessay. (Chateau de Versailles Spectacles: *www.chateau versaillesspectacles.fr*)

INSIDER TIP:

Save your visit to the grounds for late afternoon, when the setting sun transforms the palace's gardens, statues, and walls.

—GILLES MINGASSON
National Geographic photographer

with names like "Bacchus Basin," "Apollo Baths," and "Room of Chestnut Trees."

The groves were equipped with a sophisticated system of fountains, created to accompany the festivities organized by Louis XIV. The most famous of these, held in 1664, was dedicated ostensibly to his wife, Marie-Thérèse, but was actually in honor of his favorite mistress, Mademoiselle de La Vallière. The playwright Molière wrote several plays, including *Tartuffe*, for the week-long celebration, and the entire château and gardens were turned into a backdrop for ballets, fireworks, tournaments, waterworks, and ornate banquets.

Today, the Grandes Eaux celebrations, held every weekend from early April through October, re-create something of the ambience of these events.

Louis demanded that the flowers in his gardens flourish all year long. Through the ingenuity of Jean-Baptiste de La Quintinye, the king ate strawberries in March and lettuce in January. The **King's Kitchen Garden,** which has produced fruit and vegetables continuously for three centuries, is also open to the public.

Grand & Petit Trianons

Versailles was sometimes too large and too public, even for Louis XIV. With nearly 10,000 people occupying the palace, there was no way to escape the jostling courtiers. The king, therefore, asked Hardouin-Mansart to build the Grand Trianon, a pink marble mini-palace, in his gardens. Only slightly less magnificent than Versailles, the Grand Trianon became a getaway for several royal families. The building was renovated under General de Gaulle and used as the official residence for foreign heads of state.

After Louis XIV's death, Louis XV continued to live at Versailles, where he constructed the Petit Trianon in 1769 as a place where he could meet his mistress, Madame de Pompadour. When Marie-Antoinette became queen, she created an English-style garden and a miniature mock-hamlet, complete with farm animals.

Visiting the Château

Several different tickets are available, depending on what you want (or have the energy) to see. The basic "Palace" ticket, which includes an audio guide, admits you to the Hall of Mirrors, King and Queen's Grand Apartments, the King's Bedchamber, the Dauphin's apartments, and Mesdames' Apartments (on weekends only). The more costly "Passport" ticket includes all of the above, plus the Trianon Palaces and Marie-Antoinette's Estate, temporary exhibitions, and musical fountains (when they are in operation). A less expensive ticket admits you only to the Trianon Palaces, their gardens, and Marie-Antoinette's Estate. Other tickets include the Academy of Equestrian Arts and dressage demonstrations.

Buy your ticket online to avoid standing in two separate lines at the always crowded château. Plan on spending at least two hours visiting the château, and about the same for the Trianon Palaces. It takes about half an hour to walk through the park to Marie-Antoinette's Estate, but a little train can take you there faster.

The gardens are free, except during the "Grandes Eaux" performances, when the 32 pools and fountains are turned on as part of a musical display. ■

Versailles's formal gardens were intended to show the mastery of the human hand over nature.

Cathédrale St.-Denis

St.-Denis, the cathedral that inspired Gothic architecture in France, stands in an unlikely setting in the working-class suburb of St.-Denis, 5 miles (8 km) north of Paris. More than 800 years separate the two monuments for which the town is famous: the cathedral, a landmark in the evolution of Gothic architecture; and the Stade de France, a major stadium.

The Cathedral of St.-Denis was a pioneer of Gothic styles.

St.-Denis
🅰 212 D3

**Cathédrale
St.-Denis**
✉ Place de
la Légion
d'Honneur
☎ 01 48 09 83 54
💲 €€
🚇 Métro: Line 13
to St.-Denis-
Basilique.
By car: via A1
**www.saint-denis
.monuments-
nationaux.fr**

The official burial site for French monarchs since 1122, St.-Denis represents a turning point in the history of architecture. The Abbey of St.-Denis, built around 475, was already powerful when Abbot Suger improved the existing Merovingian basilica by adding intersecting ribbed vaults on a large scale throughout the church—an innovation for the time. The master builders of the other great cathedrals that followed (including Chartres and Senlis) drew their inspiration from this prototype. Unfortunately, the church was badly damaged during the Revolution, and most of its treasures are now in the Louvre.

Royal Monuments

The crypt represents a fascinating chronology of the French monarchy. Sometime around 1260, Saint Louis commissioned images of his predecessors, starting with the seventh century. From the 14th century on, the heart and viscera of deceased royals were removed and dispersed to separate monuments, while the bodies were buried at St.-Denis.

For centuries, almost every king, queen, and royal child was buried here, from Dagobert through Louis XVIII. The most interesting funerary monuments are those of Dagobert, Henri II, Catherine de Médicis, Pépin the Short, Charles Martel, Louis XII, and François I. ■

Disneyland Paris

Disneyland Resort Paris has expanded beyond the original Disneyland theme park opened in 1992 and now features the Disney Village, a golf course, La Vallée outlet shopping center, and the much hyped new attraction, the Walt Disney Studios Park. Visitors will find the same beaming "cast members," attractions similar to the U.S. versions, and the same turreted Sleeping Beauty's Castle—a somewhat hollow edifice in a country overrun with real châteaus.

If you're traveling with children who balk at visiting one more museum, Disneyland can provide an entertaining break from Paris. The youngest kids love **Fantasyland,** where Disney habitués will recognize such rides as "It's a Small World" and the "Alice in Wonderland" maze, complete with trick fountains. Older kids and adults head straight for **Discoveryland** and "Space Mountain," a heart-stopping roller coaster that literally shoots you off the starting line. The nearby "Star Tours" is a popular simulator ride. **Frontierland** offers a few other thrills, notably the "Big Thunder Mountain" roller coaster.

Somewhere between the gentle Fantasyland and the other looping rides is **Adventureland,** with

"Indiana Jones and the Temple of Peril," another wild attraction, and the "Pirates of the Caribbean" boat trip. Small pockets of calm include the "Critter Corral" for young kids and the "Pocahontas Indian Village," a parent-free playground. There are lots of restaurants—where, at least in some establishments, Disney has taken into account French culture by allowing wine to be served.

Outside the park itself is the **Disney Village,** a complex with restaurants, a disco, and shops. And finally, the newest addition, the **Walt Disney Studios Park** *(separate admission ticket),* where the secrets of Hollywood come alive, with attractions such as "Animagique," "Cinémagique," and the "Stunt Show Spectacular" (a big favorite). ■

Disneyland Paris

🅰 213 E3

✉ 20 miles (32 km) east of Paris in Marne-la-Vallée

☎ 08 25 30 60 30

💲 €€€€€

🚗 By car: A4 toward Nancy-Metz, exit 14. By train: RER A, exit Marne-la-Vallée-Chessy. Shuttles from Roissy & Orly airports

www.disneyland paris.com

Especially for Kids

Aside from Disneyland Paris, there are other local options for kids. At the **Thoiry Wildlife Reserve** *(Réserve Africaine et Parc Zoologique, tel 01 34 87 53 76, www.thoiry .net, €€€€€)* west of Paris on the D11, animals roam free as you drive through the park; there is also a traditional zoo.

North of Paris on the A1 at Plailly is an entire theme park devoted to a French favorite, the plucky comic hero Astérix. **Parc Astérix** *(tel 08 26 30 10 40, www*

.parcasterix.fr, closed Sept.–Easter except school holidays, shuttle buses leave from the Louvre and Eiffel Tower, €€€€€) comes complete with rides and attractions.

Parc France Miniature *(tel 08 26 30 20 40, www.franceminiature.com, closed Nov.–Feb., €€€–€€€€)* is a little known attraction beyond Versailles. More than 150 of France's famous monuments have been reconstructed at a tiny fraction of their size at a 12.3-acre (5 ha) park.

Vaux-le-Vicomte & Blandy

Vaux-le-Vicomte is one of the best examples of the Louis XIV style. If you can schedule a visit on Saturday night, don't miss the special Candlelight Evenings, when 2,000 candles illuminate the castle and gardens.

The magnificent Vaux-le-Vicomte is protected by a moat.

Vaux-le-Vicomte
- 212 D2
- 30 miles (50 km) southeast of Paris
- 01 64 14 41 90
- Open April–Oct. Thurs.–Tues.; daily July–Aug.
- €€€
- By train: Gare de Lyon to Melun, then taxi or shuttle bus

www.vaux-le-vicomte .com

Château Forteresse de Blandy-les-Tours
- 30 miles (50 km) southeast of Paris
- 01 60 59 17 80
- Closed Tues.
- €€

Vaux-le-Vicomte was built for Nicolas Fouquet by the greatest 17th-century French architects and designers—Louis Le Vau, Charles le Brun, and André Le Nôtre. However, Fouquet's fatal mistake was to create a palace even more radiant than the Sun King's, with most of the building funds embezzled from the French government.

Fouquet was one of the most powerful men in the kingdom when he began work on Vaux-le-Vicomte in 1653. For six years, he spent lavishly to create his splendid château and landscaped gardens. In 1661, fearful that he had fallen from the king's favor, Fouquet invited Louis XIV to a celebration that included 6,000 guests, fireworks, and complex waterworks.

A jealous Louis had him arrested that month and thrown into prison, where he remained until his death 15 years later. The king then requisitioned the furniture, statuary, tapestries, and the same architect to build Versailles.

Highlights include the oval salon, Le Brun's painted ceilings in the Salon des Muses, the restored kitchen, and the terraced gardens.

Blandy's Fortress

Just a few miles to the east of Vaux-le-Vicomte (*Map 213 E2*) is Blandy-les-Tours, the last remaining medieval fortress in the Île de France. The ruins lie in a valley, their stone towers lacking only colorful banners to make you believe you have stumbled into the Middle Ages. ∎

Provins

Every spring and summer, this hilltop town, a World Heritage site, transports visitors 800 years into the past, with knights in armor astride charging steeds, catapults assaulting ancient stone ramparts, falconry shows, and costumed actors.

Provins was an economic capital of the Champagne region as early as the tenth century; it traded in expensive silks, exotic spices, and wool during its twice-annual fair, which brought traders from all over Europe. A good place to discover the past is at the **Grange aux Dîmes,** a wax museum on Rue St.-Jean.

INSIDER TIP:

When in this village of yore, be sure to catch the fascinating equestrian falconry show.

—BARBARA A. NOE
National Geographic senior editor

The ancient upper town has been restored and now has 58 historical monuments that form the backdrop for colorful reenactments of medieval life *(April–Oct.).* A jousting tournament re-creates a battle in 1230, when Comte Thibaud de Champagne saved Provins from besieging armies. Every summer nearly 80 birds of prey swoop over the crowds in a demonstration of falconry.

A self-guided walking tour of the town (brochure available from tourist office) explores the 11th-century ramparts that extend nearly a mile around the old town. The César Tower stands high above the town, offering a fine view over the Brie region.

Both the upper and lower towns are honeycombed with nearly 6 miles (9.6 km) of ancient tunnels linking dozens of vaulted cellars. The walls bear the mysterious marks of various secret societies (including the Freemasons), who once used these underground galleries for their meetings.

A medieval feast is held during a weekend in June, and other events, including concerts and a sound-and-light show, are scheduled throughout the summer. ■

Provins

🔺 213 F2

✉ 50 miles (80 km) east of Paris

🚗 By car: A4 toward exit 13 at Serris, follow signs to Provins (D231). By train: Paris Gare de l'Est to Provins

Visitor Information

✉ Chemin de Villecran

☎ 01 64 60 26 26

www.provins.net

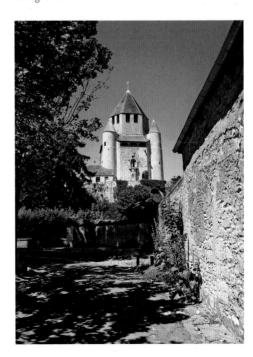

The César Tower in medieval Provins

Fontainebleau & Nearby

Fontainebleau is one of the most popular weekend destinations for Parisians, who flock to the forest to enjoy hiking, rock climbing, and riding. While Versailles reflects a single monarch's glory (Louis XIV), the royal abode of Fontainebleau has evolved constantly during the reigns of 30 different rulers of France, and much of its charm is due to the disparate elements and odd series of buildings they created. Like Versailles, however, it is immense.

The Château of Fontainebleau housed generations of French rulers, beginning in 1137.

The Château

Drawn by the abundant game in the forest, Louis VII began building here in 1137. Subsequent kings, similarly attracted to hunting, remodeled and expanded the property. The first major work was undertaken in 1530 by François I, who preferred Fontainebleau to his other royal palaces. He brought Italian artists (including Leonardo da Vinci, whose "Mona Lisa" hung on the walls at Fontainebleau before being transferred to the Louvre) and craftsmen to construct a magnificent mannerist palace to replace the existing modest hunting lodge; the frescoes and stucco work in the François I Gallery remain from this period.

Henri II continued his father's projects, including the 98-foot-long (30 m) ballroom—a dazzling display of Renaissance style, with a coffered ceiling by architect Philibert Delorme and frescoes by Italian artist Francesco Primaticcio. The exterior horseshoe staircase was constructed by Louis XIII; it is where Napoleon I famously addressed his men in 1814 before being sent into exile.

The emblems of various rulers can be spotted in different rooms: the interlaced "H" and "C," for Henri II and Catherine de Médicis (intended to be interpreted as a "D," for his mistress, Diane de Poitiers); Napoleon's insignia of golden bees, emblazoned on red velvet in the throne room; and François I's salamander. There is also a museum of Chinese works collected by Empress Eugénie as well as a Napoleon Museum.

Fontainebleau Forest

Covering 61,750 acres (25,009 ha), the forest is crisscrossed with roads, 200 miles (320 km) of marked paths, and countless lanes. The Fontainebleau tourist office provides maps of the forest and information for excursions. Although the elevation never climbs above 482 feet (127 m), the forest is popular with rock climbers. Bicycles can also be rented. Some of the more popular sites include the Apremont Gorges, the Franchard Gorges, and the Béatrix Grotto.

Other Places Nearby

The area around Fontainebleau is legendary in the history of painting. The village of **Barbizon** nearby *(Map 212 D2, tel 01 60 66 41 87)* was a mecca for 19th-century landscape painters including Daubigny, Corot, and Millet. The single main street is lined with antique dealers and art galleries, as well as a couple of museums: the **Auberge Ganne,** and the house-studios of both Millet and Theodore Rousseau.

Thoméry *(Map 213 E1, visitor information available at Fontainebleau),* nestled in a loop of the Seine, has long been famous for its Chasselas Doré grapes. The fortified town of **Moret-sur-Loing** *(Map 213 E1, tel 01 60 70 41 66),* immortalized by painters such as Camille Pissarro, hosts a spectacular sound-and-light show on Saturday nights from mid-June through mid-September. And **Samois-sur-Seine** *(Map 212 D1),* in the middle of Fontainebleau Forest, hosts the annual summer Django Reinhardt Jazz Festival. ∎

Fontainebleau

- 212 D1
- 40 miles (60 km) southeast of Paris near Melun

Visitor Information

- 4 rue Royale, Fontainebleau
- 01 60 74 99 99
- **www.fontainebleau-tourisme.com**

Château de Fontainebleau

- 01 60 71 50 70
- Closed Tues.
- €€–€€€
- By car: A6 south, exit at Fontainebleau. By train: Paris Gare de Lyon to Fontainebleau-Avon, then take bus A to château.
- **www.musee-chateau-fontainebleau.fr**

EXPERIENCE: A Walk in the Royal Forest

Art, history, nature, and photography lovers—not to mention rock-climbing enthusiasts—all owe themselves a walk through the **Fontainebleau Forest** *(www.fontainebleau-tourisme.com).* Pathways lead you through the trees of this surprisingly large woodland, popular with weekend visitors from Paris and beyond.

In the 19th century, this was the favorite spot for painting *en plein air* for Barbizon School artists Camille Corot, Gustave Courbet, Théodore Rousseau, and others. Bring a sketchbook or a camera—you are sure to be inspired by the surrealistic rock formations, carved by the sands of an ancient sea, and by the wealth of vegetation (some 5,000 plant species).

Don't be surprised if a family of roe deer, one of 6,600 animal species living in the forest, goes leaping by. The occasional poetry-inscribed 19th-century fountain or grotto in the middle of the forest adds to its romantic atmosphere.

Rambouillet & Around

Although not the most beautiful château in the Île de France region, Rambouillet (now a presidential retreat) sits in the middle of a magnificent forest, with plenty of nearby excursions.

Once a lodge for Louis XVI, Rambouillet now hosts heads of state.

Château de Rambouillet

 212 B2

✉ 30 miles (50 km) southwest of Paris

☎ 01 34 83 00 25

🕐 Closed Tues.

💲 €€

www.chateau-rambouillet.monuments-nationaux.fr

Rochefort-en-Yvelines

🔼 212 C2

✉ 10 miles (16 km) southeast of Rambouillet

Montfort-l'Amaury

🔼 212 B3

✉ 16 miles (26 km) north of Rambouillet

The Château

Rambouillet was renovated and modified by successive owners. Louis XVI, a frequent guest on hunting expeditions, acquired the long-coveted property in 1784, adding several rustic features for Queen Marie-Antoinette—including a dairy and sheepfold. Since 1897, the château has been used by France's heads of state.

Visitors can tour the château, apartments, queen's dairy and National Sheepfold, and magnificent French-style water gardens with their large artificial lakes. One of the château's most famous rooms is the Napoleon I bathroom decorated with a mock ancient fresco in 1807. There is also a cottage adorned inside with seashells, mother of pearl, and marble.

Nearby Places

Southeast of Rambouillet, **Rochefort-en-Yvelines** has hardly changed for centuries. An 11th-century village, **Montfort-l'Amaury** is one of the prettiest in the area, its château visible atop the hillside. ■

Abbaye de Vaux-de-Cernay

Founded in 1148, the Abbaye de Vaux-de-Cernay *(Map 212 C2, tel 01 34 85 23 00)*, 6 miles (10 km) northeast of Rambouillet, is spectacular, with vaulted ceilings and stone walls. It functioned as a prosperous Cistercian abbey until the Revolution and is now a luxury hotel.

Auvers-sur-Oise

Auvers is something of a pilgrimage site for people seeking traces of van Gogh. A series of panels representing famous paintings by van Gogh, Cézanne, and others have been placed all over town on the exact sites where they were painted. The tourist office has suggestions for walks, taking in the Auberge Ravoux, where van Gogh died after a self-inflicted bullet wound on July 29, 1890, and the church and cornfields immortalized by the painter.

Van Gogh lived here for only 70 days, under the care of close friend Dr. Gachet (homeopathic doctor to the artists of Auvers-sur-Oise), but he worked frenetically, producing 70 paintings and numerous drawings. He is buried in the local cemetery next to his brother.

INSIDER TIP:

If you favor the taste of anise, try some modern absinthe, prepared in the traditional way with cold sugary water.

—PATRICIA DANIELS
National Geographic contributor

Before van Gogh arrived, Auvers was already a favorite destination of 19th-century landscape painters. Charles Daubigny, a member of the Barbizon school, moored a houseboat here in 1857 and was soon followed by many other artists, who used his **studio** (*61 rue Daubigny, tel 01 34 48 03 03, open Sat.–Sun. Easter–Oct., €€*), established in 1861 on what is now Rue Daubigny, as a meeting place. Daubigny campaigned for younger painters like Renoir,

Monet, and Cézanne, who also visited him, along with Corot and Daumier. Daubigny's paintings and memorabilia are in the **Daubigny Museum** (*Colombières Manor, Rue de la Sansonne, tel 01 30 36 80 20, closed Mon.–Tues. & a.m. except Sat.–Sun. April–Oct., €*).

Two other museums are worth visiting in Auvers: The **Absinthe Museum** (*44 rue Alphonse Callé, tel 01 30 36 83 26, closed Nov.–Feb., call for opening times, €*) explores the elixir known as "the green peril"; and the **Château d'Auvers** (*2 rue de Léry, tel 01 34 48 48 48, closed Mon. & Christmas–mid-Jan., €€€*) offers a presentation on the Impressionists. ∎

Auvers-sur-Oise
- 🅰 212 C4
- ✉ 22 miles (35 km) north of Paris
- 🚆 By train: Paris Gare du Nord to Auvers-sur-Oise (via Pontoise) April–Nov.; direct train on weekends

**www.auvers-sur-oise
.com**

Auberge Ravoux
- ✉ Place de la Mairie
- ☎ 01 30 36 60 60
- 🕐 Closed Mon. & Tues. & Dec.–Feb.
- 💲 €

Van Gogh painted cottages in Auvers in 1890, shortly before his death.

Chartres Cathedral

For nearly 800 years, Chartres Cathedral has stood like a beacon, seemingly alone amid the flat fields of the Beauce region. Little has changed since the 13th century. Despite fires, revolutions, two world wars, and overzealous restorers, the church has remained almost intact from the day it was consecrated in 1260.

The glowing beauty of Chartres has remained intact since the Middle Ages.

The present cathedral stands on the site of earlier churches dating from the eighth century. The most important event in its history was the gift of the "Sancta Camisia," a priceless relic presented by Charles the Bald, Charlemagne's grandson. This was the tunic supposedly worn by Mary as she gave birth to Christ, and it transformed Chartres into one of the most popular pilgrimage shrines in Europe (the relic is still stored in the Treasury). In the tenth century, the School of Chartres was one of the most prestigious centers of learning in Europe.

A series of fires destroyed the successive churches, but the most serious one was in 1194, when the entire city went up in flames, destroying everything but the Royal Portal and the western towers of the church. The local townspeople were mortified to think that the precious relic had been lost. Three days later, as the church lay smoldering, a procession appeared holding the relic. This miracle was seen as a sign from Mary that Chartres would be an ever greater church, and the rebuilding project was begun immediately with great zeal. The result is this breathtaking Gothic cathedral. Its architectural and sculptural unity is chiefly due to the fact that it was constructed almost entirely in less than 30 years.

"Chartres Blue" Stained Glass

The cathedral's stained-glass windows, with the unique "Chartres blue" color, are famous throughout the world. They form the most complete collection of medieval glass anywhere. The 12th-century Royal Portal survived the great fire, as did its glass and the spectacular window known as "the Blue Virgin." The 13th-century windows in the rest of the church form radiant illustrations of biblical and historical scenes, peopled with knights, peasants, kings, noble ladies in furs, and craftsmen at work, providing a fascinating record of religion and daily life in medieval times. Each panel tells a story to be read from left to right, and bottom to top.

Statuary & Maze

The statuary on the three main portals completes the iconography of the church. The North Porch shows the story of Creation (on the left side), leading to the Fall of Adam and Eve (right), followed by Old Testament figures, and a nativity scene. The South Porch depicts scenes of the Last Judgment.

Unfortunately, the rows of chairs now in the nave hide the best-preserved stone labyrinth in France, where pilgrims used to make their way through the 953-foot-long (291 m) maze on their knees.

What to See & Do

Take a tour (in English) by resident historian Malcolm Miller, who offers a look at the glass, sculptures, and history of the cathedral. Check times with the tourist office.

If you have a few extra hours, the old town is worth exploring. The tourist office provides maps of a Circuit Touristique that takes you to the former **Episcopal Palace** and the **Fine Arts Museum** and down to the river, which winds past an old mill and half-

INSIDER TIP:

As you gaze at the cathedral's stained glass, think of how advanced it must have seemed to pilgrims in the Middle Ages.

—DIANA PARSELL
National Geographic contributor

timbered Renaissance houses and over stone bridges. A small train runs during the tourist season and follows much the same itinerary through the town.

Don't miss the **St.-Pierre Church** nearby at Place St.-Pierre. Usually overshadowed by the more famous cathedral, it also contains some fine 13th- and 14th-century stained glass. ∎

Chartres

 212 B2

✉ 52 miles (83 km) southwest of Paris

🚗 By car: Take the A6, then A10, then A11 toward Le Mans & follow signs to Chartres. By train: Paris Gare Montparnasse to Chartres. Tel 08 92 35 35 35 for national lines, tel 3658 for Île de France. SNCF information: www.voyages-sncf.com

www.diocese chartres.com/ cathedrale

Visitor Information

✉ Place de la Cathédrale

☎ 02 37 18 26 26

www.chartres-tourisme.com

Giverny

In 1883, Claude Monet moved with his family to this house, where he remained until his death in 1926. The house and gardens were an unceasing source of inspiration for the painter. Wherever he lived, Monet always had a garden, but at Giverny it became his life's work: There he created in nature the motifs that became his obsession, transposing the water lilies, boats, and bridges of his garden onto his canvases.

Monet's carefully tended gardens at Giverny are reflected in his art.

Giverny

 212 B4

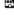 49 miles (78 km) northwest of Paris

 By car: Autoroute de l'Ouest (A13/ E05) from Pont de St.-Cloud, toward Rouen. Exit at Bonnières, follow the D201 to Giverny. By train: from Paris-Gare St.-Lazare on the Rouen line, get off at Vernon, & take a local bus or a taxi, or walk the 3 miles.

By 1966, when his son Michel donated Giverny to the Académie des Beaux-Arts, the floors and ceiling beams had rotted away. It took ten years to restore the house and the gardens; the museum eventually opened in 1980, and now hosts nearly 500,000 visitors every year.

Gardens

Whatever season you arrive, the garden is as much a profusion of color as it was in Monet's lifetime. When the family first moved here, the garden was a modest orchard of about 2 acres, enclosed within high stone walls. The painter transformed it, creating patterns and perspectives by planting clumps and shapes of color that changed with every month. Monet detested the formal French garden and instead created rose-covered archways entwined with trailing nasturtiums, dividing the garden into brilliant flower beds filled with hollyhocks and annuals.

Ten years after he moved to Giverny, Monet bought the land on the other side of the railroad tracks, intending to divert the Epte River to create a pond and water garden. He had an artificial lake dug and then created an exotic garden with bamboo plants, wisteria, willows, and, of course, the famous water lilies. A local craftsman built the graceful Japanese bridge; a wooden boat still floats at one end of the pond.

House & Studio

The house, with its pink, roughcast facade and green shutters, was the scene of frequent entertaining for Monet's many guests. Friends such as Sacha Guitry, Stéphane Mallarmé, and Pierre-Auguste Rodin gathered in the blue-tiled kitchen and sunny yellow dining room.

Monet loved Japanese engravings, and his precious collection (which inspired his design of the water garden) is displayed in several of the rooms. On the walls of the modest living room hung Monet's personal collection of works he particularly admired, including a dozen Cézannes, a few Renoirs, eight Manets, a couple of Degas, and two bronzes by Rodin. Now

dispersed to collections around the world, these works have been reproduced to re-create the interior in Monet's day.

Visitors enter through the huge Nympheas studio, which was constructed in 1916 to give Monet the room and light he needed to paint the giant "Water Lilies," which were commissioned by his friend Georges Clemenceau for the Musée de l'Orangerie in Paris (see p. 140). Today, the studio exhibits reproductions of his work and includes a souvenir shop.

To avoid the crowds, come on a weekday. (Wednesdays can also be busy.) Tour buses often leave around 4 p.m., but the gardens stay open until 6 p.m., which is a lovely time to enjoy them.

Museum of Impressionisms

Also worth seeing is the Museum of Impressionisms, which has replaced the Museum of American Art. Devoted to Impressionism and its evolution in the 20th century, the museum holds both thematic and one-artist exhibitions. ∎

Claude Monet Museum
- ✉ 84 rue Claude Monet
- ☎ 02 32 51 28 21
- 🕐 Open April–Oct.
- 💲 €€

www.fondation-monet.com

Museum of Impressionisms
- ✉ 99 rue Claude Monet
- ☎ 02 32 51 94 65
- 🕐 Closed March–Nov.
- 💲 €€

www.museedes impressionismes giverny.com

EXPERIENCE: Art Classes en Plein Air

Learn to paint in Monet's garden and around his beloved village of Giverny. English-language artistic retreats are run by the venerable **ArtStudy/Giverny** (www.giverny.org/artists/schools/artstudy .com), with hands-on workshops taught by professional artists. In 8- or 11-day sessions, painters and photographers at every level of skill have a chance to capture the en plein air spirit at sites made

famous by French and American Impressionist painters.

There is daily instruction in watercolors, pastels, oils, and acrylics. The teaching is based on the classic principles of fine art with emphasis on analyzing composition and color directly from nature. Students are asked to assume the Impressionist point of view that observation is the key to the creative imagination.

More Places to Visit Around Paris

Château de Chantilly & Forest

Set in the middle of a romantic moat in the heart of the forest, Chantilly is one of the most beautiful châteaus around Paris. It was destroyed during the Revolution but has been re-created and is now home to the **Condé Museum,** an art collection put together by the Duc d'Aumale in the 19th century.

What sets Chantilly off from other châteaus, however, is the **Horse Museum and Great Stables** (circa 1719–1735; tel 03 44 57 13 13), housed in a monumental stone building that at its height held 240 horses and 300 hounds. The public can attend dressage demonstrations daily, except Tuesdays. Chantilly is also the site of one of France's major horse-racing tracks.

Other sites nearby include the Cistercian **Abbaye de Royaumont** (Map 212 D4, Asnières-sur-Oise, tel 01 30 35 59 00) and the ancient royal town of **Senlis** (Map 212 D4). www.chateau dechantilly.com

🅰 212 D4 ✉ Chantilly, 25 miles (40 km) north of Paris ☎ 03 44 27 31 80 🕐 Closed Tues. 💲 €€€ 🚇 By car: Take the A1 to the Chantilly exit, then the D924A to Chantilly. By train: Gare du Nord or RER Line D to Chantilly-Gouvieux (then a short walk).

Château de Malmaison

Josephine purchased this property when Napoleon was still the First Consul. He found his official residence, the Tuileries Palace, too depressing and retreated to Malmaison whenever he could. Josephine kept the château after Napoleon divorced her, and she devoted considerable sums to the house and gardens, creating the first great collection of roses here. The house is now a museum devoted to Napoleonic history and Empire memorabilia. www. chateau-malmaison.fr

🅰 212 C3 ✉ 1 avenue du Château, Rueil-Malmaison ☎ 01 41 29 05 55 🕐 Closed Tues. 💲 €€ 🚇 By Métro or

RER: Line A to Grande Arche de la Défense, then bus 258

Écouen Château & Museum

Many of the works in the collection of this Renaissance museum came from the Musée de Cluny in Paris. The magnificent 16th-century château was constructed by some of the most famous artists of the time, including Le Rosso and Jean Clouet; the south wing has remained nearly intact since that time. The collection includes a series of 16th-century tapestries depicting the story of David and Bathsheba. www.musee-renaissance.fr

🅰 212 D3 ✉ Écouen, 12 miles (19 km) north of Paris off N16 ☎ 01 34 38 38 50 🕐 Closed Tues. 💲 € 🚇 By train: Gare du Nord to Écouen-Ézanville, then bus No. 269

Château de Saint-Germain-en-Laye

This magnificent pile of medieval and Renaissance architecture stands on a plateau in the center of the town of Saint-Germain-en-Laye, about 25 minutes from Paris by train (RER A to Saint-Germain-en-Laye). The royal château, which now houses the **National Museum of Archaeology** (tel 01 39 10 13 00, www.musee-antiquitesnationales. fr, closed Tues., €€) is a stunning sight. The 13th-century chapel was the work of Pierre de Montreuil, architect of Saint-Chapelle in Paris, and is a smaller model of that church. Louis XIV was born at Saint-Germain-en-Laye and turned it into a luxurious residence, complete with terraced gardens. The chapel and the gardens, with their lovely views over the valley of the Seine, with Paris in the distance, can be visited for free.

Travelwise

A parking spot is a rarity in Paris.

TRAVELWISE

PLANNING YOUR TRIP
When to Go

If you visit in late summer, when many residents are vacationing, you'll find that some stores and restaurants are closed. However, Paris has a special, sometimes villagelike quality in August. The city has less traffic and pollution and offers free activities like Paris Plages, concerts in the parks, and outdoor movies at La Villette. Another advantage of the summer months is that it is low season for the hotels, and many offer reduced rates. Reservations are also easier to obtain, as there are no major conventions or events being held.

In fall, the Parisians return, the weather is good, and the city bustles again. Winter and spring are often cold and rainy, but the Christmas holidays can light up the city.

Climate

Paris has moderately cold winters, with little snow; cool springs and falls; and moderately hot, humid summers.

What to Take

Be prepared for rain in any season, and always pack a sweater, even in the summer. Other necessities: comfortable walking shoes, a dressy outfit for evenings out, and a major credit card with an international PIN number (check with your bank) so you can withdraw cash from money machines. Don't forget the essentials: passport, driver's license, and insurance documentation.

Insurance

Make sure you have adequate coverage for medical treatment and expenses, including repatriation, and baggage and money loss.

Passports

For U.S. and Canadian citizens only a passport is needed to enter France for a stay of up to 90 days. No visa is required.

HOW TO GET TO PARIS
Airports

Roissy–Charles de Gaulle (north of Paris), tel 3950
Orly (south of Paris), tel 3950
Airport information: www .aeroportsdeparis.fr
Direct flights to Paris are available from most major cities via Air France (tel 800/237-2747) and many other international airlines. Paris has two airports: Roissy-Charles de Gaulle and Orly. To get into town from Roissy-Charles de Gaulle, take a taxi (around €50); the Air France bus (stops at Porte Maillot, Étoile, Gare Montparnasse, Gare de Lyon); the Roissybus (stops at Opéra); or the RER, the regional mass-transport train (Line B stops at Gare du Nord, Châtelet, St.-Michel, Luxembourg, Port-Royal, and Denfert-Rochereau). From Orly, take a taxi (around €45); the Orlybus (stops at Denfert-Rochereau); the Air France bus (stops at Gare Montparnasse, Invalides, Étoile); or the Orlyval train (connects with RER at Antony station).
You can arrange for a door-to-door shuttle:
Paris Limousine Shuttle (tel 01 48 41 41 28, www.paris-ls .com, chauffeured car for up to 3 persons: €90; up to 7: €110)
Super Shuttle Paris (tel 01 43 65 55 55, www.supershuttleparis.fr, from €20 per person)

• **Blue Airport Shuttle Paris** (tel 01 30 11 13 00, www.paris-blue-airport-shuttle.fr, from €27 per person)

GETTING AROUND
By Car
Car Rentals in France

Ada, tel 08 25 16 91 69, www.ada.fr
Avis, tel 08 20 05 05 05, www.avis.fr
Europcar, tel 08 25 35 83 58, www.europcar.fr
Hertz, tel 01 41 91 95 25, www.hertz.fr
Driving in Paris is not advised—the traffic is heavy, street parking scarce, and you can get wherever you want to go using the good urban-transport system or plentiful taxis. However, if you wish to rent a car, check with your travel agent at home first before trying the agencies in France, as prices are often lower when a car is booked from the United States.

Driving Regulations

An international driver's license is not required for short-term visitors. When driving, keep all relevant documents in the car. Remember that at unmarked intersections, the car coming from the right has priority and will not stop; slow down and look to the right when crossing an intersection. Seat belts are required for all passengers, even in the back seat. Children under ten are not allowed to ride in the front seat unless a special seat is provided for them. It is illegal to use a cell phone while driving.

In the absence of speed-limit signs, the limit is 30 mph/50 kph in villages, towns, and cities; 55 mph/90 kph (50 mph/80 kph in wet weather) on country roads; 70

mph/110 kph (60 mph/100 kph in wet weather) on divided roads and highways in urban areas; and 80 mph/130 kph (70 mph/110 kph in wet weather; 30 mph/50 kph in foggy conditions) on highways. If you have had more than two glasses of wine, you are over the legal limit and should not drive. If your car is towed or clamped in Paris, go to the nearest police station to find out how to retrieve it.

Car Breakdown
Europ Assistance, tel 01 41 85 85 85 or 08 10 00 50 50
SOS Dépannage, tel 01 47 07 99 99
For rental cars, check the package of information in the glove compartment for the emergency number. Europ Assistance offers a towing service that costs at least €150. For 24-hour car repairs, call SOS Dépannage. Otherwise, look for a *garagiste* (garage) along the road. An "N" symbol means that it is open at night. There is one repair service open in every town on Sunday. Call the police (17) or the local *gendarmerie* (police station) if you can't find a garage. On *autoroutes* (highways), emergency phones are located alongside the road at regular intervals.

Public Transportation
Métro
tel 3646, www.ratp.fr
Operates: 5:30 a.m.–12:30 a.m., (1:30 a.m. on Fri.–Sat.)

Noctilien (Night Bus)
Operates: 12:30 a.m.–5:30 a.m.

Balabus
Operates: noon–9 p.m., May–Sept.

RER
Operates: 5:30 a.m.–12:45 p.m.
Métro The Parisian subway,

known as the Métro, is operated by the Regie Autonome des Transports Parisiens (RATP). A map is posted in every station, or ask for a free *Plan du Métro* when you buy your ticket. Each line has a number, and is identified by the names of the station at either end: The east–west line 1, for example, is La Défense–Château de Vincennes.

Individual tickets are available, but a *carnet* (book) of ten tickets is better value if you plan to use the Métro frequently. Passe Navigo Découverte is good for unlimited trips on the Métro, RER, and buses for one month or one week *(Mon.–Sun.)*. You will need a passport-size photo for the Passe. These tickets should not be validated on buses, just shown to the driver. A Paris Visite card, available from ticket booths in the Métro, good for one, two, three, or five days, entitles you to unlimited use of public transportation in Paris and the Île de France and discounts at some sightseeing attractions. The Mobilis card, also available from ticket booths in the Métro, is good for one day only, exclusively for transportation.

Do not throw away a one-use ticket until you have left the station; a *contrôleur* (conductor) may ask to see your ticket, and will fine you if you do not have one.
RER The suburban train network, the RER, has stops in Paris, and you can use a Métro ticket to travel on it within Paris. Prices are higher for destinations outside the city.
Buses Métro tickets can also be used on city buses (validate one-use tickets in the machine behind the driver) or tickets can be purchased from the driver (exact change not required). A map of bus lines is posted at bus shelters. Some bus lines do not operate after 8:30 p.m., or on Sundays and holidays. This information is posted at bus stops. Forty-seven late-night bus lines, called

Noctilien, leave from Châtelet, Montparnasse, Gare de l'Est, Gare St.-Lazare, and Gare de Lyon. The **Batobus** *(www.batobus .com)* river buses run between the Eiffel Tower and the Jardin des Plantes. **L'Open Tour** *(tel 01 42 66 56 56, www.parislopentour.com),* a sight-seeingbus line, has four routes. One-, two-, or three-day passes are sold. Commentaries are in ten languages (on headphones). The tours operate seven days a week, year-round.

Taxis
Taxis can be hailed on the street or found at a *station de taxi* (taxi stand) at major intersections. When the entire light on top is glowing, the taxi is available, but if only the small bulb is lit, it is not. Some new cabs have green/red lights to indicate availability. Extra charges are added to the fare for pickups at train stations, luggage weighing over 12 lbs/5 kg, a fourth passenger (drivers can refuse to take more than three people), and an animal (except a seeing-eye dog). Tipping is at your discretion, but about ten percent of the fare is customary.

If you call for a taxi, the meter starts running when the driver receives the call, and the fare can be expensive. It is a good idea to ask for a receipt in case you leave something behind, or have a problem with the driver. Fares go up at night and when the cab passes the city limits.

Any complaints about Paris taxis should be addressed to Service des Taxis, Préfecture de Police, 36 rue des Morillons, Paris 75015, tel 01 55 76 20 05.

Radio-Dispatched Taxis
Alpha-Taxis, tel 01 45 85 85 85, www.alphataxis.fr
Taxis G7, tel 01 47 39 47 39, www.taxisg7.fr

Taxis Bleus, tel 01 49 36 10 10, www.taxis-bleus.com

Motorcycle taxis
(with driver, helmet supplied):
City Bird, tel 08 26 10 01 00, www.city-bird.com

Limousine services
Executive Car, tel 01 42 65 54 20, www.executive-car.com
Prestige Limousines, tel 01 47 30 54 54, www.prestige-limousines .com

Trains
SNCF The national French railroad, the SNCF (Société Natio-nale des Chemin de Fer) links Paris and all major cities.
Information and reservations, tel 08 92 35 35 35 (7 a.m.–10 p.m.); for suburban lines, tel 3658.

The Paris mainline SNCF train stations (each with a Métro station of the same name) are the Gare de Lyon (for traveling to/from the southeast of France and Italy); the Gare du Nord (Brussels, London, and other northern destinations); the Gare de l'Est (the east); the Gare St.-Lazare (the northwest, including Normandy); the Gare d'Austerlitz (Spain and the south-west); and the Gare Montparnasse (the west, including Brittany). Phone for times and reservations, reserve online at www.voyages-sncf .com, or buy your ticket at the sta-tion (phone service is expensive).

TGV The high-speed *Train à Grande Vitesse* (TGV) will get you to Marseilles in just over three hours, Brussels in one-and-a-half hours, or London in two-and-a-quarter (by Eurostar via the Channel Tunnel). Reserve in advance for all TGV and Eurostar trips.

Before boarding any train, it is essential to *composter* (validate) your ticket in one of the yellow machines at the start of each journey. You may be fined by the conductor if you don't.

Tours & Organized Sightseeing
Bus Tours
Tours of the city and its monu-ments:
Balabus, www.ratp.info
Cityrama, tel 01 44 55 61 00, www.pariscityrama.com
Paris Vision, tel 01 42 60 30 01, en.parisvision.com
Paris L'Open Tour, tel 01 42 66 56 56 (also see p. 235)

Walking Tours
A variety of tours, from museums and monuments to historic districts:
Paris Walks, tel 01 48 09 21 40, www.paris-walks.com
Classic Walks, classicwalksparis .com

Bicycle & Segway Tours
Tours of different neighborhoods and parks; some night tours available:
Paris à Vélo C'est Sympa, 22 rue Alphonse Baudin, 75011, tel 01 48 87 60 01, www.parisvelosympa .com
City Segway Tours, 24 rue Edgar Faure, 75015, tel 01 56 58 10 54. citysegwaytours.com/paris

Boat Tours
The following companies offer regular hour-long Seine tours all day long, starting at around 10 a.m. and ending between 10 p.m. and 11 p.m. (later in summer). Some also offer dinner cruises.
The Seine
Bateaux-Mouches, Pont de l'Alma, 75008, tel 01 42 25 96 10, www.bateaux-mouches.fr, Métro: Alma-Marceau.
Bateaux Parisiens Tour Eiffel, Port de la Bourdonnais, 75007, tel 08 25 01 01 01 or 01 44 11 35 35, www.bateauxparisiens.com, Métro: Bir Hakeim.
Vedettes de Paris, Port de Suffren, 75007, tel 01 47 05 71

29, www.vedettesdeparis.com, Métro: Bir-Hakeim.
Bateaux Vedettes du Pont Neuf, Square du Vert-Galant, Île de la Cité, 75001, tel 01 46 33 98 38, www.vedettesdupontneuf.com, Métro: Pont-Neuf.

The Canals
Canauxrama, 13 quai de la Loire, tel 01 42 39 15 00 (reservations required), www.canauxrama.com. Three-hour canal cruise. Departs: Bassin de la Villette (Métro: Jaurès) 9:45 a.m. and 2:45 p.m.; Port de l'Arsenal (Métro: Bastille), 9:45 a.m. and 2:30 p.m.
Paris Canal, Port de Solferino, tel 01 42 40 81 60 (reservations required): The Canal St.-Martin and the Seine in three hours. Departs: Quai Anatole France, near Musée d'Orsay (Métro: Solferino), 9:30 a.m.; Parc de la Villette (Métro: Jaurès), 2:30 p.m.

PRACTICAL ADVICE
Communications
Post Offices
Main Branch: 52 rue du Louvre, 75001, tel 3631, www.laposte .fr, Métro: Louvre or Les Halles. Open: 24 hours daily. Local branches open: Mon.–Fri., 8 a.m.–7 or 8 p.m.; Sat., 8 or 9 a.m.–noon or 1 p.m.

Known as "La Poste," the French postal service has branches in every neighborhood. To receive mail there, letters should be addressed with your name clearly printed, followed by "Poste Restante" and the post office's address. All Paris postal codes begin with 75, and end with the number of the arrondissement, or quarter. For example, 75010 is in the 10th arrondissement, 75002 in the 2nd arrondissement, and so on.

Mailboxes Yellow *boîtes postales* (mailboxes) are located outside every post office. They may have separate compartments for local mail, *départemental* (mail within the départemente, and *autres départe-ments/étranger* (elsewhere in France and foreign).

Telephones
To call France from the United States, dial 011-33 (international and French country code) and the nine-digit number (leaving out the initial zero).

To make a domestic call from a telephone booth within France, buy a *télécarte* (phonecard) in a post office or *tabac* (tobacco shop). The following instructions will appear on the telephone's screen: *"décro-chez"* (pick up the receiver); *"insérez votre carte"* (insert your card); *"pati-entez"* (wait); *"numérotez/composez"* (dial the number); and *"raccrochez"* (hang up).

All French phone numbers have ten digits, with Paris-region numbers beginning with 01. The four other national prefixes are: 02 for the northwest; 03 for the northeast; 04 for the southeast; and 05 for the southwest. Numbers beginning with 08 00 are toll free. There is an extra charge for other numbers beginning with 08.

To make an international call, dial 00, followed by the country code (1 for the United States and Canada), the area code, and the number. American long-distance operators include World Phone: 01 30 25 94 10; and Sprint: 01 53 75 69 20.

To reach French directory assistance, dial 12. For international directory assistance, dial 118-700. For French directory assistance, dial 118-712 or go to www.pages blanches.fr (individuals) or www .pagesjaunes.fr (businesses).

Newspapers
Most kiosks (newsstands) sell some English-language newspa-pers, including the *International Herald Tribune*, *USA Today*, *The Wall Street Journal*, *The Financial Times*, and sometimes other British or Irish dailies. The major French

daily papers are the left-wing *Libération*, the left-leaning *Le Monde*, and the conservative *Le Figaro*. The only paper published on Sunday is the *Journal du Dimanche*.

Television
The basic stations available on non-cable TVs are TF1, France 2, France 3, Arte, and M6. Most programs are in French. Cable stations include Canal+, a movie channel with some films in the original language, CNN, France 24 (news), BBC Prime, MTV, MCM (music videos), Eurosport, Planète (nature and science), RAI Uno (Italian), TVE 1 (Spanish), and Euronews. Many programs can be viewed in either the original language or in French. Look for the "VM" option in the TV guide.

Radio
For a mix of pop, rock, jazz, and classical with no commercials, try FIP (105.1 FM). Radio Nova (101.5 FM) offers rap, soul, and other forms of African-American, African, or Afro-Caribbean music; Radio Latina (99 FM) Latin music; France-Info (105.5 FM) 24-hour news in French; Skyrock (96 FM) pop; RFM (103.9 FM) pop and rock; Radio Classique (101.1 FM) classical music; and TSF Jazz (89.9)

Movies & Books Set in Paris
The romantic setting of Paris has provided the background for innumerable works of film and literature. The list is endless.

Movies
An abbreviated list of some well-known American and international movies set here includes: *An American in Paris, Love in the Afternoon, Funny Face, Desire, Paris When It Sizzles, Paris by Night,*

Paris Calling, National Lampoon's European Vacation, The 400 Blows, Small Change, Breathless, The Last Métro, Last Tango in Paris, Frantic, French Kiss, Amélie, Midnight in Paris. If you want to see any or all of these films, visit the Forum des Images *(2 & 4 rue du Cinéma),* which has an archive of just about every film having anything to do with Paris. For a small fee, you can watch any of them on your own video screen.

Books
The following novels and mem-oirs are steeped in Parisian ambi-ence: *Tropic of Cancer* and *Quiet Days in Clichy* by Henry Miller; *Quartet* by Jean Rhys; *A Moveable Feast* by Ernest Hemingway; *The Autobiography of Alice B. Toklas* and *Paris France* by Gertrude Stein; *Being Geniuses Together* by Robert McAlmon and Kay Boyle; *Shakespeare and Company* by Sylvia Beach; *The Paris Edition* by Waverly Root; *Down and Out in Paris and London* by George Orwell; *The Secret Paris of the 30s* by Brassaï; *The Diary of Anaïs Nin* by Anaïs Nin; *Force of Circumstance* by Simone de Beauvoir; *Paris Notebooks* by Mavis Gallant; *Paris Journal* and *Paris Was Yesterday* by Janet Flanner; *Paris Journal* by M.F.K. Fisher; *Paris* by Julian Green; *Paris in the '50s* by Stanley Karnow. The ultimate work set in Paris is Marcel Proust's *Remem-brance of Things Past.*

Electricity
French circuits use 220 volts; a transformer and adapter plug are needed for American appliances that operate on 110 volts. Many appliances are equipped with switches that convert them from one voltage to the other, but an adapter plug is still needed. Ask at a *droguerie* (hardware store) or in the basement of the BHV store at 52 rue de Rivoli.

Local Customs

Say "bonjour" and "au revoir" to the staff when entering and leaving a shop, restaurant, or café. The French tend to keep to themselves more than Americans do, but as elsewhere a friendly approach usually gets a friendly response, and certainly the natives are always more than willing to give directions. If you are invited to dinner at a French person's home, bring flowers rather than wine.

Money Matters

Banque de France, 31 rue Croix-des-Petits-Champs, 75001, tel 01 42 92 42 92, Métro: Palais-Royal **American Express,** 11 rue Scribe, 75009, tel 01 47 77 77 07 or 01 47 77 70 00, Métro: Opéra

In early 2011, one U.S. dollar equaled .72 euro. One euro equals 100 centimes, which come in coins of 1, 2, 5, 10, 20, and 50. The euro comes in coins of 1 and 2, and bills of 5, 10, 20, 50, 100, and 500, although many shops may not accept bills over 50.

Commercial currency exchanges are located in train stations, airports, and numerous locations around the city. Bank branches that exchange currency display a sign saying *"Change."* A commission is usually charged. The Banque de France usually has the best exchange rate. Cash withdrawals against a credit card are possible at banks and currency exchanges. The American Express office exchanges currency, offering special services to Amex cardholders.

ATMs are the easiest way to get money, but an international PIN number is required. Check with your bank before leaving. In France, credit and debit cards now often have a chip containing the ID. Foreign cards usually have this information on a magnetic strip, which may occasionally cause problems. A fee is usually charged for credit card advances, but the exchange rate

may be more advantageous than those offered by banks.

National Holidays

January 1, Easter Monday, May 1, May 8, Ascension (40 days after Easter), Pentecost Monday (10 days after Ascension), July 14, August 15, November 1, November 11, December 25.

Opening Times

Most banks are open Monday to Friday, from 9 a.m.–5 p.m. Some close at lunchtime or open on Saturday morning. Major department stores are open from about 9:30 a.m.–7 p.m., and some stay open till 10 p.m. one night of the week. Boutiques open around 10 a.m. and close at 7 p.m. or 8 p.m.; they may be closed on Monday and at lunchtime, usually between 1 p.m. and 2:30 p.m. More and more shops are staying open on Sunday, but check first. Cafés are open from early morning until 8 p.m., 10 p.m., or 2 a.m. Most restaurants are open from noon–3 p.m. and 7:30 p.m.–11 p.m. Many stores and restaurants close in August.

Time Differences

Paris is one hour ahead of Greenwich mean time. If it is midnight in Paris, it is 6 p.m. in New York, 3 p.m. in California.

Tipping

All restaurant bills include a 15 percent service charge. It is usual to leave a small additional tip for the waiter if the service has been good. It is customary to tip taxi drivers 10 percent, though this is not obligatory. It is usual to give porters, doormen, tour guides, and hairdressers a tip of €1–2, ushers and cloakroom attendants 50 centimes. There is no need to leave a tip for hotel maids unless you have required out of the ordinary service.

Toilets

The self-cleaning toilets on the street (now wheelchair-accessible) are free, and should not be used by children under ten unless accompanied by an adult. Some Métro stations have public toilets. Large department stores have public rest rooms. If you are desperate, go into a café and head for the *"toilette"* sign. They are usually free, although a few may charge 50 centimes, but don't be surprised if you are asked to buy a coffee. Your chances of not being noticed are better in a large, busy café.

While all restaurants are required to have rest rooms, they are not always up to the highest standards of cleanliness, and a few still have squat toilets.

Tourist Offices

In the U.S.
New York, tel 212/838-7800
Los Angeles, tel 310/271-6665
Office de Tourisme de Paris
(Paris Tourist Office)
Main office: 25 rue des Pyramides, 75001, tel 01 49 52 42 63, www.parisinfo.com, Métro: Tuileries. Open: daily 9 a.m.–7 p.m.

Staff will answer questions and help with hotel reservations. There are branches at airports and train stations (see p. 9).

Travelers with Disabilities

Information: Office de Tourisme de Paris (Paris Tourist Office), 25 rue des Pyramides, 75001, tel 01 49 52 42 63, Open: daily, 9 a.m.–7 p.m.

The new Météor metro line is wheelchair accessible. Aihrop runs adapted vehicles to and from airports, tel 08 10 64 64 64 (call in advance), or request a Renault-Espace taxi when calling any taxi service.

Access to the Métro is nearly impossible for anyone in a

wheelchair, and only a few RER stations are easily accessible. Cité Universitaire, Auber, and Charles-de-Gaulle–Étoile have public elevators. At the following stations, you must ask a station employee to accompany you as the elevators require a key: Châtelet–Les Halles, Gare de Lyon, Grande Arche de la Défense, Denfert-Rochereau, St.-Michel-Notre-Dame, Porte de Clichy, Porte Maillot, Avenue Foch, Avenue Henri-Martin, Boulainvilliers, Avenue du Président-Kennedy, and Invalides. Other stations are not accessible. Of the bus lines, only Line 20 (Gare St.-Lazare–Gare de Lyon) is wheelchair-accessible. Spaces are reserved for wheelchairs in the high-speed TGV trains, and there are accessible toilets.

Taxis are obliged to accept passengers with disabilities even if they require assistance, and to accept seeing-eye dogs. Persons with disabilities do not have to wait in line for a taxi at an airport or train station. When calling for a taxi, ask for a Renault-Espace van (see Taxis, pp. 235–236). Hertz and Avis (see Car Rentals, p. 234) have adapted cars; reserve 48 hours in advance.

Most hotel elevators are usually too small for a wheelchair, and bathrooms can be tiny. Large, modern hotels are the most likely to be accessible. There is a ramp at the curb on every street corner. Street toilets are not accessible.

For the visually impaired, there is a strip of bumps on the edge of Métro quays (platforms) and tactile numbers on elevator buttons.

U.K. publisher RADAR puts out Access in Paris, an English-language guide for disabled travelers. J'accede also publishes an annual guide listing accessible places. Their website (www.jaccede.com) also provides useful information. The Paris Tourist Office has information on the accessibility of transportation, museums, and monuments. Pamphlets on train and Métro accessibility are available at all stations.

Always clearly describe your needs when booking any travel service.

Escort Services for Travelers with Disabilities
Auxiliaires des Aveugles, 71 avenue de Breteuil, 75015, tel 01 43 06 94 30. Free escorts for the visually impaired.
Les Compagnons du Voyage, 34 rue Championnet, 75008, tel 01 58 76 08 33, www .compagnons.com

EMERGENCIES
Embassies & Consulates
United States Embassy, 2 avenue Gabriel, 75008, tel 01 43 12 22 22; Consulate, 2 rue St.-Florentin, 75001, tel 01 43 12 22 22, Métro: Concorde.
Canadian Embassy & Consulate, 35 avenue Montaigne, 75008, tel 01 44 43 29 00, Métro: Franklin D. Roosevelt.

For legal assistance in an emergency, contact your embassy or consulate for a list of English-speaking lawyers.

Emergency Phone Numbers/Addresses
Any emergency, tel 112
Police, tel 17
Fire or **emergency medical assistance,** tel 18
Ambulance, tel 15 or 01 44 49 23 23
Poisoning, tel 01 40 05 48 48
SOS Médecin, tel 01 47 07 77 77 or 08 20 33 24 24. Medical emergency house calls.
Urgences Dentaires de Paris, tel 01 42 61 12 00. Emergency dental service from 8 a.m.–10 p.m. Sun. and holidays.
American Hospital, 63 boulevard de Victor-Hugo, Neuilly, tel 01 46 41 25 25. Métro: Pont de Levallois or Pont de Neuilly. Bus: 82. For 24-hour bilingual emergency medical and dental services.
24-hour pharmacy, Pharmacie les Champs-Élysées, 84 avenue

des Champs-Élysées, 75008, tel 01 45 62 02 41. Métro: George-V. (Closed pharmacies post a sign in the window with the address of the nearest one open.)
SOS Help, tel 01 46 21 46 46. English-language crisis hotline, 3 p.m.–11 p.m.

Lost Property
Bureau des Objets Trouvés (Lost & Found Bureau), 36 rue des Morillons, 75015, tel 08 21 00 25 25. Métro: Convention. Open: Mon.– Thurs. 8:30 a.m.–5 p.m., Fri. 8:30 a.m.–4:30 p.m.
RATP lost and found: tel 3246

Lost credit cards
American Express, tel 01 47 77 72 00
Diners Club, tel 08 10 31 41 59
MasterCard, tel 0800 90 13 87
Visa, tel 08 92 70 57 05

Hotels & Restaurants

Parisian hotels (listed here by location, price, then in alphabetical order) are officially rated from no stars to four stars. Only the larger hotels have in-house restaurants, noted in the listings. Unless otherwise mentioned, all these hotels have private bathrooms with shower and/or bathtub. Value-added tax and service are included in the prices, but a hotel tax per person per night will be added to the bill.

Most hotels now charge extra for breakfast, usually continental style (bread, croissant, jam, and tea or coffee), but sometimes buffet style. Where two prices are given, the first is for continental breakfast, the second is for a buffet breakfast.

Street parking is extremely difficult to find in Paris, and most hotels do not have parking lots or garages. Reservations are recommended for all restaurants: The greats are often booked well in advance, and the small ones fill up quickly. All the following restaurants serve French cuisine unless otherwise noted.

Little has been done to make the city's hotels and restaurants accessible to the disabled. "Accessible room" means that a wheelchair would be able to get into a room and move around, and "adapted" means that the bathroom is up to standards. However, there are no specific facilities for the disabled, and buildings may have steps to navigate before entering. Travelers with disabilities should check when booking to make sure the hotel or restaurant meets their needs.

If your hotel is on a main street, ask for a room at the back where you will not be disturbed by traffic. Hotels in this directory are listed by price, then in alphabetical order.

Grading System

★★★★Four stars indicate a hotel with a restaurant and all rooms with private bath/shower rooms.

★★★Three-star hotels have at least 80 percent of the rooms with bath/shower, and offer breakfast in the room.

★★Two-star establishments must have 40 percent of the rooms with bath/shower and a telephone in each room.

★One-star hotels offer plain but adequate accommodation. Room price categories are given only for guidance and do not take into account seasonal variations.

In high season, always try to book in advance, if possible confirming by e-mail or fax. You may be asked for a deposit or credit card number.

Restaurants

One of the great pleasures of visiting Paris is its glorious food. Many hotels have their own restaurants, and some restaur-ants also have rooms to rent. Restaurants in this directory are listed by price, then in alphabetical order.
L = lunch
D = dinner
See also the menu reader on pp. 263–264.

Credit & Debit Cards

Many hotels and restaurants accept all major cards. Smaller ones may accept only some, as shown in their entry. Abbreviations used are: AE American Express, DC Diners Club, MC MasterCard, V Visa.

Dining Hours

Lunch usually starts around midday, and continues until 2 p.m. Dinner is usually eaten around 8 p.m., but may start about 7 p.m.

Menus must by law be displayed outside any establishment

PRICES

HOTELS
An indication of the cost of a double room in the high season is given by € signs.

€€€€€	Over €300
€€€€	€220–300
€€€	€150–220
€€	€100–150
€	Under €100

RESTAURANTS
An indication of the cost of a three-course meal without drinks is given by € signs.

€€€€€	Over €90
€€€€	€60–90
€€€	€40–60
€€	€25-40
€	Under €25

---

serving food, and studying and comparing these before making your choice is part of the pleasure. Most restaurants offer one or more *prix-fixe* menus, set menus at a fixed price, sometimes including wine. Otherwise (and usually more expensively), you order individual items à la carte—from the menu. The French usually eat a salad after the main course and sometimes with the cheese course, which always comes before dessert. Bread and water are supplied free. (French tap water is safe to drink.)

Smoking is forbidden in all public places in France. The smokers now congregate on the sidewalk.

Cafés

Cafés remain a French institution, good for morning coffee, leisurely drinks, modest meals, or just people-watching. They are usually busy all day, opening early to serve the traditional *grand crème* (large cup of white coffee) with croissants to people on their way to work.

Tipping

A 15 percent service charge is always included in the bill. Only add more if the service has been particularly good.

■ THE ISLANDS

The Île de la Cité and the Île St.-Louis, while major sightseeing attractions, are home to mostly minor restaurants. There are, however, a few charming hotels, especially on the Île St.-Louis.

HOTELS

⊞ DU JEU DE PAUME
€€€€ ★★★★
54 RUE ST.-LOUIS-EN-L'ÎLE, 75004
TEL 01 43 26 14 18
FAX 01 40 46 02 76
www.jeudepaumehotel.com
A 17th-century tennis court creatively converted into a hotel with striking mezzanines. Rooms are comfortable and attractive, but small. Garden. Breakfast: €18.
🛏 30 🚇 Pont Marie ⬆ 🚭
🖑 All major cards

⊞ DES DEUX ÎLES
€€€ ★★★
59 RUE ST.-LOUIS-EN-L'ÎLE, 75004
TEL 01 43 26 13 35
FAX 01 43 29 60 25
www.deuxiles-paris-hotel.com
Located on the chic Île St.-Louis. Small, attractive rooms with exposed wooden beams. Breakfast: €13.
🛏 17 🚇 Pont Marie ⬆ 🚭
🖑 AE, MC, V

⊞ DE LUTÈCE
€€€ ★★★
65 RUE ST.-LOUIS-EN-L'ÎLE, 75004
TEL 01 43 26 23 52
FAX 01 43 29 60 25
www.paris-hotel-lutece.com
A fire burns in the lobby's fireplace, and each modest room has an interesting detail, like exposed beams or a pretty mirror. Breakfast: €13.
🛏 23 🚇 🚇 Pont Marie
⬆ 🖑 AE, MC, V

⊞ HENRI IV
€ ★
25 PLACE DAUPHINE, 75001
TEL 01 43 54 44 53
For those on a tight budget. Clean and basic. Breakfast included.
🛏 15 🚇 Pont Neuf or Cité
🖑 MC, V

■ QUARTIER LATIN

Small hotels are the rule in the famous student quarter, which has hundreds of cheap restaurants (often of dubious quality), as well as one of the most expensive, La Tour d'Argent.

HOTELS

⊞ LE CLOS MÉDICIS
€€€ ★★★
56 RUE MONSIEUR-LE-PRINCE, 75006
TEL 01 43 29 10 80
FAX 01 43 54 26 90
www.closmedicis.com
Designer furnishings amid stone walls and exposed beams in this mid-19th-century hotel. Small, comfortable rooms, charming staff, fireplace, and garden. Breakfast: €13.
🛏 37 + 1 suite 🚇 Odéon, RER: Luxembourg ⬆ 🚭
🖑 All major cards

⊞ PARC SAINT-SÉVERIN
€€€ ★★★
22 RUE DE LA PARCHEMINERIE, 75005
TEL 01 43 54 32 17

FAX 01 43 54 70 71
www.esprit-de-france.com
An attractively decorated hotel with a mix of modern and antique furnishings on a quiet street. Bright, spacious rooms, some with rooftop terraces. Breakfast: €11.
🛏 27 🚇 St.-Michel or Cluny–La Sorbonne ⬆ 🚭 🖑 All major cards

⊞ HOTEL DES GRANDS HOMMES
€€/€€€ ★★★
17 PLACE DU PANTHÉON, 75005
TEL 01 46 34 19 60
FAX 01 43 26 67 32
www.hoteldesgrands hommes.com
Ask for a room with a view of the Panthéon across the street in this pretty, comfortable hotel. Some rooms have canopy beds and exposed beams. Breakfast: €10.
🛏 31 🚇 Maubert Mutualité, RER: Luxembourg ⬆ 🚭 🖑 All major cards

⊞ MAXIM QUARTIER LATIN
€€ ★★
28 RUE CENSIER, 75005
TEL 01 43 31 16 15
FAX 01 43 31 93 87
www.maximparishotel.com
Recently redecorated in a simple modern style. Near the Jardin des Plantes. Breakfast: €9.
🛏 36 🚇 Censier Daubenton ⬆ 🚭 🚭 🖑 All major cards

⊞ GAY-LUSSAC
€ ★
29 RUE GAY-LUSSAC, 75005
TEL 01 43 54 23 96
FAX 01 40 51 79 49
www.paris-hotel-gay-lussac.com
Cheap, clean, comfortable, and located near the Luxembourg Garden. Breakfast: €6.
🛏 35 (some without private bathrooms) 🚇 RER: Luxembourg ⬆ 🖑 DC, MC, V

🚭 Nonsmoking 🚭 Air-conditioning 🏊 Indoor Pool 🏊 Outdoor Pool 🏋 Health Club 🖑 Credit Cards

RESTAURANTS

🍴 LA TOUR D'ARGENT
€€€€€
15 QUAI TOURNELLE, 75005
TEL 01 43 54 23 31
www.latourdargent.com
Its reputation may have slipped
a little, and it now has only one
Michelin star instead of three,
but it's still a great favorite with
visitors for its duckling and its
spectacular views of the Seine
and Notre-Dame. Fixed-price
L menu.
🚇 Maubert Mutualité
🕐 Closed Sun.–Mon., Aug.
🔁 🔆 🔷 All major cards

🍴 L'AVANT-GOUT
€€€
26 RUE BOBILLOT, 75013
TEL 01 53 80 24 00
www.lavantgout.com
This bistro is farther afield, near
the Place d'Italie, but it's small,
cozy, and one of the city's greatest. Fixed-price menus.
🚇 Place d'Italie 🕐 Closed
Sun.–Mon. 🔷 MC, V

🍴 ITINERAIRES
€€
5 RUE DE PONTOISE, 75005
TEL 01 46 33 60 11
www.restaurant
itineraires.com
Young husband-and-wife team
offer fresh, creative takes on
tradition and friendly service in
a comfortable, quiet, modern
setting.
🚇 Maubert Mutualité
🕐 Closed Sun.–Mon. 🔆
🔷 AE, MC, V

🍴 LE PRÉ VERRE
€€
8 RUE THÉNARD, 75005
TEL 01 43 54 59 47
www.lapreverre.com
Jazzy, modern restaurant with
an Asian twist, adding tamarind,
cinnamon, and other exotic
spices to classic dishes.
🚇 Maubert Mutualite
🕐 Closed Sun., Mon., & first
two weeks of Aug. 🔷 MC, V

◼ ST.-GERMAIN &
MONTPARNASSE
The chic and beautiful neighborhood of St.-Germain-des-Prés
has many charming hotels, some
of them quite reasonably priced,
as well as many interesting little
restaurants. Lively Montparnasse
is more downmarket, but it has
plenty of points of interest.

HOTELS

🏨 L'HÔTEL
€€€€€ ★★★★
13 RUE DES BEAUX-ARTS, 75006
TEL 01 44 41 99 00
FAX 01 43 25 64 81
www.l-hotel.com
Has a marvelous, round
stairway and extravagantly
decorated rooms. Oscar Wilde
died in room 16. Breakfast: €16.
ℹ️ 20 inc. suites 🚇 St.-Ger-
main-des-Prés 🔁 🔆
🔷 All major cards

🏨 RELAIS CHRISTINE
€€€€€ ★★★★
3 RUE CHRISTINE, 75006
TEL 01 40 51 60 80
FAX 01 40 51 60 81
www.relais-christine.com
Discreet, Left Bank luxury in
a former convent, in whose
vaulted, 13th-century kitchens
breakfast is served. Garden and
courtyard. Breakfast: €25–30.
ℹ️ 51 + suites 🚇 Odéon,
St.-Michel 🅿️ 🔁 🔆
🔷 All major cards

🏨 DE L'ABBAYE
€€€€ ★★★
10 RUE CASSETTE, 75006
TEL 01 45 44 38 11
FAX 01 45 48 07 86
www.hotel-abbaye.com
Charming 18th-century building
with a courtyard garden on a
quiet street. Four duplex suites
with terraces. Some rooms are
small. Breakfast included.
ℹ️ 44 inc. suites 🚇 St.-Sulpice
🔁 🔆 🔷 AE, MC, V

🏨 LUTÉTIA
🍴 €€€€ ★★★★
45 BOULEVARD RASPAIL, 75006
TEL 01 49 54 46 46
FAX 01 49 54 46 00
www.lutetia.com
A stunning, art deco pile whose
past residents include James
Joyce, Pablo Picasso, and Henri
Matisse. Reasonable packages.
Breakfast: €26.
ℹ️ 241, inc. suites 🚇 Sèvres-
Babylone 🔁 🔆 🔷 All major
cards

🏨 PULLMAN PARIS
🍴 MONTPARNASSE
€€€€ ★★★★
19 RUE COMMANDANT RENÉ
MOUCHOTTE, 75014
TEL 01 44 36 44 36
FAX 01 44 36 49 00
www.pullmanhotels.com
A modern, high-rise hotel with
business facilities and good
views from the upper floors.
Choice of two restaurants.
Breakfast: €25.
ℹ️ 953 inc. suites 🚇 Montpar-
nasse-Bienvenue 🔁 🔆 🔷 All
major cards

🏨 D'ANGLETERRE SAINT-
GERMAIN-DES-PRÉS
€€€ ★★★
44 RUE JACOB, 75006
TEL 01 42 60 34 72
FAX 01 42 60 16 93
www.hotel-dangleterre.com
A friendly staff, historical
associations (Washington Irving
and Ernest Hemingway stayed
here), and loads of charm in
individually decorated rooms
keep regulars coming back.
Breakfast included.
ℹ️ 26 🚇 St.-Germain-des-Prés
🔁 🔷 All major cards

🏨 LENOX ST.-GERMAIN
€€€ ★★★
9 RUE DE L'UNIVERSITÉ, 75007
TEL 01 42 96 10 95
FAX 01 42 61 52 83
www.lenoxsaintgermain.com
A fashionable, intimate, Left
Bank hotel with smallish rooms.

🏨 Hotel 🍴 Restaurant ℹ️ No. of Guest Rooms 🅿️ Parking 🚇 Métro 🕐 Closed 🔁 Elevator

Bar. Breakfast: €11–15.

🛈 34 inc. suites 🚇 St.-Germain-des-Prés or Rue du Bac
🔁 🅰️ 🅰️ All major cards

LEFT BANK ST.-GERMAIN BEST WESTERN
€€€ ★★★

9 RUE DE L'ANCIENNE COMÉDIE, 75006

TEL 01 43 54 01 70

FAX 01 43 26 17 14

www.hotelleftbank
saintgermain.com

In the heart of the Left Bank, this small hotel has an antique-filled lobby, wooden beams, and marble bathrooms. Breakfast included in price of room.

🛈 31 🚇 Odéon 🔁 🅰️
🅰️ All major cards

HÔTEL DE L'ODÉON
€€€ ★★★

13 RUE ST.-SULPICE, 75006

TEL 01 43 25 70 11

FAX 01 43 29 97 34

www.paris-hotel-odeon.com

Antiques and tapestries in this 16th-century manor house create a romantic setting. Most rooms overlook garden. Breakfast: €14.

🛈 27 🚇 Odéon 🔁 🅰️
🅰️ All major cards

ODÉON-HÔTEL
€€€ ★★★

3 RUE DE L'ODÉON, 75006

TEL 01 43 25 90 67

FAX 01 43 25 55 98

www.odeon-paris-hotel.com

A quiet location between the Boulevard St.-Germain and the Luxembourg Garden, with individually decorated rooms. Breakfast: €12.

🛈 33 🚇 Odéon 🔁 🅰️
🅰️ All major cards

HÔTEL DES SAINTS-PÈRES
€€€ ★★★

65 RUE DES STS.-PÈRES, 75006

TEL 01 45 44 50 00

FAX 01 45 44 90 83

www.paris-hotel-
saints-peres.com

Beloved of the fashion crowd, most of its antique-furnished rooms have views of the garden. Breakfast: €14.

🛈 39 🚇 St.-Germain-des-Prés
🔁 🅰️ 🅰️ AE, MC, V

ISTRIA–ST.-GERMAIN
€€ ★★★

29 RUE CAMPAGNE-PREMIÈRE, 75014

TEL 01 43 20 91 82

FAX 01 43 22 48 45

www.hotel-istria-paris.com

A well-kept, comfortable hotel on a quiet street near Montparnasse; its past guests have included such greats as Rainer Maria Rilke, Marcel Duchamp, and Man Ray. Breakfast: €10.

🛈 26 🚇 Raspail 🔁 🅰️
🅰️ All major cards

RIVE GAUCHE
€ ★★

25 RUE DES STS.-PÈRES, 75006

TEL 01 42 60 34 68

FAX 01 42 61 29 78

www.hotel-rive-gauche.net

Clean, comfortable rooms, and a cheap price for this classy location. Breakfast: €9.50.

🛈 21 🚇 St.-Germain-des-Prés
🔁 🅰️ All major cards

RESTAURANTS

CLOSERIE DES LILAS
€€€€€

171 BOULEVARD MONTPARNASSE, 75006

TEL 01 40 51 34 50

www.closeriedeslilas.fr

A new chef has improved the quality of the food at this famous Montparnasse bar/brasserie/restaurant, a former hangout of Hemingway, Picasso and more. A good place to drink amid the literary crowd. Fixed-price menus available.

🚇 Vavin 🅰️ All major cards

LES BOUQUINISTES
€€€€

53 QUAI DES GRANDS-AUGUSTINS, 75006

TEL 01 43 25 45 94

www.lesbouquinistes.com

A fashionable bistro on the quays of the Seine, owned by top chef Guy Savoy. Try the lamb with wild mushrooms, or the foie gras with celeriac and cassis. Fixed-price lunch menus available.

🚇 St.-Michel 🅰️ 🅰️ All major cards

LE DÔME
€€€€

108 BOULEVARD MONTPARNASSE, 75014

TEL 01 43 35 25 81

Fine fish in the lively ambience of this famous Montparnasse brasserie. À la carte menu.

🚇 Montparnasse, Vavin 🅰️
🅰️ All major cards

LE DUC
€€€€

243 BOULEVARD RASPAIL, 75014

TEL 01 43 20 96 30

Fresh fish, prepared simply and served in a yacht-like setting. Fixed-price menus available.

🚇 Raspail 🕐 Closed Sat. L, Sun.–Mon., & public hols.
🅰️ 🅰️ All major cards

BRASSERIE LIPP
€€€

151 BOULEVARD ST.-GERMAIN, 75006

TEL 01 45 48 53 91

A place to go for its historical and literary connections (patrons have included Ernest Hemingway and F. Scott Fitzgerald), and its wonderful, intact, turn-of-the-20th-century decor, but not for the indifferent food and service.

🚇 St.-Germain-des-Prés 🅰️
🅰️ All major cards

CAFÉ DE FLORE
€€€

172 BOULEVARD ST.-GERMAIN, 75006

TEL 01 45 48 55 26

www.cafedeflore.fr

The prices are astronomical, but it's worth a visit for the art deco interior, classy service, and celebrity-spotting opportunities.

🚇 St.-Germain-des-Prés 🛗 🍽 All major cards

🍽 LA CAGOUILLE
€€€

10 PLACE CONSTANTIN BRAN-CUSI, 75014
TEL 01 43 22 09 01
www.la-cagouille.fr
Exquisite seafood, yummy desserts, and friendly service in a stark setting. Outdoor terrace in summer. Fixed-price menus available.

🚇 Gaité 🍽 MC, V

🍽 LA COUPOLE
€€€

102 BOULEVARD MONTPAR-NASSE, 75014
TEL 01 43 20 14 20
www.flobrasseries.com/coupoleparis
A lively, art deco brasserie with great service, good food, and impeccable historical credentials—everyone who was anyone came here in the 1920s. Fixed-price menu available.

🚇 Montparnasse, Vavin 🛗 AE, MC, V

🍽 ZE KITCHEN GALERIE
€€€

14 RUE DES GRANDS AUGUS-TINS, 75006
TEL 01 44 32 00 32
www.zkg.fr
Colorful contemporary art decorates the walls of this bright, cheery (but noisy) restaurant. Kitchen workers toil away in full view of diners as they whip up chef William Ledeuil's equally colorful, artistically presented and Asian-influenced dishes.

🚇 St.-Michel 🕐 Closed Sat. L, Sun. 🍽 All major cards

🍽 LA ROTISSERIE D'EN FACE
€€€

2 RUE CHRISTINE, 75006

TEL 01 43 26 40 98
www.jacquescagna.com
A lower-priced annex of well-known chef Jacques Cagna's restaurant, with creative bistro food and a cozy atmosphere. Fixed-price menus available.

🚇 St.-Michel 🕐 Closed Sat. L & Sun. 🛗 🍽 All major cards

🍽 LA BASTIDE ODÉON
€€

7 RUE CORNEILLE, 75006
TEL 01 43 26 03 65
www.bastide-odeon.com
Provençal cooking with a modern twist in a pretty setting. Fixed-price lunch menus available.

🚇 Odéon 🕐 Closed Sun.–Mon. & Aug. 🍽 AE, MC, V

🍽 L'OS À MOELLE
€€

3 RUE VASCO DE GAMA, 75015
TEL 01 45 57 27 27
Trained by Christian Constant, the young chef makes a serious effort to provide refined cuisine at low prices. Fixed-price menus available.

🚇 Lourmel 🕐 Closed Sun.–Mon., & Aug. 🍽 All major cards

🍽 POLIDOR
€€

41 RUE MONSIEUR-LE-PRINCE, 75006
TEL 01 43 26 95 34
www.polidor.com
A 19th-century bistro that serves classics like boeuf bourguignon at basic prices. Fixed-price menus available.

🚇 Odéon 🍽 AE, MC, V

🍽 LE PETIT SAINT BENOÎT
€

4 RUE ST.-BENOÎT, 75006
TEL 01 42 60 27 92
Cheap, funky, old-time bistro with decent food.

🚇 St.-Germain-des-Prés 🕐 Closed Sun. 🍽 No credit cards

PRICES

HOTELS
An indication of the cost of a double room in the high season is given by € signs.

€€€€€ Over €300
€€€€   €220–300
€€€   €150–220
€€   €100–150
€   Under €100

RESTAURANTS
An indication of the cost of a three-course meal without drinks is given by € signs.

€€€€€ Over €90
€€€€   €60–90
€€€   €40–60
€€   €25-40
€   Under €25

■ CHÂTELET & LES HALLES

The heart of the city is noisy and congested, but the hotels listed below are on relatively quiet streets. Many of the area's restaurants are throwbacks to the days when Les Halles was the major food market; they serve hearty, copious meals that are heavy on meat.

HOTEL

🏨 BRITANNIQUE
€€€ ★★★

20 AVENUE VICTORIA, 75001
TEL 01 42 33 74 59
FAX 01 42 33 82 65
www.hotel-britannique.fr
Cozy, British-style comfort on a quiet street in the busy city center. Breakfast: €13.

🛏 40 🚇 Châtelet 🛗 🛗 🍽 All major cards

SOMETHING SPECIAL

🏨 SAINT-MERRY
€€€ ★★★
78 RUE DE LA VERRERIE, 75004
TEL 01 42 78 14 15
FAX 01 40 29 06 82
This used to be a presbytery of the St.-Merri Church, whose flying buttresses form part of the decor of room 9. Expensive rooms have authentic, carved-wood Gothic furnishings; cheaper ones might not have private bathrooms, but do have showers, and are charmingly decorated with matching wallpaper, bedspreads, and curtains. Breakfast: €11.
🛏 12 inc. 1 suite 🚇 Hôtel de Ville 🏧 AE, MC, V

RESTAURANTS

🍽 GÉRARD BESSON
€€€€€
5 RUE DU COQ-HÉRON, 75001
TEL 01 42 33 14 74
www.gerardbesson.com
The chef serves the freshest produce in his creatively prepared, classic dishes.
🚇 Les Halles, Louvre, Rivoli 🕐 Closed Sat. L, Sun., Mon. L 🏧 🏧 All major cards

🍽 LA POULE AU POT
€€€
9 RUE VAUVILLIERS, 75001
TEL 01 42 36 32 96
A popular, all-night restaurant serving traditional food that attracts a variety of night-owls and theater people. Fixed-price menu available.
🚇 Les Halles 🕐 Closed Mon., open other days until 5 a.m. 🏧 🏧 MC, V

🍽 L'AMBASSADE D'AUVERGNE
€€
32 RUE DU GRENIER ST LAZARE, 75004
TEL 01 42 72 31 22
www.ambassade-auvergne.com
Hearty country food from the Auvergne in a rustic setting, with specialities like aligot (creamy cheese and potato), lentils, duck, and cured ham.
🚇 Rambuteau 🕐 Closed mid-July–mid-Aug. 🏧 AE, MC, V

🍽 LE HANGAR
€€
12 IMPASSE BERTHAUD, 75003
TEL 01 42 74 55 44
Welcoming popular local bistro close to the Beaubourg serves traditional fare from steaks to rabbit, salads, and chocolate soufflé.
🚇 Rambuteau 🕐 Closed Sun., Mon. & Aug. 🏧 No credit cards

🍽 AU PIED DE COCHON
€€
6 RUE COQUILLIÈRE, 75001
TEL 01 40 13 77 00
www.piedecochon.com
Lively, all-night restaurant specializing in such brasserie fare as pig's feet and shellfish. Fixed-price menus available.
🚇 Louvre, Châtelet–Les Halles 🕐 Open 24 hours a day, 🏧 All major cards

🍽 BISTROT BEAUBOURG
€
25 RUE QUINCAMPOIX, 75004
TEL 01 42 77 48 02
Lively, bohemian atmosphere, with decent, inexpensive food, near the Pompidou Center.
🚇 Rambuteau 🏧 MC, V

▮ LE MARAIS & BASTILLE
The historic Marais does not have many hotels, but there are a few interesting options, as well as lots of good, small restaurants. The bustling Bastille area is slowly moving upscale, thanks to the opera house, but is still not the most desirable area to stay.

HOTELS

🏨 CROWNE PLAZA HOTEL RÉPUBLIQUE
€€€€€ ★★★★
10 PLACE DE LA RÉPUBLIQUE, 75011
TEL 01 43 14 43 50
FAX 01 47 00 32 34
www.ichotelsgroup.com
International-style rooms in a turn-of-the-century building. Garden, bar. Breakfast: €25.
🛏 328 🚇 République 🏧 🏧 🏧 All major cards

🏨 PAVILLON DE LA REINE
€€€€€ ★★★★
28 PLACE DES VOSGES, 75003
TEL 01 40 29 19 19
FAX 01 40 29 19 20
www.pavillon-de-la-reine.com
Antique-furnished rooms, some with four-poster beds. Garden. Breakfast: €28/34.
🛏 54 🚇 St.-Paul 🅿 🏧 🏧 🏧 All major cards

🏨 CARON DE BEAU-MARCHAIS
€€€ ★★★
12 RUE VIEILLE-DU-TEMPLE, 75004
TEL 01 42 72 34 12
FAX 01 42 72 34 63
www.carondebeaumarchais.com
The 18th century brought back to life in this pretty hotel. Breakfast: €13.
🛏 19 🚇 St.-Paul, Hôtel de Ville 🏧 🏧 🏧 AE, MC, V

🏨 HÔTEL DE NICE
€€ ★★
42 BIS RUE DE RIVOLI, 75004
TEL 01 42 78 55 29
FAX 01 42 78 36 07
www.hoteldenice.com
Antique furnishings and a central location at reasonable prices. Breakfast: €8.
🛏 23 🚇 Hôtel de Ville 🏧 🏧 MC, V

🏧 Nonsmoking 🏧 Air-conditioning 🏊 Indoor Pool 🏊 Outdoor Pool 🏋 Health Club 🏧 Credit Cards

🏨 GRAND HÔTEL JEANNE D'ARC
€ ★★
3 RUE DE JARENTE, 75004
TEL 01 48 87 62 11
FAX 01 48 87 37 31
www.hoteljeannedarc.com
A fine little hotel, much in demand because of its location and low prices. Breakfast: €7.
🛏 35 🚇 St-Paul 🛗 🏧 MC, V

🏨 GRAND HÔTEL DU LOIRET
€ ★★
8 RUE DES MAUVAIS-GARÇONS, 75004
TEL 01 48 87 77 00
FAX 01 48 04 96 56
Clean, cheap, modest hotel on the evocatively named street of "bad boys." Breakfast: €7.
🛏 27 🚇 Hôtel-de-Ville 🛗 🏧 AE, MC, V

RESTAURANTS

🍴 L'AMBROISIE
€€€€€
9 PLACE DES VOSGES, 75004
TEL 01 42 78 51 45
www.ambroisie-placede vosges.com
Classic three-Michelin-star French food by chef Bernard Pacaud.
🚇 St-Paul 🕐 Closed Sun.–Mon., Aug. & school vacation in Feb. 🅿 🏧 AE, MC, V

🍴 LE TRAIN BLEU
€€€€
GARE DE LYON, 20 BOULEVARD DIDEROT, 75012
TEL 01 43 43 09 06
Go for a drink to see the belle epoque decoration in this train-station restaurant rather than for its pricey food. Fixed-price menu available.
🚇 Gare de Lyon 🛗 🏧 All major cards

🍴 BISTRO DU DÔME
€€€

2 RUE DE LA BASTILLE, 75004
TEL 01 48 04 88 44
Good seafood at lower prices than in the original Dôme on the Left Bank.
🚇 Bastille 🅿 🏧 AE, MC, V

🍴 LE 404
€€€
69 RUE DES GRAVILLIERS, 75003
TEL 01 42 74 57 81
Moroccan restaurant with fine couscous and tagines. Fixed-price L menu available.
🚇 Arts et Métiers 🅿 🏧 AE, MC, V

🍴 LE PAMPHLET
€€€
38 RUE DEBELLEYME, 75003
TEL 01 42 72 39 24
A comfortable, quiet, rather old-fashioned restaurant with solid, high-quality traditional French food. Eating here is a relaxing, enjoyable experience
🚇 Filles du Calvaire 🕐 Closed Sat. L, Sun., Mon. L 🏧 All major cards

🍴 AU BASCOU
€€
38 RUE RÉAUMUR, 75003
TEL 01 42 72 69 25
www.aubascou.fr
Basque and French specialties prepared in a lively restaurant. Fixed-price L menu available.
🚇 Arts et Métiers 🕐 Closed Sat., Sun., Aug. & Christmas week 🏧 AE, MC, V

🍴 CHEZ JANOU
€€
12 RUE ROGER VERLOMME, 75003
TEL 01 42 72 28 41
www.chezjanou.com
Lively, crowded, friendly, and trendy, this bistro serving solid, well-prepared Provençal specialties has a great outdoor terrace in summer and a fixed-price menu at lunch.
🚇 Bastille 🏧 AE, MC, V

🍴 CHEZ OMAR
€€
47 RUE DE BRETAGNE, 75003
TEL 01 42 72 36 26
Excellent couscous, old-fashioned bistro decor, and extra-friendly service.
🚇 Temple 🏧 No credit cards

SOMETHING SPECIAL

🍴 CLOWN BAR
€€
114 RUE AMELOT, 75011
TEL 01 43 55 87 35
This unusual restaurant/wine bar next to the Cirque d'Hiver (Winter Circus), with 1920s art nouveau decor and colorful, original, clown-motif tiles, guarantees a lively evening. Creative, quality French cooking, warm ambience, and a good selection of reasonably priced wines. Reservations recommended.
🚇 Filles-de-Calvaire 🕐 Closed Sun., Mon. L, Tues. L 🏧 No credit cards

🍴 LES COTELETTES
€€
4 IMPASSE GUÉMÉNÉE, 75004
TEL 01 42 72 08 45
www.lescotelettes.com
Good-quality, unpretentious French cooking served by a friendly crew in a Marais restaurant where Georges Simenon (of Inspector Maigret fame) used to dine.
🚇 St.-Paul, Bastille 🕐 Closed Sat. L, Sun., Mon. 🅿 🏧 AE, MC, V

SOMETHING SPECIAL

🍴 LA BELLE HORTENSE
€
31 RUE VIEILLE DU TEMPLE, 75004
TEL 01 48 04 71 60
www.cafeine.com
This wine bar/café/book-shop/wine shop (you can buy a bottle to go) offers two distinct ambiences. The small

bar in the front is crowded and friendly, while the back room is a quiet oasis where you can read a book. Exhibitions, literary readings, and a good sound system are added attractions. If you're hungry, they will send out for a meal from their sister restaurant on the same block.

🚇 Hôtel de Ville, St.-Paul
💳 MC, V

🍴 LE PETIT FER À CHEVAL
€

30 RUE VIEILLE-DU-TEMPLE, 75004
TEL 01 42 72 47 47
Fashionable little bar/restaurant; one of the few places in the Marais where you can eat at any time until 1 a.m.

🚇 St.-Paul, Hôtel de Ville
💳 MC, V

🍴 LE TRUMILOU
€

84 QUAI DE L'HÔTEL-DE-VILLE, 75004
TEL 01 42 77 63 98
An old-time bistro on the Seine. Fixed-price menus available.

🚇 Hôtel de Ville, Pont Marie
💳 MC, V

■ THE LOUVRE & PALAIS-ROYAL

A few grand hotels and some chic restaurants can be found in this palatial neighborhood.

HOTELS

🏨 DU LOUVRE
🍴 €€€€€ ★★★★

1 PLACE ANDRÉ MALRAUX, 75001
TEL 01 44 58 38 38
FAX 01 44 58 38 01
www.hoteldulouvre.com
Pissarro painted the view from his window in this luxury hotel. Café. Breakfast: €28.

🛈 177 🚇 Palais-Royal
🔌 💺 💳 All major cards

🏨 MEURICE
€€€€€ ★★★★

228 RUE DE RIVOLI, 75001
TEL 01 44 58 10 10
FAX 01 44 58 10 15
www.meuricehotel.com
This lavish hotel was once Salvador Dalí's favorite in Paris. Business facilities. Breakfast: €36/48.

🛈 160 🚇 Concorde, Tuileries
🔌 💺 💺 💳 All major cards

🏨 THE WESTIN
🍴 PARIS
€€€€€ ★★★★

3 RUE CASTIGLIONE, 75001
TEL 01 44 77 11 11
FAX 01 44 77 14 60
www.thewestinparis.fr
The century-old splendor of this hotel has been refurbished. Two restaurants, spa. Breakfast: €28/38.

🛈 450 🚇 Tuileries 🔌 💺
🏊 💳 All major cards

🏨 HÔTEL DE LA PLACE DU LOUVRE
€€€ ★★★

21 RUE DES PRÊTRES-ST.-GERMAIN-L'AUXERROIS, 75001
TEL 01 42 33 78 68
FAX 01 42 33 09 95
www.paris-hotel-place-du-louvre.com
Facing the Louvre. Breakfast (€14) served in an ancient, vaulted basement.

🛈 20 🚇 Louvre or Pont Neuf
🔌 💺 💳 All major cards

🏨 AU RELAIS DU LOUVRE
€€€ ★★★

19 RUE DES PRÊTRES-ST.-GERMAIN-L'AUXERROIS, 75001
TEL 01 40 41 96 42
FAX 01 40 41 96 44
www.relaisdulouvre.com
A cozy little hotel between the Louvre and St.-Germain-l'Auxerrois. Breakfast: €13.

🛈 21 + suites 🚇 Louvre, Pont Neuf 🅿 🔌 💺 💳 All major cards

RESTAURANTS

🍴 CARRÉ DES FEUILLANTS
€€€€€

14 RUE CASTIGLIONE, 75001
TEL 01 42 86 82 82
www.carredesfeuillants.fr
Excellent traditional, southwestern French cuisine: variations on foie gras and truffles. Fixed-price menus available.

🚇 Concorde, Tuileries
🕐 Closed Sat. L, Sun., & Aug.
💺 💳 All major cards

SOMETHING SPECIAL
🍴 LE GRAND VÉFOUR
€€€€€

17 RUE DE BEAUJOLAIS, 75001
TEL 01 42 96 56 27
www.grand-vefour.com
The most romantic restaurant in Paris has a decor unchanged since the mid-19th century, a fine Savoyard chef, charming staff, and an amazing list of historical customers (Napoleon, Cocteau, Colette, Garbo). This two-Michelin-star restaurant is the place for those who want to splurge. Recommended dish: *lièvre à la royale* (hare cooked in red wine and stuffed with foie gras and truffles). Fixed-price menus available.

🚇 Palais-Royal, Bourse
🕐 Closed Fri. D, Sat.–Sun., Aug. & Easter week 💺 💳 All major cards

🍴 SPRING
€€–€€€€

6 RUE BAILLEUL, 75001
TEL 01 45 96 05 72
www.springparis.blogspot.com
Dinner here is pricey and customers eat what American chef Daniel Rose has decided to serve that evening (there is no menu), but divine food and an enjoyable evening are practically guaranteed. Lunch (a bouillon full of ingredients du jour) and meals in the vaulted wine cellar are less expensive. Reserve far in advance.

🚇 Louvre-Rivoli 🕐 Closed Sat.
L, Sun.–Mon., Tues. L 🛗 🅂 V

🍴 MACÉO
€€€

15 RUE DES PETITS-CHAMPS,
75001
TEL 01 42 97 53 85
www.maceorestaurant.com
A trendy restaurant. Second
Empire decor and creative cui-
sine with an international flavor.
Fixed-price menus available.
🚇 Pyramides 🕐 Closed Sat. L
& Sun. 🅂 DC, MC, V

🍴 CAFÉ MARLY
€€€

COUR NAPOLÉON, 93 RUE
DE RIVOLI, 75001
TEL 01 49 26 06 60
Incredible setting in the
Louvre for a chic, designer
café-restaurant with fine inter-
national food.
🚇 Palais-Royal 🛗 🅂 AE,
MC, V

🍴 AUX BONS CRUS
€€

7 RUE DES PETITS-CHAMPS,
75001
TEL 01 42 60 06 45
A wine bar that's been around
for nearly a century, with a
corresponding ambience and
traditional dishes.
🚇 Bourse, Pyramides
🕐 Closed Sun. & Mon. D 🛗
🅂 AE, MC, V

🍴 LE GRAND COLBERT
€€

2 RUE VIVIENNE, 75002
TEL 01 42 86 87 88
www.legrandcolbert.fr
Attractively restored brasserie
decor, friendly service, and
respectable food. Fixed-price
menu available.
🚇 Bourse 🅂 AE, DC, V

🍴 JUVENILES
€€

47 RUE DE RICHELIEU, 75001
TEL 01 42 97 46 49
Small, laid-back, wine bar

with tasty food and excellent
international wines. Fixed-price
menus available.
🚇 Palais-Royal 🕐 Closed Sun.,
Mon. L 🅂 AE, MC, V

🍴 WILLI'S WINE BAR
€€

13 RUE DES PETITS-CHAMPS,
75001
TEL 01 42 61 05 09
www.williswinebar.com
Even the French like it, although
it's owned by an Englishman.
Top-notch wines, fine cooking,
debatable service. Fixed-price
menu available.
🚇 Bourse 🕐 Closed Sun.
🅂 DC, MC, V

■ CHAMPS-ÉLYSÉES & 16TH ARRON- DISSEMENT

The Champs-Élysées isn't what
it used to be, but most of the
palace hotels are located in its
environs, along with some top
restaurants. The 16th and 17
arrondissements are a stylish
residential area with some equally
stylish hotels and restaurants.

HOTELS

🏨 HÔTEL BALTIMORE
🍴 PARIS
€€€€€ ★★★★

88 BIS AVENUE KLÉBER, 75116
TEL 01 44 34 54 54
FAX 01 44 34 54 44
www.accorhotels.com
Wood paneling, tapestries, and
plush period furnishings for a
homey feel. Bertie's restaurant
serves English haute cuisine.
Breakfast: €26
ⓘ 103 🚇 Boissière 🅿 ⬆
🛗 🛗 🛗 🅂 All major cards

🏨 BALZAC
🍴 €€€€€ ★★★★

6 RUE BALZAC, 75008
TEL 01 44 35 18 00
FAX 01 44 35 18 05
www.hotelbalzac.com

PRICES

HOTELS
An indication of the cost of
a double room in the high
season is given by € signs.

€€€€€	Over €300
€€€€	€220–300
€€€	€150–220
€€	€100–150
€	Under €100

RESTAURANTS
An indication of the cost of
a three-course meal without
drinks is given by € signs.

€€€€€	Over €90
€€€€	€60–90
€€€	€40–60
€€	€25-40
€	Under €25

Luxurious, elegant, belle
epoque building with huge
rooms. The restaurant is the
home of the great chef Pierre
Gagnaire (see Pierre Gagnaire,
p. 250). Breakfast: €28/38.
ⓘ 79 🚇 George-V
⬆ 🛗 🅂 All major cards

🏨 HÔTEL CASTILLE
🍴 €€€€€ ★★★★

33–37 RUE CAMBON, 75001
TEL 01 44 58 44 58
FAX 01 44 58 44 00
www.castille.com
Venetian-style luxury near the
Place Vendôme in a former
annex of the Ritz. Italian restaurant with terrace. Breakfast:
€28.
ⓘ 108 🚇 Madeleine
🅿 ⬆ 🛗 🛗 🛗 🅂 All major
cards

🏨 CRILLON
🍴 €€€€€ ★★★★★

10 PLACE DE LA CONCORDE,
75008

🏨 Hotel 🍴 Restaurant ⓘ No. of Guest Rooms 🅿 Parking 🚇 Métro 🕐 Closed ⬆ Elevator

TEL 01 44 71 15 00
FAX 01 44 71 15 02
www.crillon.com
One of the great palace hotels, with views over the Place de la Concorde toward the Eiffel Tower. There are two restaurants: the gourmet Les Ambassadeurs (see p. 250) and L'Obelisque, more modest and less expensive. Winter garden, tea room, and English bar. Breakfast: €38/49/62.

[i] 148 🅿 Concorde
🔁 🅰 🎾 🅲 All major cards

FOUR SEASONS
HOTEL GEORGE V
€€€€€ ★★★★★
31 AVENUE GEORGE V, 75008
TEL 01 49 52 70 00
FAX 01 49 52 70 10
www.fourseasons.com/paris
This venerable palace hotel with its fine antiques and tapestries reopened in 1999 after renovation. Courtyard garden and in-house restaurants. Breakfast: €38/44/49.

[i] 245 🅿 George-V
🔁 🅰 🏊 🎾 🅲 All major cards

HOTEL MARIGNAN
CHAMPS ELYSÉES
€€€€€ ★★★★
12 RUE MARIGNAN, 75008
TEL 01 40 76 34 56
FAX 01 40 76 34 34
www.hotelmarignan.fr
Antique furnishings, a Beauvais tapestry in the salon, and comfortable, simply decorated rooms. Tea room. Breakfast: €27

[i] 57 + 16 duplex suites
🅿 Franklin D. Roosevelt 🔁
🅰 🅲 All major cards

MÉRIDIEN ÉTOILE
€€€€€ ★★★★
81 BOULEVARD GOUVION ST.-CYR, 75017
TEL 01 40 68 34 34
FAX 01 40 68 31 31
www.lemeridien-etoile.com
Modern high-rise with standard comforts and little charm.

The Lionel Hampton Jazz Club in the lobby presents live concerts every night. Two restaurants. Breakfast: €25.

[i] 1,025 🅿 Porte Maillot
🔁 🅰 🅲 All major cards

LE PAVILLON DES
LETTRES
€€€€€ ★★★★
12 RUE DES SAUSSAIES 75008
TEL 01 49 24 26 26
FAX 01 49 24 26 27
www.pavillon-des-lettres.com
A brand-new "literary" hotel run by Le Pavillon de la Reine, with each room devoted to a different writer or poet (from Shakespeare to Proust) and decorated in the appropriate period style, with excerpts of the author's writing on the wall.

[i] 26 🅿 Miromesnil
🔁 🅲 All major cards

LE PLAZA ATHÉNÉE
€€€€€ ★★★★
25 AVENUE MONTAIGNE, 75008
TEL 01 53 67 66 65
FAX 01 53 67 66 66
www.plaza-athenee-paris.com
Rooms in Louis XV, Louis XVI, and Regency styles, chandeliers, and potted palms in the lobby. Two restaurants (see Restaurant Alain Ducasse, p. 250), bar, business facilities. Breakfast: €33/50/69.

[i] 191 🅿 Franklin D. Roosevelt
🔁 🅰 🅰 🎾 🅲 All major cards

PRINCE DE GALLES
€€€€€ ★★★★
33 AVENUE GEORGE V, 75008
TEL 01 53 23 77 77
FAX 01 53 23 78 78
www.hotelprincedegalles.fr
An art deco palace now owned by Starwood; nicely spruced-up rooms with Toile-de-Jouy fabric and modern amenities. Business facilities. Breakfast: €26.

[i] 168 🅿 George-V
🔁 🅰 🅲 All major cards

RAPHAËL
€€€€€ ★★★★★
17 AVENUE KLÉBER, 75116
TEL 01 53 64 32 00
FAX 01 53 64 32 01
www.raphael-hotel.com
Truly classy, luxury hotel with a painting by Turner in the lobby. Spacious rooms amid elegant furnishings. Wonderful, wood-paneled bar. Business facilities. Breakfast: €38/39.

[i] 82 🅿 Charles-de-Gaulle–Étoile 🔁 🅰 🅲 🎾
🅲 All major cards

HOTEL RENAISSANCE
PARIS LE PARC
TROCADERO
€€€€€ ★★★★
55 AVENUE RAYMOND-POINCARÉ, 75116
TEL 01 44 05 66 66
FAX 01 44 05 66 00
www.marriot.fr
Elegant decor in this luxury hotel in five buildings, with a garden. Titular chef Alain Ducasse. Business facilities. Breakfast: €27.

[i] 116 + suites 🅿 Trocadéro
🔁 🅰 🅲 🅰 🎾 🅲 All major cards

ROYAL MONCEAU
€€€€€ ★★★★★
37 AVENUE HOCHE, 75008
TEL 01 42 99 88 00
FAX 01 42 99 89 90
www.royalmonceau.com
Just reopened with a new owner (Raffles) and a new decor by Philippe Starck. Rooms and suites in neutral colors are designed to feel like a home, with artworks and a mixture of styles. Breakfast: €28.

[i] 85 + 61 suites + 3 apts.
🅿 Charles-de-Gaulle–Étoile
🅿 🔁 🅰 🅰 🎾 🅰 🅲 All major cards

VERNET
€€€€€ ★★★★
25 RUE VERNET, 75008
TEL 01 44 31 98 00
FAX 01 44 31 85 69
www.hotelvernet.com

🅲 Nonsmoking 🅲 Air-conditioning 🏊 Indoor Pool 🅰 Outdoor Pool 🎾 Health Club 🅲 Credit Cards

A highly intimate, luxurious gem. Fireplace and piano in the lobby, and Jacuzzis in all the bathrooms. Belle epoque gourmet restaurant; access to the Royal Monceau's spa and pool. Breakfast: €20/30.

🛈 51 🚇 George-V 🅿 ⬍ 🔄 🍳 AE, MC, V

🏨 ASTOR ST.-HONORÉ
🍴 €€€€ ★★★★
11 RUE D'ASTORG, 75008
TEL 01 53 05 05 05
FAX 01 53 05 05 30
www.astorsainthonore.com
Elegant Regency-revival decor on a quiet street in a tiny neighborhood. Some rooms have balconies or terraces. Gourmet restaurant. Breakfast: €18.

🛈 128 inc. suites 🚇 Champs-Élysées–Clemenceau ⬍ 🔄 🍳 🌾 🍳 All major cards

🏨 BEST WESTERN PREMIER HOTEL PERGOLÈSE
€€€€ ★★★★
3 RUE PERGOLÈSE, 75016
TEL 01 53 64 04 04
FAX 01 53 64 04 40
www.parishotelpergolese.com
Warm, modern, designer decor with marble bathrooms. Near the Bois de Boulogne and Arc de Triomphe. Bar. Breakfast: €17.

🛈 40 🚇 Argentine ⬍ 🔄 🍳 🍳 All major cards

🏨 CAMBON
€€€€ ★★★★
3 RUE CAMBON, 75001
TEL 01 44 58 93 93
FAX 01 42 60 30 59
www.hotelcambon.com
Stylish, modern comfort near the Place de la Concorde. Breakfast: €19.

🛈 40 🚇 Concorde ⬍ 🔄 🍳 All major cards

🏨 MAJESTIC
€€€€ ★★★★
30 RUE LA PEROUSE, 75116
TEL 01 45 00 83 70

FAX 01 45 00 29 48
www.majestic-hotel.com
Bourgeois comfort, with period furnishings and spacious rooms, near the Arc de Triomphe. Breakfast: €27/34.

🛈 52 🚇 Kléber ⬍ 🔄 🍳 🌾 🍳 All major cards

🏨 GALILÉO
€€€ ★★★
54 RUE GALILÉE, 75008
TEL 01 47 20 66 06
FAX 01 47 20 67 17
An Aubusson tapestry hangs in the lounge, and the rooms are comfortable in this wonderfully refined small hotel. Breakfast: €13.

🛈 27 🚇 George-V ⬍ 🔄 🍳 AE, MC, V

RESTAURANTS

🍴 LES AMBASSADEURS
€€€€€
HÔTEL DE CRILLON
10 PLACE DE LA CONCORDE, 75008
TEL 01 44 71 16 16
www.crillon.com
Opulent marble decor, formal service, and chef Christopher Hache, who is upholding the standards of this fine restaurant. Fixed-price menus available.

🚇 Concorde 🕐 Closed Sun.–Mon. 🔄 🍳 All major cards

🍴 ASTRANCE
€€€€€
4 RUE BEETHOVEN, 75016
TEL 01 40 50 84 40
Elegant, exclusive restaurant with stylish original dishes and superb service. Book well ahead.

🚇 Passy 🕐 Closed Sat.–Mon. & Aug. 🔄 🍳 All major cards

🍴 GUY SAVOY
€€€€€
18 RUE TROYON, 75017
TEL 01 43 80 40 61
www.guysavoy.com
This excellent restaurant offers specialties such as artichoke

soup with parmesan and black truffles or sea bass with spicy vanilla sauce.

🚇 Charles de Gaulle–Étoile 🕐 Closed Sat. L, Sun.–Mon., Aug. & Christmas 🍳 All major cards

🍴 LEDOYEN
€€€€€
8 AVENUE DUTUIT, 75008
TEL 01 53 05 10 01
www.ledoyen.com
One of the greats, three-star chef Christian Le Squer, has a perfect setting for his specialties (notably seafood) from Brittany in this 18th-century pavilion. The elegant Napoleon III dining room looks out on the gardens of the Champs-Élysées. Fixed-price menus available.

🚇 Champs-Élysées–Clemenceau 🅿 🕐 Closed Sat.–Sun., Mon. L, & Aug. 🔄 🍳 All major cards

🍴 PIERRE GAGNAIRE
€€€€€
HÔTEL BALZAC (see p. 248)
6 RUE BALZAC, 75008
TEL 01 58 36 12 50
www.pierre-gagnaire.com
One of France's greatest chefs has opened this three-Michelin-star restaurant and is wowing the city with his artistic haute cuisine. Specialties include encornets (small squid) with walnuts. Fixed-price menus available.

🚇 George-V 🕐 Closed Sat. & Sun. L & mid-July–mid-Aug. 🔄 🍳 All major cards

🍴 RESTAURANT ALAIN DUCASSE
€€€€€
HÔTEL LE PLAZA ATHÉNÉE
25 AVENUE MONTAIGNE, 75008
TEL 01 53 67 65 00
www.alain-ducasse.com
The three-star restaurant in this classy hotel serves up langoustines au caviar and the famous Bresse chicken.

🚇 Franklin D. Roosevelt 🕐 Closed Sat., Sun., Mon.–

Wed. L, mid-July–mid-Aug.
& Christmas 🚭 ❄ All major cards

🍴 SPOON, FOOD & WINE
€€€€
14 RUE DE MARIGNAN, 75008
TEL 01 40 76 34 44
Alain Ducasse's haute-design restaurant offers the best "fusion food" in Europe. The eclectic menu features offerings such as spareribs with *sauce diable* and grilled loin of rabbit.
🚇 Franklin D. Roosevelt 🚭 ❄ All major cards

🍴 LE RELAIS DE L'ENTRECÔTE
€€€
15 RUE MARBEUF, 75008
TEL 01 49 52 07 17
www.relaisentrecote.fr
When you are not in the mood to decide what to eat, line up at the Relais de l'Entrecôte (the line moves quickly). Once you are seated, a waitress in a black uniform, frilly white apron and high heels will ask you how you want your steak cooked. It comes with a green sauce full of herbs and great shoestring fries, preceded by a simple green salad with walnuts. If you take dessert, you actually have a choice. Reliable quality, efficient service, great fun.
🚇 Franklin D. Roosevelt 🚭 ❄ MC, V

🍴 LE RELAIS DU PARC
€€€
57 AVENUE RAYMOND-POIN-CARÉ, 75016
TEL 01 44 05 66 10
For those who can't afford Alain Ducasse, this lower-priced bistro is supervised by the master.
🚇 Victor-Hugo 🚭 ❄ All major cards

🍴 MINI PALAIS
€€–€€€
GRAND PALAIS (PONT ALEXANDRE III SIDE), AVENUE

WINSTON-CHURCHILL, 75008
TEL 01 42 56 42 42
www.minipalais.com
Three-star chef Eric Frechon of the Bristol created the menu for the newly revamped restaurant in the Grand Palais, which is now quiet and comfortable in spite of its high ceiling and cavernous size. Exquisite ingredients, fine preparation, and top-level service, all for quite reasonable prices, make this a great place to eat.
🚇 Champs-Élysées, Clemenceau ❄ AE, MC, V

SOMETHING SPECIAL

🍴 ANGÉLINA
€€
226 RUE DE RIVOLI, 75001
TEL 01 42 60 82 00
Join the ladies-who-shop and the fashion crowd for a cup of sinfully rich, "African" hot chocolate in this elegant, turn-of-the-20th-century Viennese tea room. Busy weekends.
🚇 Tuileries ⬌ ❄ AE, MC, V

◼ LES GRANDS BOULEVARDS
Pockets of tranquility, like the ritzy Place Vendôme, along with a few fine restaurants and brasseries, can be found here.

HOTELS

🏨 BRISTOL
🍴 €€€€€ ★★★★★
112 RUE DU FAUBOURG ST.-HONORÉ, 75008
TEL 01 53 43 43 00
FAX 01 53 43 43 01
www.lebristolparis.com
Top luxury and discretion for the rich and/or famous, with fine works of art and antiques, Gobelin tapestries, Persian carpets. Garden, bar, tea room. Breakfast: €30/50.
🛏 187 🚇 Miromesnil ⬌ 🚭 🏊 🏋 ❄ All major cards

🏨 COSTES
🍴 €€€€€ ★★★★
239 RUE ST.-HONORÉ, 75001
TEL 01 42 44 50 00
FAX 01 42 44 50 01
In Paris, the name "Costes" guarantees good design and fashionableness. Lavish, neoclassic decor. Bar, business facilities. Breakfast: €32.
🛏 82 🚇 Tuileries 🚭 🏊 🏋 ❄ All major cards

🏨 LE GRAND HÔTEL
🍴 INTERCONTINENTAL
€€€€€ ★★★★
2 RUE SCRIBE, 75009
TEL 01 40 07 32 32
FAX 01 40 07 32 02
www.intercontinental.com
The public rooms are truly grand, but some rooms are small. Home of the famous Café de la Paix; two other restaurants. Breakfast: €39.
🛏 470 + suites 🚇 Opéra 🅿 ⬌ 🚭 🏋 ❄ All major cards

🏨 RITZ
🍴 €€€€€ ★★★★★
15 PLACE VENDÔME, 75001
TEL 01 43 16 30 30
FAX 01 43 16 31 78
www.ritzparis.com
All the gilt, crystal chandeliers, and hushed luxury you would expect from the legendary Ritz. Gourmet restaurant (see L'Espadon p. 252), bar, health spa. Breakfast: €38/50/67.
🛏 169 + suites 🚇 Concorde ⬌ 🚭 🏊 🏋 ❄ All major cards

🏨 AMARANTE BEAU MANOIR
€€€€ ★★★★
6 RUE DE L'ARCADE, 75008
TEL 01 53 43 28 28
FAX 01 53 43 28 88
www.hotelbeaumanoir.com
An Aubusson tapestry, antique furnishings, marble bathrooms, and a quiet location. Breakfast: €20.
🛏 60 + suites 🚇 Madeleine 🅿 ⬌ 🚭 ❄ All major cards

🚭 Nonsmoking 🚭 Air-conditioning 🏊 Indoor Pool 🏊 Outdoor Pool 🏋 Health Club ❄ Credit Cards

🏨 MERCURE STENDHAL PLACE VENDÔME
€€€€ ★★★★
22 RUE D. CASANOVA, 75002
TEL 01 44 58 52 52
FAX 01 44 58 52 00
www.mercure.com
Stendhal once lived in this little hotel with charming, individually decorated rooms. Breakfast: €18.
🛏 20 + suites 🚇 Opéra 🛗
📶 🅰 All major cards

🏨 BANKE HOTEL
€€€–€€€€ ★★★
20, RUE LAFAYETTE, 75009
TEL 01 55 33 22 22
FAX 33 1 55 33 22 23
www.derbyhotels.com
Set in a former belle epoque bank, this new hotel has a splendid two-story-high lobby in the round with a glass cupola and a magnificent mosaic floor. The rooms are decorated with rich yet sober furnishings. Near the Opéra and major department stores.
🛏 94 🚇 Chausée d'Antin– La Fayette, Le Peletier
🛗 📶 📺 🅰 All major cards

🏨 GAILLON OPÉRA BEST WESTERN
€€€ ★★★
9 RUE GAILLON, 75002
TEL 01 47 42 47 74
FAX 01 47 42 01 23
www.hotel-paris-gaillon-opera.com
A helpful staff runs this tastefully decorated little hotel near the Opéra Garnier. Breakfast: €13.
🛏 25 + 1 suite 🚇 Opéra
🛗 📶 🅰 All major cards

🏨 HÔTEL JULES
€€€ ★★★★
49 RUE LAFAYETTE, 75009
TEL 01 42 85 05 44
FAX 01 49 95 06 60
www.hoteljules.com
New owners have given this hotel a colorful, kicky 1970s décor with touches of '50s and '60s. Breakfast: €14.
🛏 101 + suites 🚇 Le Peletier
🛗 📶 🅰 All major cards

🏨 MANSART
€€€ ★★★
5 RUE DES CAPUCINES, 75001
TEL 01 42 61 50 28
FAX 01 49 27 97 44
www.paris-hotel-mansart.com
Next door to the Ritz, with spacious, individually decorated rooms and striking decoration in the lobby—an homage to Mansart, Louis XIV's architect. Breakfast: €14.
🛏 57 🚇 Opéra 🛗 📶 🅰 All major cards

RESTAURANTS

🍴 L'ESPADON
€€€€€
RITZ HÔTEL
15 PLACE VENDÔME, 75001
TEL 01 43 16 30 80
It's the Ritz, and the setting and service are as they should be, though the food has its ups and downs. Fixed-price menus available.
🚇 Concorde 📶 🅰 All major cards

🍴 SENDERENS
€€€€€
9 PLACE DE LA MADELEINE, 75008
TEL 01 42 65 22 90
Chef Alain Senderens has reinvented his famed haute cuisine restaurant with modern interior and eclectic original dishes like duck foie gras with figs and licorice.
🚇 Madeleine 📶 🅰 All major cards

🍴 TERMINUS NORD
€€
23 RUE DE DUNKERQUE, 75010
TEL 01 42 85 05 15
Bustling brasserie with handsome decor, perfect for a late dinner. Fixed-price menus available.
🚇 Gare du Nord 📶 📶
🅰 All major cards

🍴 LE VAUDEVILLE
€€
29 RUE VIVIENNE, 75002
TEL 01 40 20 04 62
Art deco decor, amiable, efficient service, lively ambience, and reasonable brasserie fare. Fixed-price menus available.
🚇 Bourse 🅰 All major cards

◼ TOUR EIFFEL & LES INVALIDES
A quiet, upper-class, residential area with some lovely hotels and fine eateries.

HOTELS

🏨 DUC DE SAINT-SIMON
€€€€€ ★★★★
14 RUE ST.-SIMON, 75007
TEL 01 44 39 20 20
FAX 01 45 48 68 25
www.hotelduducdesaintsimon.com
A luxurious haven on the Left Bank, with exquisite antique furnishings. Courtyard garden,

charming basement breakfast room. Breakfast: €15.

🛈 34 + suites 🚇 Rue du Bac ⊟ 🚭 All major cards

🏨 🍴 **MONTALEMBERT**
€€€€€ ★★★★

3 RUE MONTALEMBERT, 75007

TEL 01 45 49 68 68

FAX 01 45 49 69 49

www.montalembert.com

Fashionable hotel with designer lobby and attractive, contemporary- or traditional-style rooms. Business facilities, Le Montalembert restaurant. Breakfast: €24.

🛈 54 + suites 🚇 Rue du Bac 🅿 ⊟ 🚭 🚭 All major cards

🏨 **LE BELLECHASSE**
€€€€ ★★★★

8 RUE BELLECHASSE, 75007

TEL 01 45 50 22 31

FAX 01 45 51 52 36

A short walk from the Musée d'Orsay, with a new designer decor. Breakfast: €21.

🛈 34 🚇 Solferino ⊟ 🚭 🚭 All major cards

🏨 **BERSOLY'S**
€€€ ★★★

28 RUE DE LILLE, 75007

TEL 01 42 60 73 79

FAX 01 49 27 05 55

www.bersolys-paris-hotel.com

A quiet hotel with small but attractive rooms. Breakfast: €10.

🛈 16 🚇 Rue du Bac 🅿 🔒 Closed Aug. ⊟ 🚭 🚭 AE, MC, V

🏨 **DE L'ACADÉMIE**
€€€ ★★★

32 RUE DES STS.-PÈRES, 75007

TEL 01 45 49 80 00

FAX 01 45 44 75 24

www.kleber.com

A 17th-century building with exposed beams in rooms and 18th-century furnishings. Breakfast: €14.50.

🛈 34 + suites 🚇 St.-Germain-des-Prés 🅿 ⊟ 🚭 🚭 All major cards

🏨 **DE L'UNIVERSITÉ**
€€€ ★★★

22 RUE DE L'UNIVERSITÉ, 75007

TEL 01 42 61 09 39

FAX 01 42 60 40 84

www.hoteluniversite.com

Antique-furnished hotel distinguished by attention to detail. Two rooms have private terraces. Breakfast: €13.

🛈 27 🚇 St.-Germain-des-Prés ⊟ 🚭 🚭 All major cards

RESTAURANTS

🍴 **L' ARPÈGE**
€€€€€

84 RUE DE VARENNE, 75007

TEL 01 47 05 09 06

www.alain-passard.com

Alain Passard, one of Paris's top chefs, runs this highly rated restaurant with a modern decor. Try the sole with ginger and lime, or the baby onion fondue with herbs and broad beans. Fixed-price menus available.

🚇 Varenne 🔒 Closed Sat.–Sun. 🚭 🚭 All major cards

🍴 **LE DIVELLEC**
€€€€€

107 RUE DE L'UNIVERSITÉ, 75007

TEL 01 45 51 91 96

www.le-divellec.com

The "big fish" among Parisian seafood restaurants, with a big bill at the end of the meal. Fixed-price menus available.

🚇 Invalides 🔒 Closed Sat.–Sun., Aug. & Christmas 🚭 🚭 All major cards

🍴 **LE JULES VERNE**
€€€€€

EIFFEL TOWER, 2ND FLOOR 75007

TEL 01 45 55 61 44

www.lejulesverne-paris.com

A gourmet restaurant with sleek, modern decor in one of the world's most famous monuments. Dinner with a view, and chef Alain Ducasse. Fixed-price menus available.

🚇 Trocadéro 🚭 🚭 All major cards

🍴 **LES FABLES DE LA FONTAINE**
€€€€

131 RUE ST.- DOMINIQUE, 75007

TEL 01 44 18 37 55

www.lesfablesdelafontaine.net

Cramped but excellent fish restaurant with high-quality products, founded by two chefs trained by Christian Constant.

🚇 École Militaire 🚭 🚭 All major cards

🍴 **VIOLON D'INGRES**
€€€€

135 RUE ST.-DOMINIQUE, 75007

TEL 01 45 55 15 05

www.leviolondingres.com

Christian Constant, the former chef at Les Ambassadeurs, provides the same high-quality cuisine at lower prices here. Fixed-price menus available.

🚇 École Militaire 🚭 🚭 All major cards

🍴 **LES COCOTTES DE CHRISTIAN CONSTANT**
€€

135 RUE ST.-DOMINIQUE, 75007

TEL 01 45 50 10 31

Same chef as the Violon d'Ingres, same high-quality products but lower prices and a livelier ambiance. Diners sit on stools at high tables.

🚇 École Militaire 🔒 Closed Sun. 🚭 🚭 AE, V

🍴 **L'OEILLADE**
€€

10 RUE ST.-SIMON

TEL 01 42 22 01 60

A cozy little restaurant where you can count on creative cooking. Fixed-price menu available.

🚇 Rue du Bac 🔒 Closed Sat. L, Sun. 🚭 🚭 MC, V

🍴 **AU PIED DE FOUET**
€

45 RUE DE BABYLONE, 75007

TEL 01 47 05 12 27

www.aupieddefouet.com

Small family restaurant with 19th-century decor, homey atmosphere, and low-priced

---

🚭 Nonsmoking 🚭 Air-conditioning 🏊 Indoor Pool 🏊 Outdoor Pool 🏋 Health Club 🚭 Credit Cards

selection of French classics.
🚇 Sèvres-Babylone 🕐 Closed
Sun. 💳 MC, V

■ MONTMARTRE

Montmartre still has a bohemian
feel, and Pigalle is becoming
less sleazy as more fashionable
nightspots open.

RESTAURANTS

🍴 CASA OLYMPE
€€€
48 RUE ST.-GEORGES, 75009
TEL 01 42 85 26 01
www.casaolympe.com
Celebrated chef Dominique
Versini offers luxurious cuisine
with abundant truffles and foie
gras, in a simple setting.
🚇 St.-Georges 🕐 Closed Sat.–
Sun. & Aug. 💳 AE, MC, V

🍴 CHAMARRÉ MONTMARTRE
€€€
52 RUE LAMARCK, 75018
TEL 01 42 55 05 42
Sleek, modern setting for chef
Antoine Heerah's sophisticated
cuisine with a spicy touch.
Fixed-price menus.
🚇 Lamarck Caulaincourt 🕐
💳 All major cards

🍴 LA MASCOTTE
€€€
52 RUE DES ABBESSES, 75018
TEL 01 46 06 28 15
www.la-mascotte-mont
martre.com
Old-time Paris the way we like
it in this lively brasserie, where
the waiters still wear the traditional vest and long apron and
like to joke with the customers
while they sample their seafood
and steaks.
🚇 Abbesses 💳 V

🍴 CHÉRI BIBI
€€
15 RUE ANDRÉ-DEL-SARTE, 75018
TEL 01 42 54 88 96
A trendy young crowd
frequents this lively place

furnished with flea market
furniture to dine on traditional
French dishes made with quality
ingredients. Dinner only.
🚇 Château Rouge 🕐 Closed
Sun. & 3 weeks in Aug. 💳 DC,
MC, V

🍴 LA CLOCHE D'OR
€€
3 RUE MANSART, 75009
TEL 01 48 74 48 88
www.alaclochedor.com
A lively actors' hangout that
serves decent, basic meals till
4 a.m.
🚇 Blanche 🕐 Closed Sun. &
Aug. 💳 MC, V

■ AROUND THE PÉRIPHÉRIQUE

These are areas not often visited
by tourists, but the restaurants
listed below provide good reasons
to make an excursion.

RESTAURANTS

🍴 LA GRANDE CASCADE
€€€€€
BOIS DE BOULOGNE,
ALLÉE DE LONGCHAMP, 75016
TEL 01 45 27 33 51
www.grandecascade.com
Second Empire restaurant in
a beautiful setting in the Bois
de Boulogne with Provençal-
influenced dishes. Fixed-price
menus available.
🚇 Porte Maillot, then Bus
244 (till 8 p.m.) 🅿 🕐 Closed
Christmas 💳 All major cards

🍴 LE PRÉ CATELAN
€€€€€
ROUTE DE SURESNES, 75016
TEL 01 44 14 41 14
www.precatelanparis.com
Talented chef Eric Anton livens
up the cuisine of this lovely
restaurant with a garden terrace
in the Bois and three Michelin
stars. Fixed-price menus
available.
🚇 Porte Maillot, then Bus 244
(till 8 p.m.) 🕐 Closed Sun.–
Mon. 💳 All major cards

🍴 BRASSERIE FLO
€€
7 COUR DES PETITES-ÉCURIES,
75010
TEL 01 47 70 13 59
A sparkling, 19th-century
Alsatian brasserie near the Gare
de l'Est with typical dishes and
friendly service. Fixed-price
menus available.
🚇 Château d'Eau 🕐 🕐 💳 All
major cards

🍴 LES GRANDES TABLES DU 104
€€
5 RUE CURIAL, 75019
TEL 01 42 05 38 40
The restaurant with a Gascon
chef in Paris's new cultural center, the Centquatre, has a sleek
decor to go with the setting
(the city's former mortuary). Still
finding its way, but looks promis-
ing, with creative dishes.
🚇 Riquet 🕐 Closed Sun. D,
Mon. 💳 MC, V

🍴 LA RÉGALADE
€€
49 AVENUE JEAN-MOULIN, 75014
TEL 01 45 45 68 58
Chef Bruno Doucet packs them
in with haute cuisine at *petits
prix* (small prices) in this
restaurant in southern Paris.
Fixed-price menu available.
🚇 Alésia 🅿 🕐 Closed Sat.–
Mon. 🕐 💳 MC, V

Shopping in Paris

Spending money is easy in this shopper's paradise, where tempting window displays abound. Shop owners are required to price each item displayed, so you'll know what you're in for, but bring a little extra cash if you don't want to go home frustrated. Items purchased include a 19.6 percent sales tax that is refundable to visitors from outside the European Union on purchases over €175 made from the same shop on the same day (ask the assistant for a *détaxe* form).

Accessories

Frenchwomen seem to be born with a knack for accessorizing. Ask the salesperson for tips on tying that *foulard*.

Axes et Soirs 8 rue Caffarelli, 75003. tel 01 42 74 43 06. Closed Sun.–Mon. Métro: Temple. Flamboyant handmade hats and other accessories.

Bains Plus 51 rue des Francs-Bourgeois/corner of rue Vieille du Temple, 75004. tel 01 48 87 83 07. Closed Mon. a.m. & Sun. a.m. Métro: St.-Paul. A Marais boutique with luxurious bathing and lounging accessories.

Droguerie 9–11 rue du Jour, 75001. tel 01 45 08 93 27. Closed Mon. a.m. & Sun. Métro: Les Halles. Colorful yarns, feathers, unusual buttons and beads, and other trimmings.

Groom 21 rue Debelleyme, 75003. tel 01 49 96 57 04. www .groomparis.com. Métro: Filles du Calvaire.

13 rue du Cherche-Midi, 75006, tel 01 45 48 49 36. Métro: St.-Sulpice.

Cashmere-lined leather gloves, a handsome line of colorful handbags and small leather goods, scarves, and other tasteful accessories.

Jean-Claude Monderer 22 rue des Francs-Bourgeois, 75003. tel 01 48 04 51 41. Closed Sun. a.m. Métro: St.-Paul. Men's and women's accessories that are trendy but not ridiculously expensive.

Kabuki 25 rue Etienne Marcel, 75002. tel 01 42 33 55 65. Closed Sun. Métro: Etienne Marcel. Wild shoes for wild women, by designers like Marc Jacobs and Barbara Bui.

Madeleine Gély–Alexandra Sojfes 218 boulevard St.-Germain, 75007. tel 01 42 22 63 35. Closed Sun. Métro: Rue du Bac. A truly Parisian shop more than 150 years old, stuffed with every type umbrella and cane imaginable.

Michel Perry High-style, high-priced, and very high-heeled women's shoes. Boutiques at:

42 rue de Grenelle, 75007. tel 01 42 84 12 45. Closed Sun. –Mon. Métro: Rue du Bac.

243 rue St.-Honoré, 75001. tel 01 42 44 10 07. Closed Sun. Métro: Bourse.

Sentimentale 14 rue du Roi-de-Sicile, 75004. tel 01 42 78 84 04. Closed Mon. & weekday a.m. Métro: St.-Paul. Off-the-beaten-track men's and women's shoes, custom made to fit your feet; not too expensive.

Tati Or 19 rue de la Paix, 75008. tel 01 40 07 08 86. Closed Sun. Métro: Opéra. Bargain prices on gold jewelry, near Cartier and other fine jewelers on Place Vendôme.

Antique Shops

Antique shops can be found on the Quai Voltaire, Rue de Beaune (*Métro: Rue du Bac*), and neighboring streets, where exclusive dealers sell museum-quality pieces; the Louvre des Antiquaires (*Closed Mon., Métro: Palais-Royal*) has 250 boutiques. At the Village St.-Paul (*Closed Tues. & Wed., Métro: St.-Paul*), the '50s seem to be the most popular era.

Books & Music

Paris has many English-language bookshops, and even the French

stores listed below carry some foreign-language books.

Abbey Bookshop 29 rue de la Parcheminerie, 75005. tel 01 46 33 16 24. Closed Sun. Métro: St.-Michel. New and used English-language books.

La Chaumière à Musique 5 rue de Vaugirard, 75006. tel 01 43 54 07 25. Closed Sun. a.m. RER: Luxembourg. A huge collection of used CDs at low prices, great for classical music fanatics.

FNAC 74 avenue des Champs-Élysées, 75008. tel 08 25 02 00 20. Open till midnight. Closed Sun. a.m. Métro: Franklin D. Roosevelt. Every record and (French) book imaginable is sold in the newest branch of this chain. All CDs can be tested on headphones.

Galignani 224 rue de Rivoli, 75001. tel 01 42 60 76 07. Closed Sun. Métro: Tuileries. English and French books in an Old World–style shop with wooden shelves.

Shakespeare and Company 37 rue de la Bûcherie, 75005. tel 01 43 25 40 93. Open 11 a.m.–11 p.m. Métro: St.-Michel. Nothing to do with Sylvia Beach's original bookstore, though it co-opted its name. The daughter is gradually taking over from Paris fixture George Whitman. Its stacks are dusty, but it still attracts plenty of tourists.

Virgin Megastore 52 avenue des Champs-Élysées, 75008. Tel 01 49 53 50 00. Open till midnight. Closed Sun. a.m. Métro: Franklin D. Roosevelt. Huge selection of CDs, cassettes, books, and videos, plus a restaurant and bar.

The Village Voice 6 rue Princesse, 75006. tel 01 46 33 36 47. Closed Mon. a.m. & Sun. a.m.

Métro: St.-Germain-des Prés. The
finest selection of English-language
books in Paris.

Boutiques

The real joy of shopping in Paris,
however, is boutiquing. Wander
through the Marais, Mont-
martre, St.-Germain-des-Prés,
Sèvres-Babylone, or the Place des
Victoires to discover your own
favorite boutique.

Children

Even W.C. Fields went all gooey at
the sight of the unbelievably cute
children's clothing in Paris. Prices
are just as unbelievably high.

C'est Ma Chambre 8 rue du
Petit Thouars, 75003. tel 01 48
87 26 67. Closed Sun.–Mon.
Métro: Hôtel de Ville. Parents
and children alike will fall in love
with the children's furnishings
and bedroom accessories in this
Marais shop.
 Jacadi 17 rue Tronchet,
75008. tel 01 42 65 84 98. Closed
Sun. Métro: Madeleine. Flagship
chainstore selling traditional French
children's clothing.
 La Maison du Cerf-Volant 7
rue du Prague, 75012. tel 01 44 68
01 86. Closed Sun.–Mon. Métro:
Ledru-Pollin. Put some wind in your
sails—go fly a kite. All shapes and
sizes—butterflies, galleons, birds,
and beasts.
 Du Pareil au Même 128
boulevard Courcelles, 75017. tel 01
47 66 03 31. Closed Sun. Métro:
Ternes. The main store of a chain
with great prices on colorful, quality
children's clothes.
 Petits Petons 23 rue Tronchet,
75008. tel 09 61 39 08 16. Closed
Sun. Métro: Madeleine.
 135 rue du Faubourg St.-
Antoine, 75011. tel 09 61 49 04 16.
Closed Sun. Métro: Ledru-Rollin.
The cutest, most colorful kiddie
shoes imaginable.

Clothing

The boutiques of the top designers are concentrated on Rue du
Faubourg-St.-Honoré, Avenue
Montaigne, and in St.-Germain-
des-Prés. Along with these, the
other boutiques listed here have
something a little different, with
many offering bargain prices on
designer labels.

Act 2 2 rue des Trois-Frères,
75018. tel 01 42 54 01 56. Closed
2 p.m.–3 p.m. Métro: Abbesses.
For the fashionable man who
wants to look just a little bit out
of the ordinary.
 Agnes B 6 rue du Jour, 75001.
tel 01 45 08 56 56. Closed Sun.
Métro: Les Halles. Reliable quality
and stylish cuts from this much
loved designer, for men, women,
and children.
 Alternatives 18 rue du Roi-de-
Sicile, 75004. tel 01 42 78 31 50.
Sat. by appt. Closed Sun.–Mon.
Métro: St.-Paul. Carefully selected
used clothing (mostly for women),
much of it with designer labels.
 Anna Kaszer 16 rue de
Turenne, 75004. tel 01 42 71 51
10. Closed Sun. a.m. & Mon. a.m.
Métro: St.-Paul. For funky clothes
and exquisitely cut jackets, plus
accessories and T-shirts. Kaszer uses
classic materials and jazzes them up
in an original way.
 Azzedine Alaïa 7 rue de
Moussy, 75004. tel 01 42 72 19
19. Closed Sun. Métro: Hôtel de
Ville. The lovely Marais boutique
of a unique designer whose clothes
make women look sexy.
 Chanel 31 rue Cambon, 75001.
tel 01 44 50 66 00. Closed Sun.
Métro: Concorde. The sacred,
snooty precincts of Chanel fashion,
designed by Karl Lagerfeld.
 Christian Dior 30 avenue
Montaigne, 75008. tel 01 40 73 73
73. Closed Sun. Métro: Franklin D.
Roosevelt. Extravagant creations in
the plush setting of the refurbished
Dior salons off the Champs-Élysées.
 Colette 213 rue St.-Honoré,

75001. tel 01 55 35 33 90. Closed
Sun. Métro: Tuileries. Cool designer
clothing to sophisticated electronic
gadgets, in a minimalist shop with
a basement café. Prices range from
reasonable to ridiculously high.
 Come On Eileen 16 rue des
Taillanders, 75011. tel 01 43 38 12
11. Métro: Ledru-Rollin. Huge shop
packed with vintage clothing, good
quality though not particularly
cheap.
 L'Eclaireur A judicious selection
of clothing and accessories by
designers including Dries
van Noten and Helmut Lang.
Boutiques at:
 40 rue de Sévigné, 75004. tel
01 48 87 10 22. Closed Sun. Métro:
St.-Paul. Women's fashions in new
shop with spectacular design.
 12 rue Mahler, 75004. tel 01
44 54 22 11. Closed Sun. Métro:
St.-Paul. Men's fashions.
 26 avenue des Champs-Élysées,
75008. tel 01 45 62 12 32. Closed
Sun. Métro: Champs-Élysées. Men's
fashions.
 133 galerie de Valois, 75001. tel
01 40 20 42 52. Closed Sun. Métro:
Palais-Royal. Tableware and jewelry.
 Fifi Chachnil 231 rue St.-
Honoré, 75001. tel 01 42 61 21
83. Closed Sun. Métro: Madeleine.
Designer Fifi Chachnil sells real lingerie in the kitten miaow tradition
in her lollipop pink boutique. Sexy
color mixes and ensembles with
bows and trim.
 Giorgio Armani 149 boulevard
St.-Germain, 75006. tel 01 53 63
33 50. Métro: St.-Germain-des-
Prés. The Italian designer's huge
new store in the heart of St.-
Germain-des-Prés, all stark-white
clean lines.
 Jean-Paul Gaultier boutique
44 avenue George V, 75008. tel 01
44 43 00 44. Closed Sun. Métro:
George V. Jean-Paul Gaultier's
men's and women's ready-to-wear,
lower-priced Gaultier jeans, accessories, and perfumes.
 L'Habilleur 44 rue de Poitou.
75003. tel 01 48 87 77 12. Closed

Sun. Métro: Sebastien Froissart. New, seriously discounted designer clothes from Helmut Lang, Dries van Noten, and others, and shoes from Patrick Cox.

Hermès 24 rue du Faubourg-St.-Honoré, 75008. tel 01 40 17 47 17. Closed Sun. Métro: Madeleine. Famous for its silk *foulards* (scarves), this venerable house is trying to liven up its classic image with Christophe Lemaire designing its women's collection.

Marché Saint-Pierre 2 rue Charles-Nodier, 75018. tel 01 46 06 92 25. Closed Sun. & Mon. a.m. Métro: Anvers. This five-floor Montmartre store sells all kinds of fabric amid dozens of other nearby fabric shops.

La Marelle 21–25 galerie Vivienne, 75002. tel 01 42 60 08 19. Closed Sat. a.m. & Sun. Métro: Bourse. Upscale used clothing in perfect condition, by the likes of Dior and Chanel.

NapoliParis 8 rue de la Grange aux Belles, 75010. tel 01 42 49 00 71, www.napoliparis.com. Métro: Jacques Bonsergent. Handmade, one-of-a-kind women's clothing by Italian designer Carmen Ragosta at reasonable prices in this little boutique near the Canal St.-Martin. Simple styles with a twist, and great accessories.

Nina Jacob 23 des Francs-Bourgeois, 75004. tel 01 42 77 41 20. Métro: St.-Paul. Hip yet feminine, colorful women's clothing in a pretty Marais boutique.

Vanessa Bruno 12 rue Castiglione, 75001. tel 42 61 44 60. www.vanessabruno.com. Métro: Tuileries.

25 rue St.-Sulpice, 75006. tel 43 54 41 04. Métro: Odéon

100 rue Vieille-du-Temple, 75003. tel 01 42 77 19 41. Métro: Filles de Calvaire.

Designer Vanessa Bruno's sophisticated but easy to wear women's clothing with great cuts are prized by Parisiennes.

Yves St. Laurent 38 rue du Faubourg-St.-Honoré, 75008. tel 01 42 65 74 59. Closed Sun. Métro: Madeleine. Current designer Stefano Pilati has scored a hit with his updated interpretations of the late master's high style.

Department Stores

For those who prefer large department stores where they can find everything in one place, next-door neighbors Galeries Lafayette and Printemps *(closed Sun., Métro: Havre-Caumartin or Chaussée-d'Antin)* have it all. The smaller Bon Marché *(closed Sun., Métro: Sèvres-Babylone)* is less crowded and more exclusive. BHV *(closed Sun., Métro: Hôtel de Ville)* is a mid-market department store. The low-priced chain Monoprix *(Closed Sun.)* has branches all over town, and is interesting for children's clothes, cosmetics, and accessories. Attractive, youthful women's fashion at reasonable prices can be found at specialist chain stores like Naf Naf, Promod, Zara, and H&M.

Flea Markets

There are several permanent flea markets on the edges of Paris: the enormous Puces de St.-Ouen *(Closed Tues.–Fri., Métro: Porte de Clignancourt)*, specializing in antiques; the more junk-oriented Puces de Montreuil *(Open Sat.–Mon., Métro: Porte-de-Montreuil)*; and the Puces de Vanves *(Open Sat. a.m. & Sun., Métro: Porte-de-Vanves)*, with some antiques and lots of miscellaneous stuff. As with most flea markets, the rules are: Go as early in the a.m. as possible, and don't hesitate to bargain. Prices are generally high, especially for antiques, but there are a lot of finds.

Housewares & Interior Design

The French claim to know the most about about *l'art de vivre* (the art of living). The following stores sell some of the elements that go into this fine art.

La Chaise Longue Cheap, chic accessories for the kitchen and the bathroom. Boutiques at:

30 rue Croix-des-Petits-Champs, 75001. tel 01 42 96 32 14. Closed Sun. Métro: Palais-Royal.

8 rue Princesse, 75006. Tel 01 43 29 62 39. Closed Sun. Métro: St.-Germain-des-Prés.

20 rue des Francs-Bourgeois, 75003. tel 01 48 04 36 37. Closed Sun. a.m. Métro: St.-Paul.

The Conran Shop 117 rue du Bac, 75007. tel 01 42 84 10 01. Closed Sun. Métro: Sèvres-Babylone. Terence Conran's design domain, with attractive, amusing furniture and home accessories.

Diners en Ville 27 rue de Varenne, 75007. tel 01 42 22 78 33. Closed Sun. & Mon. a.m. Métro: Varenne. Cheerful, colorful, elegant tableware.

Galerie VIA 33 avenue Daumesnil, 75012. tel 01 46 28 11 11. Métro: Gare de Lyon. A gallery promoting avant-garde French furniture designers in a row of art- and crafts-related shops.

Maison de Famille 29 rue St-Sulpice, 75006. tel 01 40 46 97 47. Closed Sun. Métro: St.-Sulpice. Kitchen gadgets to bedding and decorative objects, plus selected men's and women's clothing.

Matins Bleus 85 avenue du Général Leclerc, 75006. tel 01 42 22 94 40. Closed Sun.–Mon. Métro: Alesia. Fine bed linens, as only the French know how to make. **Merci** 111 boulevard Beaumarchais, 75011. tel 01 42 77 00 33. www.merci-merci.com. Closed Sun. Métro: Saint Sébastien-Froissart. This trendy concept store in a huge multilevel space with a glass roof sells home furnishings and much, much more: kitchenware, fresh flowers, vintage and new clothing, books, etc. Café and restaurant. Profits are used to help orphans in Madagascar.

Muriel Grateau 37 rue de Beaune, 75007. tel 01 40 20 42 82. Closed Sun.–Mon. Métro: Rue du Bac. Luxurious, 100-percent linen bedsheets in a palette of colors, and tableware with pure, modern, elegant lines.

Sté. Déhillerin 20 rue Coquillière, 75001. tel 01 42 36 53 13. Closed Sun. L. Métro: Les Halles. A fantastic array of kitchen utensils and cookware at this emporium, open since 1820.

Villa Marais 40 rue des Francs-Bourgeois, 75003. Tel 01 42 78 42 40. Métro: Hôtel de Ville. Exotic furniture and fun, decorative items for your home.

Miscellaneous

Art du Bureau 47 rue des Francs-Bourgeois, 75004. tel 01 48 87 57 97. Closed Sun. a.m. Métro: St.-Paul. Elegant, unusual supplies for the well-dressed office.

CSAO 9 rue Elzévir, 75003. tel 01 42 71 33 17. Closed Sun. a.m. Métro: St.-Paul. Stepping into CSAO, on a street in the Marais called "la petite Afrique," is like entering an African bazaar. There's an amazing variety of color handcrafted fabrics, naïve paintings on glass, gas-can lamps, pottery, baskets, and household furnishings—many made from recycled and salvaged goods. CSAO works with local African craftsmen and has helped certain villages survive. It also has a gallery featuring African art next door at 9 bis.

Perfume

This is a city where any man can name the scent being worn by a woman. Your preferred Poison (Christian Dior) may not be Opium (Yves St. Laurent), but you will surely find a fragrance to your liking.

Parfumeries Bernard Marionnaud 23 boulevard de la Madeleine, 75001. tel 01 40 20 08 80. Closed Sun. Métro: Madeleine.
A wide selection of brand-name perfumes offered by this chain. Call for other locations.

Sephora 70 avenue Champs-Élysées, 75008. tel 01 53 93 22 50. Métro: Franklin D. Roosevelt. The ultimate perfume and cosmetics store, with testers of nearly every brand in existence. Open till midnight.

Salons du Palais Royal Shiseido 142 galerie de Valois, 75001. tel 01 49 27 09 09. Closed Sun. Métro: Palais-Royal. Luxurious boutique where you can pamper yourself with a custom-designed perfume.

Shopping Centers

Paris has few American-style shopping centers. The notable exceptions are the Forum des Halles (*Métro: Les Halles*), a rather unsavory underground mall full of chain-store branches, and the shops under the Carrousel du Louvre. The beautiful, 19th-century Galerie Vivienne (*Métro: Bourse*) and the 18th-century arcades of the Palais-Royal (*Métro: Palais-Royal*) might be called forerunners of the mall, but they are worlds apart from the modern U.S. version.

Taste Treats

Barthélemy 51 rue de Grenelle, 75007. tel 01 45 48 56 75. Métro: Sèvres-Babylone. Closed Sun.–Mon. Some of the best cheeses in Paris, in a charming, old-fashioned shop.

Berthillon's 31 rue St.-Louis-en-Île, 75004. tel 01 43 54 31 61. Métro: Pont Marie. Closed Mon.–Tues., Aug. & during school vacations, except Christmas. Makers of the famous Parisian ice cream, also sold in other outlets throughout Paris.

Demoulin Patisserie 6 boulevard Voltaire, 75011. tel 01 47 00 58 20. Closed Sun. L & Mon. Métro: République. This pastry shop makes mouth-watering almond croissants and incredible chocolate tarts.

Fauchon 24, 26, 30, place de la Madeleine, 75008. tel 01 70 39 38 00. Closed Sun. Métro: Madeleine. The finest of foodstuffs.

Goumanyat 3 rue Charles-François Dupuis, 75003. tel 01 44 78 96 74. www.goumanyat.com. Closed Sun.–Mon., Aug. Métro: Temple. Hidden on a back street near the Marché des Enfants Rouges, this shop is heaven for foodies with its wide variety of artisanal peppers, spices, and mustards, plus fine coffees, teas, chocolate, homemade ice cream and high-quality kitchen utensils.

Izraël 30 rue François-Miron, 75004. tel 01 42 72 66 23. Closed Sun.–Mon. & L on weekdays. Métro: St.-Paul. Don't miss this imported-food shop, redolent of spices and filled with good food.

Legrand 1 rue de la Banque, 75002. tel 01 42 60 07 12. Closed Sun. Métro: Bourse. One of the best wine merchants in Paris; also sells carafes, other wine accessories, and French regional food specialties.

Nicolas Main store: 31 place de la Madeleine, 75008. tel 01 42 68 00 16. Closed Sun. Métro: Madeleine. A chain of franchised wine shops with a reliable selection and knowledgable (often English-speaking) owners. Branches in all Parisian neighborhoods.

Poujauran 20 rue Jean Nicot, 75007. tel 01 43 17 35 20. Closed Sun.–Mon. Métro: Latour Maubourg. Top bakery known throughout the city for its baguettes, as well as its chocolate cake.

Entertainment

As a major world capital, Paris has more than its share of entertainment possibilities. Parisians love to go out, so many performances are sold out in advance—try to book tickets ahead of time for the theater, concerts, dance performances, and the opera. For details on concert times and movie listings, buy a copy of the weekly *Pariscope* or *l'Officiel des Spectacles* at any newsstand. Both come out on Wednesday. *Le Monde* has a Wednesday section on entertainment.

Bars/Nightclubs

Paris nightlife offers something for everyone: "bobos" (bourgeois bohemians) who like to gossip and smoke (outdoors only!) in funky cafés with flea-market furniture (Le Charbon, Lou Pascalou); lounge lizards who enjoy relaxing in comfy armchairs to the mellow sounds of chill-out music (Buddha Bar); sophisticates who want to sip a martini (Pershing Hall, Harry's Bar); and clubbers who refuse to go to bed before dawn spreads its rosy fingers behind the Eiffel Tower (Le Bus Palladium, La Machine).

Le Baron 6 avenue Marceau, 75008. tel 01 47 20 04 01. www .clublebaron.com. Métro: Alma-Marceau. A tiny, exclusive club that's still hard to get into even though it has been around since 2004! Dress for the occasion: cool. Eclectic theme nights, occasional concerts, and star sightings.

Barrio Latino 46–48 rue du Faubourg St.-Antoine, 75012. tel 01 55 78 84 75. Open daily. Métro: Bastille. A three-floor 900-seat bar/club and restaurant with a neo-Cuban decor. Owned by the same people who run the Buddha Bar. It's worth a trip just for an eyeful.

Bizz'art 167 quai de Valmy, 75010. tel 01 40 34 70 00. www .bizzartclub.com Métro: Louis Blanc. Bar, club and restaurant (French/fusion) with soul, Latin, funk, and R&B concerts. Package deals for meal with concert and/or club.

Buddha Bar 8 rue Boissy-d'Anglas, 75008. tel 01 53 05 90 00. Métro: Concorde. Huge basement restaurant/bar for beautiful people, with an enormous Buddha statue.

Le Bus Palladium 6 rue Fontaine, 75009. tel 01 45 26 80 35. www.lebuspalladium.com. Métro: Blanche. Live music on Tues. & Thurs. DJs on Fri. & Sat. Nightclub Thurs.–Sat. Argentinian/American restaurant.

Cabaret Sauvage 59 boulevard MacDonald, 75019. tel 01 42 09 03 09. www.cabaretsauvage.com Métro: Porte de la Villette. In a round building with a peaked roof like a circus tent, with a bar in the center and a stage on one side. Hosts concerts (world, electro/techno, jazz/funk, hip-hop, reggae, and more), cabaret shows, and dance parties. Restaurant.

La Casbah 18–20 rue de la Forge-Royale, 75011. tel 01 43 71 04 39. Métro: Ledru Rollin. The lavish Moroccan decor is the main interest of this restaurant/club. House, R&B, pop, and dance music.

La Chapelle des Lombards 19 rue de Lappe, 75011. tel 01 43 57 24 24. Closed Sun.–Wed. Métro: Bastille. Latin rhythms, R&B, funk, and live concerts in a warm and friendly atmosphere. Free admission Sun.–Thurs.

Le Charbon 109 rue Oberkampf, 75011. tel 01 43 57 55 13. Métro: Parmentier. A former music hall, this was the first hip café to open on this street, now lined with funky, inexpensive bars. Its decor must be seen (high ceiling, turn-of-the-century mural of cabaret dancers), but avoid the crowds on weekend nights. Also check out **Nouveau Casino** at the same address (tel 01 43 57 57 40). Now part of the Charbon, it has live techno, alternative rock, and pop music.

Chez Georges 11 rue des Canettes, 75006. tel 01 43 26 79 15. Closed Sun.–Mon. Métro: St.-Germain-des-Prés. Friendly, unpretentious, cheap bar in a classy neighborhood.

Chez Jeannette 47 rue du Faubourg St.-Denis, 75010. tel 01 47 70 30 89. www.chezjeannette .com. Métro: Château d'Eau. This old-fashioned neighborhood café taken over by a good-natured crew of young people is now a popular watering hole and meeting place for a hard-partying crowd. Decent food, too.

Chez Moune 54 rue Jean Baptiste Pigalle, 75009. tel 01 45 26 64 64. www.chezmoune.fr. Métro: Pigalle. Closed Sun.–Tues. Long a lesbian cabaret (hence the sign depicting a tuxedoed lady with a cigarette), now one of the hottest clubs in town. Edith Piaf herself used to hang out here.

Le China 50 rue de Charenton, 75012. tel 01 43 46 08 09. www .lechina.eu. Métro: Ledru Rollin. The atmosphere and decor of old Shanghai in Paris. Bar, Asian restaurant, and concerts of blues, jazz, jam, and world music.

Le Comptoir Paris-Marrakech 14 rue Vauvilliers, 75001. tel 01 40 26 26 66. Métro: Les Halles. A good place to enjoy a drink amid a designer decor with a Moroccan flavor.

Le Folie's Pigalle 11 place Pigalle, 75009. tel 01 48 78 55 25. www.lefoliespigalle.com. Métro: Pigalle. Once a strip joint, this disco attracts its share of drag queens and an otherwise mixed crowd.

Harry's Bar 5 rue Danou, 75002. tel 01 42 61 71 14. Métro: Opéra. The venerable American bar in Paris where the Bloody Mary was first concocted.

L'International 5 rue Moret, 75011. tel 01 49 29 76 45. www.linternational.fr. Métro: Ménilmontant. Exactly what Parisian nightlife was lacking: a place with free admission and reasonably priced drinks where you can listen to live music: folk, rock, world, and more.

Lou Pascalou 14 rue des Panoyaux, 75020. tel 01 46 36 78 10. Métro: Ménilmontant. One of the original trendy/funky bars in the Ménilmontant area, just to the north of Rue Oberkampf. Free concerts on Sunday evenings.

La Machine 90 boulevard de Clichy. tel 01 53 41 88 92. www .lamachinedumoulinrouge.com. Métro: Blanche. Enormous three-level club with concerts and DJ nights, featuring rock, electro, and world music.

Pershing Hall 49 rue Pierre Charron, 75008. tel 01 58 36 58 00. Métro: George V. Come here for a soothing cocktail and admire Andrée Putman's chic, sleek decor in the lounge bar. The courtyard features a wall entirely covered in plants. Definitely upmarket. Lounge music.

Raidd Bar 23 rue du Temple, 75004. tel 01 42 77 04 88. Métro: Hôtel de Ville. *The* trendy gay bar of the moment, with butch bartenders who occasionally leave their post to take a public shower in a glass booth. Women sometimes admitted. Open until 5 a.m.

Queen 102 avenue des Champs-Élysées, 75008. tel 01 53 89 08 90. Métro: George V. Still the hottest gay disco in town, with mostly house music and theme nights that attract straights also (women are generally frowned upon and not welcome on Sunday nights).

Le Sans Souci 65 rue Jean-Baptiste Pigalle, 75009. tel 01 53 16 17 04. Métro: Pigalle. A neighborhood bar and restaurant that has profited from the popularity of

Chez Moune, across the street, and has become a hangout for young people, enlivened by a DJ.

Sanz Sans 49 rue du Faubourg St.-Antoine, 75011. tel 01 44 75 78 78. Métro: Bastille. A bar/restaurant with a found-object decor and DJ, packed with trendy youngsters.

Satellit' Café 44 rue de la Folie-Méricourt. tel 01 47 00 48 87. Closed Mon. Métro: Oberkampf. Concerts or a DJ after midnight. Salsa music on Sundays.

Le Sous Bock 49 rue St.-Honoré, 75001. tel 01 40 26 46 61. Métro: Pont Neuf, Les Halles. A large pub serving food 24 hours a day.

Cabaret

These famous, Vegas-type shows with topless dancing girls are expensive, and attended mostly by busloads of tourists. If going, skip the overpriced, mediocre meals and just have a pricey drink at the bar.

Crazy Horse Saloon 12 avenue George-V, 75008. Tel 01 47 23 32 32. Métro: Alma-Marceau. Considered the most erotic of the cabarets. The dancers have names like "Kismy Patchwork," with shows like "Teasing."

Folies-Bergère 32 rue Richer, 75009. tel 08 92 68 16 50. Métro: Grands Boulevards. Musical comedies and variety shows in a beautiful old theater.

Lido 116 bis avenue des Champs-Élysées, 75008. tel 01 40 76 56 10. Métro: George V. The Bluebell Girls sing, dance, and ice skate in fabulous costumes.

Moulin Rouge 82 boulevard de Clichy, 75009. tel 01 53 09 82 82. Métro: Blanche. The Doriss Girls still do the can-can in thousands of varied costumes. Dance numbers are interspersed with circus acts.

Cinema

Parisians are movie-mad; they love everything from the latest

American blockbuster to the most intellectual East European offering. Many cinemas regularly show the classics as well, from the Marx Brothers to Frank Capra. Cinema snobs go only to films in "VO" *(version originale)*, so you will find many screenings in English. "VF" means *version française*, and the film will be dubbed into French. Make sure you check before you buy your ticket. On Friday and Saturday nights there are long lines outside cinemas on the Champs-Élysées and les Grands Boulevards. Don't be surprised if you have to sit through up to 20 minutes of advertising before the film starts; this is standard practice. The following are a few of the more interesting cinemas.

Accatone 20 rue Cujas, 75005. tel 01 46 33 86 86. Métro: Luxembourg, Cluny–La Sorbonne. Artsy offerings like *Hiroshima Mon Amour* and erotic classics like *The Empire of the Senses*. Classics only.

Action Rive Gauche 5 rue des Écoles, 75005. tel 01 43 29 11 30. Métro: Cardinal Lemoine, Jussieu. Art-house movies, with festivals of everything from Tennessee Williams to the Marx Brothers.

Le Champo 51 rue des Écoles, 75005. tel 01 43 54 51 60. Métro: St.-Michel, Odéon. Woody Allen and Monty Python classics, recent films you may have missed, and new releases.

La Cinémathèque Française 51 rue de Bercy. 75012. tel 01 71 19 33 33; www.cinemathequefrancaise .com. Métro: Bercy. A stunning new Frank Gehry building houses the new Cinémathèque, with four screens, a bookshop, and a restaurant.

Max Linder Panorama 24 boulevard Poissonnière, 75009. tel 01 48 24 00 47. Métro: Grands Boulevards. New releases in a serious cinema with good seating, digital

THX sound, and a balcony.

MK2 Bibliothèque 128/162 avenue de France, 75013. tel 08 92 69 84 84. Métro: Bibliothèque F. Mitterrand, Quai de la Gare. Artsy films for the masses at the latest MK2 multiplex: 14 screens, three restaurants, a bar, and "love seats" for couples in the theaters.

La Pagode 57 bis rue de Babylone, 75007. tel 01 45 55 48 48. Métro: St.-François-Xavier. Cinema in an imitation pagoda with a tea room in the lovely garden.

Studio Galande 42 rue Galande, 75005. tel 01 43 26 94 08. Métro: St.-Michel. The *Rocky Horror Picture Show* is shown every Fri. and Sat. at 10:30 p.m. plus other recent and not-so-recent films.

Opera/Dance/Classical Music

All the international greats in the worlds of classical music, opera, and both modern dance and ballet eventually perform in Paris. Many churches regularly hold concerts of classical music. Check *Pariscope* or the *Officiel des Spectacles* for details, or call 01 44 62 00 55, or Musique Sacré à Notre-Dame de Paris (tel 01 42 34 56 10). You can book online for major shows at www .fnacspectacles.com, but you will still have to pick up your tickets at a FNAC store. Also for concerts: www.concertclassic.com

Cité de la Musique 211 avenue Jean-Jaurès, 75019. tel 01 44 84 44 84. Métro: Porte de Pantin. The concert hall in this lovely building designed by Christian Portzamparc presents an eclectic repertory of world music, jazz, and classical.

Opéra-Comique 5 rue Favart, 75002. tel 01 42 44 45 40. Métro: Richelieu Drouot. Operas, operettas, and classical concerts are staged in this beautiful, sumptuously decorated 100-year-old theater, built by Louis Bernier.

Opéra National de Paris-Bastille 120 rue de Lyon, 75012. tel 08 92 89 90 90, www.operadeparis .fr. Métro: Bastille.Major opera and dance productions in the new opera house that Parisians love to hate, but flock to anyway.

Opéra National de Paris Palais-Garnier Place de l'Opéra, 75009. tel 08 92 89 90 90. Métro: Opéra. Opera and dance performances (by the Ballet de l'Opéra National de Paris and visiting companies) in this wonderfully overdecorated, 19th-century opera house with frescoes by Chagall.

Salle Gaveau 45 rue de la Boétie, 75008. tel 01 49 53 05 07. www.sallegaveau.com. Métro: Miromesnil. The belle epoque Salle Gaveau, which seats 1,020, is known for its fine acoustics and was restored to a faithful version of its early-20th-century appearance a decade ago. It features primarily piano and chamber music, along with occasional orchestral concerts.

Salle Pleyel 252 rue du Faubourg-St.-Honoré, 75008. Tel 01 42 56 13 13. Métro: Ternes. This prestigious venue, recently restored, is the home base of the Orchestre Philharmonique and stages classical and jazz concerts.

Théâtre des Champs-Élysées 15 avenue Montaigne, 75008. tel 01 49 52 50 50. Métro: Alma-Marceau. Hosts the Orchestre National de Paris, plus visiting orchestras and opera companies.

Théâtre du Châtelet place du Châtelet. Tel 01 40 28 28 40. Métro: Châtelet. Musicals, classical concerts, and dance productions are held in this attractive theater.

Théâtre de la Ville 2 place du Châtelet, 75004. tel 01 42 74 22 77. Métro: Châtelet. The major venue for an adventurous program of dance performances by all the best international companies.

Pop/Rock/Jazz

The French have adopted American jazz and made it their own,

with many Parisian basement jazz clubs. They can get very crowded; arrive early but don't expect things to get going before 11 p.m.

Bilboquet 13 rue St.-Benoît, 75006. tel 01 45 48 81 84. Métro: St.-Germain-des-Prés
This Left Bank, belle epoque-style club in the heart of St.-Germain-des-Prés has been around for half a century and is very popular with tourists. It offers dinner and New Orleans–style jazz.

Caveau de la Huchette 5 rue de la Huchette, 75005. tel 01 43 26 65 05. Métro: St.-Michel. A smoky, Latin Quarter basement club with '50s-style rock, boogie, and swing. Still going strong.

La Cigale 124 boulevard Rochechouart, 75018. tel 01 49 25 89 99. Métro: Pigalle. Rock concerts by international and local groups in a former theater.

Le Divan du Monde 75 rue des Martyrs, 75018. tel 01 42 52 02 46. Métro: Pigalle. All types of music—rock, *chansons française* (French songs), gospel, and Central European.

Duc des Lombards 42 rue de Lombards, 75001. tel 01 42 33 22 88. Métro: Châtelet. The club heats up with lively jazz concerts beginning around 10 p.m.

Élysée-Montmartre 72 boulevard Rochechouart, 75018. tel 01 44 92 45 36. Métro: Anvers. A former Pigalle music hall with good rock and rap concerts.

Instants Chavirés 2 rue Émile Zola, 93100 Montreuil. tel 01 42 87 25 91. www.instantschavires.com. Métro: Robespierre. Just outside of Paris, this friendly club is the best for avant-garde jazz.

Jazz Club Lionel Hampton Hôtel Meridien, 81 boulevard Gouvion St.-Cyr, 75017. tel 01 40 68 30 42. Métro: Porte Maillot. Good, live jazz and blues in the lobby of the otherwise unexciting Méridien hotel.

New Morning 7–9 rue des Petites-Écuries, 75010. tel 01

45 23 51 41. www.newmorning .com. Métro: Château d'Eau. Top jazz, blues, African, and South American musicians perform in this smoky club.

Olympia 28 boulevard des Capucines, 75009. tel 08 92 68 33 68. Métro: Opéra. Recently renovated concert hall with a variety of music acts, including many French *chanteurs* and *chanteuses* (singers).

Point Ephémère 200 quai de Valmy, 75010. tel 01 40 34 02 48; restaurant: 01 40 34 04 06. www .pointephemere.org. Métro: Gare de l'Est. Lively cultural center with art exhibitions, events, and a wide variety of pop, rock, and dance concerts for a young crowd. Restaurant with terrace overlooking the Canal St.-Martin.

Petit Journal Montparnasse 13 rue du Commandant-Mouchotte, 75014. tel 01 43 21 56 70. Métro: Montparnasse. Live jazz, blues, and rock in this popular club.

Petit Journal 71 boulevard St.-Michel, 75005. tel 01 43 26 28 59. RER: Luxembourg. Basement club featuring New Orleans–style jazz.

Le Sunset 60 rue des Lombards, 75001. tel 01 40 26 46 60. Métro: Châtelet. Central, basement jazz club with good French and international groups.

Zénith 211 avenue de Jean-Jaurès, 75019. tel 08 90 71 02 07. www.le-zenith.com. Métro: Porte de Pantin. Cavernous rock venue where international superstars perform.

Theater

Going to the theater in Paris provides an opportunity to soak up the ambience, but otherwise there is not much point unless your command of French is excellent—most of the plays are in French. However, a few theaters occasionally stage plays in English (listed below; otherwise, in French). Booking usually starts two weeks in advance.

Café-théâtres are small theaters

(without cafés), with the equivalent of off-off-Broadway plays and stand-up comedy of varying quality, but don't go unless your French is really good.

Bouffes du Nord 37 bis boulevard de la Chapelle, 75010. tel 01 46 07 34 50. Métro: La Chapelle. Director Peter Brook stages plays of excellent quality—many in English—in a handsome old theater.

Café de la Gare 41 rue du Temple, 75004. tel 01 42 78 52 51. Métro: Hôtel de Ville. A café-théâtre presenting plays and comedy sketches.

Cartoucherie-Théâtre du Soleil route du Champ-de-Manoeuvres, 75012. tel 01 43 74 24 08. Métro: Château-de-Vincennes, then shuttle service or bus. Acclaimed director Ariane Mnouchkine's troupe performs plays in an old warehouse near the Bois de Vincennes.

Comédie Française 1 place Colette. tel 01 44 58 14 00. Métro: Palais-Royal. Molière's company was the founding troupe of this venerable theater next to the Palais-Royal; his works are performed, along with pieces by Chekhov, Corneille, Racine, Shakespeare, Anouilh, and others. The acting is usually superb. French language only.

Odéon-Théâtre de l'Europe 2 rue Corneille, 75006. tel 01 44 85 40 40, www.theatre-odeon .fr. Métro: Odéon, Luxembourg. A terrific and eclectic repertoire, with theater companies from all over Europe and performances in many languages.

Point Virgule 7 rue St.-Croix-de-la-Bretonnerie, 75004. Tel 01 42 78 67 03. Métro: Hôtel-de-Ville. A small, popular café-théâtre with mostly comic sketches.

Théâtre MC93 Bobigny La Maison de la Culture, 1 boulevard Lénine, Bobigny. tel 01 41 60 72 72. Métro: Bobigny–Pablo Picasso. Avant-garde pieces (Robert Wilson,

Peter Sellars) are the mainstay of this modern theater in one of Paris's "red" suburbs.

Théâtre de Nesle 8 rue de Nesle, 75006. tel 01 46 34 61 04. Métro: Odéon. Tiny Left Bank theater with occasional English-language plays by Pinter and others.

Théâtre du Rond Point 2 bis avenue Franklin D. Roosevelt, 75008. tel 01 44 95 98 10. Métro: Franklin D. Roosevelt. Marcel Maréchal's company presents classic plays, as well as works by Samuel Beckett and Harold Pinter to name but two, in this skating-rink-turned-theater. French language only.

Théâtre du Vieux-Colombier 21 rue du Vieux-Colombier, 75006. tel 01 44 39 87 00. Métro: St.-Sulpice. A smaller, Left Bank outpost of the Comédie Française, with a selection of both classic and modern pieces.

Théâtre National de Chaillot 1 place du Trocadéro, 75016. tel 01 53 65 30 00, www.theatre-chaillot. fr. Métro: Trocadéro. Enormous theater directed by Jérôme Savary, who presents lavish spectacles. Free mini-concerts are sometimes held in the Grand Foyer at the cocktail hour or on Sunday afternoon.

Language Guide

General

Yes *Oui*
No *Non*
Excuse me *Excusez-moi*
Hello *Bonjour*
Hi *Salut*
Please *S'il vous plaît*
Thank you (very much) *Merci (beaucoup)*
You're welcome *De rien*
Have a good day! *Bonne journée!*
OK *D'accord*
Goodbye *Au revoir*
Good night *Bonsoir*
Sorry *Pardon*
here *ici*
there *là*
today *aujourd'hui*
yesterday *hier*
tomorrow *demain*
now *maintenant*
later *plus tard*
right away *tout de suite*
this morning *ce matin*
this afternoon *cet après-midi*
this evening *ce soir*
Do you have . . . ? *Avez-vous . . . ?*
Do you speak English? *Parlez-vous anglais?*
I am American *Je suis Américain* (man); *je suis Américaine* (woman)
I don't understand *Je ne comprends pas*
Please speak more slowly *Parlez plus lentement, s'il vous plaît*
Where is . . .? *Où est. . . ?*
I don't know *Je ne sais pas*
No problem *Ce n'est pas grave*
That's it *C'est ça*
Here it is *Voici*
There it is *Voilà*
What is your name? *Comment vous-appelez-vous?*
My name is . . . *Je m'appelle . . .*
Let's go *On y va*
At what time? *À quelle heure?*
When? *Quand?*
What time is it? *Quelle heure est-il?*

In the hotel

Do you have . . .? *Avez-vous . . . ?*
a single room *une chambre simple*
a double room *une chambre double*
with/without bathroom/shower *avec/sans salle de bain/douche*

Help

I need a doctor/dentist *J'ai besoin d'un médecin/dentiste*
Can you help me? *Pouvez-vous m'aider?*
Where is the hospital? *Où est l'hôpital?*
Where is the police station? *Où est le commissariat?*

Shopping

I'd like . . . *Je voudrais . . .*
How much is it? *C'est combien?*
Do you take credit cards? *Est-ce que vous acceptez les cartes de crédit?*
size (clothes) *la taille*
size (shoes) *la pointure*
cheap *bon marché*
expensive *cher*
Have you got . . .? *Avez vous. . . ?*
I'll take it *Je le prends*
Anything else? *Avec ça?*
enough *assez*
too much *trop*
bill *la note*

Shops

bakery *la boulangerie*
bookshop *la librairie*
drugstore *la pharmacie*
delicatessen *la charcuterie/le traiteur*
department store *le grand magasin*
fishmonger *la poissonnerie*
grocery *l'alimentation/l'épicerie*
junk shop *la brocante*
library *la bibliothèque*
supermarket *le supermarché*

Sightseeing

visitor information office *l'office de tourisme/le syndicat d'initiative*
open *ouvert*
closed *fermé*
every day *tous le jours*
all year round *toute l'année*
all day long *toute la journée*
free *gratuit/libre*

abbey *l'abbaye* (**f**)
castle, country house *le château*
church *l'église* (**f**)
museum *le musée*
staircase *l'escalier* (**m**)
tower *la tour* (**La Tour Eiffel**)
tour (walk or drive) *le tour*
town *la ville*
old town *la vieille ville*
Town Hall *Hôtel de Ville/la mairie*

Menu Reader

breakfast *le petit déjeuner*
lunch *le déjeuner*
dinner *le dîner*
I am on a diet *Je suis au régime*
I'd like to order *Je voudrais commander*
Is service included? *Est-ce que le service est compris?*

Le Menu

menu à prix fixe **meal at set price**
à la carte **dishes from the menu, charged separately**
entrée/hors d'oeuvre **first course**
le plat principal **main course**
le plat du jour **dish of the day**
le dessert **dessert**
boisson compris **drink included**
carte des vins **wine list**
l'addition **the bill**

Les Boissons Drinks

café **coffee**
au lait ou crème **with milk or cream**
deca/decaffeine **decaffeinated coffee**
express/noir **espresso/black**
filtre **American filtered coffee**
thé **tea**
le lait **milk**
eau minérale **mineral water**
gazeux **fizzy**
non-gazeux **non-fizzy**
citron pressé **fresh lemon juice served with sugar**
orange pressée **fresh squeezed orange juice**
frais, fraîche **fresh or cold**
bière **beer**
en bouteille **bottled**

à la pression **on tap**
panaché **mixed**
le panaché **shandy**
la carafe/le pichet **pitcher of tap water or wine**
la demi-carafe **half liter**
un quart **quarter of a liter**
vin de maison **house wine**
vin de pays **local wine**
digestif **after-dinner drink**

Le Repas The Meal
le pain **bread**
le poivre **pepper**
le potage **soup**
le sel **salt**
le sucre **sugar**

Meat Dishes
l'agneau **lamb**
l'andouille **tripe sausage**
le bifteck **steak**
à point **just cooked**
bien cuit **well done**
bleu **very rare**
contre-filet **cut of sirloin steak**
entrecôte **rib steak**
faux-filet **sirloin steak**
grillé **grilled**
hachis **chopped**
saignant **rare**
bordelaise **with red wine and shallots**
bourguignonne **cooked in red wine, onions, and mushrooms**
le canard **duck**
la carbonnade **stew of beef in beer**
le carré d'agneau **rack of lamb**
le cassoulet **stew of beans, sausages, pork, and duck**
la choucroute **sauerkraut**
le confit **duck or goose preserved in its own fat**
le coq au vin **chicken in red wine**
le côte d'agneau **lamb chop**
les cuisses de grenouille **frog's legs**
la daube **stew with red wine, tomatoes, and onions**
le dinde **turkey**
l'escargot **snail**
farci **stuffed**
le jambon **ham**
le lapin **rabbit**
le magret de canard **breast of duck**
le médaillon **round piece of meat**
l'oie **goose**

le porc **pork**
le pot-au-feu **casserole of beef and vegetables**
le poulet **chicken**
le poussin **young chicken**
les rognons **kidneys**
rôti **roast**
la saucisse **fresh sausage**
le saucisson **salami**
le veau **veal**

Fish Dishes
l'anchois **anchovy**
l'anguille **eel**
le belon **Brittany oyster**
la bouillabaisse **fish soup**
le cabillaud **cod**
le colin **hake**
le coquillage **shellfish**
la coquille Saint-Jacques **scallop**
la crevette **shrimp**
la daurade **sea bream**
l'encornet **squid**
le flétan **halibut**
les fruits de mer **seafood**
l'homard **lobster**
l'huître **oyster**
la langoustine **large shrimp**
la limande **lemon sole**
la lotte **monkfish**
la moule **mussel**
moules marinières **mussels in white wine and onions**
la poulpe **octopus**
le saumon **salmon**
le thon **tuna**
la truite **trout**

Some Sauces
aïoli **garlic mayonnaise**
américaine **sauce of white wine, tomatoes, butter, and Cognac**
béarnaise **egg, butter, wine, and herbs**
forestière **mushrooms and bacon**
hollandaise **egg, butter, and lemon**
meunière **butter, lemon, and parsley**
meurette **red wine sauce**
Mornay **cream, egg, and cheese**
Provençale **usually tomatoes, garlic, and olive oil**

Légumes Vegetables
l'ail **garlic**
l'artichaut **artichoke**

les asperges **asparagus**
l'aubergine **eggplant**
l'avocat **avocado**
le champignon **mushroom**
les chips **potato chips**
le chou **cabbage**
le chou-fleur **cauliflower**
le concombre **cucumber**
le cornichon **pickle**
la courgette **zucchini**
cru **raw**
les crudités **raw vegetables**
les épinards **spinach**
le haricot **dried bean**
les haricots rouges **kidney beans**
les haricots verts **green beans**
les lentilles **lentils**
le maïs **corn**
le mange-tout **snow pea**
le mesclun **mixed leaf salad**
la noisette **hazelnut**
la noix **nut, walnut**
l'oignon **onion**
le poireau **leek**
le pois **pea**
le poivron **bell pepper**
les pommes de terre **potatoes**
les pommes frites **french fries**
le riz **rice**
la salade verte **green salad**
la truffe **truffle**

Fruits
l'ananas **pineapple**
la cerise **cherry**
le citron **lemon**
le citron vert **lime**
la figue **fig**
la fraise **strawberry**
la framboise **raspberry**
le pamplemousse **grapefruit**
la pêche **peach**
la poire **pear**
la pomme **apple**
la prune **plum**
le pruneau **prune**
le raisin **grape**

Snacks
le croque-monsieur **toasted ham and cheese sandwich**
l'oeuf à la coque **boiled egg**
oeufs au jambon **ham and eggs**
oeufs brouillés **scrambled eggs**
oeufs sur le plat **fried eggs**
le yaourt **yogurt**

INDEX

ILLUSTRATIONS CREDITS

All photographs by Gilles Mingasson unless otherwise noted.

2-3, Stephen Alvarez/NationalGeographicStock.com; 8, Rob Wilson/Shutterstock; 18-19, Scala/White Images/Art Resource, NY; 24, Scala/White Images/Art Resource, NY; 28-29, Réunion des Musées Nationaux/Art Resource, NY; 30, Bettmann/Corbis; 33, Lionel Bonaventure/AFP/Getty Images; 66, Bridgeman/Getty Images; 110, Patrick Kovarik/AFP/Getty Images; 114, The Gallery Collection/Corbis; 127, Huang Yuetao/Shutterstock; 129, pseudolongino/Shutterstock; 131, Réunion des Musées Nationaux/Art Resource, NY; 150, Pascal Le Segretain/Getty Images; 151, Vladislav Gurfinkel/Shutterstock; 153, Daniel Beltsazar/iStockphoto.com; 166, Scala/White Images/Art Resource, NY; 182, Erich Lessing/Art Resource, NY; 198, Amy Toensing; 201, Annie Greenwood/iStockphoto.com; 213, Richard Bord/Getty Images; 216, Jose Ignacio Soto/Shutterstock; 219, Tupungato/Shutterstock; 223, Chris Green/Shutterstock; 227, Réunion des Musées Nationaux/Art Resource, NY.

National Geographic
TRAVELER
Paris

Published by the National Geographic Society
John M. Fahey, Jr., *Chairman of the Board and Chief Executive Officer*
Timothy T. Kelly, *President*
Declan Moore, *Executive Vice President; President, Publishing*
Melina Gerosa Bellows, *Executive Vice President, Chief Creative Officer, Books, Kids, and Family*

Prepared by the Book Division
Barbara Brownell Grogan, *Vice President and Editor in Chief*
Jonathan Halling, *Design Director, Books and Children's Publishing*
Marianne R. Koszorus, *Director of Design*
Barbara Noe, *Senior Editor*
Carl Mehler, *Director of Maps*
R. Gary Colbert, *Production Director*
Jennifer A. Thornton, *Managing Editor*
Meredith C. Wilcox, *Administrative Director, Illustrations*

Staff for This Book
Patricia Daniels, *Project Editor*
Jane Menyawi, *Illustrations Editor*
Kay Kobor Hankins, *Art Director*
Linda Makarov, *Designer*
Michael McNey and Mapping Specialists, *Map Production*
Rosemary Bailey, Sheila Buckmaster, Christel Cherqaoui, Anne Randerson, Jane Sunderland, *Contributors*
Rob Waymouth, *Illustrations Specialist*

Manufacturing and Quality Management
Christopher A. Liedel, *Chief Financial Officer*
Phillip L. Schlosser, *Vice President*
Chris Brown, *Technical Director*
Nicole Elliott, *Manager*
Rachel Faulise, *Manager*
Robert L. Barr, *Manager*

First edition: Edited and designed by AA Publishing (a trading name of Automobile Association Developments Limited, whose registered office is Norfolk House, Priestley Road, Basingstoke, Hampshire, England RG24 9NY. Registered number: 1878835).

Area map illustrations drawn by Chris Orr Associates, Southampton, England
Cutaway illustrations drawn by Maltings Partnership, Derby, England

The National Geographic Society is one of the world's largest nonprofit scientific and educational organizations. Founded in 1888 to "increase and diffuse geographic knowledge," the Society works to inspire people to care about the planet. National Geographic reflects the world through its magazines, television programs, films, music and radio, books, DVDs, maps, exhibitions, live events, school publishing programs, interactive media and merchandise. *National Geographic* magazine, the Society's official journal, published in English and 33 local-language editions, is read by more than 40 million people each month. The National Geographic Channel reaches 370 million households in 34 languages in 168 countries. National Geographic Digital Media receives more than 15 million visitors a month. National Geographic has funded more than 9,600 scientific research, conservation and exploration projects and supports an education program promoting geography literacy. For more information, visit www.nationalgeographic.com.

For more information, please call 1-800-NGS LINE (647-5463) or write to the following address:

National Geographic Society
1145 17th Street N.W.
Washington, D.C. 20036-4688 U.S.A.

For information about special discounts for bulk purchases, please contact National Geographic Books Special Sales: ngspecsales@ngs.org

For rights or permissions inquiries, please contact National Geographic Books Subsidiary Rights: ngbookrights@ngs.org

The information in this book has been carefully checked and to the best of our knowledge is accurate. However, details are subject to change, and the National Geographic Society cannot be responsible for such changes, or for errors or omissions. Assessments of sites, hotels, and restaurants are based on the author's subjective opinions, which do not necessarily reflect the publisher's opinion.

National Geographic Traveler: Paris (Third Edition)
ISBN: 978-1-4262-0819-5

Printed in China
11/TS/1